A History of the Canadian Peoples

A History of the Canadian Peoples

J.M. Bumsted

Toronto Oxford New York
OXFORD UNIVERSITY PRESS
1998

To Wendy

Oxford University Press
70 Wynford Drive, Don Mills, Ontario M3C 1J9

Oxford New York
Athens Auckland Bangkok
Calcutta Cape Town Chennai Dar es Salaam Delhi
Florence Hong Kong Istanbul Karachi
Kuala Lumpur Madrid Melbourne
Mexico City Mumbai Nairobi Paris Singapore
Taipei Tokyo Toronto Warsaw

and associated companies in
Berlin Ibadan

Oxford is a trade mark of Oxford University Press

Canadian Cataloguing in Publication Data

Bumsted, J. M., 1938–
    A history of the Canadian peoples

Abridged ed. of: The peoples of Canada
Includes bibliographical references and index.
ISBN 0-19-541200-1

1. Canada – History. I. Bumsted, J. M., 1938–. The peoples of Canada. II. Title.
FC164.B862 1997   971   C97-931361-9
F1026.B952 1997

Cover illustration: James Wilson Morrice, *Return from School, c.* 1901, oil on
canvas, 44.5 x 73.7 cm. ART GALLERY OF ONTARIO, TORONTO. Gift from
the Reuben and Kate Leonard Canadian Fund, 1948.
Editor: Valerie Ahwee
Design: Max Gabriel Izod

Oxford University Press Canada web site: http://www.oupcan.com

Contents

�֍

Maps

✤

Tables

✿

Acknowledgements

❁

The following previously published materials are reproduced with permission of the publishers:

A.B. BENSON: Excerpt from *Peter Kalm's Travels in North America*, vol. 2, A.B. Benson, ed. New York: Dover Publications, 1937. Reprinted by permission of Dover Publications Inc.

MARGARET FAIRLEY: Extract from *The Selected Writings of William Lyon Mackenzie*, edited by Margaret Fairley. Toronto: Oxford University Press Canada, 1960. Reprinted by permission of Oxford University Press Canada.

JOHN GRAY: Extract from *The Winter Years: The Depression on the Prairies* by James Gray © 1966. Reprinted by permission of Macmillan Canada.

BARBARA GRAYMONT: Map 'Iroquois Country, 1776' from *The Iroquois in the American Revolution*, Barbara Graymont, Syracuse University Press, 1972, p. xii.

M. JOHNSTON: Extract from *Corvettes Canada: Convoy Veterans of WWII Tell Their True Stories* by M. Johnston. Whitby, Ontario: McGraw-Hill Ryerson, 1994. Reprinted by permission of McGraw-Hill Ryerson.

G. KEALEY: Extract from *Canada Investigates Industrialism* (The Royal Commission on the Relations of Labour and Capital, 1889, abridged), edited by G. Kealey. Toronto: University of Toronto Press, 1973. Reprinted by permission of University of Toronto Press Inc.

FRANCES V. McCOLL: Extract from *Vignettes of Early Winnipeg* by Frances V. McColl. Quoted by permission.

MARGARET MACDONELL: Extract from *The Emigrant Experience: Songs of Highland Emigrants in North America* by Margaret MacDonell. Toronto: University of Toronto Press, 1982. Reprinted by permission of University of Toronto Press Inc.

J.R. MILLER: Map 'The Numbered Treaties, 1871–1921' from *Skyscrapers Hide the Heavens*, Revised Edition, by J.R. Miller. Toronto: University of Toronto Press, 1991. Reprinted by permission of University of Toronto Press Inc.

R.B. MORRISON AND C.R. WILSON: Extract from *Native Peoples: The Canadian Experience* by R.B. Morrison and C.R. Wilson. Toronto: McClelland and Stewart, 1995. Reprinted by permission of the authors and Oxford University Press Canada.

W.L. MORTON: Extract from *Monck Letters and Journals 1863–1868: Canada from Government House at Confederation*, W.L. Morton, ed. Toronto: McClelland & Stewart, 1970. Reprinted by permission.

MARY BIGGAR PECK: The selection from Sadie Harper's diaries is excerpted from *A Full House and Fine Singing: Diaries and Letters of Sadie Harper Allen*, edited by Mary Biggar Peck 1992, with the permission of Goose Lane Editions.

M.M. QUAIFE: Extract from *The Western Country in the 17th Century: The Memoirs of Antoine Lamothe Cadillac and Pierre Liette*, M.M. Quaife, ed. New York: The Citadel Press, 1962.

K.J. REA: Table 'Expenditures on Personal Health Care as a Percentage of Gross Provincial Product and Personal Income, Ontario, 1960–1975' from *The Prosperous Years: The Economic History of Ontario 1939–75* by K.J. Rea. Toronto: University of Toronto Press, 1985. Reprinted by permission of University of Toronto Press Inc.

JOHN SAYWELL: Extract from *Quebec 70: A Documentary Narrative* by John Saywell. Toronto: University of Toronto Press, 1971. Reprinted by permission of University of Toronto Press Inc.

STATISTICS CANADA: Table 'Offences by Type, 1987–1991' reproduced by authority of the Minister of Industry, 1997, Statistics Canada, *Canada Yearbook 1994*, cat. no. 11–402, p. 222.

Table 'Immigrants Arriving by Place of Birth, 1981–1990' reproduced by authority of the Minister of Industry, 1997, Statistics Canada, *Canada Yearbook 1994*, cat. no. 11–402, p. 116.

Table 'Federal Government Debt' reproduced by authority of the Minister of Industry, 1997, Statistics Canada, *Canada Yearbook 1994*, cat. no. 11–402, p. 304.

PHILIP STRATFORD: Extract from *Memoirs* by René Lévesque, translated by Philip Stratford. Used by permission, McClelland & Stewart, Inc. *The Canadian Publishers*.

J.A. WILLIAMSON: Extract from *The Cabot Voyages and British Discoveries under Henry VII*, J.A. Williamson, translator. Cambridge: The Hakluyt Society, 1962. Reprinted by permission of David Higham Associates.

Major Events in the Early History of the First Nations

12,000 BC	Mammal retaining stone weapon killed in New Mexico.
11,000 BC	Glacial retreat escalates with warming trend.
10,000 BC	Continued warming alters physical environment as ice retreats.
9000 BC	Fluted Point people spread across North America.
7000 BC	Maritime Archaic culture develops the harpoon.
5500 BC	Maritime Archaic culture develops burial mounds. Mound at L'Anse Amour is filled with harpoon and walrus tusk. Notched projectile points appear in British Columbia.
3000 BC	Forest reaches its northernmost extension.
2000 BC	Paleo-Eskimos and other Archaics begin displacing Maritime Archaics on eastern seaboard and Arctic regions.
1000 BC	Ceramic pottery appears in Great Lakes area and spreads east.
500 BC	Dorset people appear in Arctic Canada. Climate deteriorates.
AD 500	Maize cultivation begins in southern Ontario. Climate begins improving.
600	Beothuk culture replaces the Dorset Eskimos in Newfoundland.
1000	Norse settle in eastern North America.
1150	Dorset culture is replaced by Thule culture among Inuit.
1350	Squash and bean cultivation are added in southern Ontario.
1498	First Europeans since Vikings reach northern North America.
1634ff	Beginning of the destruction of the Huron nation.
1730	Horses reach the northern great plains.

Major Events in the Early European Exploration of Northern North America

982–5	Eric the Red explores Greenland.
c. 1000	L'Anse aux Meadows is established by the Vikings.
1497	John Cabot sights Newfoundland.
1500	Gaspar Corte-Real lands at Tierra Verde (Newfoundland).
1501	Gaspar Corte-Real brings the first Aboriginals to Europe.
1534	Jacques Cartier erects a cross in Gaspé Harbour on his first voyage to the St Lawrence.
1576	Martin Frobisher's first voyage to Baffin Island.
1585	John Davis enters Davis Strait.
1611	Henry Hudson enters Hudson Bay.
1615	Étienne Brûlé investigates New York and Pennsylvania.
1616	Robert Bylot sails through Davis Strait.
1651	Pierre Radisson is captured by Mohawks.
1659	Radisson begins partnership with Médard Chouart Des Groseilliers.
1660	Radisson and Groseilliers return from Hudson Bay with a rich haul of furs.
1669	René-Robert Cavelier de La Salle heads out on his first expedition.

1
The Beginning

Once upon a time, a history of Canada would typically begin with the arrival of the European 'discoverers' at the end of the fifteenth century. These events at best mark only the moment at which the land and its people enter the European historical record, not the beginning of its history. Thousands of years of human development had preceded the Europeans' appearance. The Native inhabitants of North America have their own history. The work of countless modern specialists, chiefly linguistic scholars and archaeologists, has only begun to touch the bare outlines of the pre-European period. The record of human settlement clearly does not begin with the Europeans.

THE FIRST IMMIGRANTS

Unlike other continents on this planet, North America did not produce indigenous archaic human forms going back thousands of generations. No evidence suggests that any of the many ancestors of *Homo sapiens* developed on this continent. There was no Old Stone Age as in Africa, Asia, or Europe. Instead, the first humanlike inhabitant of North America was *Homo sapiens* herself, arriving as an immigrant in the New World during the last Great Ice Age—which ended 10,000 years ago—probably across a land bridge stretching between what is now Siberia and Alaska.

The 30,000 years or more of the human occupation of the North American continent before the arrival of the Europeans around 1500 was, until very recently, usually labelled as 'prehistoric'. The term has now fallen out of common usage, however, because it produces so many misconceptions. There may have been no written record of North American development before the Europeans, but to assume that 'history' begins only with writing is totally misleading. Plenty of earlier records of human activity exist. From them a fascinating picture of the early history of what is now Canada can be created. That picture is hardly a static one. Instead, it is one of constant movement, adaptation, and change. These early people did not attempt to modify their environment so much as adapt to it. That environment was continually shifting, perhaps not over a single season but over several generations.

One of the chief factors influencing the early inhabitants of North America was climate. Until very recently—as the history of the planet goes—most of what is now Canada was covered with glacial ice, which began retreating about 10,000 years ago. There were several ice-free corridors running from Alaska south, through which the first immigrants from Asia probably travelled into the warmer regions of the continent. While some inhabitants adapted to ice and snow, most people began moving northward as the ice began melting. By the time of Christ around 2,000 years ago, most of Canada had acquired a natural environment recognizable to us today. The land had also acquired permanent Native inhabitants. What we know about these people and their history comes to us in the form of physical artefacts, chiefly bones and tools or weapons.

Because of the limited nature of the evidence, the early history of humankind in Canada is usually described in terms of the surviving tools and weapons, especially projectile points. Archaeologists can infer much from tool-making technology and its geographical spread across the continent. Using various dating techniques, including laboratory testing of organic substances to determine what remains of a radioactive carbon isotope called carbon-14, it has been possible to provide some overall sense of chronological development. The first incontestable evidence of human habitation in North America comes in the form of fluted projectile points chipped from various rocks by taking long flakes (or flutes) from the base to the tip. Between 9500 and 8000 BC people using these points spread from Alaska through the central plains and eastern woodlands. They were hunters and gatherers who lived in small units, although not in total isolation from neighbours. There is evidence of trade and exchange of goods.

As the ice melted and the glaciers moved northward, the hunters who made the fluted points spread more widely across the continent. These people have come to be known by archaeologists as the Plano People because of their distinctive projectile-point technology. They flourished from 8000 to 6000 BC. By 4000 BC a number of regional offshoots from the Plano People had developed. Over the next 3,000 years these cultures stabilized to some extent, although there was still substantial physical movement. On the western plains, a culture organized around communal bison-hunting emerged, perhaps as early as 3000 BC. The High Arctic was occupied by Paleo-Eskimos, who gradually moved to the south into the Barren Lands west of Hudson Bay. The northeastern seaboard was occupied between 2000 and 1000 BC. On the West Coast, a semisedentary lifestyle based on the salmon had developed by 2000 BC.

From 1000 BC to AD 500, substantial cultural changes occurred across North America. Once we stop trying to compare these developments with what was going on in Europe and see them instead in their own terms, we can appreciate how substantial the technological innovations of this period were. The bow and arrow spread rapidly, for example, completing altering hunting techniques. In the same years, pottery making moved from the Yukon to eastern

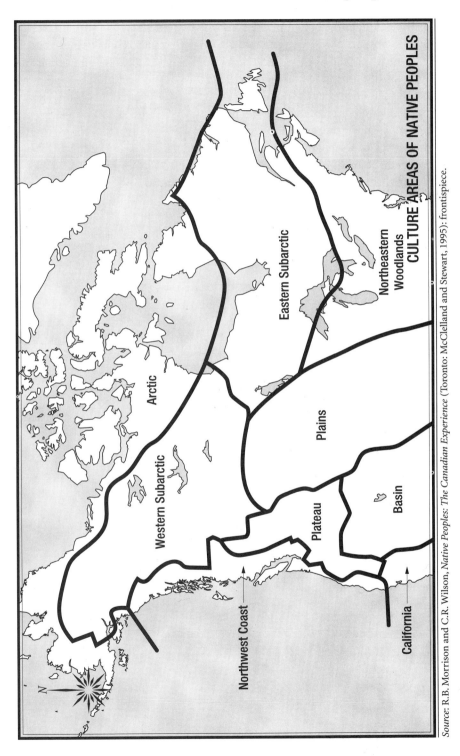

CULTURE AREAS OF NATIVE PEOPLES

Arctic

Western Subarctic

Eastern Subarctic

Northeastern Woodlands

Plains

Plateau

Basin

Northwest Coast

California

Source: R.B. Morrison and C.R. Wilson, *Native Peoples: The Canadian Experience* (Toronto: McClelland and Stewart, 1995): frontispiece.

districts. The introduction of the pot changed food preparation substantially, but also provides evidence of rapidly changing aesthetic sensibilities as ornamentation was added to design. Archaeologists have shifted their classification systems from the projectile point to the pot for the peoples of this era. Another new development was the rapid expansion from the south of new funeral practices, chiefly burial in large mounds. This, of course, helped provide a new self-consciously created richness of physical evidence. The relatively rapid diffusion of these technologies and aesthetics suggests a substantial amount of personal interaction and trade among the peoples of this period.

In the 1,000 years before the arrival of the Europeans, another substantial technological leap occurred. Cultivation of plants gradually spread north from Mexico and was adopted in southern Ontario along the Mississippi River water basin sometime after AD 500. Corn was rapidly followed by sunflowers, beans, squash, and eventually tobacco. In the north, the Thule culture expanded out of Alaska and spread relatively rapidly eastward across the Arctic after AD 1000. Except for this development, however, most of the inhabitants in the northern part of the continent spent the millennium before 1500 in relative physical stability. As a result, the era was one of considerable cultural consolidation, including the development of distinctive regional languages based on a few common language groups, chiefly Algonquian and Iroquoian in the east and Athapaskan in the northwest.

THE ABORIGINAL POPULATION AROUND 1500

Although on the eve of European intrusion all Aboriginal peoples lived in a reciprocal relationship with nature, not all had the same relationship. Much depended on the resources of the region in which they lived and the precise combination of survival skills they had. Most of the many groups were hunters and gatherers, organized into mobile bands that followed the seasons and the cycles of the game. On the coasts, fishing replaced hunting as the principal means of collecting a food supply. In the north, as in many other areas, whether one fished or hunted depended on the season. On the

Indians fishing, drawn by John White
(Copyright © British Museum).

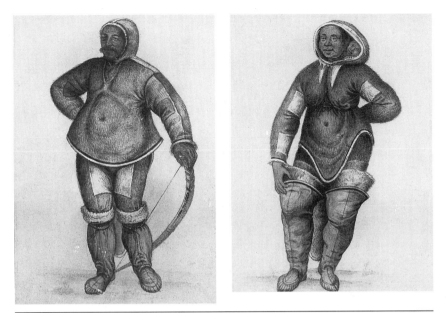

Three Baffin Island Inuit—a man, a woman, and her child—whom Martin Frobisher took prisoner on his second expedition to the Arctic in 1577, all died a month or so after arriving in England (Copyright © British Museum 205220 and 234062).

Pacific Slope, the rich resource base of salmon and cedar made possible considerable accumulations of wealth. The Pacific peoples demonstrated that it was not essential to farm in order to prosper. Only one group of people, those living in the area of the Great Lakes, pursued horticulture. This activity, involving the planting of corn, tobacco, beans, squash, and sunflowers, led to the establishment of semipermanent villages.

Despite the differences in their lifestyles, all Native peoples were singularly ingenious at adapting to their environment. None were more successful at adaptation than the Inuit, who inhabited an ice-bound world in the north. At sea they used the speedy kayak and on land the dog-sled. They lived in a domed snow-hut (the igloo) in winter and in skin tents in summer. Caribou hides served as the basic clothing material. The Inuit were extremely skilful at making tools and weapons. Their use of bone and ivory for such equipment was extensive.

With the possible exceptions of the horticulturalists of southcentral Canada and the fisherfolk of the Pacific Slope, the economies of the Native inhabitants were quite simple ones. They were organized around the food supply, offering seminomadic people little scope for the acquisition of material possessions that would only have to be abandoned at the next—and imminent—move. Nevertheless, these *were* economies, and those within them functioned according to their inner logic. Food was not cultivated but pursued. The movement of fish and game had certain rhythms, but was at least potentially capricious. When

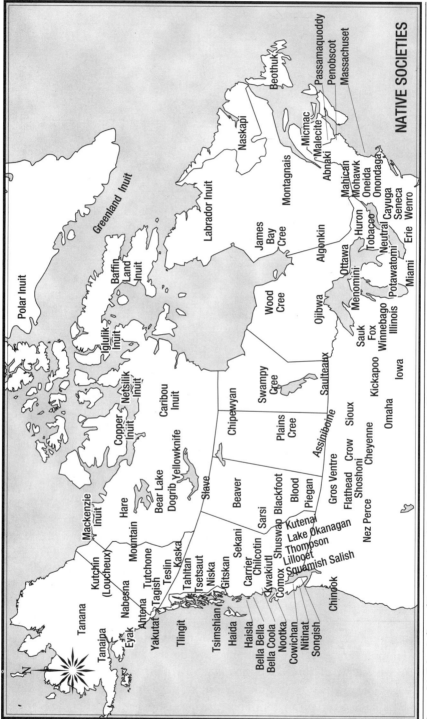

NATIVE SOCIETIES

Polar Inuit

Greenland Inuit

Baffin Land Inuit

Igulik Inuit

Copper Inuit

Netsilik Inuit

Caribou Inuit

Mackenzie Inuit

Labrador Inuit

Naskapi

Beothuk

Micmac
Malecite
Abnaki
Passamaquoddy
Penobscot
Massachuset

Montagnais

James Bay Cree

Mahican
Mohawk
Oneida
Onondaga
Cayuga
Seneca
Wenro

Algonkin

Huron
Tobacco
Neutral
Erie

Ottawa

Menomini

Potawatomi
Miami

Wood Cree

Ojibwa

Sauk
Fox
Winnebago
Illinois

Kickapoo

Iowa

Chipewyan

Swampy Cree

Saulteaux

Hare

Bear Lake

Dogrib Yellowknife

Slave

Plains Cree

Assiniboine

Mountain

Beaver

Sarsi

Sioux
Crow
Gros Ventre
Flathead
Shoshoni
Cheyenne

Omaha

Tanana

Tanaina

Kutchin (Loucheux)

Nabesna

Ahtena

Tutchone

Eyak

Yakutat Tagish

Teslin

Tahltan

Tsetsaut

Kaska

Niska

Gitskan

Sekani

Carrier

Chilcotin

Shuswap Blackfoot
Blood
Piegan

Kutenai

Lake Okanagan
Thompson
Lillooet
Squamish Salish

Nez Perce

Chinook

Tlingit

Tsimshian

Haida

Haisla

Bella Bella
Bella Coola
Kwakiutl
Comox
Nootka
Cowichan
Nitinat
Songish

Source: J.A. Price, *Indians of Canada: Cultural Dynamics* (Toronto: Prentice-Hall, 1979): viii–ix.

food was available, the population galvanized into action, gathering as much as possible and consuming it almost immediately. When food ran out, energetic questing for new supplies did not necessarily begin immediately. The people knew the general patterns of the wildlife and vegetation they sought, and hurry often did little good. It was, for example, useless to hunt for berries in February. In any event, these economies put no premium on the disciplined pursuit of goals, or on the deferral of expectations. Nor did they encourage the sort of unremitting hard labour familiar to the European newcomers.

The numbers of Aboriginals living in Canada on the eve of European intrusion has become the subject of considerable debate. One point seems clear. The Native population, lacking immunities to a variety of European diseases, was quickly decimated by epidemics, which spread silently across the land, often in advance of the actual appearance of a European carrier. Measles, small-pox, typhus, typhoid, venereal disease, and tuberculosis were as much European imports as the gun, the horse, and the wheel. The size of the population observed by the first European arrivals may have already been considerably modified by disease brought by the earliest fishermen, who may well have preceded the recorded explorers. The indigenous precontact population of Canada was probably substantially larger than the most generous estimates of all the first-contact observers.

THE FIRST INTRUDERS

As every schoolchild now knows, Norsemen made the first documented European visitations to North America. There is contemporary evidence of these visits in the great Icelandic epic sagas, confirmed in our own time by archaeological excavations near L'Anse aux Meadows on the northern tip of Newfoundland. The sagas describe the landings to the west of Greenland made by Leif Ericsson and his brother Thorvald. They also relate Thorfinn Karlsefni's colonization attempt at a place Leif had called Vinland, an attempt that was thwarted by hostile Aboriginals labelled in the sagas as 'Skraelings'. It is tempting to equate Vinland with the archaeological discoveries, although there is no real evidence for doing so.

Later Greenlanders may have timbered on Baffin Island. They may also have intermarried with the Inuit. Attempts have been made to attribute the Thule culture of the Inuit to such racial mixings. But Greenland gradually lost contact with Europe, and the Icelandic settlement there died away in the fifteenth century. For all intents and purposes, the Norse activities became at best part of the murky geographical knowledge of the late Middle Ages.

In our own time the uncovering of a world map executed in the mid-fifteenth century, showing a realistic Greenland and westward islands including inscriptions referring to Vinland, created much speculation about Europe's geographical knowledge before Columbus. This Vinland map has never been

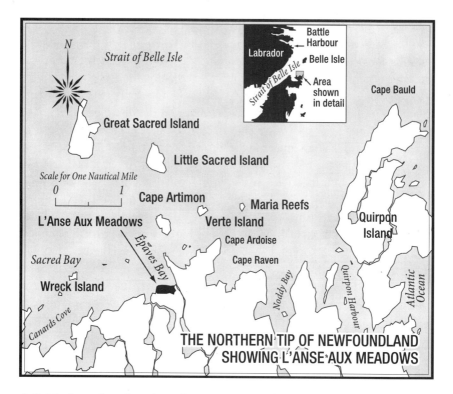

THE NORTHERN TIP OF NEWFOUNDLAND SHOWING L'ANSE AUX MEADOWS

definitively authenticated, and many experts have come to regard it with considerable scepticism. Like the Vinland map, none of the various candidates for North American landfalls before Columbus—except for the Vikings in Newfoundland—can be indisputably documented. In the fifteenth century, Portuguese and possibly English fishermen may have discovered the rich fishing grounds off the Grand Banks. An occasional vessel may have even made a landfall. The fishermen did not publicize their knowledge, although many scholars insist that it was probably in common circulation in maritime circles by the close of the fifteenth century.

EUROPE AROUND 1500

The arrival of Europeans in the Americas at the end of the fifteen century was a collaborative effort by mariners and scholars of many nations, behind which were profound changes in economies and polities. The ambition to visit new lands was fuelled by the surge of intellectual confidence and the explosion of knowledge associated with the Renaissance. By the end of the fifteenth century, geographers—led by Paolo dal Pozzo Toscanelli, an Italian cosmographer in Portuguese service—were convinced that Europe and Asia were closer than the ancients had conjectured. The schemes of Christopher Columbus were influ-

The sighting rod on an astrolabe could be turned to point at the sun or bright stars. A mariner could thus estimate the altitude of the sun or star above the horizon as an aid in navigation (Canadian Museum of Civilization, image number 77-401).

The compass, like this Italian example (*c.* 1580), was every mariner's most valuable navigational tool to avoid losing direction when out of sight of land (National Maritime Museum London).

enced both by Toscanelli and by Portuguese notions of oceanic islands. Geographical speculation and ship design and navigational aids pointed towards transatlantic voyages. Some time in the twelfth century, the Germans developed the cog, a single-masted ship decked over and fitted with rudder and tiller. In the early fifteenth century the cog's hull was lengthened and the vessel was given two additional masts, becoming the carvel (or caravel). Early explorers found smaller ships more manoeuvrable than larger ones and came to prefer them on their

The lateen rig is shown on this model of a fourteenth-century Mediterranean ship (Science & Society Picture Library).

voyages. Rigging also improved, particularly with the addition of the square sail to the earlier lateen (triangular) variety.

The art of navigation showed parallel development to ship design, a gradual result of trial and error by countless mariners. The greatest advance was in written sailing directions based on taking latitudes in relation to Polaris and the sun. Longitudes were still based largely on guesswork, mainly on a mariner's estimates of his vessel's speed. In addition to the compass, seamen used quadrants and astrolabes to determine latitude, and were familiar with the need to transfer their data on latitude and longitude onto charts ruled for these variables. *Routiers*—coastal pilot charts of European waters—were readily available, but none of the early explorers who reached North America had the

John Cabot Reaches Land Across the Atlantic, 1497

[Over the winter of 1497–8, the English merchant John Day wrote a letter to 'El Gran Almirante', probably Christopher Columbus, giving him an account of a recent voyage by John Cabot. This account provides some of our best evidence for Cabot's landfall. Source: J.A. Williamson, ed., *The Cabot Voyages and British Discoveries under Henry VII* (Cambridge: Hakluyt Society of the University Press, 1962):211–14.]

From the said copy [of 'the land which has been found', which is no longer extant] your Lordship will learn what you wish to know, for in it are named the capes of the mainland and the islands, and thus you will see where land was first sighted, since most of them was discovered after turning back. Thus your Lordship will know that the cape nearest to Ireland is 1800 miles west of Dursey Head which is in Ireland, and the southernmost part of the Island of the Seven Cities is west of Bordeaux River, and your Lordship will know that he [Cabot] landed at only one spot of the mainland, near the place where land was first sighted, and they disembarked there with a crucifix and raised banners with the arms of the Holy Father and those of the King of England, my master; and they found tall trees of the kind masts are made, and other smaller trees, and the country is very rich in grass. In that particular spot, as I told your Lordship, they found a trail that went inland, they saw a site where a fire had been made, they saw manure of animals which they thought to be farm animals, and they saw a stick half a yard long pierced at both ends, carved and painted with brazil, and by such things they believe the land to be inhabited. Since he was with just a few people, he did not dare advance inland beyond the shooting distance of a cross-bow, and after taking in fresh water he returned to his ship. All along the coast they found many fish like those which in Iceland are dried in the open and sold in England and

faintest idea of the hazards he was risking. The most remarkable feature of the first known voyages was the infrequency with which mariners ran into serious problems with rocks, shoals, and tides. Such master mariners had an instinctive 'feel' for the sea. They were able to read and deduce much from its colour and surface patterns.

Though the early explorers had their blind spots, they were without exception skilled sailors, suitably cautious in uncharted waters, which may explain many glaring failures to uncover rivers and bays obvious on any modern map. Once ashore, however, the first Europeans to reach North America threw caution to the winds, particularly in collecting rumours of rich mineral deposits or routes to Asia. Neither they nor their sponsors were at all interested in the scientific accumulation of knowledge. What they sought was wealth, equivalent to the riches the Spaniards were already taking out of their territories to the south. While other motives—such as national advantage and

other countries, and these fish are called in English 'stockfish'; and thus following the shore they saw two forms running on land one after the other, but they could not tell if they were human beings or animals; and it seemed to them that there were fields where they thought might also be villages, and they saw a forest whose foliage looked beautiful. They left England toward the end of May, and must have been on the way 35 days before sighting land; the wind was east-north-east and the sea calm going and coming back, except for one day when he ran into a storm two or three days before finding land; and going so far out, his compass needle failed to point north and marked two rhumbs below. They spent about one month discovering the coast and from the above mentioned cape of the mainland which is nearest to Ireland, they returned to the coast of Europe in fifteen days. They had the wind behind them, and he reached Brittany because the sailors confused him, saying that he was heading too far north. From there he came to Bristol, and he went to see the King to report to him all the above mentioned; and the King granted him an annual pension of twenty pounds sterling to sustain himself until the time comes when more will be known of this business, since with God's help it is hoped to push through plans for exploring the said land more thoroughly next year with ten or twelve vessels—because in his voyage he had only one ship of fifty 'tonnes' and twenty men and food for seven or eight months—and they want to carry out this new project. It is considered certain that the cape of the said land was found and discovered in the past by the men from Bristol who found 'Brasil' as your Lordship well knows. It was called the Island of Brasil, and it is assumed and believed to be the mainland that the men from Bristol found.

Since your Lordship wants information relating to the first voyage, here is what happened: he went with one ship, his crew confused him, he was short of supplies and ran into bad weather, and he decided to turn back.

missionary fervour directed at Aboriginal inhabitants—also entered the picture, the easy and rapid exploitation of the resources of the New World long remained the principal inspiration.

THE EUROPEAN ENTRY INTO NORTH AMERICA

John Cabot went ashore briefly at 'newfoundland'. Cabot, originally an Italian, had convinced Henry VII of England to finance one small ship of 50 tons and a crew of eighteen to sail west and find a short route to Asia. Cabot was lost at sea on a second voyage, and his mantle fell to a number of Portuguese mariners, some in English service, who produced a more clearly defined Newfoundland. Most of the sixteenth-century place names in Newfoundland were Portuguese rather than English. Portugal actually attempted to settle a colony on the Newfoundland coast under the leadership of Juan Fagundes, who had earlier sailed as far as the Gulf of St Lawrence.

Jacques Cartier Encounters Native Peoples, 1534

[Jacques Cartier sailed from St Malo on 20 April 1534 with two ships manned by sixty-one men each. A navigator apparently familiar with the Gulf of St Lawrence, he had been commissioned by Francis I of France to explore in North America. The following account is of one of the earliest encounters between Europeans and Native peoples on the northern part of the continent. *Source*: H.B. Stephens, *Jacques Cartier and His Four Voyages to Canada: An Essay with Historical, Explanatory and Philological Notes* (Montreal: W. Drysdale & Co., 1890):31–3.]

On the twenty-fourth [of July 1534] we made a large cross, thirty feet high; this was made in the presence of some of the savages at the point at the entrance of the harbor, on the middle of which cross we put a shield (escutcheon) in relief with three fleur-de-lys, above which was cut in large letters:

VIVE LE ROY DE FRANCE,

and we erected it in their presence on the point, and they looked at it keenly, both when we were making it and while erecting it. Having erected it we all joined hands and knelt down in adoration of it before their eyes, and we made signs to them, looking and pointing to heaven, that in this was our salvation. This astonished them greatly; they turned to each other and looked at the cross. Having gone back to our ships, their captain (chief) came to us in a canoe, wearing an old black bearskin, with his three daughters and his brother; they did not come as close as usual. The chief made a long speech, pointing to the cross and making a representation of it with his two fingers. Then he pointed to the district round us, as if to say it was all his, and that we should not have erected the cross without his permission. Having finished we showed him a ring or hatchet, as if we wished to exchange it for his bearskin, which attracted him, and he gradually came close to our ships. One of our sailors who was in the ship's boat laid his hand on the canoe, and instantly jumped into it with two or three more, and obliged them to go on board ship, at which they were much astonished. But our captain at once assured them they would receive no hurt, making signs of friendship to them, welcoming them to eat and drink. After this, we gave them to understand by signs that the cross was placed as a guide and mark to enter the harbor, and that we wished to return here shortly and that we would bring iron tools and other things, and that we wished to take with us two of his sons and that we would return again to this harbor. And we dressed each of the sons in a shift, a colored sack, and a red capo, and we placed a brass chain around the neck of each, which pleased them immensely. They gave their old clothes to those who returned. We gave a hatchet and some knives to each one of the three we sent back; these having reached shore and related what had passed to the others, about noontime six of their canoes, with five or six men in each, came to the ships, bringing fish to the chief's daughters and bid them adieu, and said some words to them which we could not understand. They made signs that they would not remove the cross. . . .

Portrait of Cartier from the frontispiece of *The Voyages of Jacques Cartier* by H.P. Biggar (Thomas Fisher Rare Book Library).

Fagundes ended up on Cape Breton Island, where his little settlement was destroyed by Natives, who 'killed all those who came there'. Nevertheless, by 1536 Newfoundland was sufficiently familiar, if exotic, to Europeans that a tourist voyage to the island was organized. London merchant Richard Hore (*fl.* 1507–40) signed up 120 passengers, 'whereof thirty were gentlemen'. When provisions ran short on the Newfound-land coast, some participants allegedly resorted to eating their compatriots. Those surviving were understandably relieved to get back to England.

In 1523 the French entered the picture through the activities of Italian master mariner Giovanni da Verrazzano (*c.* 1485–*c.* 1528). Of high birth, Verrazzano persuaded Francis I to sponsor a voyage of exploration. He made three voyages in all, opening a French trade with Brazil and convincing himself that what he was investigating was not Asia but a totally new continent. Verrazzano was succeeded by Jacques Cartier (1491–1557), who allegedly had been to Brazil and Newfoundland. In 1534 Francis I ordered him to uncover new lands 'where it is said that a great quantity of gold, and other precious things, are to be found.' There is little evidence of concern for the conversion of indigenous peoples in Cartier's efforts. He made three voyages: the first to make a great discovery, a second to locate some mineral resource there that would attract investors and the royal court, and a final large-scale effort that failed to produce any profit.

On his first voyage in 1534 Cartier explored the Gulf of St Lawrence. His second voyage in 1535 took him up-river as far as Mont Royal. He visited several Native villages and wintered at one of them, Stadacona. Here he heard about the fabulous kingdom of the Saguenay, somewhere farther west. A third voyage was actually headed by a great nobleman, the Sieur de Roberval (*c.* 1500–60). It was a disaster, finding little wealth to exploit and accomplishing nothing. The gold and diamonds Cartier brought back turned out to be iron pyrites and quartz. 'False as Canadian diamonds' became a common French expression of the time.

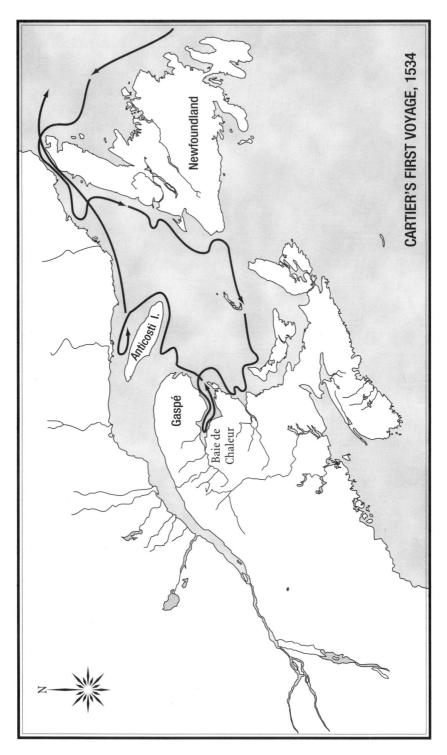

CARTIER'S FIRST VOYAGE, 1534

Newfoundland

Anticosti I.

Gaspé

Baie de Chaleur

N

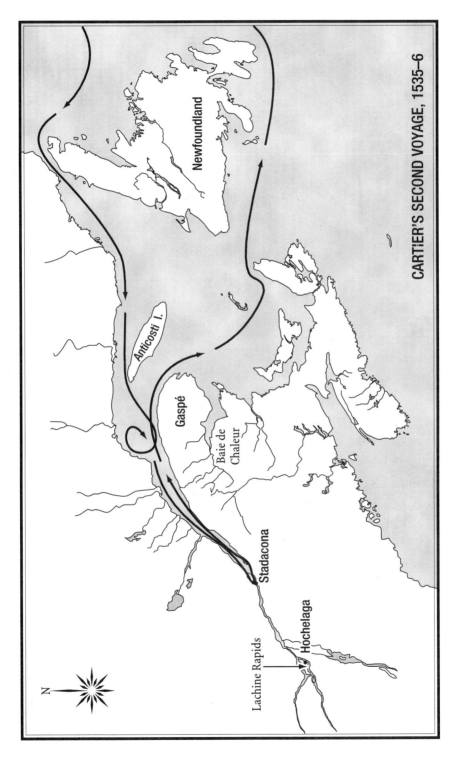

CARTIER'S SECOND VOYAGE, 1535–6

Newfoundland

Anticosti I.

Gaspé

Baie de Chaleur

Stadacona

Hochelaga

Lachine Rapids

N

Martin Frobisher made three voyages between 1576 and 1578 in search of the Northwest Passage (Poole painting 50, The Bodleian Library, University of Oxford).

Marooned in the Arctic, 1620

[Jens Munk was in what is now southern Norway. In 1611 he joined the Danish navy and later served with the Danish whaling fleet before being selected by King Christian IV of Denmark to search for a northwest passage. He left Copenhagen on 9 May 1619 and returned on 21 September 1620, having spent a winter with his crew near the modern town of Churchill, Manitoba. Most of the men died, mainly from scurvy. Of the crew of sixty-four men, only two returned to Norway alive. *Source*: W.A. Kenyon, ed., *The Journal of Jens Munk, 1619–1620* (Toronto: Royal Ontario Museum, 1980):30–1.

On 27 March [1620] I opened the surgeon's chest to examine its contents in detail, for as we no longer had a surgeon, I had to do whatever I could myself. And then I discovered what a serious oversight had been made in not providing a list that would tell us what the medicines were good for, and how they were to be used. I would also stake my life on the opinion that even the surgeon did not know how those medicines were to be used, for all the labels were written in Latin, and whenever he wished to read one, he had to call the priest to translate it for him.

The weather continued to be rather mild till 29 March, when Ismael Abrahamsen and Christian Gregersen

Despite the lack of accomplishment, a French claim to the St Lawrence region had been established, and the French would ultimately return there.

The next major adventurer to what is now Canada was the Englishman Martin Frobisher (1539?–94), who spent several years searching for the Northwest Passage and great wealth in the Arctic region. Frobisher was a leading English 'sea dog', part pirate and part merchant. In 1576 he raised the funds for an expedition to sail west through northern waters. He did not find the passage-

died. They were buried that same day, as we had both the opportunity and the ability at that time. Suend Arffuedsen, one of the carpenters, died on 30 March during a very sharp frost. My greatest sorrow and misery started at that time, and soon I was like a wild and lonely bird. I was obliged to prepare and serve drink to the sick men myself and to give them anything else I thought might nourish or comfort them. I was not accustomed to such duties, however, and had but little knowledge of what should be done. Johan Petterson, my second mate, died on 31 March, after a long illness during which he was confined to his bed, and my nephew, Erich Munk, died the following day. Both bodies were placed together in a single grave.

On 3 April there was such a fearfully sharp frost that none of us could get out of bed; nor did I have any men left to command, for they were all lying under the hand of God. Amidst all that misery and sorrow, Iffuer Alsing died. Next day the weather was so bitterly cold that it was impossible for anyone to dig a grave to bury the dead bodies that were in the ship. Then, on the fifth, Christoffer Opsloe and Rasmus Clemedsen, my chief gunner and mate, both died; and later that same day Lauritz Hansen also died. By that time the number of healthy men was so small that we could scarcely muster a burial party.

On 8 April William Gordon, my chief mate, died after a long illness; and that evening Anders Sodens also died. We buried them, too, in a common grave. We who were still alive managed to bury them, but only with great difficulty because of the miserable weakness that was upon us. We were so weak that not one of us was able to fetch wood from the forest. For fuel, we were forced to break up anything in the ship that would burn, even our own shallop. . . .

On 13 April I took a bath in a wine cask. I added to the water some of each of the different herbs that we found in the medicine chest and that we thought might be helpful. After me, those men who still had the strength to move about also took a bath. Thanks be to God, that bath did us much good, me in particular. The next day there was a sharp frost, and only four men besides myself were strong enough to sit up in their berths to hear the homily for Good Friday. Anders Oroust and Jens, the cooper, died on Easter Day, 16 April, after a long illness; and as the weather was fairly mild, we managed to bury them that same day. Although he was ill himself, I immediately promoted my quartermaster to the position of master so that he might assist me with whatever strength he could still muster. For by that time I was quite miserable and felt abandoned by the entire world, as you may imagine.

way, but did bring back mineral samples from Baffin Island. These were pronounced to be gold-bearing, leading to a second expedition in 1577, which brought back 200 tons of ore. A third voyage brought more ore, which was finally identified as iron pyrites. Frobisher's quest for the Northwest Passage in Arctic waters inspired a series of explorers, mainly Englishmen backed by English capital, over the next fifty years. The best known of them was Henry Hudson

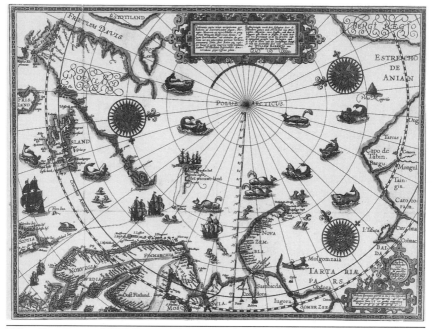

Willem Barent's map of 1598 illustrated European explorations through the polar regions (National Archives of Canada).

(d. 1611), who sailed under both English and Dutch auspices. On his last voyage in 1610 he entered Hudson Bay and navigated its eastern coastal waters southward into James Bay.

The great voyages of discovery were largely completed by the end of the sixteenth century, even though much of the North American continent remained to be mapped and charted. They occurred against a complex European backdrop of dynastic manoeuvring, the rise of the modern nation-state, the religious disputes of the Protestant Reformation and the Catholic Counter-Reformation, and the growth of capitalistic enterprise fuelled by the infusion of new wealth in the form of gold and silver bullion from the Indies. In the sixteenth century Henry VII and Elizabeth I of England joined Francis I of France as important patrons of master mariners who set sail for the West, hoping to obtain wealth and national advantage from the voyages they sponsored. The dissolution of an earlier alliance between Spain and England in the wake of the latter nation's becoming Protestant, as well as the complex relationships between the ruling houses of the two countries, encouraged Elizabeth to turn her 'sea dogs' loose on the Spanish empire. English exploration was inextricably bound up with 'singeing the Spanish beard' and with political hostility to Spain heightened by religious sentiments. English adventurers often combined the activities of explorer, pirate, and even colonizer. The French entered the American sweepstakes in the hopes of competing with the Spaniards and Portuguese. After Cartier's pioneering (and unsuccessful) voyages of 1534, 1535–6, and 1541–2, France became more wrapped up in its internal dynastic struggles than in overseas adventuring. The country did not show much state interest in North America until the end of the century, by which time Henry IV had stabilized the monarchy.

In both France and England, overseas investment by an emerging mercantile class took over gradually from the earlier efforts of intrepid mariners

This drawing by John White shows Inuit using bows and arrows to attack the Englishmen, who fire back with muskets, a conflict that was described in accounts of Frobisher's second expedition (Copyright © British Museum 202756).

backed by the Crown. Cartier's third voyage marked for France the transition from public to private enterprise, and the 1576 voyage of Martin Frobisher in search of the Northwest Passage to the East demonstrated the new importance of mercantile investment to the English.

By the end of the sixteenth century Europe had established that there were no wealthy Native civilizations to be conquered on the eastern seaboard, nor readily apparent sources of rich mineral wealth to be exploited. When it was clear that what the continent possessed were fish and furs, a more complex pattern of exploitation was developed that required the year-round presence of settlers. Both France and England shifted their energies from maritime thrusts to colonization.

EUROPEAN CONTACT AND THE DEVELOPMENT OF CULTURAL CONFLICT

The intrusion of Europeans greatly altered the dynamics of Aboriginal development, while providing us with a somewhat misleading version of the nature of the population at the moment of contact and beyond. Recorded history was, after all, monopolized by those who had written languages and could make records. In the centuries following European arrival, virtually everything written about the indigenous population of Canada was produced from the European perspective. That perspective, moreover, tended to involve considerable misunderstanding of Aboriginal culture and behaviour.

In many ways, there was no justification to the assumption of superiority over the indigenous population, which was the common response of the European observer. The visitors' veneer of civilization was a thin one at best, and often wore away quite quickly. The sixteenth century was still a nasty, brutish, and violent age. Most Europeans still ate with their fingers, bathed as seldom as possible, and enjoyed such amusements as bear-baiting, in which dogs were pitted against captive bears in fights to the death. The institutions of the ruling classes allowed heretics to be tortured in the name of Jesus Christ, witches to be burned at the stake, and thousands, whose beliefs or backgrounds were different from those in charge of church and state, to be executed. Public executions were guaranteed crowd-pleasers, especially if the victim could be drawn and quartered while still alive. In some parts of Europe a popular entertainment at fairs was watching blind men in pens attempt to beat each other to death with clubs. Garbage and animal excrement were piled high in the streets of European cities, 'piss-pots' were still emptied into the streets, and one of the major motivations behind European expansion was the search for new and more powerful scents to help disguise the stench of daily life. The term *sauvages* (savages), which the Europeans often used to refer to the Aboriginal peoples of North America, is, to the modern mind, ironic and, to Natives of today, insulting.

Native elder or chief, woman, and conjuror (Copyright © British Museum 315522, 315508, 315394).

At the same time, Europe had achieved a different stage of development than the indigenous peoples they visited. It had advanced to a new level of technology, based on the book and the wheel, although much of its technological glitter would prove relatively useless in the wilderness of the New World. Successful Europeans in Canada would for several centuries adopt Aboriginal technology to survive. Nevertheless, their inventions helped to give them a sense of superiority, as did their emerging capitalist economic order, their new political organization into nation-states, and

The Tradition of the Flood

[Antoine Lamothe Cadillac (1658–1730) was one of those immigrants to Canada who arrived with no previous history and who proved to be a wily if unscrupulous fur trader, operating mainly in the Michilimackinac and Detroit areas. At the end of the seventeenth century he prepared a manuscript memoir describing the Native peoples of the region. Are there alternative explanations to his for the flood traditions he discusses? *Source*: M.M. Quaife, ed., *The Western Country in the 17th Century: The Memoires of Antoine Lamothe Cadillac and Pierre Liette* (New York: The Citadel Press, 1962):52–60.]

All these tribes, without exception, have a tradition of the Flood; we shall see what their ideas are on this subject. They say that such a great quantity of snow and rain fell that all the waters, being gathered together, rose higher than the highest mountains, so that people went about everywhere in canoes and the earth was changed into a vast lake. But they maintain that in this universal flood, in which everyone perished, an old man in each tribe was saved, with all his family, because they had the sense when they saw the waters rising to build a very big canoe in which they put provisions and animals of all kinds, and after spending many days in great discomfort they threw an otter out of the boat to see whether he could not get to land somewhere; but they say the otter was drowned, for after some days he was seen floating on the water, on his back. After some time the old man sent a beaver in the opposite direction to see whether he could not find land. They say he found a sort of dam of dry wood, but because he was hungry he returned to the canoe, bringing back a big stump, which made the old man conclude that the waters were beginning to fall; then they turned their canoes toward the spot from which they had seen the beaver returning and at length they saw in the distance a great pile of wood, which had collected in the following manner:

They say that an enormous turtle fell from the sky and floated under

especially their Christian system of values and beliefs. These pronounced differences between Europeans and indigenous Canadians prevented the visitors from comprehending the people they encountered. The Europeans quite unconsciously, often quite subtly, judged Aboriginals by their own standards.

The Native economies did not produce political institutions on a European scale. Semisedentary people had no need for political organizations larger than the band, which was based on the consolidation of a few family units. Even where horticulture was developed, with its large semipermanent villages, political structure was not complex by European standards. 'Chiefs' were not kings. They may not even have been 'head men' in any European sense. Such a concept of rulership was introduced and imposed on the indigenous population by the newcomers. As is now well known, the Native notion of property, especially involving land, was well beyond the comprehension of the Europeans. While

water; and as there was a quantity of dry wood around, and other trees with their roots and branches carried hither and thither by the wind and the water, those which came against the turtle fastened to him and remained there, so that in a short time such a large quantity accumulated that one could walk on it as on a raft. When the old man saw this, he landed on it, and finding a little earth on the roots of the trees he collected it and offered it as a sacrifice to the sun, which dried it. Then the old man, after reducing it to dust, sowed it broadcast over the waters, so that it drank up the water with which the earth was covered. Each tribe maintains that the turtle which fell from the sky stopped on the highest mountain in their part of the country, so that there is no agreement where the place was.

If the statements set forth in this chapter are considered attentively the reader may think, as I do, that all these tribes are descended from the Hebrews and were originally Jews, which may also be observed from the terms they use in conversation and in their speeches and customs. . . .

It may be thought that if the Indians are really descended from the Jews they would at least have retained their language, since it is not natural that children should forget what their fathers and mothers have taught them from the time they began to lisp; and it is much more probable that habits, manners, and customs should pass away than the operations of the mind, which cannot be expressed nor known except by means of signs and words, which are lost only by the decay of the organs of the human body.

It seems to me that we may reply to this objection, that a language that is badly taught rusts and perishes completely, as everything else does in the course of time. Reason and experience teach us that a language becomes disfigured and weakened in proportion to its neglect and use. . . . Nor is it surprising that a people who have been wanderers and vagrants for so many centuries, and never accustomed to writing or reading—which are the foster-mothers of a language—should have so corrupted and debased it that scarcely any trace of it now remains.

some Native groups could conceive of territory as 'belonging' to them, the concept was one of usage rather than ownership. Natives erroneously identified as kings were quite happy to 'sell' to the European newcomers land that neither they nor their people owned, at least as Europeans understood ownership.

Lacking much inclination to create hierarchical political organizations, the Natives practised war according to different rules than those employed in Europe, where institutions of church and state went to war for 'reasons of state'. Indian wars were mainly raids by a few warriors, conducted partly because success in battle was an important test of Indian manhood. They were often used to capture women and children to replace those lost within the band. Individual prowess in battle was valued, while long-term military strategy and objectives were not. Indians had their own military agendas, and were notoriously fickle allies from the European perspective. Only the Iroquois—who in the seventeenth century may have developed a militarily viable form of political organization partly based on European models—were able to compete with the newcomers and withstand their military power.

Nowhere was the gulf between Natives and newcomers more apparent than in the spiritual realm. Aboriginal religious beliefs were complex, although not readily apparent to the outside observer. They were part of an intricate religio-magical world that the Native peoples inhabited and shared with the flora and fauna. Given the hunting orientation of most groups, it is hardly surprising that animals were endowed with spiritual significance. The very act of food consumption often acquired deep religious meaning, becoming a form of worship of the spirit world through everyday activity. Many peoples had legends about the origins of the world, and some may have believed in a single Creator, although this is what missionaries wanted them to believe. The mixture of authentic Indian lore with European thought and missionary teaching that has coloured Indian legends and tales over the last 350 years has made it difficult—perhaps even impossible—to separate one from the other. Formal religious ceremonies were not readily apparent to the visitors, except for the activities of the shamans, who claimed supernatural powers and engaged in several kinds of folk medicine ranging from herbal treatment to exorcism. Shamans were no more priests than Native leaders were kings, but Europeans tended to consider their activities to be at the core of Native religion. The newcomers found it impossible to grasp that for the Native peoples, objects in nature were alive and had their own powers, or that rituals connected with the ordinary round of daily life could have deep religious significance. That Native religion had no buildings, no hierarchy, and no institutional presence further disoriented the Europeans.

Tolerance for alternative spiritual values and belief systems was hardly one of Europe's strong suits in the Age of Discovery. The period of European arrival in North America coincided with the Protestant Reformation and the Catholic Counter-Reformation. Christianity was undergoing profound alteration, with traditional Catholicism subjected to reform from both within and without. Protestants and Catholics alike were quite capable of fierce persecution of any deviation from official belief and practice, and both could agree that what was being encountered in Canada was pagan supernaturalism that needed to be uprooted as quickly as possible and replaced with a 'true faith'. That Europeans themselves could not agree on the truth perplexed some Native peoples, such as the Iroquois, who were exposed to competing French, English, and Dutch missionaries.

The European intruders could not grasp the notion that Christianity was part of a well-developed European value system, or that indigenous religious beliefs and practices were integral to Native existence. Views of the world and

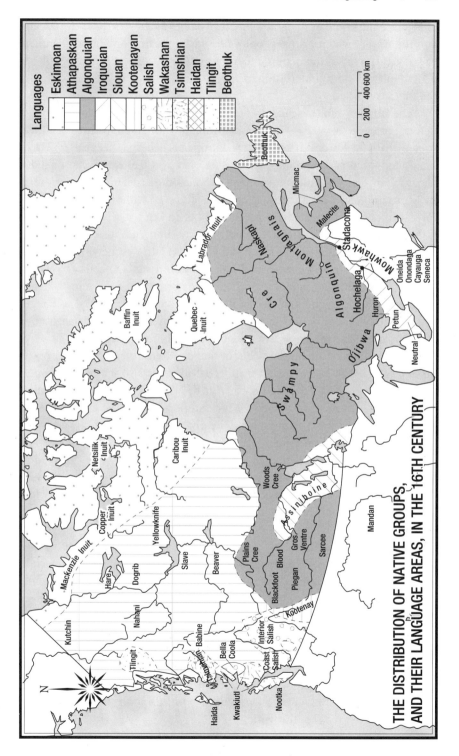

Languages
- Eskimoan
- Athapaskan
- Algonquian
- Iroquoian
- Siouan
- Kootenayan
- Salish
- Wakashan
- Tsimshian
- Haidan
- Tlingit
- Beothuk

0 200 400 600 km

THE DISTRIBUTION OF NATIVE GROUPS, AND THEIR LANGUAGE AREAS, IN THE 16TH CENTURY

one's place in it were as integral to life for Natives as they were for Europeans, and the way in which Native peoples related spiritually to their environment was a critical part of their culture. Europe could not convert Native peoples to Christianity without undermining the very basis of their existence. Naturally, the Indians resisted.

The almost total absence of seeking complex long-term goals through deferral of expectations was easily one of the most marked features of Indian society from the European perspective. Europeans believed that goals had to be inculcated at an early age through a series of repressive tactics that included heavy reliance on corporal punishment, although monastic orders were continually proving that the same results could be achieved without the overt use of force. Children were treated like adults and put to work at an early age. Native Canadians, on the other hand, treated their children with affectionate indulgence, seldom inflicting reprimands and totally eschewing corporal punishment. Young warriors learned stoic self-control and an ability to endure hardship and physical pain, but Indian self-control was more the ability to endure than the capacity to obey. Though circumscribed, controlled, and regulated by ritual, tradition, and custom (what we today would call 'socialization'), most Indians hated taking orders, particularly from Europeans.

While commenting on the freedom that children were allowed, European observers of every Native group from coast to coast also wrote that women were badly exploited. European society at the time could scarcely be called liberal in its treatment of women. What the newcomers saw as exploitation reflected their inability to comprehend the divisions of labour within a warrior society. Men hunted and fought, while women were responsible for just about everything else. Ironically enough, when European women were captured by raiding parties and integ-rated into Native life, many chose to remain with their captors instead of accepting repatriation back into colonial society. What this says about the treatment of women by the respective cultures can only be surmised.

As for morality, particularly sexual, the Europeans and the Natives seemed about equally matched. The generosity of the males in some tribes in permitting their women to bestow sexual favours on the newcomers speaks volumes about the male prerogative in Native society. While some observers felt obliged to comment on Indian promiscuity, a few had the decency to recognize that Europeans were not blameless in this regard. In the saga of European intrusion around the world over the centuries, Europe sent only males, particularly as exploiters and traders in the presettlement period, so Native females were employed for sexual purposes. The pattern in western Canada of European male coupling with Indian female produced a mixed-blood society that had its parallels in other parts of the world.

Almost from the outset, European newcomers to Canada had two contra-dictory responses to the peoples they were contacting and describing. On the one hand, much of what they saw of Native life, particularly beyond mere superficial observation, struck them as admirable, giving rise to the idea of the 'noble savage'. The Indians exhibited none of the negative features of capi-talistic society, such as covetousness and rapaciousness, and they revered freedom while eschewing private property. On the other hand, there was the equally powerful image of the Indian as brutal savage and barbarian, partic-ularly in the context of war. The newcomers kept trying to 'civilize' the Natives by converting them to Christianity and forcibly educating them in European ways. But Mère Marie de l'Incarnation, the head of the Ursuline School for girls at Quebec, admitted of her Native charges in 1668 that they 'find docil-ity and intelligence in these girls, but when we are least expecting it, they clamber over our wall and go off to run with their kinsmen in the woods, finding more to please them there than in all the amenities of our French houses' (Marshall 1967: 341).

Europeans would blunder on for centuries in their attempts to come to terms with the indigenous peoples of North America. The Natives would prove tenacious in maintaining their own identity and culture in the face of much effort to Europeanize them, but they lacked the physical power to prevent either constant encroachment on their territory, or the continual undermining of the basic physical and spiritual substance of their way of life. The cultural contact between Native and newcomer was a true tragedy. Reconciliation of the two cultures was quite impossible, and the failure of reconciliation resounds still today.

THE FIRST EUROPEAN COMMUNITIES

When generations of experience taught Europeans that there was no quick road to wealth by exploiting the indigenous peoples or the resource base of North America, men's hopes turned to transplanting Europeans who could take advantage of fish and furs. The shift occurred at the beginning of the seven-teenth century. There were a variety of motives in the minds of the early promoters of settlement, few of whom ever planned to set foot on North American soil. National advantage, religion, humanitarianism, greed, personal ambition, and sheer fantasy were all present in various combinations. European monarchs and their supporters were flattered by the 'enlarging of Dominions'. Missions to the Natives and the possibilities of refuge from religious persecu-tion at home excited the pious. Many a promoter saw colonization as a way to rid Europe of unwanted paupers and petty criminals. Investors were tempted with talk of titles and large land grants. In the pursuit of great profits, men easily lost their common sense. Although large-scale colonization activities

Champlain's rendition of the *Habitation* at Port Royal, which was built in 1605 on the north shore of the Annapolis Basin. The parts of the closed quadrilateral complex are identified in his *Voyages* in an accompanying key: for example, 'A. Artisans' quarters'; 'B. Platform for cannon'; 'C. The storehouse' (National Archives of Canada NC-8760).

were begun by the English in Virginia in 1607, the ventures undertaken in the northern latitudes were typically more modest. They consisted mainly of trading posts and fishing settlements.

English familiarity with Newfoundland led London merchants to attempt colonization there beginning in 1610. The London and Bristol Company for the Colonization of Newfoundland (usually known as the Newfoundland Company) was organized by forty-eight subscribers who invested £25 each. The plan was that permanent settlers employed by the company would quickly dominate the fishery over those who came in the spring and went home in the autumn. Europe was desperately short of a protein food for the poor, and dried cod found a ready market, especially in Catholic companies. The first settlement of the company was established by John Guy (d. 1629), who led forty colonists from Bristol to Cupid's Cove on Conception Bay in July 1610, only months after the company was granted the entire island and the venture was funded by sale of stock. The company did not appreciate how difficult local agriculture would be, given the soil and the climate, or how unlikely it was in the vast expanses of the New World that settlers could be kept as landless employees labouring solely for the profit of their masters. Its fishing settlements prospered no more than did those of courtiers like George Calvert, First Baron

Baltimore (1579/80–1632), who began a plantation at Avalon in 1623, which he subsequently moved to Maryland.

The French were marginally more successful than the English at establishing colonies in the northern regions, both at Acadia (the region vaguely bounded by the St Lawrence to the north, the Atlantic Ocean to the east and south, and the St Croix River to the west) and at Canada in the St Lawrence Valley. An early effort by the Marquis La Roche de Mesgouez (*c.* 1540–1606) on Sable Island failed dismally, with a settler rebellion murdering their local leaders over the winter of 1602–3. The island was subsequently evacuated. A similar result occurred at a settlement at the mouth of the Saguenay River. In May 1604 Pierre Du Gua de Monts (1558?–1628) arrived on the Nova Scotia coast with a young draftsman named Samuel de Champlain (*c.* 1570–1635). The two men were searching for a suitable site to establish a settlement, a condition of de Monts's grant of a trading monopoly in the region. They tried first on an island in the mouth of the St Croix River. In 1605 the settlement was moved to Port Royal in the Annapolis Basin, where de Monts built a *habitation,* a supposed replica of which still exists as a historic site. In 1606 the Paris lawyer Marc Lescarbot (*c.* 1570–1642) joined the colony and kept a narrative of its development, published in 1609 as *Histoire de la Nouvelle France.* In this work Lescarbot noted the foundation of *L'Ordre de Bon Temps* in 1607, a sort of dining club with extemporaneous entertainment. He also described the masque he wrote for it (the first play composed and performed in North America). The colonists were obliged to leave in 1607 when de Monts was forced to relinquish his monopoly, but a French presence would continue in Acadia from the first establishment of Port Royal, usually in the form of a handful of individuals trading with the Natives.

As for Samuel de Champlain, he headed up the St Lawrence in 1608 to found a new trading post for de Monts. Another *habitation* was erected, this one including three buildings of two storeys—connected by a gallery around the outside, 'which proved very convenient', wrote Champlain—surrounded by a moat and palisades. Champlain provided a careful drawing of this *habitation* in his *Voyages.* He was forced to put down a conspiracy and face a devastating attack of scurvy in the first year. The post survived, however, and Champlain gradually allied himself with the local Native peoples, who supplied him with furs and drew the French into war against the Iroquois. Champlain had little alternative to an alliance against the Iroquois, and they became mortal enemies of the French. There were only about fifty Frenchmen on the St Lawrence by 1615. Among the early settlers, only Louis Hébert (1595?–1627), who came to Quebec in 1617 after lengthy service at Port Royal as a surgeon, showed an interest in cultivating the land. But Hébert was most useful for his medical and apothecary skills; the trading company actually attempted to discourage him from agriculture. Not until 1618—when Champlain outlined a grand scheme for the colonization of New France in reports to the king and the French Chamber of Commerce—did anything approaching the plans of the Newfoundland Company enter the French vision. Earlier French activities, including those of Champlain himself, had been underfinanced by a succession of individual entrepreneurs and small syndicates. Trading posts, rather than settlement colonies, were the goal.

Until 1618, Champlain had served as an agent for others rather than as a colonial promoter in his own right. In that year, however, he combined arguments for major investors with a scheme designed to appeal to the imperial pretensions of the Crown. New France and the St Lawrence not only held the possibility of a short route to Asia but could produce 'a great and permanent trade' in such items as fish, timber, whale oil, and furs. The annual income was projected at 5,400,000 *livres*, virtually none of it coming from agriculture and less than 10 per cent coming from furs. Champlain requested that priests, 300 families of four people each, and 300 soldiers be sent to his base on the St Lawrence. Amazingly enough, French response was enthusiastic, and Louis XIII instructed the syndicate employing Champlain to expedite his plans. The partners and Champlain, however, were unable to agree upon terms or make any progress in establishing the colony. Not until 1627, when Cardinal Richelieu assumed supervision of New France and established the Company of One Hundred Associates, did Champlain's grandiose schemes receive substantial backing.

THE BEGINNINGS OF OVERLAND EXPLORATION

The geographical shakedown of European colonization activity in the late sixteenth and early seventeenth centuries determined that it would be the French who would take the lead in exploring the interior of the continent, and that their activities would extend far beyond the boundaries of what is now Canada. While the English, Scots, Dutch, and Swedes established settlements along the eastern seaboard, the French founded their settlements on the St Lawrence River. Providing access to the Great Lakes and to most of the major river systems of the continent, this river would confer enormous power and influence on the nation that controlled it. It focused the French need for new sources of furs to supply the major export commodity of New France, and the ability of young Frenchmen to adapt themselves to the ways of the Native inhabitants. Its access to the interior ensured that most of the great feats of inland exploration would be executed by the French.

Champlain himself was active in moving inland to investigate territory previously unknown to Europe, but he was not a typical figure. The first major

French overland explorer, in many ways quintessential, was Étienne Brûlé (*c.* 1592–1633), who lived with the Hurons near Georgian Bay, Lake Huron, in 1612, and may have been the first European to sight lakes Superior and Erie. A shadowy elusive figure, Brûlé, like many early explorers, left no written accounts of his life or adventures. It is likely that he had volunteered in 1610 to live with the Indians and learn their language, and he was probably the young man to whom Champlain referred in 1611 as 'my French boy who came dressed like an Indian' (quotes in *Dictionary of Canadian Biography* 1966, I:131). In 1615 Brûlé accompanied a party of Huron braves into the territory of the Susquehanna to the south of the Iroquois, in what is now southwestern New York state. He took advantage of the opportunity to investigate the neighbouring regions, perhaps reaching Chesapeake Bay, and certainly tramping around modern Pennsylvania. Brûlé subsequently journeyed to the north shore of Georgian Bay, and then in the early 1620s along the St Mary's River to Lake Superior. Like many Europeans who 'went native', Brûlé's compatriots respected him as an interpreter, even though they were intensely suspicious of his new persona. In Brûlé's case, his moral character and behaviour were criticized by Champlain even before his final 'treachery' in 1629 when he entered the employment of the Kirke brothers, who had successfully captured the tiny French colony. By pursuing his own agenda rather than observing the abstract national loyalties dear to European hearts and values, he had thus established a familiar pattern for those early Europeans who had come to terms with North America. By 1633 Brûlé was dead, reportedly killed and eaten by Hurons.

Over the course of the seventeenth century, the interpreter—as represented by Brûlé—would be transformed into the *coureur de bois*—the 'runner of the woods' or 'bushloper'—as the English often called him. These men would be responsible for most of the constantly broadening geographical knowledge of the North American continent. Their desire was less to improve cartography than to exploit new sources of wealth, particularly furs, and above all to enjoy a free and adventurous life in the woods. Whether or not these wilderness bravoes became completely assimilated into Indian society and culture (some did), they all learned skills from the Native peoples that made them crucial figures in the economy of New France. Marine skills like sighting latitude or reading the surface of the water were replaced by the ability to live off the land, to paddle a canoe for long distances with few breaks, to hunt animals for food, and of course to communicate successfully with a local Indian population, not merely at the level of language but at one of genuine empathy. These inland explorers travelled in exposed parties and had no defensive structure such as a ship to protect them from attack. They lived by their wits and had to be constantly adaptable. They made splendid guerrilla warriors as Europe moved into warfare for control of the continent.

By the mid-1620s the first period of European intrusion in what is now Canada had been completed. Exploration of the new continent's eastern seaboard was done, and Europe could construct a fairly decent map of that coastline. What lay beyond was beginning to be investigated. Europe was on the verge of deciding that major transplantations of people were going to be necessary if this new northern land were to be exploited. As for the indigenous population, they had been buffeted by epidemic disease, the causes of which were beyond their comprehension, but they had not yet been marginalized. The Native peoples could still meet the newcomers on what appeared to be equal terms. In retrospect, we can see how ephemeral this equality really was.

Major Events, 1627–1758

1627 Cardinal Richelieu establishes the Company of One Hundred Associates.

1629 The Kirke brothers capture Quebec.

1632 Treaty of St-Germain-en-Laye restores Canada and Acadia to France.

1633 Champlain returns to the St Lawrence.

1634 Jesuits set up permanent missions in Huronia.

1635 Champlain dies.

1639 Jesuits establish Ste-Marie-aux-Hurons.

1640 Iroquois begin attacking the Huron.

1642 Montreal is established.

1645 Company of One Hundred Associates surrenders its monopoly to local interests. Madame de La Tour surrenders Fort La Tour.

1647 Canada adopts government by central council.

1649 Iroquois destroy St-Louis and St-Ignace; martyrdom of Jean de Brébeuf and Gabriel Lalemant.

1654 English capture Acadia.

1659 Bishop Laval arrives in Canada.

1662 French establish first Newfoundland colony at Placentia Bay.

1663 Earthquake strikes Canada. French royal government takes over New France and institutes the *Coutume de Paris*.

1665 Carignan-Salières regiment arrives in New France. Jean Talon arrives as first intendant.

1667 English return Acadia to France.

1670 Hudson's Bay Company is granted a charter by Charles II.

1689 War of the League of Augsburg begins.

1690 Port Royal captured by the English; Quebec is unsuccessfully invaded.

1697 Treaty of Ryswick ends War of the League of Augsburg.

1702 War of Spanish Succession begins.

1713 By the Treaty of Utrecht, which ends the War of Spanish Succession, France surrenders Nova Scotia and Newfoundland claims to Great Britain.

1720 Louisbourg is established.

1737 First iron forge at St-Maurice is established.

1744 War of the Austrian Succession begins.

1745 Louisbourg is captured by joint Anglo-American military force.

1748 Treaty of Aix-la-Chapelle ends the War of the Austrian Succession.

1749 British establish Halifax.

1755 General Braddock is defeated on the Monongahela River near Fort Duquesne. Acadians are expelled from Nova Scotia.

1756 Seven Years' War officially begins.

1758 Louisbourg is taken by force under General James Wolfe. Acadians are rounded up and again expelled. Nova Scotia's first elected assembly meets. Nova Scotia's government advertises for settlers in New England.

2

Struggling for a Continent, 1627–1758

✿

Cardinal Richelieu, as drawn by François Ragot (National Archives of Canada C-041620).

In 1627 Cardinal Richelieu, Louis XIII's 'grey eminence', assumed supervision of New France and established the Company of One Hundred Associates. However, Richelieu's company, unlike the English Newfoundland Company, was organized from the top of the government rather than from grassroots interest in the profits of colonization. It was to be capitalized at 300,000 *livres*, each participant contributing 3,000, and profits were not to be distributed initially. Of the 107 members listed in May 1629, only twenty-six were merchants and businessmen, mainly from Paris. The remainder were courtiers and state officials. The company's initial venture—at a cost of 164,270 *livres*—was to send four ships containing 400 people and carrying 'all necessary commodities & quantities of workmen & families coming to inhabit & clear the land and to build & prepare the necessary lodging' to Quebec in 1628 (quoted in Trudel 1973:118). Unfortunately, England and France had gone to war in 1627, and in July 1628 the company's ships were captured off Gaspé by an Anglo-Scottish armed expedition led by the brothers Kirke. Thus began a military struggle lasting more than a century between France and Britain for control of North America.

The nineteenth-century American historian Francis Parkman wrote of a 'Half Century of Conflict', but it was really much longer and more protracted. The conflict would transcend a straightforward European rivalry, increasingly involving as it did both the population of the colonies and the Native peoples of the continent—each often fighting with their own agendas—as well as other remote corners of the world. The French colonies of North America felt the effects of this contest far more than their British counterparts to the south. The

Champlain's New France

In 1603 Pierre Du Gua de Monts (1558?–1628) was granted a trading monopoly in northeastern North America in return for an obligation to settle sixty colonists each year and to establish missions among the Aboriginals. Among the first settlers he recruited was a young draftsman, Samuel de Champlain (c. 1570–1635), who had been to Tadoussac in 1603 and would serve as geographer and cartographer for de Monts's expedition. Thus Champlain continued a commitment to explore and colonize the New World that would end only with his death on Christmas Day. Unlike his English contemporaries, William Bradford at Plymouth Plantation or John Winthrop at Boston, Champlain had not been able to lead a prospering colony through the problems of internal growth and the establishment of permanent institutions. Instead, much of his career was spent dealing with the preliminaries of settlement, in the interests of which he sailed to France nine times to further his plans for colonization or to resist attempts to negate them.

As a successful geographer and intrepid explorer who was equal to the most arduous demands of wilderness life, and who was capable in complex dealings with Native peoples, Champlain also left a literary legacy. The three volumes of his *Voyages* (published in Paris in 1613, 1619, and 1632) provide much of what we know about New France during this period. This map of New France by Champlain appeared in the last volume of his *Voyages*. It includes the territories he explored, which are rendered with considerable accuracy, along with inevitably inaccurate renderings of regions for which he had only second-hand information (National Archives of Canada).

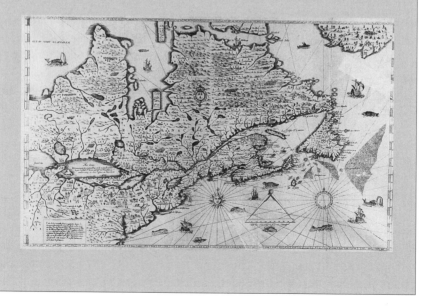

much smaller population in New France was more often in the front lines of the fighting, which frequently occurred on French territory. Between 1627 and the final military defeat of New France more than a century later, the French experienced only one protracted period (from 1713 to the early 1740s) when they were not constantly at war or under severe military threat, either from native peoples or the British. The pervasiveness of the international rivalry came equally to affect British colonists and British policy in the northern region.

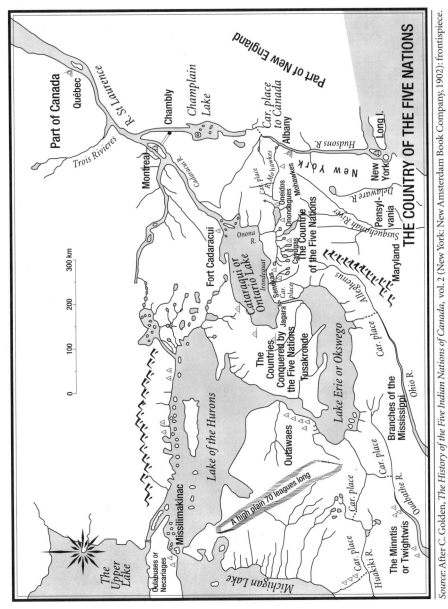

Source: After C. Golden, *The History of the Five Indian Nations of Canada*, vol. 2 (New York: New Amsterdam Book Company, 1902): frontispiece.

NEW FRANCE FIGHTS FOR SURVIVAL

In July 1629 Lewis and Thomas Kirke, who were at the head of an Anglo-Scottish armed expedition, forced Champlain's little outpost on the St Lawrence to surrender. In 1629 an attempt by the Company of One Hundred Associates to reoccupy Quebec failed dismally. The colony was restored to France in 1632 under the Treaty of St-Germain-en-Laye. One of the first French arrivals that year was Father Paul Le Jeune (1591–1664), recently appointed superior-general of the Jesuit missions in Canada. The Jesuits were to be the principal missionary order in the colony. Le Jeune soon began sending the first of the annual reports, the famous *Jesuit Relations*, which were forwarded to the provincial Father of the Society of Jesus in Paris to explain and promote in the mother country the missionaries' efforts. They combine a wealth of detail about life in New France, the Native peoples, Iroquois warfare, the Huron missions, exploration and travel, as well as accounts of various miracles. Champlain returned to Quebec in May 1633 after a four-year exile, tired but optimistic. He would die on Christmas Day 1635, his vision of a prosperous colony still beyond his grasp. At the time there were but 150 settlers on the St Lawrence.

Over the next few decades, the forces along the St Lawrence that met in bitter rivalry were less France and Britain and more Catholic evangelical energy on the one hand and resistance from the indigenous population on the other. The struggle was over the control of the fur trade. Conflict along the Atlantic seaboard had more traditional European overtones, while in Canada the long rivalry between the Iroquois and the Indian trading allies of the French created much fear and havoc, with disastrous consequences for the Huron people caught in the middle.

The Huron had access to a seemingly inexhaustible supply of furs from the northwest, and the French were determined to keep the supply flowing to Montreal and Quebec. The Huron had once greatly outnumbered the Iroquois, but in the 1630s their numbers were greatly reduced by diseases contracted from the French missionaries who lived among them. In 1634, the year the Jesuits set up permanent missions in Huronia, the Natives suffered an epidemic of measles. In 1639 the Jesuits oversaw the building of an elaborate fortified headquarters, Ste-Marie-aux-Hurons, on the Wye River. It eventually comprised twenty buildings, including a residence for priests, a church, a hospital, outbuildings for farming, residences for lay workers and Indian converts, as well as a canal with three locks.

The Iroquois—supplied by the Dutch with firearms, which the French were reluctant to give to their Indian allies—were equally determined to control the flow of furs. They ambushed the Huron fur-fleets on the Ottawa River, and between 1640 and 1645 they blockaded the river, while also attacking the settlements on the St Lawrence from 1643 onwards. Under the force of the assault, the Company of One Hundred Associates virtually withdrew from

New France in 1645, giving its fur-trading monopoly to the *Communauté des Habitants*, an organization of Canadian merchants, which agreed to continue to pay for the administration of the colony. While the devolution of the fur trade to local interests was a positive move for the colony, the new company soon felt the effects of Iroquois hostility, which limited the fur trade for an entire decade. The Iroquois soon turned their full attention to Huronia. In July 1648 Senecas destroyed the mission of St-Joseph and killed 700 Huron. In March 1649 a party of 1,200 Iroquois destroyed St-Louis and St-Ignace, where the priests Jean de Brébeuf (1593–1649) and Gabriel Lalemant (1610–49) were tortured to death. The weakened Huron were killed, surrendered, or fled. Before the Iroquois could reach Ste-Marie, the Jesuits there 'applied the torch to the work of our own hands' and fled with some 300 families to Christian Island in Georgian Bay. Most died of starvation or malnutrition. The next year the missionaries returned to Quebec with a few hundred Huron, the pathetic remnant of a once-powerful nation.

The Huron were early victims of European ethnocentrism. As for the missionaries themselves, only the Jesuits' profound faith and misguided intentions—to educate the Natives in French ways and induct them into a completely alien form of religion—kept them on their indomitable rounds of travel and life under extremely harsh and tense conditions. Many of the Natives turned against the missionaries, blaming their problems with disease and with the Iroquois on the Christian interlopers. Indeed, by exposing the Natives to disease and weakening their culture by introducing alien religious beliefs, the missionaries may have inadvertently contributed to the destruction of Huronia.

In 1647 Canada adopted government by a central council, with elected representatives of the districts of Quebec, Trois-Rivières, and Montreal employed for consultative purposes. Such a government was both responsive to the wishes of the inhabitants and autonomous of the mother country, but the arrangement was more a result of emergency conditions than a genuine reform. With the Huron destroyed, the Iroquois turned the full brunt of their fury on the French at Montreal. Dollier de Casson observed in the autumn of 1651 that 'not a month of this summer passed without our roll of slain being marked in red at the hands of the Iroquois' (Dollier de Casson 1928:155). The attacks subsided over the course of the decade, but the menace never entirely disappeared. The period of the Indian wars was a difficult one for the French fur traders. Not surprisingly, many headed northwestward to avoid the Iroquois. Among these adventurers was Pierre Radisson (*c.* 1640–1710) and his brother-in-law Médard Chouart Des Groseilliers (*c.* 1618–96?). Radisson was born in France, but had been captured by Mohawks in 1651 and adopted by a prominent family, and was thus forced to learn Native ways in order to survive. In 1659 this pair took a journey to Lake Superior that excited their interest in exploiting the fur-bearing region that they knew extended as far north as

Pierre-Esprit Radisson

Few *coureurs de bois* had the time or inclination to keep detailed records of their adventures or accounts of their personal lives. However, one of the greatest, Pierre-Esprit Radisson, left accounts of his six 'voyages' into the interior of North America in the form of a series of autobiographical narratives. They constitute some of the most fascinating documents of the early period of European settlement and expansion across the continent, a world where the rules were quite different from those in Europe. Radisson (*c.* 1640–1710) was born in France. As an eleven-year-old in 1651 he was kidnapped by a Mohawk raiding party and adopted by a prominent family, rapidly acquiring Native ways. After meeting another Frenchman in similar circumstances on a hunting trip, the two young men murdered their Native companions and escaped, but were soon recaptured. He eventually managed to escape in 1654 and later accompanied some Jesuit missionaries to the Iroquois village at Onondaga in present-day New York state. Radisson employed his knowledge of the Natives to plan an escape. In the spring the Natives were invited to a great feast given by the French, who provided large quantities of food, drink, and entertainment, insisting that their guests could not rest until everything had been consumed. Eventually the Natives fell into a sated (perhaps drugged) state, and the Europeans left. The Jesuits prevented

Radisson and his secular companions from slaughtering the sleeping Natives.

In 1659 Radisson began his partnership with Médard Chouart Des Groseilliers (*c.* 1618–96?) to extract furs from the Hudson Bay region. When the bureaucracy in New France harassed them for trading without a proper licence, they did not hesitate in turning to the English, first in Boston and then in London. They subsequently changed their national allegiance several times before retiring from the fur trade.

In 1684 Radisson persuaded his nephew (Groseilliers's son), who was in charge of a French post on the Nelson River, to defect to the English. The two escaped with a huge cargo of furs only one step ahead of a French relief expedition. This line drawing of Radisson was copied from an old Paris print (National Archives of Canada B-70).

Hudson Bay. They returned to Montreal in August 1660 with a vast haul of beaver skins, which was seen as the colony's salvation. However, the two fur traders were not themselves well received; their furs were confiscated and both men were prosecuted for trading without official permission. Not surprisingly, they wound up in Boston in 1664, where the English were quite enthusiastic about the Hudson Bay fur trade.

Marie de l'Incarnation

Born in Tours, the daughter of a master baker, Marie Guyart (1599–1672) was a devout child who married at the age of seventeen. Her husband died two years later, leaving her with a son. Soon after she had a mystical experience of conversion. Taking vows of chastity, poverty, and obedience, she lived for some years with her sister and brother-in-law and worked with them in their business. At the age of twenty-seven, she had another experience of the 'inner paradise' and joined the Ursuline Order of nuns. After taking her vows in 1633, Marie had a dream in which God told her to go to Canada. She sailed there in 1639, founded her school, and spent the remainder of her life running it successfully. Mère Marie had an extraordinary ability to combine her fervent spiritual life with her skills as a competent administrator and perceptive observer of the secular life around her. She wrote extensively, as well as educating young girls, providing food for hungry Natives and catechizing them, studying Native languages, preparing dictionaries in French-Algonquin and French-Iroquois and an Iroquois catechism. Her writings included spiritual autobiographies, lectures on faith, notes on prayer, and over 13,000 letters (most of them to her son), of which relatively few survive. In her correspondence, Mère Marie dealt not only with spiritual matters but with the business of the entire colony. Her letters are one of the two best sources, along with the *Jesuit Relations*, for the history of New France in the mid-seventeenth century. This oil portrait has been attributed to Abbé Hugues Pommier (1637–86) (Archives des Ursulines de Québec, Québec).

By the early 1660s the tensions within the colony on the St Lawrence were manifesting themselves in strange forms. A general state of panic was produced by an incident of alleged witchcraft, and in the midst of carnival season in February 1663 the colony was struck by an earthquake. Mère Marie de l'Incarnation noted, 'we were all so frightened we believed it was the eve of Judgement, since all the portents were to be seen' (Marshall 1967:288–9). About this time the French Crown formally withdrew trading privileges and land ownership from the Company of One Hundred Associates and made New France a Crown colony. Given the tensions and problems of the colony, most of its 3,035 inhabitants were happy to trade autonomy for French financial and military assistance. In June 1665 four companies of the Carignan-Salières regi-

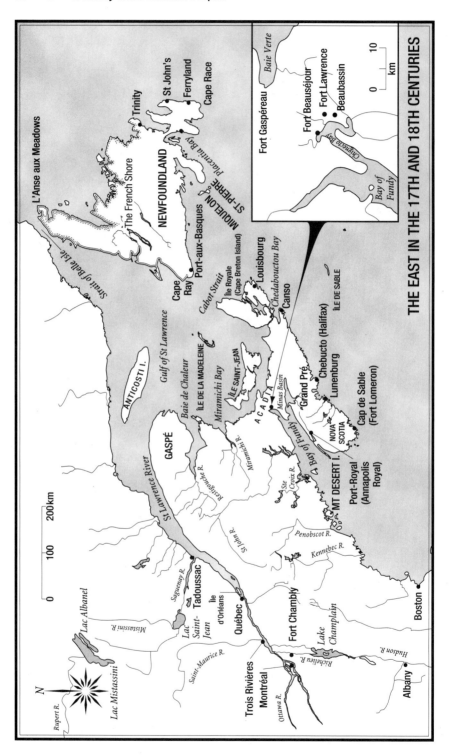

THE EAST IN THE 17TH AND 18TH CENTURIES

ment arrived to quell the Iroquois. In September of that year an intendant (or chief administrative officer), Jean Talon (1626–94), arrived to revitalize the colony. One of the royal government's first aims was to increase the population, and the *filles du roi* (orphan girls who had been raised at the king's expense) were sent over to effect this goal. Mère Marie reported that 100 girls had arrived in 1665, and more would come later. How long the French Crown would continue such support was uncertain, but it certainly rejuvenated the colony. The government had begun making a concerted effort to deal with the Iroquois menace and to reform both the administrative and economic structure of New France. It would shortly attempt to establish a foothold in Newfoundland and regain control over Acadia. Although success would hold within it the seeds of destruction, the French in 1665 were on the eve of almost a century of expansion and dominance in North America.

THE ATLANTIC REGION TO 1667

In the Atlantic region, overtones of Europe could be detected in the complex conflicts of the seventeenth century, although local forces were probably more influential. Much of the confusing history of Acadia after 1624 is wrapped up in the activities of the La Tour family, which illustrate the fluid and violent nature of the period. In 1629, when Quebec was captured by the Kirkes, a tiny trading post at Cape Sable (on the southeastern tip of present-day Nova Scotia), headed by Charles de Saint-Étienne de La Tour (1598–1666), was all that was left of a French presence in North America. La Tour's father, Claude de La Tour (*c.* 1570–after 1636), had already returned to France to plead for assistance, but on the return voyage was captured and taken to England, where he quickly made himself at home. Accepted at court, he married one of the Queen's ladies-in-waiting. He also accepted Nova Scotia baronetcies for himself and his son from Sir William Alexander, a Scottish courtier, who had been granted Nova Scotia in 1621 by James VI of Scotland (also James I of England).

Returning with his bride to Acadia in May 1630 as part of a Scots-English expedition, Claude stopped at Cape Sable to persuade his son to join him. Charles replied that 'he would rather have died than consent to such baseness as to betray his King' (MacBeath 1966:593). Declaring his son an enemy, Claude led an unsuccessful attack on the fort at Cape Sable and retreated to Port Royal, only to discover that the English planned to abandon it. He was forced to throw himself on his son's mercy and confess to his wife that he could not return to Europe. Acadia, like Canada, was returned to France by the English with the Treaty of St-Germain-en-Laye in 1632. The English monarch Charles I needed French financial subsidies as he attempted to govern without meeting Parliament.

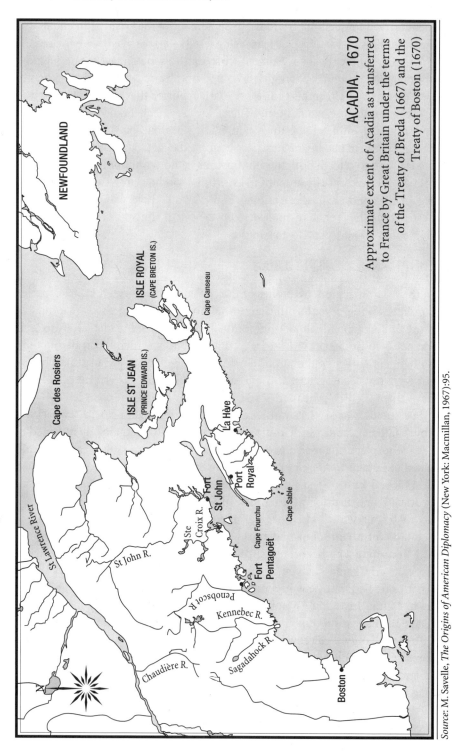

ACADIA, 1670

Approximate extent of Acadia as transferred to France by Great Britain under the terms of the Treaty of Breda (1667) and the Treaty of Boston (1670)

NEWFOUNDLAND

ISLE ROYAL
(CAPE BRETON IS.)

Cape Canseau

ISLE ST JEAN
(PRINCE EDWARD IS.)

Cape des Rosiers

La Hève

Port Royal

Cape Sable

Fort St John

Ste Croix R.

Cape Fourchu

St John R.

Fort Pentagoët

Penobscot R.

Kennebec R.

St Lawrence River

Sagadahock R.

Chaudière R.

Boston

Source: M. Savelle, *The Origins of American Diplomacy* (New York: Macmillan, 1967):95.

Charles de La Tour continued to lead an embattled life, coming into conflict with others who claimed royal authority in the region. In 1642 his chief rival, Charles de Menou d'Aulnay (*c.* 1604–50), returned to Acadia with the official order that La Tour appear before the French king to answer charges of treason. La Tour decided to send his wife, Françoise-Marie, to represent him at the royal court, where she successfully argued her husband's case in 1642, then returned in a French warship, carrying supplies for La Tour. In 1644 she again went to France, but this time was unable to protect her husband's interests. Early in 1645, with her husband again off in Boston negotiating with the Puritans, Madame de La Tour commanded the defence of Fort La Tour against an attack by Charles d'Aulnay. Her forty-five defenders held out for four days against an invading force of 200, but she eventually surrendered. All the captives were hanged, and Madame de La Tour died scant weeks later. D'Aulnay ruled Acadia until his death in 1650.

Charles de La Tour returned to France after d'Aulnay's death to demand an enquiry into his case, and was completely vindicated and again received into royal favour. Returning to Port Royal with a few new settlers in 1653, he successfully courted d'Aulnay's widow. Pursued by his debtors, he was forced in 1654 to surrender his garrison of seventy at Fort La Tour to an invading English expedition of 500 men. La Tour was taken to England, where Oliver Cromwell refused to restore his Acadian property but did agree to recognize the long-dormant baronetcy of Nova Scotia (negotiated earlier by Claude) if Charles would accept English allegiance and pay his English debts. Twenty-five years after denying his father and asserting his loyalty to the French Crown, Charles de La Tour accepted Cromwell's terms. He eventually sold out his rights in Acadia to English partners, and retired to Cape Sable with his wife and family.

For more than forty years La Tour and his family had kept French interests alive in Acadia, but he was a trader, not a colonizer. The few settlers he brought to the New World were only incidental to his economic and military activities. Unlike Champlain in Canada, La Tour had no vision of a settled agricultural presence in Acadia. After his surrender to the English in 1654, the scattered Acadian settlers (only a few hundred) were very much on their own until formal French occupation was restored in 1667. While the period of English control from 1654 to 1667 left little internal impress on the region, it did isolate Acadia from official French rethinking of its American empire in the early 1660s. Thus Acadia was not initially part of the Crown's decision in 1663 to take a more active interest in its American colonies. As a result, its subsequent status was never properly clarified, leading to an administrative weakness that encouraged its population to have an autonomous outlook and France to be willing (in 1713) to surrender large parts of the region to the English under pressure.

THE PEOPLING OF NEWFOUNDLAND, 1650–1750

Although there was no organized settlement activity in Newfoundland after the collapse of the Newfoundland Company, the island continued to grow steadily in resident population. At the Treaty of Utrecht in 1713, the British conceded permanent fishing rights to the French, who agreed to evacuate their inhabitants and to maintain neither permanent residences nor fortifications. Obtaining exclusive sovereignty over Newfoundland was the most positive action the British government took with regard to the island. The substantial growth of permanent population on the island developed independently of government policy or supervision. It was the product of the decisions of countless fisherfolk to remain behind rather than to return to Europe with their vessels at the close of the fishing season. Initially the population was almost entirely of English origin (especially from Cornwall, Devon, and Dorset), but in the eighteenth century the new arrivals came mainly from Ireland.

By the 1750s there were over 7,000 permanent residents. The island began to develop a deep schism in its population that was simultaneously ethnic, religious, and economic. The chief economic division was between those who owned boats and those who did not. Not all Protestant West Countrymen owned boats, but few Catholic Irish did. Parallel to the increase of permanent population came a shift in fishing practice. After 1714 the English summer visitors abandoned the inshore fishery and turned instead to fishing directly from the offshore banks. After 1750 there were already signs of depletion of the fish stock, at least inshore. The result was not efforts at conservation but diversification, with many Newfoundlanders moving into the seal fishery.

CANADA, 1665–1760

That part of New France along the St Lawrence known as 'Canada' mixed French origins and North American environment in a way that defied easy generalization. The French background provided institutions, a terminology with which to express them, and a set of assumptions about how society ought to be ordered and operated. The French assumed an ordered and hierarchical society in which the various social orders stayed in their place and duly subordinated themselves to the good of the whole, as defined by the Crown. As a complication, the French Crown did not simply attempt to replicate the familiar institutions of the Old World in North America but to reform them by stripping them of centuries of European tradition that decentralized power and limited royal authority. At the same time, the environment provided a set of daily realities that worked against European institutions and assumptions, modifying and altering—while never totally negating—efforts to imitate the mother country. The result was a society that refracted the metropolis in France

This portrait of Jean Talon is a nineteenth-century copy attributed to Théophile Hamel (1817–70) of a seventeenth-century painting by Frère Luc (Claude François, 1614–85) (National Archives of Canada C-7100).

through the dual prisms of royal reform and North American experience. The external observer was often struck at first glance by the presence of familiar European patterns and terminology, while beneath the surface different designs were constantly evolving.

The royal take-over of 1663 put French administrative policy for the colonies and its execution in the hands of two men, Jean-Baptiste Colbert and Jean Talon. Colbert was Louis XIV's chief bureaucrat, a highly experienced civil servant. His major tasks both at home and abroad were to strengthen royal government and expand the French economy. As minister of marine, he served as the seventeenth-century equivalent of colonial secretary, in addition to a myriad of other responsibilities. To implement policy in the colony, Colbert decided to establish the position of intendant, a royal official who, in France, had been developed to cut through the accretion of centuries of devolution of royal power and to act decisively on behalf of the state. Beginning with Talon's first appointment as intendant in 1665, the colony's administration was greatly reorganized and centralized. The governor, although still the titular head, was responsible for military affairs, external relations, and the colony's connections with the Church (which included education). Over the years the governor would invariably be a member of the French nobility and an experienced military man, but routine administration was in the hands of the intendant, a career civil servant. There would be some classic confrontations between intendants and governors, particularly during the regime of Louis Buade de Frontenac (1620–98, governor 1672–82 and 1689–98). But the royal regime consistently backed the former.

Colbert and Talon not only managed to put the colony on its feet but established its administrative and institutional structure for the entire century of French royal control. Their task was not easy. Political institutions had to be established that were simultaneously responsive to the royal will and satisfactory to the inhabitants. External threats had to be confronted. Population growth had to be encouraged. Some kind of economic viability had to be created that would not endanger the mother country. Out of all these factors would emerge a society and culture of enormous tenacity, possessing many resources for regeneration and change.

Canada was ruled by the Sovereign Council made up mainly of the colony's élite and presided over by the intendant. No regularly elected political body represented the inhabitants. Instead the colony used informal means to test public opinion, including the public protest (or 'riot'), which was a typical feature of life in both Europe and America at the time. Most Canadian riots were over food shortages, to which the government usually responded. The Church was one of the institutions comprising the government of Canada. Its main political task was to help establish, within the ranks of its communicants, due subordination to spiritual and secular authority. During the French regime the Church often found this job beyond its capabilities, partly because it was chronically understaffed. In 1759, for example, there were only seventy-three parish priests among 200 clergymen, hardly enough to provide religious services for everyone in the colony, especially outside the towns. In the symbiotic relationship between church and state, moreover, the state dominated. It appointed bishops, granted seigneuries, and provided much of the revenue for religion. At the same time, the subordinate role of the Church did not mean that Canada was irreligious or that Catholicism did not permeate deeply the lives of most of its inhabitants. Canada had been born in deep Catholic piety, and Catholic orthodoxy remained the norm.

Because Canada spent most of its existence in a state of siege, the role of the military was crucial. France was prepared to spend money on the military that it would not have allowed for civilian matters. The soldiers' pay was an important source of money for the Canadian economy, and the army was the best local customer for Canadian merchants. Regular soldiers served as a source of labour and as potential additions to the civilian population, which they were encouraged to join upon expiration of their enlistments. Regular troops were not regarded as a sufficient military force, and from 1669 the entire adult male population of the colony between the ages of sixteen and sixty was required to serve in the militia, locally commanded by *capitaines de milice* chosen from the ranks of the inhabitants. After 1684 the militia was used regularly in every war. Virtually every able-bodied Canadian male served in at least one campaign. Much of this militia service was in collaboration with Indians in the form of raiding parties, designed to keep the English colonies off balance and prevent them from using their superior numbers to invade the St Lawrence. Foreign observers were always impressed with the martial spirit of the Canadians. For many Canadian élite families, military service in an officer class was preferable to entrance into commerce and industry, just as in France itself. By the eighteenth century the Canadian élite provided most of the officers for the *Troupes de la Marine*, and even expected commissions to be reserved for the sons of serving officers.

One of Canada's major disadvantages in its constant wars against the English was the small size of its population. After 1660 French Canada matched the English colonies by doubling in population every twenty-five years, but it could never keep pace numerically. In 1715 the population of New France was 20,000, while that of the English colonies was 434,000. By 1754 the gap had grown even wider, with 70,000 in New France and 1,485,000 in the American colonies to the south. After 1672 few French immigrants arrived in the colony, either publicly sponsored or privately motivated. The absence of agrarian dislocation and the insatiable demands of the French military for manpower both prevented the development of a discontented and displaced population available for colonial migration on a massive scale. The traditional juxtaposition of the French and British colonial experiences is in many ways misleading. In relation to the colonies of most European nations in America, New France was successful and typical. The British colonies were the ones unusual in their numbers and dynamism. Unfortunately for the French, the British had not merely two or three colonies in America but at least thirteen, which were both economically vibrant and located on the exposed flanks of New France and Louisiana. In the imperial rivalries that inevitably ensued, the French were at a considerable disadvantage.

At the time of the royal take-over in 1663, both Colbert and Talon attempted to diversify the economy. They were concerned about the colony's heavy dependence on the fur trade. Colbert even saw the fur trade as a menace. 'It is to be feared', he wrote, 'that by means of this trade, the *habitants* will remain idle a good part of the year, whereas if they were not allowed to engage in it they would be obliged to apply themselves to cultivating their land' (quoted in Eccles 1983:104). What the French authorities wanted was an agricultural surplus and the exploitation of timber resources, which would enable the colony to supply the French West Indies with goods currently being obtained from the English, but the economy was slow to diversify. Part of the problem was that the fur trade kept expanding, contributing to a circular effect. The successful French quest for furs not only deflected from other enterprises but brought the colony into conflict with the English to the south. The ensuing struggle made it virtually impossible to limit the fur traders, since they were the ideal shock troops for engaging the enemy.

The numbers involved in the fur trade (the *voyageurs* and *engagés*) grew in number from 200 at the end of the seventeenth century to nearly 1,000 by the mid-eighteenth century. The work was both physically and emotionally demanding. Perhaps as many as one-quarter of able-bodied Canadian males were involved in the fur trade at some point in their lives, usually in their younger years before they settled down with a wife and family in sedentary occupations along the St Lawrence. Many left Native families behind when they

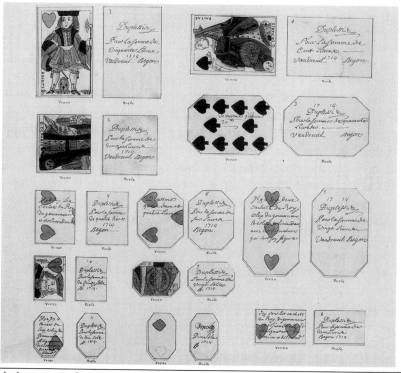

In the late seventeenth century, when Quebec lacked currency, playing cards, marked with amounts, were turned into money—refundable when funds arrived from France. These copies were painted in watercolour and ink by Henri Beau (1863–1949) (National Archives of Canada C-17059).

retired. A few rose to be specialists in the trade, some remaining in the West throughout their lives. A few became *marchands equipeurs* (or outfitters), who organized the parties and provided the credit. Unlike transatlantic merchants, the fur trade merchants were almost exclusively Canadian-born.

A complex commercial and small-scale artisanal life did develop in New France. There was a small merchant class, particularly at the transatlantic level. Overseas trade was complex and dangerous, and most merchants operated through family and clan connections. Marriage alliances established new branches of family firms in distant ports, and after the deaths of their husbands, women frequently took over the local enterprise. The trading economy over which the merchants presided required peace and stability to perform at its best. It also suffered from a chronic shortage of a circulating medium of exchange, which led the colony to print its own paper money by using decks of playing cards inscribed in various denominations and signed by the intendant. Officially the cards represented promissory notes, but they and the military *ordonnances* that circulated as legal tender after 1735 were both inflationary. There was a constant demand for the local production of skilled artisans, particularly those master craftsmen who worked for the Church, providing the furniture, ornaments, and decorations for the many churches of the colony. Two major attempts to industrialize New France were made, both in the 1730s. One was an ironworks near Trois-Rivières (Les Forges du St-Maurice), the other a shipyard at Quebec. Both required large amounts of state subsidy to survive, but both demonstrated that Canadian workmen could be mobilized for industrial activity and could manufacture serviceable goods on a large scale.

Despite the growth of trade and industry, agriculture was always the dominant form of economic activity along the St Lawrence, functioning around the French seigneurial system brought to the valley in 1627 and governed after 1663 by the *Coutume de Paris*. Seigneurialism in New France worked less to order society than to provide a means of ordering settlement. The state made property concessions to landlords, who were supposed to find settlers to serve as tenants. Although the *censitaire* (or tenant) owed various rents and feudal dues to his seigneur, these amounted to very little so long as there was more land than settlers. Moreover, after the Edict of Marly in 1711, the seigneur could no longer withhold land from settlement in anticipation of price increases if there were settlers demanding it. Since they did not own the means of production, the *censitaires* seldom treated agriculture as a business enterprise. The seigneurial system did not tie settlers to the soil and did not encourage large-scale, staple-crop farming but rather family farms on small holdings. The system was not really feudal, since military obligation in the colony was not tied to land tenure. Not until the end of the French period was there sufficient pressure on the land to benefit the seigneur economically. He did acquire social status, however, and by the mid-eighteenth century the typical seigneur was an absentee landlord who lived in one of the towns and was involved in a variety of economic and political activities. A seigneury was part of a diversified portfolio of investment for an élite in whose ranks little specialization of function had yet occurred.

By the mid-eighteenth century, Swedish visitor Peter Kalm was able to describe the heartland of French Canada along the St Lawrence as 'a village beginning at Montreal and ending at Quebec, which is a distance or more than one hundred and eight miles, for the farmhouses are never above five *arpents* [293 metres] and sometimes but three apart, a few places excepted' (Benson 1937, II:416–17). Each farmhouse, usually of three or four rooms built of stone and timber, stood alone. Tiny villages occasionally, but rarely, gathered around the churches. Three towns punctuated this continuous village: Quebec towards the eastern end, Trois Rivières in the middle, and Montreal towards the west. Quebec and especially Montreal contained impressive and concentrated public and private buildings, but by our standards, both towns were quite small in population and area. On their peripheries, the dominant landscape pattern of

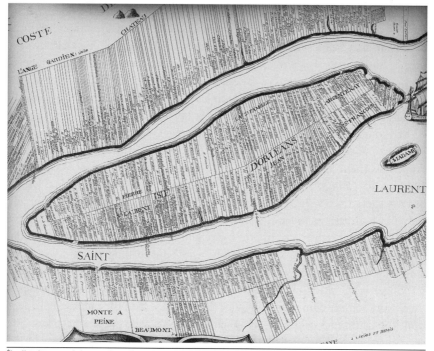

Île d'Orléans and the north and south shores of the St Lawrence opposite, showing the boundaries of the land grants with names of the seigneurial families in 1709, mapped by Gédeon Catalogne (1662–1729) and drawn by Jean-Baptiste de Couagne—a detail of a larger map of the Quebec region (National Archives of Canada NMCOO48248).

the separate but contiguous farmstead was quickly resumed. Narrow lots ran back for large distances from the river, and while there were new rows (or *rangs)* of lots behind the first, population was slow to move into the *rangs* behind those along the waterfront. Thus French Canada replicated neither the European medieval village, whence many of its rural settlers had come, nor the English colonial tendency towards isolated farmsteads in the middle of large holdings separated from one another by considerable distances.

Although Montreal and Quebec were not large, they did give Canada an urban life and a proportionately larger urban population than those of most North American colonies. These towns were the centres of government, of the direction of economic activity, and of the Church and its social services, such as health care and education. They inevitably included a heavy concentration of the upper classes of French Canada, and had an impressive, polite society. While there were, doubtless, gradations of wealth and status, French North America was fundamentally divided into two orders: those with, and those without, access to government largesse and patronage. The law was available to all, but only *some* could expect public appointments, government contracts,

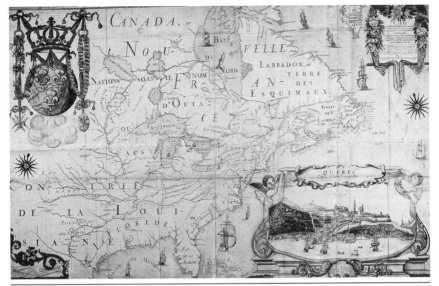

This is perhaps the most beautiful map of the cartographer Jean-Baptiste-Louis Franquelin, who worked at Quebec from 1671 to 1692 as both 'king's geographer' and 'king's hydrographer'. Elaborately decorated and delicately coloured, it shows the known territory of New France in 1688, with a portrait of Quebec (National Archives of Canada, Cartographic and Architectural Archives Division PH/1000/1688).

and seigneurial grants. There was the possibility of upward mobility, but most observers agreed that the typical *Canadien* worked no harder than necessary, spent a disproportionate amount of time pursuing his own pleasures and interests (which included racing horses and disappearing into the bush), was far more prosperous and enjoyed considerably more personal liberty than his European counterpart.

As for the roles and status of women, they did not undergo a remarkable transformation in the New World. The organization of society continued to be fundamentally patriarchal, with the woman in the traditional role of helpmate and child bearer. Both the shortage of marriageable women and the frequent absence of men away on the frontier or in the military somewhat moderated the oppression. There was some limited protection for the property rights of married women, and the autonomous rights of widows were well safeguarded by law and custom. In truth, however, historians do not know very much about women in early Canada, chiefly because of the male orientation of the documentation. While Canada always had a substantial number of women in holy orders, most women in the colony married (at the average age of twenty-two) and raised a family. If marriage and remarriage rates were high, so too were birth rates and the number of children. Throughout the eighteenth century, raw birth rates ran over fifty per 1,000 inhabitants per annum, and women on average bore seven children, but these demographic characteristics were typical of

A Swedish Visitor Observes New France

[In 1770 an English translation of the travel diary of the Swedish botanist Peter Kalm was published in London. Kalm had visited Canada in 1749. *Source*: A.B. Benson, ed., *Peter Kalm's Travels in North America*, vol. 2 (New York: Dover Publications, 1937):510–11.

Kitchen Gardens. Near each farm there is a kitchen garden in which onions are most abundant, because the French farmers eat their dinners of them with bread, on Fridays and Saturdays, or fasting days. However, I cannot say the French are strict observers of fasting, for several of my rowers ate meat to-day, though it was Friday. The common people in Canada may be smelled when one passes by them on account of their frequent use of onions. Pumpkins are also abundant in the farmers' gardens. They prepare them in several ways, but the most common is to cut them through the middle, and place each half on the hearth, open side towards the fire, till it is roasted. The pulp is then cut out of the peel and eaten. Better class people put sugar on it. Carrots, lettuce, Turkish beans, cucumbers, and currant shrubs, are planted in every farmer's little kitchen garden.

Tobacco. Every farmer plants a quantity of tobacco near his house, in proportion to the size of his family. It is necessary that one should plant tobacco, because it is so universally smoked by the common people. Boys of ten or twelve years of age, as well as the old people, run about with a pipe in their mouth. Persons of the better class do not refuse either to smoke a pipe now and then. In the northern parts of Canada, they generally smoke pure tobacco; but further north and

all colonial societies. Childbirth was difficult and dangerous. Canada's menfolk were constantly exposed to the dangers of wartime battle, but their wives faced equal or greater danger every time they gave birth.

In many ways the most difficult feature of early French Canada to comprehend has been its culture. In New France, language came to be the French of the Paris region, spoken extremely well, although with a modified accent and wonderful new vocabulary adopted from the indigenous peoples. Emphasizing the spoken language rather than the written word is important, for the colony never had a printing press or a newspaper. Formal culture was visual and oral rather than written. The locus of the formal artistic and aesthetic life of Canada was largely in the ritualistic requirements of the Church, involving the visual and the aural senses. There was a great emphasis on music, both for the Church and among the people, who brought with them to the New World a rich heritage of song, dance, and music for dance. A literary culture was expressed through folk-tales and songs, but it too was oral rather than written. Most expression of culture among ordinary *Canadiens* was part of the ritual of everyday life and of experience in *habitant* households in rural parishes. Those

around Montreal, they take the inner bark of the red Cornelian cherry (*Cornus sanguinea L.*), crush it, and mix it with the tobacco, to make it weaker. People of both sexes, and of all ranks, use snuff very much. Almost all the tobacco which is consumed here is the product of the country, and some people prefer it even to Virginia tobacco: but those who pretend to be connoisseurs reckon the last kind better than the other.

Manners and Customs. . . . When one comes into the house of a Canadian peasant or farmer, he gets up, takes his hat off to the stranger, invites him to sit down, puts his hat on and sits down again. The gentlemen and ladies, as well as the poorest peasants and their wives, are called Monsieur and Madame. The peasants, and especially their wives, wear shoes which consist of a piece of wood hollowed out, and are made almost as slippers. The boys and the old peasants themselves wear their hair behind in a queue, and most of them wear red woolen caps at home and sometimes on their journeys.

Food. The farmers prepare most of their food from milk. Butter is seldom seen, and what they have is made of sour cream, and therefore not so good as English butter. A good deal of this butter has a slight taste of tallow. Congealed sour milk is found everywhere, in stone vessels. Many of the French are very fond of milk, which they eat chiefly on fast days. However, they have not so many methods of preparing it as we have in Sweden. The common way is to boil it, and put bits of wheat bread and a good deal of sugar into it. The French here eat nearly as much meat as the English on those days when their religion allows it. For excepting the soup, the salads and the dessert, all their other dishes consist of meat variously prepared.

few examples of early wooden house furnishings that survive are much admired for their elegant, functional lines.

The St Lawrence colony of France had considerable vitality and, left to its own devices, would doubtless have flourished mightily. But New France itself was eventually overwhelmed by the exigencies of imperial rivalry, finding herself no longer an integral part of overseas France but rather an alien component of a vastly expanded British empire in North America.

THE FIRST THREE ANGLO-FRENCH WARS

Although sporadic warfare had occurred in North America since the early seventeenth century, a protracted struggle for the continent between the British and the French—in which the Native peoples were important players—began only in 1689. The North American hostilities had their own dynamic, although they were always associated with the larger international rivalry of the mother countries. There were four wars. The first three were the War of the League of Augsburg (1689–97), settled by the Treaty of Ryswick; the War of the Spanish

Source: M. Savelle, The Origins of American Diplomacy (New York: Macmillan, 1967): 149.

EUROPEAN POSSESSIONS IN NORTH AMERICA
AND THE CARIBBEAN AFTER THE PEACE OF UTRECHT, 1713

Major-General Sir William Pepperell at the siege of Louisbourg (Metropolitan Toronto Reference Library).

Succession (1702–13), settled by the Treaty of Utrecht; and the War of the Austrian Succession (1744–8), settled by the Treaty of Aix-la-Chapelle. The North American aspects of these first three wars shared a good deal in common. The American fighting in these first conflicts was conducted mainly by the colonists themselves employing their methods. Occasionally the mother country would undertake a brief initiative, usually disastrously. Much of the conflict occurred on the frontiers and in the back country, involving the Native peoples, who joined the battles for reasons of their own.

The strategy of New France was to send out raiding parties on land and sea at the outset to keep the British colonies disunited and off balance, so that they would not be able to utilize their superior manpower, resources, and command of the sea (the British controlled the Atlantic for all but brief periods throughout these wars) to invade and capture French territory. The British unsuccessfully—and disastrously—attempted to invade the St Lawrence in the first two wars. In the third, New England troops and British naval strength captured Louisbourg in 1745, leading to the dispatch of a major French fleet to North America in 1746, where it met bad weather and experienced epidemic disease. The fleet limped back to France without ever confronting the enemy. France itself hoped to make sufficient military gains around the world so that any territory captured would have to be returned at the peace treaty; in this it was not always entirely successful. In 1713 it was forced to give up Acadia and its claims to Newfoundland, although in 1697 and 1748 it surrendered nothing

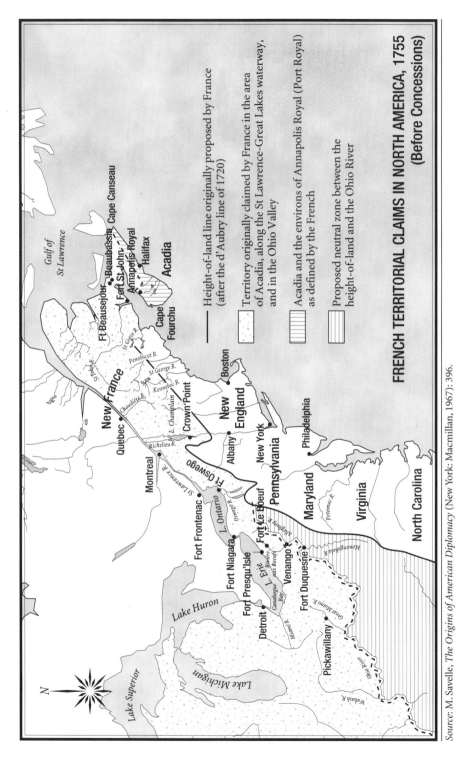

FRENCH TERRITORIAL CLAIMS IN NORTH AMERICA, 1755
(Before Concessions)

——— Height-of-land line originally proposed by France (after the d'Aubry line of 1720)

Territory originally claimed by France in the area of Acadia, along the St Lawrence-Great Lakes waterway, and in the Ohio Valley

Acadia and the environs of Annapolis Royal (Port Royal) as defined by the French

Proposed neutral zone between the height-of-land and the Ohio River

Source: M. Savelle, *The Origins of American Diplomacy* (New York: Macmillan, 1967): 396.

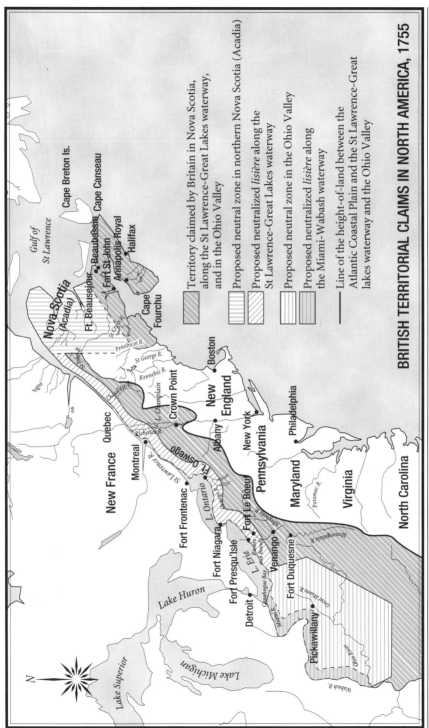

BRITISH TERRITORIAL CLAIMS IN NORTH AMERICA, 1755

Territory claimed by Britain in Nova Scotia, along the St Lawrence–Great Lakes waterway, and in the Ohio Valley

Proposed neutral zone in northern Nova Scotia (Acadia)

Proposed neutralized *lisière* along the St Lawrence–Great Lakes waterway

Proposed neutral zone in the Ohio Valley

Proposed neutralized *lisière* along the Miami–Wabash waterway

Line of the height-of-land between the Atlantic Coastal Plain and the St Lawrence–Great lakes waterway and the Ohio Valley

Source: M. Savelle, *The Origins of American Diplomacy* (New York: Macmillan, 1967): 397.

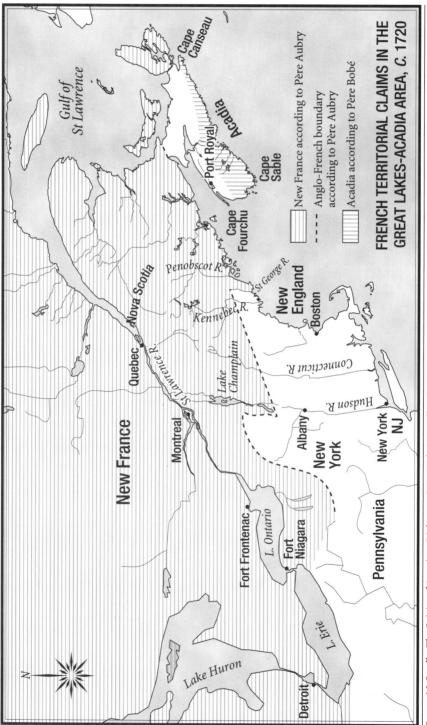

FRENCH TERRITORIAL CLAIMS IN THE GREAT LAKES-ACADIA AREA, C. 1720

New France according to Père Aubry

Anglo-French boundary according to Père Aubry

Acadia according to Père Bobé

Source: M. Savelle, The Origins of American Diplomacy (New York: Macmillan, 1967): 236.

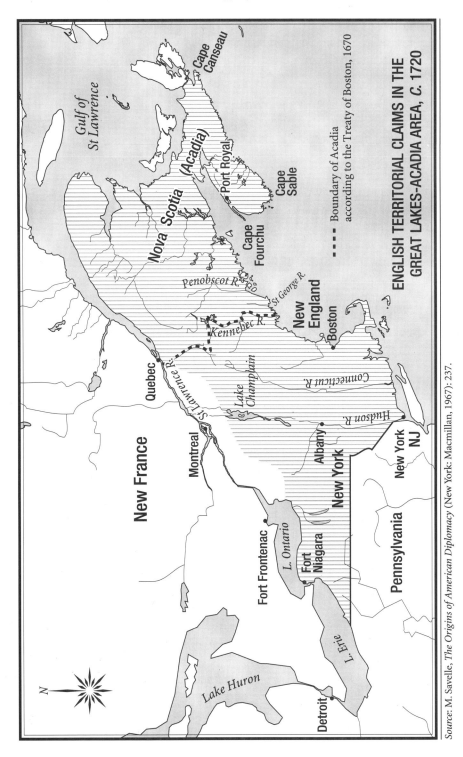

ENGLISH TERRITORIAL CLAIMS IN THE GREAT LAKES-ACADIA AREA, *C.* 1720

- - - Boundary of Acadia according to the Treaty of Boston, 1670

of substance in North America. Neither mother country considered the North American theatre anything but a sideshow until the 1750s, when the British, after settling Nova Scotia at government expense, decided to take the New World seriously.

ACADIA AND NOVA SCOTIA, 1670–1758

Acadia, the ill-defined geographical region that included more than peninsular Nova Scotia, had been contested ground between the British and the French since the first days of European settlement. Returned to France in 1670, Acadia and especially the village of Port Royal were often attacked by New Englanders. Port Royal was captured in 1690 but returned to France by the Treaty of Ryswick in 1697. New England failed to take Port Royal in 1707, but succeeded in 1710. Port Royal was not typical of all Acadia, however. The period between 1670 and 1713 saw considerable Acadian expansion, both in terms of numbers and in territory cultivated. A population of about 500 in 1670 had grown to over 1,500 in 1710, mostly through natural increase, and had planted settlements along the Minas Basin, Cobequid, and Chignecto Bay. Most of Acadia's inhabitants came from a relatively small area of southwestern France and spoke a southwestern dialect of French, which they preserved and adapted over the years. Younger members of families moved to new communities, which featured dykes that controlled the inundation of lowland areas by the high tides of the Bay of Fundy, draining marsh to allow it to be used for farming. Farms were small but extremely prosperous. Livestock, especially cattle, was the chief produce, which the Acadians illegally traded with the New Englanders. There were a few outlying fishing communities on the southwest coast. Acadia had few roads and no overland transportation. Movement was by canoe and small boat.

Government sat fairly lightly upon this population. The French never really asserted their administrative control over the region, and the Church operated solely through missionaries, who provided some contact with Canada. Culturally and politically, the Acadians remained isolated from French Canada. The family (*le clan*) and the local community were the important units for a closely knit peasant society. Acadia had developed an inherent sense of autonomy when—in the chess game that imperial warfare represented in the eighteenth century—France found itself obliged to surrender territory in North America with the Treaty of Utrecht (1713). Acadia was one of the pawns given up to the British in 1713. The *anciennes limites* of Acadia mentioned in the treaty were not defined, and the French subsequently insisted that they had only surrendered peninsular Nova Scotia, informally retaining northern Maine and New Brunswick, and formally retaining the two islands of Île-Royale (Cape Breton) and Île-St-Jean (Prince Edward Island). As

The Porte Dauphine, the entrance to the reconstructed Louisbourg, with the clock-tower of the King's Bastion and barracks in the distance (Parks Canada D-11-1).

for the population of the ceded territory, which the British called Nova Scotia to emphasize Britain's historic claims there, the inhabitants were given one year to remove to French territory or to remain as subjects of their new masters. Nobody except the French wanted the Acadians removed, so they were tacitly allowed to remain in Nova Scotia on sufferance. Questions such as their land, language, and religious rights, as well as their political and military obligations to the new rulers, went essentially unresolved. The government of Nova Scotia dealt with the Acadians on an *ad hoc* basis, accepting their insistence on political neutrality and failing to exercise much authority within the Acadian community. The Acadians were not the first nor would they be the last group to translate unofficial tolerance, born of irresolution, into enshrined 'rights'. The dealings of the Nova Scotian authorities with the Acadians on the question of loyalty before 1740 were never authorized in London, but they led the Acadians to believe that they had an understanding.

Unfortunately for the French population of Nova Scotia, their loyalties were constantly being tested by the French, who had begun after 1720 constructing a fortress at Louisbourg on the southeastern coast. The French government fortified the town, garrisoned it, and employed it as the military and economic nerve-centre of the Atlantic region. By 1734 the town site—four east-west streets on about 100 acres (40 ha)—was surrounded by walls on three sides with impressive gates. As well as a civilian population of 2,000, by the 1740s Louisbourg contained a garrison of 600 soldiers (which in the 1750s would be increased to 3,500). The fortifications, poorly located and badly built, were never completed. Captured by New Englanders in 1745, it was exchanged for Madras (in India) at the Treaty of Aix-la-Chapelle in 1748. The capture and return of Louisbourg had several important effects in Nova Scotia. One was to encourage the British to do some military settling of their own as a counterweight to Louisbourg. Another was to turn the attention of the local authorities to the Acadians. The Nova Scotia Council in 1745 declared of the Acadians that 'if they are not absolutely to be regarded as utter Enemies to His Majesty's Government they cannot be accounted less than unprofitable Inhabitants for their conditional Oath of Allegiance will not en-title them to the Confidence and Privileges of Natural British Subjects. . .' (National Archives of Canada 1745:A27). British settlement and Acadian removal were commonly coupled in the minds of British officials on both sides of the Atlantic. With the founding of Halifax an almost inexorable sequence of events was set in motion that would result in the forcible expulsion of the Acadian residents from the colony of 6,000.

The decision of the British government to use the public purse to populate a British colony—the first time Britain had done so in America, at a cost of over £600,000 between 1749 and 1764—marked a new British interest in the Atlantic region. In 1749 it recruited over 2,500 people, including some soldiers and sailors recently disbanded and some London artisans, and shipped them to Nova Scotia. They arrived to find huts, tents, and primitive conditions. The new governor, Lord Edward Cornwallis (1713–76), complained that most of the new arrivals were 'poor idle worthless vagabonds' (quoted in Bell 1990:344n). The British government soon sought a new source of more reliable settlers, turning to 'foreign Protestants' from Switzerland, France, and Germany. It employed as recruiting agent the young Scotsman, John Dick (d. 1804), who was empowered by the Board of Trade over the winter of 1749–50 to recruit up to 1,500 'foreign Protestants', who would receive land, a year's subsistence, arms and tools, but not free transportation. Dick protested that free passage would be the main inducement, but he managed to fill the order. There were again complaints about the recruits, who were labelled 'in general old miserable wretches' (Bell 1990:344n). In the end Dick sent over 2,700 Germans and Swiss, many of the latter actually French Huguenots from Lorraine. These immigrants were mainly farmers and skilled labourers. Uncertainty over land titles confined them to shanty town Halifax until the Nova Scotia government determined to remove them to a site 50 mi. (80 km) west of Halifax, renamed Lunenburg. There they resettled, an unhappy crew that was 'inconceivably

Lieutenant-Colonel John Winslow reading the proclamation for the expulsion of Acadians (National Archives of Canada C-24550).

turbulent, I might have said mutinous', according to the officer in charge of the relocation, Major Charles Lawrence (*c.* 1709–60) (Bell 1990:435).

The settlement of Halifax was only one of a series of new pressures brought upon the province's Acadians. The French were reinforcing Louisbourg and constructing new forts (Fort Beausejour and Fort Gaspéreau) on the disputed Chignecto peninsula. The French also began encouraging the Acadians in Nova Scotia to remove to French territory, especially the previously neglected Île-St-Jean, which grew to over 2,000 residents by 1752. The bulk of Nova Scotia's Acadians hung tough, but after the renewal of undeclared war in North America in 1754, the government of the colony decided to settle the question. In July 1755 the Executive Council of Nova Scotia summoned Acadian deputies into the meeting room and informed them that conditional fealty was impossible. The Acadians must immediately take the oath of allegiance in its common form. The Acadian representatives waffled overnight, but when told that if they refused to take an unconditional oath, 'effectual Measures' would be taken 'to remove all such Recusants out of the Province', some offered to concede (Akins

1869:259–60). The council refused to administer the oath, however, saying 'that as there was no reason to hope their proposed Compliance proceeded from an honest Mind, and could be esteemed only the Effect of Compulsion and Force, they could not now be indulged with such Permission' (Akins 1869: 259–60). A classic confrontation between the singlemindedness of the state and a collective minority demanding special treatment was in the closing stages of resolution. The council decided not only to expel the Acadians but to distribute them to several British colonies in the south.

Over 6,000 Acadians were summarily rounded up in the late summer and autumn of 1755 by the British military and transported by ship to the south. There was little resistance, although many escaped to the woods and headed for French territory or to the uninhabited north. The Acadians were not received with great enthusiasm in the British colonies, which had not been warned to expect them, and many gradually returned to the province. The British government never commented on the action of the Nova Scotia government, which it had never authorized, except to note that the colony had regarded it as 'indispensably necessary for the Security and protection of the Province' (quoted in Brebner 1927:230). As for those who did join the French, after the

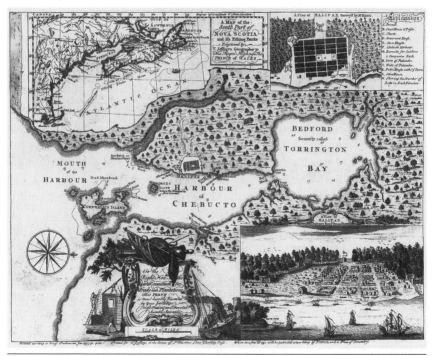

This *Map of the South Part of Nova Scotia and Its Fishing Banks* was engraved by Thomas Jefferys, printed for him in London, and published on 25 January 1750. In the upper-right corner is 'A Plan of the new town of Halifax Surveyed by M. Harris'; in the lower-right corner is 'A View of Halifax drawn from ye Top masthead' (National Archives of Canada NMC 1012).

British forced the surrender of Louisbourg in July 1758, another expulsion began. Another 6,000 Acadians, including 3,500 on Île-St-Jean, were rounded up and sent back to France. The British never succeeded in eliminating the French population from the region, however. Many escaped into the bush, others returned from their exile. What the expulsion did accomplish was to remove the Acadians from their traditional lands.

The founding of Halifax also had a substantial impact on the Native peoples of Nova Scotia, especially the 1,000 Micmacs remaining in the colony. The Micmacs had attempted to pursue their own best interests during the years of warfare between the French and the English. They understood that British concepts of land ownership and settlement were disastrous to them, declared war against the British in 1749, and were met with a policy of extermination ordered by Lord Cornwallis. A final peace treaty with the Micmacs in 1761 did not deal with land rights. No longer a military threat, the Native peoples would soon cease to be regarded as important in the colony.

In the wake of the conquest of Louisbourg, the Nova Scotia government in October 1758 sent out advertisements to New England, offering free land, trans-

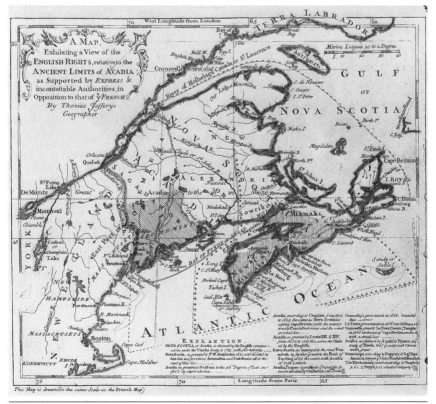

This map, which shows the British claims with regard to Acadia, is a slightly revised copy of one in *A General Cartography of North America and the West Indies* (Library of Congress).

portation to it, and initial support in the new settlements, to immigrants who would come to the colony. A few days before the advertisements were published, a legislative assembly—the first widely elected governing body in what is now Canada—met in Halifax. Nova Scotia was now a full-fledged British colony, a point reached with considerable brutality characteristic of the age.

THE SEVEN YEARS' WAR

Officially this war began in 1756 in Europe, although the North American contestants had been engaged in open conflict for several years. In the beginning, the French seemed to be doing well. They had destroyed General Braddock's army in 1754. Two years later, under General Montcalm, they took 1,700 prisoners at the surrender of the three forts of Chouaguen headed by Fort George. Hit-and-run raiders kept the American back country in an uproar along the Ohio frontier. Given their naval weakness, the French preferred to keep the British off-balance, trying to prevent a build-up of forces that would lead to an invasion.

In 1757 the French concentrated on New York as the main battlefield. Montcalm won several more notable victories, putting the French in control of the lake route into Canada. A year later, the British managed to force the surrender of the garrison at Fort Frontenac on the north shore of Lake Ontario. A sideshow in the Ohio region saw the British capture Fort Duquesne on the Ohio River. The British constantly continued to increase the number of troops at their disposal, employing their naval superiority to besiege successfully the exposed French fortress at Louisbourg in 1758. The French garrison held out just long enough to prevent the enemy from continuing on to an invasion of Quebec, but the French were pulling back militarily. The situation in New France itself was becoming desperate. The government was unable to get reinforcements of men or fresh supplies, especially of arms and munitions. Moreover, it was in terrible shape financially. Morale was very low.

By the beginning of 1759, the situation was grave for New France. After more than a century and a half of successful struggle against environment, Native peoples, and the British, the Canadians were up against the wall. A series of powerful British armies, backed by a wealthy government determined to win, was gathering for the invasion of the St Lawrence. The locus of power may finally have tided decisively against the French in North America.

Major Events, 1759–1814

1759 Battle of Quebec.

1760 Final French surrender.

1763 Treaty of Paris transfers New France and Acadia to Great Britain; the British king issues the Proclamation of 1763.

1773 The Island of St John calls its first assembly.

1774 Parliament passes the Quebec Act. It also passes Palliser's Act to regulate the Newfoundland fishery.

1775 The Americans invade Canada.

1778 Peter Pond reaches the rich Athabasca fur country. James Cook arrives at Nootka Sound.

1781 The British surrender at Yorktown; a smallpox epidemic decimates the Native peoples around Hudson Bay.

1782 The first Loyalist fleet departs for Nova Scotia.

1783 Treaty of Paris ends the War of the American Revolution by recognizing American independence.

1784 British North America is reorganized; New Brunswick is separated from Nova Scotia and given a separate government; Cape Breton gets a government but no assembly.

1786 Guy Carleton is appointed governor-general of British North America.

1787 Charles Inglis, the first Anglican bishop in North America, arrives in Halifax.

1788 King's College is established by the Nova Scotia legislature (it actually opens in 1790 at Windsor).

1789 The British and Spanish spar at Nootka Sound.

1791 Upper and Lower Canada are separated by the British Parliament's passage of the Constitutional Act of 1791.

1792 First legislature in Upper Canada is convened at Newark (Niagara-on-the-Lake). Captain George Vancouver begins his survey of the BC coast.

1793 Alexander Mackenzie of the North West Company reaches the Pacific Ocean via an overland route from Montreal.

1800 King's College (now University of New Brunswick) is founded at Fredericton.

1806 *Le Canadien*, first Francophone newspaper, is published in Quebec.

1808 Simon Fraser reaches the Pacific via the Fraser River.

1809 First steam vessel (the *Accommodation*) begins service between Montreal and Quebec.

1811 Hudson's Bay Company makes a land grant of 116,000 sq. mi. (300,420 km^2) to Lord Selkirk.

1812 Americans declare war on Great Britain and invade Canada; the first settlers arrive at Red River.

1813 York (Toronto) is sacked by the British.

1814 Treaty of Ghent inconclusively ends the War of 1812.

Becoming and Remaining British, 1759–1815

❁

The British established a foothold in Canada with their victory at the Battle of Quebec in 1759. They consolidated their position in 1760, and kept the conquest at the peace treaty in 1763. The theory was that eliminating the French would stabilize North America. It did not work out that way. Within a few years of the conquest, the American colonists had begun an armed rebellion and attempted unsuccessful invasions of Quebec and Nova Scotia. The British reorganized their North American empire after the Americans left it, taking advantage of the thousands of exiles and refugees called Loyalists whom the war had produced. Within a generation, in 1812, the Americans declared war on Great Britain and attempted another round of invasions of Canada, but were beaten back by British regulars and colonial militia with considerable

Louis-Joseph, Marquis de Montcalm

Louis-Joseph, Marquis de Montcalm (1712–59) was descended from a French family of the *noblesse du robe*. He was commissioned an ensign at the age of nine, and spent most of his life at war. In 1752 he petitioned the Crown for a pension, claiming thirty-one years of service, eleven campaigns, and five wounds. He was selected to serve in North America in 1756 because more distinguished senior officers with equal experience would not go to such a remote place. Montcalm was to be only a field commander and, not surprisingly, he soon came into conflict with the governor-general of New France, Pierre de Rigaud de Vaudreuil. His letters to the ministry were a litany of complaints about and criticisms of his superior and the Canadian militia. Despite his own victories, by 1758 he was convinced that the French could not win a war fought only with European tactics. Such defeatism was, in a sense, self-fulfilling (National Archives of Canada C-143420).

James Wolfe

James Wolfe (1727-59), the son of an army officer, was, like Montcalm, a career soldier. He came to the attention of the British command structure, and was given authority in America that was not in keeping with his experience and achievements. He appeared to fulfil this confidence with his textbook victory at Louisbourg in 1758. Technically, he was only a colonel, although he held local rank as 'Brigadier in America'. Early in 1759 Wolfe wrote his uncle: 'I am to act a greater part in this business than I wished or desired. The backwardness of some of the older officers has in some measure forced the Government to come down so low.' As Wolfe and his forces moved towards Quebec, he was already suffering from 'the gravel' (urinary tract blockage) and rheumatism, both extremely painful ailments. At Quebec he acquired an infection that produced fever and dysentery, the medical treatment (a combination of opiates and bleeding) for which made decision making difficult. The portrait is said to be a copy of a sketch by John Montresor, a British engineer, drawn from life at the Montmorency camp on 1 September 1759, only two weeks before Wolfe's death (National Archives of Canada C-14342).

difficulty. The period from 1759 to 1815 was thus one of great turmoil and change. British North America would settle down only after 1815.

THE CONQUEST AND ITS AFTERMATH

The series of abortive and aborted British attempts to seize Quebec, the administrative capital of New France (in 1690, 1711, and 1746) did not prevent another major expedition under General James Wolfe (1727–59) from trying again. The largest and best-equipped military force that North America had ever known assembled at Louisbourg over the winter of 1758–9, while the frozen ice of the St Lawrence isolated the French. It consisted of 8,600 troops, most of them regulars, and 13,500 sailors aboard 119 vessels, including twenty-two ships of the line and five frigates. This great armada required six days simply to clear Louisbourg harbour in early June 1759. On 27 June, Wolfe landed his army on the Île d'Orléans without serious French opposition. There followed over two months of skirmishing, as Wolfe attempted to land his army

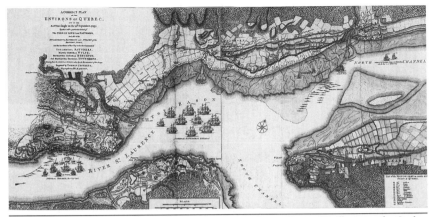

This 1760 map by Thomas Jefferys, who was then geographer to George III, illustrates the Quebec campaign in 1759. Wolfe set up camp on the Île d'Orléans (lower right); failed in July in his attempt to land at Montmorency on the north shore (above the North Channel); moved his fleet upriver past Quebec in September; and landed at l'Anse au Foulon (extreme left) to wage the brief battle on the Plains of Abraham (above) (National Archives of Canada 128079).

closer to the French forces, and the French commander-in-chief, the Marquis de Montcalm (1712–59) sought to prevent such a move. Meanwhile, Wolfe and the British admiral, Sir Charles Saunders (1713?–75), were at constant loggerheads, and Montcalm found considerable evidence that his forces, mainly French-Canadian militiamen, would not stand up to offensive action.

Wolfe tried a number of plans, all without success. He was becoming desperate. As the end of summer approached, there was less time for the massive British fleet to remain in the St Lawrence, and its commanders were pressing for a final confrontation. Finally, after partially recovering from a fever, Wolfe made a final effort. His troops found a path up the cliffs to the plain above at the Anse au Foulon, and managed to pass the French sentries unmolested. The British drew their battle lines covering the plain above the cliffs. Inexplicably, Montcalm decided to attack the British army without waiting for reinforcements. The French ranks broke first, both Wolfe and Montcalm were mortally wounded, and the British possessed Quebec. The war was not ended, for the bulk of the French army escaped and would fight on valiantly for another year. The Battle of Quebec (or of the Plains of Abraham) was probably the first military engagement in North America that was fought almost entirely in European rather than American terms. A fully professional army, well disciplined and on the day well led, defeated a partly untrained one. Backed by a government at home with regular troops and naval support, the British finally breached the defensive position that the French had enjoyed for over a century.

British reinforcements and supplies arrived first on the St Lawrence in 1760, and a traditional three-prong attack on Montreal—anchored by a large army led by General Jeffrey Amherst (1717–97) from New York—forced the surrender of that town, the final French stronghold, in early September. The fifty-five articles of capitulation would govern the British occupation of Canada until the governments in Europe finally settled matters by the Treaty of Paris in 1763. Until Europe made a final determination, Britain dealt with the colony with a fairly light hand. Canada was governed by military administrators who spoke French and accepted it as the 'language of the country'. A few of the French-Canadian élite departed for France, while a number of new suppliers (mainly American colonials tied to British and American trading patterns) made their inevitable appearance.

Peace negotiations in 1761 proved unsuccessful, not because the French had balked at sacrificing North American territory, but because war minister William Pitt had wanted more concessions around the world. When the French West Indies fell totally and the British began an assault on Spanish Havana— Spain had earlier foolishly entered the war on the side of France—the French and Spanish had their backs to the wall. The French offered to sacrifice more continental American territory. Louisiana east of the Mississippi was surrendered for Martinique and Guadeloupe. The French were granted fishing rights in Newfoundland and the tiny islands of St Pierre and Miquelon in exchange for the surrender of all other claims to territory in the northern part of the American continent. The Spanish proved no problem after the fall of Havana. In a complicated arrangement, Britain returned Havana and Puerto Rico and kept Spain's Florida, while France compensated Spain for its losses by ceding it the western half of Louisiana and the port of New Orleans.

The final arrangement was sold to the British public by emphasizing the great gains made in North America. Having stressed the security won for the American colonies as a result of the war—at monumental expense to the British people in manpower and money—the government needed an American policy. Its first effort at creating one was the notorious Proclamation of 1763. Like most British policy for its northern possessions produced over the next few years, the Proclamation of 1763 was not directly intended to effect fundamental changes for Britain's older seaboard colonies. Four new governments were created out of the American acquisitions, including Quebec, which was limited to its St Lawrence settlements. This truncated province was to be governed by British law and, as soon as possible, an elected assembly. The Island of St John and Cape Breton were attached to Nova Scotia. Land grants to retired officers and disbanded servicemen were to be readily available. In the west, beyond the river systems of the Atlantic coast, no land grants were to be made. This territory was to be reserved for the First Nations, and any trading in it was to be regulated by the imperial government.

The Proclamation had ramifications beyond the territory ceded by the French. It was preceded by a major Indian uprising in the interior, known as

Pontiac's Rebellion. Both the declaration of limits for American westward expansion and the need to finance Britain's new military responsibilities would enrage the American colonials. They began a series of provocative responses to Britain that would escalate into an organized colonial rebellion or 'revolution'. It became apparent that policy for the new territories could not be executed by Great Britain in isolation.

Although neither the Proclamation of 1763 nor any other British policy document ever elaborated a full settlement policy for what is now Canada, the outlines of that policy were perfectly plain. The British did not wish to populate their northernmost colonies with emigrants from the mother country itself. Great Britain was at the beginning of a major economic shift, usually called the Industrial Revolution. Instead of having excess population, it wanted to retain its people, both as a labour force and for military purposes. The British, however, were prepared to make land grants to disbanded soldiers, who were not regarded as very useful at home in peacetime. They were also willing to accept 'foreign Protestants' as settlers, although they hoped that colonial Americans, already acclimated to the New World, would become the principal newcomers. The creation of an Indian reserve in the west would force land-hungry Americans south and north: south to Florida, north to Quebec and Nova Scotia. The British hoped that new immigration would soon outnumber and overwhelm the French in Quebec, but they were not prepared to subsidize the movement of settlers beyond making land available to them.

FROM THE PROCLAMATION TO THE REBELLION

In Nova Scotia, a third contingent of subsidized settlers was added to the first group at Halifax and the 'foreign Protestants'. The New England 'Planters' came to the province between 1759 and 1762. Governor Charles Lawrence took advantage of a substantial annual parliamentary grant for Nova Scotia to recruit over 8,000 Yankees. He provided them with land, transportation, and subsidies until the financial tap was turned off in 1762. The New Englanders came mainly from land-hungry areas of Rhode Island, Connecticut, and south-eastern Massachusetts. They saw migration to Nova Scotia—which was an alternative to movement to northern areas of New England—as particularly attractive because it was financed by the government. The migrants tended to move in kinship groups, often as entire communities. Most were farmers, although others were fishermen seeking improved access to superior fishing grounds. The farmers settled on Acadian land in the Minas Basin, while the fishermen moved to south-shore outports they named Yarmouth and Barrington after their New England counterparts.

The Planters had been promised not only cheap land but liberty of conscience and a government 'like those of neighbouring colonies', a guarantee

Part of the Town & Harbour of Halifax in Nova Scotia, looking down Prince Street to the Opposite Shore . . ., one of six prints of drawings of Halifax made by Richard Short in 1759 (National Archives of Canada C-4294).

they took to mean that they could replicate the participatory local democracy of their former homes (quoted Bumsted 1971:8). They soon found that Nova Scotia had no intention of permitting strong local government. Political disillusionment was added to disappointment over the climate and the absence of markets. Perhaps half the newcomers left within a few years of the termination of subsidies, complaining of 'Nova Scarcity'. While Yankee farmers wheeled and dealed in small parcels of land, the élite office-holding classes (both within and without the colony) acquired large grants of wilderness land—3 million acres (1,214,100 ha) in the last few days before the Stamp Act became effective in 1765; having to buy stamped paper would greatly increase the cost of obtaining the grants. Only a handful of these speculators became active in either settlement ventures or commercial development.

Land speculation also dominated the development of the Island of St John. The entire land surface of the island was distributed to absentee owners (mainly British office holders and military men) by lottery in 1767. These proprietors were supposed to settle the land in return for their grants, but most would merely hold it in the hopes that it would become more valuable. The British allowed the proprietors on the Island of St John, which was initially attached to Nova Scotia, to petition for a separate government in 1769, on the understanding that it would not cost the mother country a penny.

In Quebec, a number of military officers (and sometimes their men) took advantage of the British offer of land grants. The anticipated stampede of American settlers to Quebec did not occur, however. The Americans were put off partly by the presence of thousands of francophone Roman Catholics and the absence of familiar institutions such as representative government and universal freehold tenure. In a classic vicious circle, the laws, government, and culture of Quebec could not very well be reconstructed until large numbers of anglophones arrived, and this immigration was not likely to happen until change had occurred. Moreover, Americans did not move north into any of the British colonies after 1763. Most of the newcomers were from Britain, mainly from Scotland, who began leaving their homes in the mid-1760s. The Scottish influx had only begun to gain momentum when it was closed down by the warfare of the American rebellion.

Everywhere in the northernmost colonies in these years, freehold land tenure and the concept of the yeoman farmer fought an uphill battle. The seigneurial system still controlled land in Quebec, the Island of St John had been distributed to proprietors who were expected to settle as tenant farmers did in Europe, and much of Nova Scotia was held by large landholders. In the absence of aggressive government settlement activity, those who acquired grants of land in North America in order to settle them were committed to replicating a European pattern of landholding, with aristocratic landlords and peasant tenants.

The administration of the new province of Quebec was not only greatly complicated by the small number of anglophones but by the emerging political turmoil to the south. The colonial authorities in Quebec began by introducing some British elements into the system, but ended up confirming many French ones. English criminal law was put into effect, but the French civil law was largely retained. The British in London agreed that British laws against Catholics did not extend to Quebec. Grand-Vicar Jean-Olivier Briand (1715–94) was chosen by his Canadian colleagues to head the Church in Quebec, and was consecrated bishop near Paris on 16 March 1766. Officially he would be only 'superintendant' of the Quebec Church, but in practice he was accepted as its bishop and the collection of tithes was officially supported. There could be no elected assembly until there were more Protestants. The process of confirmation of the institutions of the Old Regime gained a real boost from Governor Guy Carleton (1724–1808). An Anglo-Irishman, Carleton was a firm believer in a landed aristocracy, the subordination of a tenant class, and a close connection between church and state. He came to see that, with adjustments to circumstance, his overall vision for society was quite compatible with those of the Old Regime of New France. As the Americans to the south became increasingly restive and turbulent, Carleton became less

The Religious Provisions of the Quebec Act

Anno Decimo Quarto, Georgii III. Regis., Cap. LXXXIII.(An Act for making more effectual Provision for the Government of the Province of *Quebec* in *North America.*)

Whereas His Majesty, by His Royal Proclamation, bearing Date the Seventh Day of *October,* in the Third Year of His reign, thought fit to declare the Provisions which had been made in respect to certain Countries, Territories, and Islands in *America,* ceded to His Majesty by the definitive Treaty of Peace, concluded at *Paris* on the Tenth Day of *February,* One thousand seven hundred and sixty-three: . . .

And whereas the Provisions, made by the said Proclamation, in respect to the Civil Government of the said Province of *Quebec* and the Powers and Authorities given to the Governor and other Civil Officers of the said Province, by the Grants and Commissions issued in consequence thereof, have been found, upon Experience, to be inapplicable to the State and Circumstances of the said Province, the Inhabitants whereof amounted, at the Conquest, to above Sixty-five thousand Persons professing the Religion of the Church of *Rome,* and enjoying an established Form of Constitution and System of Laws, by which their Persons and Property had been protected, governed, and ordered, for a long Series of Years, from the First Establishment of the said Province of *Canada;* . . . for the more perfect Security and Ease of the Minds of the Inhabitants of the said Province, it is hereby declared, That His Majesty's Subjects, professing the Religion of the Church of *Rome* of and in the said Province of *Quebec,* may have, hold, and enjoy, the free Exercise of the Religion of the Church of *Rome,* subject to the King's Supremacy, declared and established by an Act, made in the First Year of the Reign of Queen *Elizabeth,* over all the Dominions and Countries which then did, or thereafter should belong, to the Imperial Crown of this Realm; and that the Clergy of the said Church may hold, receive, and enjoy, their accustomed Dues and Rights, with

eager for reform and more interested in pacification. Inevitably he turned to the handiest instruments at his disposal.

Instinctively grasping the need for collaborators to rule an 'alien' population, Carleton turned to the clergy and the seigneurs as natural leaders and to the protection of their rights and privileges. In the process some of the economic damage to the economy resulting from the geographical dismemberment of Quebec in 1763 could be undone. The result was the Quebec Act of 1774. Most of the ancient boundaries of Quebec were restored to the colony. His Majesty's subjects in Quebec 'professing the Religion of the Church of Rome' were granted free exercise of their religion and exempted from the traditional oaths of supremacy with a new one supplied. The Catholic clergy were allowed 'their accustomed Dues and Rights, with respect to such Persons only as shall profess the said Religion'.

respect to such Persons only as shall profess the said Religion.

Provided nevertheless, That it shall be lawful for His Majesty, His Heirs or Successors, to make such Provision out of the rest of the said accustomed Dues and Rights, for the Encouragement of the Protestant Religion, and for the Maintenance and Support of a Protestant Clergy within the said Province, as he or they shall, from Time to Time, think necessary and expedient.

Provided always, and be it enacted, That no Person, professing the Religion of the Church of *Rome,* and residing in the said Province, shall be obliged to take the Oath required by the said Statute passed in the First Year of the Reign of Queen *Elizabeth,* or any other Oaths substituted by any other Act in the Place thereof; but that every such Person who, by the said Statute is required, to take and subscribe the following Oath before the Governor, or such other Person in such Court of Record as His Majesty shall appoint, who are hereby authorised to administer the same; videlicet,

I, A.B. do sincerely promise and swear, That I will be faithful, and bear true Allegiance to His Majesty King GEORGE, *and him will defend to the utmost of my Power, against all traitorous Conspiracies, and Attempts whatsoever, which shall be made against His Person, Crown, and Dignity; and I will do my utmost Endeavour to disclose and make known to His Majesty, His Heirs and Successors, all Treasons, and traitorous Conspiracies, and Attempts, which I shall know to be against Him, or any of Them; and all this I do swear without any Equivocation, mental Evasion, or secret Reservation, and renouncing all Persons and Dispensations from any Power or Person whomsoever to the Contrary. So* HELP ME GOD.

And every such Person, who shall neglect or refuse to take the said Oath before mentioned, shall incur and be liable to the same Penalties, Forefeitures, Disabilities, and Incapacities, as he would have incurred and been liable to for neglecting or refusing to take the Oath required by the said Statute passed in the First Year of the Reign of Queen *Elizabeth.*

Provision was also made for the support of a Protestant clergy. All matters relating to property and civil rights were to be decided by the traditional laws of Canada. This clause, in effect, preserved the seigneurial system. English criminal law was continued, and the province was to be governed by a newly structured legislative council; there was no provision for an elected assembly.

Parliamentary critics of the administration that introduced this measure complained of its 'sowing the seeds of despotism in Canada' (Edmund Burke, quoted in Neatby 1972:38–9). The Americans assumed a direct connection between it and their own situation, including the Quebec Act as one of the 'Intolerable Acts' passed by the British Parliament at this time to punish the Americans for the Boston Tea Party. The legislation was certainly influenced by the need to pacify Quebec, but it was not intended to aggravate the Americans.

If the act was supposed to secure the loyalty of the *Canadiens*, however, the strategy was not entirely successful.

THE FIRST AMERICAN CIVIL WAR

In early April 1775 British troops, attempting to raid clandestine colonial arms depots in Massachusetts, were fired upon by the Americans. A long-festering imperial political crisis turned into a shooting war. From the vantage point of the American leadership, they were involved in a 'revolution' to secure their rights against the arbitrary authority of the British Crown. From the vantage point of the British government, the Americans were engaged in a 'rebellion' against duly constituted authority. Whatever its label, for many of the inhabitants in British North America the event meant involvement in an extended civil war in which brother fought brother, friend opposed friend, and many were eventually pushed into exile. Indeed, the proportion of exiles from the new United States (relative to population) exceeded that from France after 1789, from Russia after 1917, and from Cuba after 1955. Instead of seeing the people of the northernmost colonies as impotent victims of the American Revolution taking place to the south, it makes far more sense to view them as participants (although often at a distance) in a great civil war that affected the whole transatlantic region of Britain's vast empire.

The Americans moved quickly in 1775 to organize an alternative government and raise an army, under the command of George Washington of Virginia. While that force was still in embryo, the Second Continental Congress authorized an invasion of Quebec as a move to bestow 'the coup de grace to the hellish junto' governing Great Britain (quoted in Stanley 1977:27). Washington was somewhat more enthusiastic about this plan than he was about subsequent proposals to invade Nova Scotia. One army was ordered to proceed to Quebec by way of Lake Champlain and the Richelieu River. Another was authorized to travel across northern Maine and along the Chaudière River to the St Lawrence.

The sudden turn of events found the government of Quebec in a state of shock and confusion. Governor Carleton, only recently returned from London with the Quebec Act in his dispatch case, complained he had insufficient military force to withstand an invasion. A public *mandement* from Bishop Briand, ordering the population to ignore American propaganda under threat of denial of the sacraments, had little effect. The seigneurs appointed to raise a militia found it difficult to do so. Carleton's alliance with Quebec's traditional leaders proved useless, largely because he misunderstood the dynamics of the Old Regime. The Church never had much influence on habitant behaviour, and the seigneurs had never much to do with the militia. The British merchants of Quebec had never been cultivated by Carleton and proved singularly uncoop-

Sir Guy Carleton, who succeeded James Murray as governor in April 1768, was a member of the British gentry and a firm believer in a landed aristocracy, the subordination of a tenant class, and the close connection between church and state (National Archives of Canada A-197).

erative. Not even the First Nations leapt into action on Britain's behalf; most of the Iroquois would remain neutral until pushed into loyalty by the Americans later in the war.

Fortunately for the British, the Americans were neither as well organized nor as lucky as Wolfe's expedition had been in 1758–9, and the Québécois were not as enthusiastic about 'liberation from tyranny' as the invaders had hoped (Hatch 1970:60). General Richard Montgomery (1736–75), struggling to bring an invading army up the Lake Champlain route, wrote that 'the privates are all generals' and that those from different colonies did not get along together (quoted in Hatch 1970:60). Benedict Arnold (1741–1801), bringing his army across what is now Maine under horrendous late autumn conditions, lost nearly half his troops in the process. On 11 November, Montgomery and his troops arrived near Montreal and pressed on to Quebec, although his soldiers were constantly deserting. At the same time, the habitants were hardly rushing to enlist in the American army. In Quebec, Colonel Allan Maclean (1725–84), who had earlier organized two battalions of disbanded Highland soldiers, had stiffened resistance. Montgomery joined Arnold at Pointe-aux-Trembles on 3 December. He quickly determined that he lacked the force and the supplies to besiege Quebec. Instead, he decided to storm the town. The assault on 31

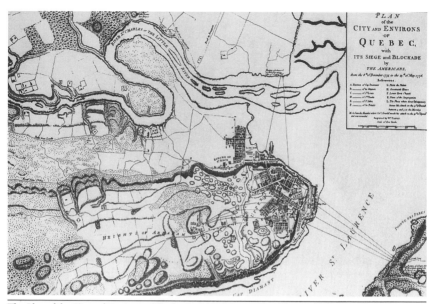

The *Plan of the City and Environs of Quebec* in 1775 (Metropolitan Toronto Reference Library).

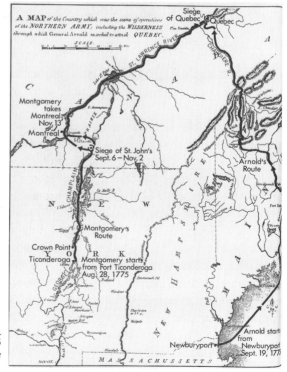

The invasion of Quebec, 1775 (Metropolitan Toronto Reference Library).

December was a desperate move by the Americans, who were suffering from smallpox as well as problems of logistics and morale.

The garrison held. The result, wrote one British officer, was 'A glorious day for us, as compleat a little victory as ever was gained' (quoted in Stanley 1977:27). General Montgomery's frozen body was found not far from the barricade against which he had led the charge. He was subsequently buried with military honours, with Guy Carleton, who had known him from earlier campaigns, as chief mourner. General Arnold took a ball through the left leg at the first battery, and over 300 Americans were taken prisoner. The American forces, now under Arnold's command, remained in military occupation of more than fifty parishes over the winter of 1775–6. Their desperate seizure of foodstuffs, sometimes paid for with worthless Continental currency, according to one American, cost the occupying army 'the affections of the people in general' (quoted in Dyer and Viljoen 1990:49). A commission from the Continental Congress, headed by Benjamin Franklin, pronounced from Montreal, 'Till the arrival of money, it seems improper to propose the Federal union of this Province with the others' (quoted in Dyer and Viljoen 1990:49). In May 1776 British reinforcements arrived at Quebec, and by mid-June the Americans had completely retreated, never to return. Quebec became an important centre for the British army, later serving as the staging point for a counterinvasion of the United States (equally unsuccessful) in 1778, led by General John Burgoyne.

The Americans had desperately wanted Quebec. George Washington wrote to Benedict Arnold early in 1776: 'To whomsoever it belongs, in their favour, probably will the balance turn. If it is ours, success, I think, will most certainly crown our virtuous struggles; if it is theirs, the contest, at least, will be doubtful, hazardous and bloody' (quoted in Dyer and Viljoen 1990:49). The Rebel leaders did not feel the same way about Nova Scotia, partly because of its protection by the British navy, partly because there was not enough visible evidence of enthusiastic residents ready to support an invading army. Some American sympathizers like Jonathan Eddy (1726/7–1804) and John Allan (1747–1805) recruited a private army in Machias and Maugerville, consisting of eighty men, who marched overland from the St John River towards the British outpost at Fort Cumberland in late October and early November 1776. This 'invasion' was joined by a few residents from the area, but was quickly suppressed by British reinforcements, leaving those Nova Scotians who had supported the Americans either abjectly explaining away their actions or quickly departing for American lines, leaving behind their wives and families to be sworn at and 'often kicked when met in the street' (quoted in Clark 1988:49). Civil wars were truly nasty ones.

An American Privateering Raid

[Simeon Perkins (1734/5–1812) was born in Norwich, Connecticut, migrating to Liverpool, Nova Scotia, in 1762. When the American Rebellion began, Perkins remained loyal to the Crown. As lieutenant-colonel of the Queen's County militia, he was responsible for the defence of Liverpool. *Source*: H. Innes, *The Diary of Simeon Perkins, 1766–1780*, vol. 1 (Toronto: Champlain Society, 1948):139–41.

Thursday, April 9th, [1778]—Pleasent [*sic*] day. Wind N.W. Capt. Hopkins, and Capt. Gorham, Capt. Dean, B. Harrington, are about going to Halifax. Some of them get to the mouth of the Harbour and discover a privateer sloop at anchor back of the Island. . . . She continues at anchor till towards night she came into the Harbour, and the wind being small, rowed up into Herring Cove and sent a boat almost up to the Bar. I went on the Point to hail them but she tacked about and returned on board the sloop. Seeing a sloop full of men come into the Harbour it was truly alarming in our defenceless condition. . . . I had some men under arms, and kept a sentry on the Point, relieved every half hour. Soon after Mr Collins return I found that the sentry, Robert Bramham, was deserted. Had left his musket, and taken a skiff from the shore, and no doubt remained but he was gone on board the privateer. This put us in some Consternation, as this Bramham . . . had

heard all our Council. The sloop soon got under way, and stood athwart the Harbour, and finally went out of sight. I then ordered a guard of one sergeant and four privates dismissed the remainder of the People, and went home. In less than two hours I was informed that the Privateer was coming in again. I immediately alarmed the People from one end of the street to the other, and mustered about 15 under arms. The sloop came in with Drum and fife going, and whuzzaing, etc. They anchored a little above the Bar, and sent a boat on board Mr Gorham's schooner, and Mr Hopkins schr. I gave orders not to speak to them or fire upon, except they offered to come on shore to rob the stores, etc. If they made any such attempt to engage them. They searched the two schrs. mentioned, and returned on board the Privateer, and hove up their anchor, and went out after daylight. They had boarded a sloop in Herring Cove, Benjamin Harrington, master, and demanded a hhd. of Rum, which was landed as she was coming in, but finally took up with 40 gallons, which Harrington produced. . . .

It is now Fryday morning, April 10th,—The Privateer is gone out. Wind S.E. All is quiet. A small schr., Prince Doan, Master, arrives from Barrington. The Privateer put a man on board her in the night, but released her this morning. I am mutch fatigued, and sleep a sound nap. In the afternoon I hear the Privateer is gone into Portmatoon.

The affair at Fort Cumberland was more typical of this war than was the earlier invasion of Quebec. Away from the armies, the opposing parties—Rebel and Loyalist—fought vicious little battles with one another for control of the uncommitted local population, often paying back old scores along the way. On the high seas, legalized pirates (called privateers) captured unarmed ships and attacked unprotected settlements along the coasts. Between 1775 and 1781 the privateers literally brought commerce to a halt in the Atlantic region, causing a number of food shortages, particularly in Newfoundland and the Island of St John. Both these colonies went for long periods without the arrival of a single vessel from overseas. On the borders between Loyalist and Rebel territory, guerrilla raiders (often including Native allies) attacked farms and villages. Since most of the population of the northernmost provinces lived on the coast or near an American border, everyone lived in constant fear of attack.

Given the insecurity of the times, it was hardly surprising that the radical preacher, Henry Alline (1748–84), should have considerable success in the Maritime region in introducing a movement of Christian pietism and rejuvenation often called The Great Awakening. Alline rejected secular affairs in favour of the self-government of the godly, emphasizing that Christ had commanded his followers 'to salute no man by the way' (quoted in Bumsted 1971:93). He travelled the countryside, composing and singing hymns, regarding music as a way to attract and hold an audience, as well as a useful vehicle on the road to salvation. At his death he left a legacy of evangelism and revivalism among his followers, who were called New Lights. In a period of confusion, Alline offered an alternative path to public involvement.

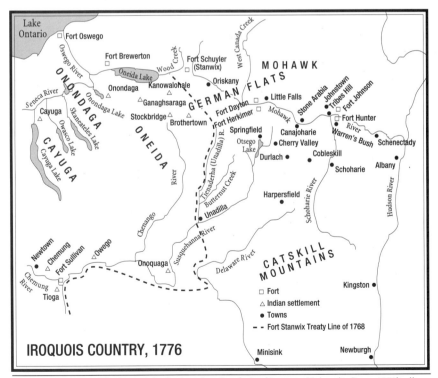

Source: B. Graymont, *The Iroquois in the American Revolution* (Syracuse University Press, 1972): xii.

Not all residents of the northernmost colonies who did make a conscious choice selected the British side. One who did not was Moses Hazen (1733–1803), a native of Massachusetts, who had settled in the Richelieu Valley of Quebec after the Conquest. After a period of fence-sitting in 1775, Hazen committed himself to the United States and was appointed by the Continental Congress to command a regiment he was to raise in Canada. Hazen successfully recruited several hundred habitants, many of whom retreated with him from Canada in June 1776 and stayed together as a unit throughout most of the war. His men (and the Nova Scotia refugees) were ultimately compensated by the American Congress with land and financial assistance.

Like many other North Americans, most Native peoples attempted to remain out of the conflict. For the Iroquois, neutrality proved impossible. One of the Mohawk leaders, Joseph Brant (Thayendanegea, 1742–1807) became persuaded that only continued active alliance with the British could protect Indian interests by preserving Indian land from the encroachment of European

Joseph Brant

This full-length oil portrait of Joseph Brant, painted perhaps as a tribute, was rendered by William Berczy after Brant died on 24 November 1807. Berczy painted him at least once from life, however, when they met at Newark in 1794. In this portrait, the Mohawk chief has his arm outstretched in a gesture of imperial authority and is majestic in a bright red blanket. Berczy wrote of Brant in 1799: '. . . he is near 6 feet high in stance, of a stout and durable texture able to undergo all the inconvenience of the hardships connected with the difficulties to carry on war through immense woods and wildernesses—His intellectual qualities compared with the phisical constructions of his bodily frame—He professes in an eminent degree a sound and profound judgement. He hears patiently and with great attention before he replies and answers in general in a precise and laconic stile. But as soon as it is a question of some topic of great moment, especially relative to the interest of his nation he speaks with a peculiar dignity—his speech is exalted energy and endowed with all the charms of complete Retorick.' This painting of Joseph Brant is by William Von Moll Berczy (National Gallery of Canada, Ottawa 5777).

settlement. Brant was unable to convince the Iroquois councils, but he recruited a force of about 300 Indian warriors and 100 Loyalist settlers, which was active in scouting and raiding operations, and in 1778 collaborated with Butler's Rangers (a Loyalist regiment) in guerrilla raids in the Mohawk Valley of New York. The Americans responded to such activity in 1779 with a major expedition into the land of the Iroquois, laying waste the country. The Indians, including Brant, were forced to retreat to Fort Niagara, where they became supplicants for British aid.

Further west in the fur trading country, Native peoples were better able to ignore the war. The western fur trade was relatively unaffected by the American Revolution. The western movement of the Montreal-based fur trade, now dominated by English-speaking traders, continued unabated. By the time of Lexington and Concord, they were pressing up the Saskatchewan River into the basin of the Churchhill River. In 1778 Peter Pond (1740–1807?) broke through into the richest fur trade country of the continent: the Athabasca region. The competition, the 'Pedlars from Quebec', as one Hudson's Bay Company man contemptuously labelled them, galvanized the English company into more aggressive action. It moved inland from its posts on the Bay to open up ones on the Saskatchewan. Trading competition was always a mixed blessing to the Native peoples. It gave them a choice and lower prices, but because the Indian consumer had a relatively inelastic need for trade goods, competition also increased the amount of non-material and non-essential consumer goods on offer, particularly tobacco and alcohol, which was a negative feature.

The revolutionary period did see one curious development in Hudson Bay. A great French fleet had been beaten by the British off Jamaica in 1781, and three of the dispersed vessels ended up in the Bay, where they caused considerable damage to Hudson's Bay Company posts before returning to France. Far more serious than the French depredations, however, was the appearance in

Capt. Cook's Ships Moored in Resolution Cove, Nootka Sound, Vancouver Island, March 1778, a watercolour by M.B. Messer after a drawing by John Webber (National Archives of Canada C-11201).

1781 and 1782 of a major epidemic of smallpox among the Native peoples, who lacked European immunities and suffered heavy mortalities.

On the Pacific coast, the American Revolution was even more remote than on Hudson Bay. From the European perspective, the major event was the appearance in March 1778 of Captain James Cook (1728–79) in Resolution Cove, Nootka Sound, off the western coast of Vancouver Island. Cook was on another quest for the Northwest Passage, spurred by new information that suggested one might exist. In Nootka Sound, he and his crews observed the Nootka Indians. The visitors were much impressed with their trading acumen and especially their principal trading commodity: the sleek, thick fur pelt of the sea otter. Cook was killed on the return voyage through the Pacific to England. An impressive account of the voyage in 1784 included descriptions of the sea otter pelts. Soon there was a rush to cash in on their obvious value, for they offered something to trade in the otherwise difficult Chinese market.

While James Cook's crews were still on the high seas returning to England, the British lost the war of the American Revolution. Whether they could ever have won it remains an open question. Military suppression of movements of national liberation has never been a very successful strategy. Once the Americans managed to hold on, assisted by considerable British military stupidity and inefficiency, they found allies in Europe. France joined the war in 1778. Unable to defeat the Americans with regular troops, the British turned increasingly to provincial Loyalist units to do the actual fighting, thus further enhancing the civil war aspect of the conflict. On the New York and Carolina frontiers, Loyalists and Rebels fought fierce battles in which no quarter was asked or given.

With the help of the French navy, the Americans finally succeeded in 1781 in trapping a large British army under Lord Cornwallis in Virginia. The surrender of Cornwallis was really the end of the line for the British. The ministry could no longer pretend that victory was just around the corner. It surrendered, allowing its critics to negotiate the peace. The final agreement worked out with the Americans, signed on 30 November 1782, gave the Rebels most of what they wanted. It recognized the independence of the United States, and allowed the new nation fishing rights in the Atlantic and gave to it the entire Ohio Valley. Equally important, the British negotiators failed to insist on any real security for either its Indian allies or the Loyalists.

ACCOMMODATING THE LOYALISTS

From the beginning of the revolutionary conflict, some colonials had supported the British. As the war continued, many more were pressured by events into choosing sides and ended up with Great Britain. The struggle had been a bitter one, and officers of the provincial Loyalist regiments insisted that they be included in any Loyalist resettlement scheme, saying 'The personal animosities that arose from civil dissension have been so heightened by the Blood that has been shed in the Contest, that the Parties can never be reconciled' (quoted in Wright 1955:41–2). The British authorities in New York, where most of the Loyalists had gathered, accepted this argument. They were allowed to join the contingents of Loyalists that departed by ship for Nova Scotia in 1782 and 1783. Other Loyalist regiments already in Quebec joined British regulars in settling there at the close of the hostilities. The British were prepared to make extensive grants of land to these new arrivals, and to support them with supplies while they remade their lives. Perhaps 40,000 people received land grants and assistance as Loyalists, with about 30,000 settling in Nova Scotia (part of which would become the province of New Brunswick in 1784), 750 on the Island of St John, 1,000 on Cape Breton, and the remainder in Quebec—mainly in what would become Upper Canada.

The Loyalists were quite a disparate group of newcomers. Of the total of 40,000, well over 3,000 were Blacks who settled in Nova Scotia, and almost 2,000 were Indians who settled in Upper Canada. Over half of the 40,000 were civilian refugees and their families; the remainder were officers and men either from former Loyalist regiments or from British regiments disbanded in America. A large proportion of both groups were neither American nor English in origin. Quite apart from the Blacks and the Indians, a disproportionate number of the new settlers came from Scotland, Ireland, or various German principalities. Anglican clergyman Jacob Bailey (1731–1808) characterized his new neighbours in the Annapolis Valley of Nova Scotia as 'a collection of all nations, kindreds, complexions and tongues assembled from every quarter of the globe and till lately equally strangers to me and each other' (quoted in Bumsted 1986:34).

Some unknown number of the Loyalist settlers were women. Most of the records of the Loyalists list only the males, who got land grants, served in the military, and received stores. But of the 3,225 individuals who presented claims to the British government for compensation of losses during the war, 468 (or about 14 per cent) were women. Only a small percentage of these women had worked outside the home, and most of them were obviously most familiar with their immediate households. Many other women and their families accompanied their husbands into their new surroundings. The loss of homes and cherished contents was probably more traumatic for Loyalist women than were property losses for men. Certainly the gradual recreation of stability was much more difficult. Men could re-establish friendships and relationships in meeting places outside the home, but women usually could not. Women—who were often not consulted about the decision to support the king or to emigrate—had sacrificed for a principle. They had every right to be bitter about their fate.

Table 3.1

Canada Census of 1784

POPULATION, SEXES, CONJUGAL CONDITION

Districts	Population	Sexes Male	Female	Married and Widowed Male	Female	Total	Children & Unmarried Male	Female	Total	Sexes & Cond.
Québec	44,760	22,064	20,570	7,911	7,280	15,291	14,153	13,190	27,343	2,126
Trois-Rivières	12,618	5,806	5,850	2,080	2,247	4,327	3,786	3,603	7,389	902
Montréal	55,634	26,134	24,339	10,140	9,272	19,867	15,994	14,612	30,606	5,161
Total	**113,012**	**54,064**	**50,759**	**20,131**	**19,354**	**39,485**	**33,933**	**31,405**	**65,338**	**8,189**

APPORTIONMENT BY AGES, &C.

Districts	Male	Female	Males Under 15	Over 15	Females Under 14	Over 14	Ser-vants	Slaves	In-firm	Tempor-arily absent	Total
Québec	7,911	7,380	10,041	4,112	8,984	4,206	1,795	88	150	93	44,760
Trois-Rivières	2,080	2,247	2,874	912	2,726	877	676	4	118	104	12,618
Montréal	10,140	9,727	11,637	4,357	10,803	3,809	4,020	212	625	304	55,634
Total	**20,131**	**19,354**	**24,552**	**9,381**	**22,513**	**8,892**	**6,491**	**304**	**893**	**501**	**113,012**

BUILDINGS, LANDS, CROPS, AND CATTLE

Districts	Houses	Agriculture Arpents under culture	Bushels sown	Horses	Oxen	Cattle Young Cattle	Cows	Sheep	Swine
Québec	7,157	628,240	126,318	9,166	8,456	12,439	16,344	41,252	22,202
Trois-Rivières	1,973	214,875	39,349	3,155	1,602	3,147	5,368	10,206	6,458
Montréal	9,794	726,703	217,682	17,825	12,036	16,620	22,579	33,238	41,805
Total	**18,924**	**1,569,818**	**383,349**	**30,146**	**22,094**	**32,206**	**44,291**	**84,696**	**70,465**

What can we learn about the colony from this data? How does the population data compare with that of Nova Scotia in 1767?

From the first days of the war, the British military authorities in America had attempted to enlist some of the half-million slaves to fight against their masters, chiefly by promising them their freedom. Thousands of Blacks found their way to British lines by whatever means possible, drawn by promises only the British could possibly honour. Loyal Blacks were usually evacuated when the British withdrew from an American district. Most of them ended up in New York with the other Loyalists and the British army. More than 3,000 were transported to Nova Scotia. Although they were free, they were not well treated. Only 1,155 of the Black Loyalists in the province actually received land grants, which averaged less than 11 acres (4.5 ha) per grant. Blacks became part of the mobile population of the region, taking up whatever employment was available. They suffered many disabilities. In Nova Scotia they were not entitled to trial by jury. In New Brunswick they were not allowed to vote. Freed Blacks were treated more harshly in the courts than White people convicted of the same or similar crimes. An unknown number of Blacks, who were brought to British North America as slaves by Loyalist masters, continued in that status until the early

Encampment of the Loyalists at Johnston, a New Settlement, on the Banks of the River S. Laurence in Canada,

This watercolour, *Encampment of the Loyalists at Johnston, a New Settlement on the banks of the St Lawrence River, June 6, 1784*, was painted by James Peachey when he was deputy surveyor-general, surveying and laying out lots for disbanded troops and Loyalists in the future Upper Canada (National Archives of Canada).

years of the nineteenth century, when local courts ruled slavery out of existence in the colonies by extending English laws. Not surprisingly, nearly half of the Nova Scotia Black Loyalists would accept with alacrity in 1791 a chance to immigrate to the African colony of Sierra Leone.

Throughout the war the British had played on the Indians' fear that the Americans intended to settle in large numbers on Native lands never recognized as belonging to the First Nations. Some Natives had joined the British, and all were punished for this choice by both sides. The Iroquois were driven from their lands in New York state. The First Nations were abandoned by the British in the rush for extrication from an unpopular and expensive war. Britain transferred to the Americans sovereignty over land south of the Great Lakes and as far west as the Mississippi River, totally ignoring the fact that most of that land was claimed by its Indian allies, who would insist they had never surrendered it to the Americans. The Native refugees were given a grant of land along the Grand River in what would become Upper Canada. Here a 1785 census showed 1,843 Native residents, including more than 400 Mohawks.

Few of the Loyalists stayed where they were initially settled. The town of Port Roseway (or Shelburne), on the southwest coast of the Nova Scotia peninsula, became notorious as a place where almost all of the 10,000 people who had been transported there left within ten years. The decade of the 1780s saw continual Loyalist relocation, sometimes within the colony of original settlement, sometimes in another colony of greater promise, and often eventually back to the United States after subsidies ran out and the initial American hostility had died down. Much of the land initially granted to the Loyalists had only limited agricultural potential, and everywhere homes had to be hewn out of a wilderness. The Loyalist settlement did reassert the principle of freehold tenure in all the colonies. The most stable newcomers were members of the office-holding élite, who tended to cluster in the provincial capitals.

If the Loyalists were a restless population physically, they were also a discontented and highly vocal one politically. Only a small fraction would receive formal compensation for property lost in the United States. All felt that they had suffered for their allegiance to the Crown, deserving of both land and government assistance. Since many of the Loyalists were former American colonials, they were accustomed to certain levels of political participation. They also shared many political assumptions with their former neighbours. Loyalists may have supported George III, but they expected to be admitted to full participation in the political process for which they had fought. Quebec Loyalists thus complained bitterly about the absence of a representative assembly in the province. Nova Scotia and Island of St John Loyalists were unhappy about the domination of government by earlier inhabitants. Loyalists were also divided among themselves, with the chief divisions between the old élite, who sought to re-establish themselves as the natural leaders of society, and the more articulate among the rank and file, who sought a more democratic and open future. The coming of the Loyalists finally provided the cadre of articulate anglophone settlers that the British had hoped for in 1763. The new settlers not only brought the speaking of English, but the speaking of English with an American accent. In most respects, except loyalty to George III, the Loyalists were thoroughly Americanized.

REINVENTING BRITISH NORTH AMERICA

The loss of the American colonies, combined with pressure from the Loyalist leadership, gradually produced a political reorganization of British North America. It is at least arguable that since the Americans were the ones who had separated, what remained of British North America carried on the imperial continuity in the New World. Stage one came in 1784, after the Treaty of Paris of 1783, when a governor-generalship was established to administer Britain's remaining North American colonies. Sir Guy Carleton, now Lord Dorchester, was the first appointee to this post in 1786. Britain also created two new provinces in 1784. New Brunswick was hived off from Nova Scotia and given a set of political officials chosen from the 'needy' Loyalist élite. The capital, Fredericton, was laid out in 1785, the year the first governor, Thomas Carleton (brother of Guy) arrived. Cape Breton was also given a separate government, administered by a lieutenant-governor and council without an assembly until it was reunited with Nova Scotia in 1820. No changes were made in the government of Newfoundland, which was still being administered by officials resident in St John's only during the summer months; there was still no assembly. There was now a court system operating on the island, however.

Nor were alterations made immediately in Quebec, although Dorchester arrived in 1786 with a new chief justice in the person of William Smith (1728–93) of New York. Smith's political views were distinctly Anglo-American. He was known to have little sympathy for the Old Regime.

In 1787 a former Loyalist pamphleteer, the Reverend Charles Inglis (1734–1816), arrived in Halifax as the first North American bishop of the Church of England. Although most Loyalists were not Anglicans, the British government wished to establish a close connection between church and state. The new bishop was also initially responsible for Quebec. Inglis worked uphill for years to bring Anglicanism to a level worthy of state support. The Loyalists pressed hard for institutions of higher learning in the colonies. William Smith of Quebec advocated a secular university for his province, Inglis helped establish King's College in Windsor, and Benedict Arnold (who lived in Saint John as an unpopular Loyalist refugee from 1786–91) spearheaded a movement for a university in New Brunswick, which did not take root at that time.

In the western part of Quebec, demands for British institutions, particularly an assembly, produced the second stage of political reorganization: the Constitutional Act of 1791. This parliamentary legislation split Quebec into Upper and Lower Canada, giving the former a lieutenant-governor—the first one was John Graves Simcoe (1752–1806)—both an executive and a legislative council, and an assembly. In theory, Upper Canada's lieutenant-governor would be responsible to the governor of Quebec, and all the chief officials in the various colonies to the governor-general, but Britain's efforts to create an administrative hierarchy was not very effective. Each colony of British North America continued to turn directly to the British government as the source of real authority.

Despite self-denying legislation by Parliament in 1777 that no direct taxes would be collected in British North America without the consent of the governed in a legislative assembly, and however much eighteenth-century British statesmen were still committed to the principle of colonial assemblies, Great Britain was reluctant to universalize these institutions. French Canada got an assembly in 1791 less because Britain felt it was entitled to one than because the Loyalist settlers up-country insisted on having one, and symmetry between Upper and Lower Canada needed to be maintained. For the British, assemblies implied that colonies had come to full maturity, including the possession of a decent revenue to control. Cape Breton, because of its small size and remote location, would have to grow into an assembly; it never did. As for Newfoundland, Britain still hesitated to grant it full colonial status, partly because of its large population of Roman Catholics. The Loyalist period, however, saw the achievement of full political privileges for Roman Catholics in most of British North America, both through local legislative initiative and parliamentary fiat (for Quebec). Only on the Island of St John (which in 1786 passed laws permitting Catholics to own land but not to vote) and in New Brunswick until 1810 were Catholics still disenfranchised politically.

A less publicized development than the introduction of assemblies and the expansion of voting franchises was the elaboration of the legal system of the various colonies. This system was based chiefly upon English law and English models except in Quebec, where English criminal law joined French civil law. The establishment of colonial courts and assemblies meant that new English statute law extended to British North America only where specifically authorized, but the colonial legal system took over earlier English statute law and the whole body of the common law, including its patriarchal treatment of women. The introduction of the law was necessary both to good government and especially to business, which would have been lost without the adjudication of the complex system of credit employed in commerce. While the law in British North America would develop its own characteristics over time, it was always closely linked to its English origins. Here was the origin of what Lord Macaulay would later describe for England as a system where 'the authority of law and security of property were found to be compatible with a liberty of discussion and individual action'.

The Loyalist migration was ended by 1786, when compensatory land grants and provisioning virtually ceased everywhere in British North America. In one decade the loyal provinces of British North America had received a substantial contingent of American settlers, well subsidized by the British government, that they had not previously been able to attract. So-called 'late Loyalists' would continue to come to Upper and Lower Canada, drawn by offers of land. The Atlantic region would never again experience a substantial American influx. For all colonies of British North America immigration and settlement would long have crucial importance, but the post-Loyalist wave would have to be managed under quite different circumstances.

Early Days in Upper Canada

[Elizabeth Posthuma Gwillim Simcoe (1766–1850) accompanied her husband John Simcoe to Upper Canada in 1792 when he took up his lieutenant-governorship there, leaving her children and family behind in England. In her diary she recounted her first 'home' in Upper Canada. *Source*: J.R. Robertson, *The Diary of Mrs John Graves Simcoe, Wife of the First Lieutenant-Governor of the Province of Upper Canada, 1792–1796* (Toronto: W. Briggs, 1911):135–6.]

Thurs. 26 July [1792]—At nine this morning we anchored at Navy Hall, opposite the garrison of Niagara, which commands the mouth of the river. Navy Hall is a house built by the Naval Commanders on this lake for their reception when here. It is now undergoing a thorough repair for our occupation, but is still so unfinished that the Governor has

IMMIGRATION AND SETTLEMENT, 1790–1815

Between 1790 and 1815 immigration to British North America came from two sources: the British Isles (mainly the Scottish Highlands and Ireland) and the United States (mainly from upper New York state, Pennsylvania, and New England). The British newcomers settled everywhere, while the Americans were almost entirely confined to the Canadas. Most of the Scots were drawn to the Maritime region, where they had already established beachheads of settlement, but some went to Lower Canada and eastern Upper Canada to join Scottish communities there. The major movement from Britain occurred in a brief interlude of European peace between 1801 and 1803, chiefly to the northeast shore of Nova Scotia, to Cape Breton, and to Prince Edward Island. Prosperity in Newfoundland and New Brunswick during the period 1812–15 drew many Irish to these colonies. More Protestant than Catholic, many came from northern Ireland.

Some of the American arrivals were Quakers and Mennonites encouraged by offers of exemption from military service in Upper Canada, but they

ordered three marquees to be pitched for us on the hill above the house, which is very dry ground and rises beautifully, in parts covered with oak bushes. . . .

Fri. 17th [August, 1792]—I desired to drive out last evening, though everyone foretold an approaching thunderstorm, which indeed came on with great violence when we were half way to the Landing. I feared that the lightning would make the horse run away, but he only started at every flash. The recollection that it was my own determination brought me into danger was very unpleasant. However, we got back safe and in time to save the marquees from being blown down. Mr Grey's and Mr Talbot's were overset, but the Governor preserved ours by having the cords held until the violence of the storm was over. The tents were so near the river that we were afraid they would be blown into it. We were so cold and wet we were glad to drink tea. It was quite dark, and too windy to allow of our burning candles, and when the forked flashes of lightning enlightened the air I was able to drink tea. I wrapped myself up in two or three great-coats, and intended, if the tent was blown down, to take shelter under the great dinner table. The rain and wind did not cease for two hours, and we had no means of drying our clothes and were obliged to sleep in a wet tent. However, we have not caught cold. I received a very pretty set of Nankeen china from England to-day, and in an hour after it was unpacked the temporary kitchen (an arbour of oak boughs) took fire, and in the hurry of moving the china it was almost all broken. . . . I sat by myself in a miserable, unfinished, damp room, looking on the lake, where it blew quite a gale, the 'Bear,' a gunboat tossing about terribly, and not a cheerful thought passing through my mind, when I had the happiness of receiving a letter. . . , which raised my spirits, though for some hours after that pleasure I felt more dejected than at all other times, from the recollection of absence from my friends.

Part of York the Capital of Upper Canada on the Bay of Toronto in Lake Ontario, 1804, painted by Elizabeth Frances Hale, shows Palace (now Front) Street, with Cooper's Tavern (facing what is now Jarvis Street), and the houses of Duncan Cameron, a merchant, William Warren Baldwin, and William Allen. In the distance can be seen the two government buildings and the town blockhouse, with flag. Elizabeth Hale, who lived in Quebec, was married to John Hale, then deputy paymaster to the British troops in the Canadas. Her painting of York, which circulated widely as a print, is somewhat similar to a painting by Edward Walsh, made the year before, and may be a copy (National Archives of Canada C-34334).

were soon joined by a large influx of settlers who took up readily available land from government or private entrepreneurs. Some of these newcomers were fleeing American policies they disliked, including the new Constitution of 1789 and the severe repression of Pennsylvania whisky distillers in the 1790s, but most were simply part of the North American moving frontier. Until 1798 the Upper Canadian government treated these arrivals as Loyalists. Between 1791 and 1812 the English-speaking population of Lower Canada (mainly American) tripled from 10,000 to 30,000 and represented 10 per cent of the province's population. The Americans were located mainly in the Ottawa Valley and the Eastern townships. In Upper Canada, by the time of the War of 1812, Americans comprised as much as 80 per cent of a population estimated by one contemporary at 136,000. As tensions grew between Britain and the United States after 1807, the British began to be worried by the predominance of Americans in Upper Canada. In both Canadas, Americans tended to recreate their own local culture and institutions rather than insist on political and legal reform of provincial political systems they regarded as oligarchical and repressive.

It was certainly the case that government and politics everywhere in British North America were, to say the least, cosy. The governments of the various provinces were dominated by a small cadre of well-paid office holders appointed chiefly in England, in collaboration with local élites represented on the councils. While serious political conflict between the elected assemblies and the provincial oligarchies that governed British North America was almost inevitable, it was slow to develop. The oligarchy associated the aspirations of the assemblies with the worst aspects of levelling republicanism—after 1789 the French Revolution succeeded the American as the chief example. Criticism of government was immediately rejected and critics were silenced by any means necessary, including violence.

In most provinces, early political opposition was sporadic and usually conducted within the ranks of the élite according to well-defined rules. Many of the early opponents of government—men like James Glenie (1750–1817) in New Brunswick, William Cottnam Tonge (1764–1832) in Nova Scotia, Robert Thorpe in Upper Canada (1764–1836), and William Carson (1770–1843) in Newfoundland—were outspoken political gadflies who

Thomas Douglas, Fifth Earl of Selkirk

Thomas Douglas, Fifth Earl of Selkirk, was the youngest son of a Scottish peer who unexpectedly came into his title because of the early deaths of four elder brothers. Educated at Edinburgh and on familiar terms with many of the leading *philosophes* of the French Revolution, he always saw himself as a 'political economist' who sought to harmonize social reform with personal self-interest and imperial unity. Before 1815, his was an almost solitary voice in Britain in support of immigration to British North America. Selkirk was convinced that colonizing vacant North American lands with oppressed and disadvantaged inhabitants of the British Isles was the ideal way of touching all bases. The colonies would benefit, the colonial promoter would benefit (either with public approbation or personal profit), and Britain would rid itself of unwanted people who very likely would eventually turn to crime or revolution. He personally sponsored three settlements in British North America: in Prince Edward Island, in

Upper Canada, and on the Red River. The last involved him in a bitter fur trade war between the Hudson's Bay Company and the North West Company, in which his reputation became a tragic casualty. This portrait is based on a painting by the distinguished Scottish artist, Sir Henry Raeburn (National Archives of Canada C-1346).

received very little consistent support from their colleagues. Only in Prince Edward Island (which the Island of St John became in 1799) and Lower Canada did something resembling political parties develop before the War of 1812. In Lower Canada, race and language created both sharp divisions and informal political bonds quite different from the usual conflicts between 'ins' and 'outs' or 'hinterland' and 'capital'. The French Canadians soon took to electoral politics, and an active group of leaders emerged from the ranks of the liberal professions in both city and countryside. After 1800 the *Canadiens* became increasingly vocal in the assembly, and a *Parti Canadien* was soon opposing the alliance of officials and merchants known as the *Château Clique*. The opposition argued that it only sought British liberty in the context of the British Constitution, both of which were being perverted by the maladministration of the province under the oligarchy.

The period before 1815 also saw the beginnings of the settlement of the west. In 1811 the Earl of Selkirk (1772–1820) received from the Hudson's Bay Company a grant of 116,000 sq. mi. (300,417 km²) covering parts of present-day Manitoba, North Dakota, and Minnesota. In return for this grant Selkirk was to supply the HBC with employees to aid it in its bitter struggle with the North West Company for control of the western fur trade. Selkirk hoped to be able to keep the colony he intended to establish at the fork of the Red and Assiniboine rivers separate from the fur trade rivalry, but this would prove impossible. Miles Macdonell (*c.* 1767–1828) was named the first governor of Assiniboia, as the territory was

A Common Soldier Fights in the War of 1812

[Shadrach Byfield was born near Bradford, England, in 1789, and joined the British army in 1807. By 1812 he was serving in Canada as a private in the 41st Foot. In the following account, written years later, he describes a battle at Brown's Town in January 1813. The account was originally published in 1828. *Source: Recollections of the War of 1812: Three Eyewitnesses' Accounts* (Toronto: Baxter Publishing Company, 1964):15–18.]

Orders were given to cross the river St Lawrence. We landed at a place called Brown's Town, and then proceeded for the river Reasin, with about 500 of our troops and a few Indians. We had to contend with about 1400 of the enemy, under the command of General Winchester. When within about two miles of the enemy, we encamped for part of the night; early in the morning, we proceeded to meet them, and under cover of a wood, we approached near to them, unperceived; we formed the line, and had a view of them as they surrounded their fires. While we were forming, the Indians marched so as to get round their right flank. We had six field pieces, which led on in front of the line. We were then discovered by one of their sentries, who challenged and discharged his piece, which killed one of our grenadiers; we then gave three cheers, and the Indians followed with a war whoop; the fight then commenced very warmly. It was on the 22nd of January, 1813. . . . As the day approached, we discovered that what had been supposed to have been the enemy's line was a made fence behind which they were sheltered, with holes in it through which they fired at us. About this time my comrade on my left hand was killed. It being now light, I saw a man come from the fence when I said to my comrade, 'There is a man, I'll have a shot at him.' Just as I said these words and pulled my trigger, I received a ball under my left ear and fell immediately; in falling I cut my comrade's leg with my bayonet. He exclaimed, 'Byfield is dead.' To which I replied, 'I believe I be,' and I thought to myself, is this death, or how do men die? As soon as I had recovered so as to raise my head from the ground, I crept away upon my hands and knees and saw a sergeant in the rear, who said, 'Byfield, shall I take you to the doctor?' I said, 'Never mind me, go and help the men.' I got to the place where the doctor was, who, when it came to my turn to be dressed, put a plaister to my neck and ordered me to go to a barn which was appointed for the reception of the wounded. As I was going, the blood

flowed so freely as to force off the plaister. I now saw a man between the woods, and asked him what he did there. He told me he was wounded in the leg. I observed to him that if I had not been wounded worse than he was, I should be back, helping the men. I then asked him to give me a pocket handkerchief to tie round my neck, to stop the blood. He replied, 'I have not got one.' I said, 'If I do not get something, I shall bleed to death.' He immediately tore off the tail of his shirt, and wound it round my neck. I then got to the bar, and laid down with my fellow sufferers. I had not been there long before the doctor came and said, 'My dear fellows, you that can had better get away, for our men are terribly cut up, and I fear we shall be all taken.' He rode away, but soon returned saying, 'My dear fellows, we have taken all of them prisoners.' At which news I exclaimed (being quite overjoyed), 'I don't mind about my wound, since that is the case.' While in the barn, I was much affected by seeing and hearing a lad, about 11 or 12 years of age, who was wounded in one of his knees. The little fellow's cries from the pain of his wound; his crying after his dear mother; and saying he should die, were so affecting that it was not soon forgotten by me. He was a midshipman, belonging to one of the gunboats; I think his name was Dickenson.

called in June 1811. On 26 July he and the first contingent of colonists left for Hudson Bay, arriving two months later at York Factory. After wintering on the Nelson River until the breakup of ice (at the end of June), they did not arrive at the junction of the Red and Assiniboine rivers until 30 August 1812. The colony soon ran afoul of the North West Company, which used the Red River region as the source of pemmican for provisioning its traders on the vast inland canoe routes it had established.

THE WAR OF 1812

After some years of worsening relations, the Americans declared war on Great Britain on 18 June 1812. There were several *casus belli*. One was British high-handedness in searching American ships on the high seas during the Napoleonic blockade, removing British subjects aboard them and recruiting them into her navy. Another was the British failure to abandon the Ohio Valley, where military posts continued to monitor the fur trade. Most of all, the Americans coveted Canada, which they proceeded again to invade in 1812 and 1813. A succession of invading armies were thrust back through the major entry points: the Detroit–Windsor corridor, the Niagara peninsula, and Lake Champlain. A relatively small number of British regulars, assisted by colonial militia and Native peoples, held the province against American armies, which were neither well trained nor well led. A number of Canadian heroes emerged from the war, their reputations to be further mythologized after it was over: General Isaac Brock, Tecumseh, and Laura Secord.

The appearance of invading American armies posed a crisis of allegiance for many of the American settlers in Upper Canada. Most remained silently on their farms, although some supported their countrymen and retreated across the border with them. A handful of Americans were arrested and tried for treason at Ancaster in 1814. Before the war had ended, York (Toronto) was burnt, the American capital at Washington was sacked in retaliation, and Fort Michilimackinac (on western Lake Huron) was captured and held by Canadian

The Battle of Queenston by Major Dennis (National Archives of Canada C-276).

Sir Isaac Brock

Sir Isaac Brock (1769–1812) began his military career in 1785. He was posted to Canada in 1802, and was a major-general by 1812, as well as president and administrator of Upper Canada. That he combined control of the army and the civil government was 'fortuitous but important because it meant that he was able to respond much more decisively to the sudden American invasion in western Upper Canada that opened the War of 1812. Brock not only rallied his forces but actually went on the offensive, surprising the invaders and encouraging his own people. His admittedly 'desperate remedies' produced a great British victory at Detroit in August 1812, thanks in large part to the assistance of Britain's Native allies. He was killed on the field of battle by an enemy sharpshooter on 13 October 1812 in the course of the British victory at Queenston Heights on the Niagara peninsula. An attractive personality,

Brock was Upper Canada's first military hero and arguably its first hero of any sort. His memory remained honoured in the province throughout much of the nineteenth century. This portrait of Brock is by John W.L. Forster (National Archives of Canada C-7760).

voyageurs. The final struggle occurred for naval control of the Great Lakes in 1814; the Americans appeared to be winning. The last battle of the war was at New Orleans, actually fought after a peace of stalemate had been signed at Ghent on 24 December 1814.

The Americans treated the War of 1812 as a second War of Independence, a necessary struggle to complete the process of separation from the mother country. National survival was taken as victory. From the British perspective, the war had been little more than a sideshow to the major struggle, which was against Napoleon in Europe. As for British North America, in the lower provinces (what the Maritime region was coming to be called), the War of 1812 was principally an opportunity to serve as a conduit for illicit trade between Britain and the United States; the region was never actively involved in the military struggle. Only in the Canadas did the War of 1812 have any great impact. In Lower Canada, the support the French Canadians gave the British demonstrated their loyalty. In Upper Canada, the war provided a demarcation point between the loyal and the disloyal, the latter composed almost entirely of Americans. During and after the fighting, the Canadian oligarchies (especially in Upper Canada) were able to appropriate Loyalism as their monopoly and use it against their American opponents. The great struggle between British and American allegiance was played out internally in Upper Canada between 1812 and 1815, and the British won. After 1815 the overt American influence on Upper Canada would gradually decline.

In the west, a little war between the Hudson's Bay Company and the North West Company ran its own course, occasionally touching on the larger Anglo-American conflict. In 1813, for example, Lord Selkirk very nearly succeeded in persuading the British government to finance the recruiting, equipping, and transporting to the Red River of a Highland Regiment to be commanded by himself. The purpose of the unit was to protect the west from American take-over. The scheme won ministerial approval, but was vetoed at the last moment by the commander-in-chief, the Duke of York, not because it would have crushed the North West Company but because it involved Highlanders. In 1816 Selkirk recruited as soldier/settlers a number of disbanded troops from several Swiss regiments that had fought for the British in North America, leading them to the Red River. As in the War of 1812, the western fur trade war was fought to an expensive draw. The two rival companies would settle matters by merging in 1821, shortly after the death of the Earl of Selkirk.

By a diplomatic convention in 1818, Great Britain and the United States would agree to declare the Great Lakes an unarmed zone and the 49th parallel to be the Anglo-American border from the Lake of the Woods to the Rocky Mountains. British policy after the war would consistently be to seek entente rather than trouble with the Americans, so in a sense the Americans had won. The final defeat of Napoleon at Waterloo in 1815, rather than the Treaty of Ghent, marked the major watershed for Britain and her North American colonies, however. After 1815 the shift from an overheated war economy to a peacetime one in the British Isles produced considerable unemployment. Even after the postwar depression had ended, a new round of industrialization and agricultural rationalization left many without work in their traditional occupations and places of residence. The result was a new era of emigration and immigration. Between 1815 and 1860 more than a million Britons would leave their homes and come to British North America. In the process they would help bring the colonies into maturity.

Major Events, 1816–1839

1816 Métis and Selkirk settlers clash at the Battle of Seven Oaks.

1817 Bank of Montreal is founded.

1818 Britain agrees to allow the French to carry on a dry fishery on Newfoundland's west coast. Britain and the United States agree in principle to extend their boundary across the 49th parallel from Lake of the Woods to the Rocky Mountains. Dalhousie University is founded in Halifax.

1820 Cape Breton is annexed to Nova Scotia.

1821 Hudson's Bay Company and the North West Company merge as Hudson's Bay Company. Bank of Canada is chartered. Contract is let for the first Lachine Canal.

1824 Canada Company is founded.

1825 Lachine Canal is completed.

1826 Canada Company is chartered and purchases most of the Crown reserves and half of the clergy reserves of Upper Canada. Rideau Canal is begun.

1827 British Parliament rejects major government resettlement scheme for Canada brought forward by Robert John Wilmot-Horton. Hudson's Bay Company establishes Fort Langley on the Fraser River.

1829 First Welland Canal is opened. King's College is founded in Toronto.

1832 John Richardson publishes *Wacousta*. Newfoundland establishes its first assembly.

1833 Slavery is abolished by the British Parliament in the British empire. First crossing of the Atlantic by a steamship (the *Royal William*).

1834 Village of York is incorporated as Toronto. The Rideau Canal is completed. Assembly of Lower Canada adopts the Ninety-two Resolutions.

1835 The Selkirk family's interests in Red River are sold to the Hudson's Bay Company, and the General Quarterly Court of Assiniboia is established.

1836 T.C. Haliburton publishes *The Clockmaker* as a book. New Brunswick legislature gains control over Crown lands in the province. The first railway in Canada completed, running 16 mi. (26 km) from La Prairie to St John's, Quebec.

1837 Rebellion erupts in Upper and Lower Canada.

1838 Lord Durham is appointed governor-general to investigate grievances. A second uprising in Lower Canada is brutally suppressed.

1839 Durham submits his report on British North America. Hudson's Bay Company establishes the office of Recorder of Rupert's Land.

4
Relying on Resources, 1815–1840

❀

Not until after the end of the War of 1812 did the various provinces of British North America really begin to develop their economies. Not surprisingly, those economies were based almost exclusively on the exploitation of the rich natural resource base of the country, with a rising merchant group serving as the commercial links to the outside world. In this period, the resource economy relied heavily on transatlantic (chiefly British) markets and took full advantage of imperial trade advantages whenever they could be found. Overseas trade to the Caribbean also expanded. While there was some trade with the United States, few in British North America concentrated on the American market. The economies of the United States and British North America were still too similar in their reliance on primary resources to develop much interdependence. The society that took shape within the resource economy depended heavily on immigration from the British Isles to fuel its growth. Like the economy, it had a fairly simple structure, dominated by a self-conscious élite, which was challenged politically towards the end of the period. In cultural terms, French Canada continued to survive and, by so doing, flourished. In many of the English-speaking provinces, there was a subtle but significant movement away from a highly derivative Americanized culture (chiefly the result of the Loyalists) to a more hybrid culture that consciously looked to Great Britain for its priorities.

THE RESOURCE ECONOMY

British North America began the postwar period of peace after 1815 with an extremely limited economy, heavily dependent upon British financial aid. By the 1840s it could boast a very active, even vibrant, commercial economy based on its rich inheritance of natural resources and a growing transatlantic carrying trade. The economic growth worked together with the appearance of new immigrants who flocked into its seaports and made their way onto its wilderness lands. Economic development was always complex, never straightforward. In most regions of European settlement it was anchored from the outset by natural resources. Fish, furs, timber, and grain—along with their ancillary industries—represented well over 90 per cent of all economic activity in British North America during this period.

Natural resources required a market, and before the 1840s Britain's colonies found the market chiefly in the United Kingdom and within the British empire, where trade policies tended to remain favourable to colonial raw materials. In the 1840s, when Britain shifted to a policy of international free trade, British North America had significant adjustments to make to fit into the new economic and commercial patterns. But for infant colonies rapidly expanding in population, British preferential treatment for colonial raw materials constituted a major boost. The mother country provided not only the market but also much of the capital with which British North Americans developed their resource base. British capital was never very adventurous. It preferred known industries and may well have constricted colonial diversification. But for a people desperately short of capital, no real alternative to British investment seemed possible. The Americans were using what capital they generated to develop their own internal economy.

A colonial economy based on natural resources was inevitably one that ultimately depended upon international and even transatlantic trade. Such an economy also had substantial implications for society and its structure. The extraction and production of the raw materials of trade was a seasonal business, for example. Rhythms depended on the commodities being produced. Fish and grain required summer labour, while timbering flourished in the winter months. Moreover, initial production was in the hands of small-scale commodity producers. These people exploited those working for them and were in turn exploited by the merchants who handled the commercial system of marketing. Most primary resource producers had little connection with the international market. They had no control over the prices they received for their products. As a result, they tended to attempt to maximize production by ruthlessly exploiting the resource regardless of economic conditions.

As a small capitalist, the typical primary producer—whether boat owner, farmer, or lumberer—identified with the commercial system rather than with his labour force, thus impeding the development of any working-class consciousness or the formation of an articulated class structure. Merchants had to be successful entrepreneurs, but found it difficult to move beyond their immediate commercial horizons. They were prepared to invest in processing raw materials within their own sphere of interest, but not outside it. The result was a highly exploitative and unadventurous economy, with a fluid and fuzzy social structure. It was an economy that could celebrate the values of an independent yeomanry at the same time that it took advantage of a labour force not composed of those yeomen.

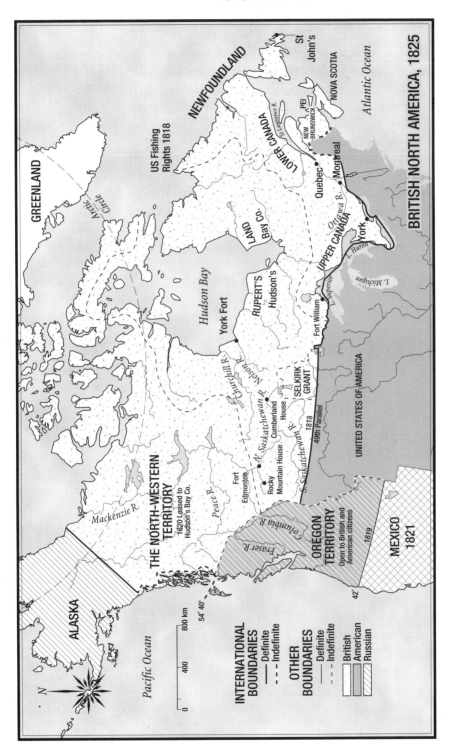

BRITISH NORTH AMERICA, 1825

GREENLAND

Arctic Circle

NEWFOUNDLAND

US Fishing Rights 1818

Atlantic Ocean

St John's

NOVA SCOTIA

PEI

NEW BRUNSWICK

Montreal

Quebec

St Lawrence R.

LOWER CANADA

Ottawa R.

York

UPPER CANADA

L. Huron

L. Michigan

L. Superior

Fort William

Hudson Bay

York Fort

LAND Bay Co.

RUPERT'S Hudson's

Churchill R.

Nelson R.

SELKIRK GRANT

Cumberland House

N. Saskatchewan R.

Saskatchewan R.

S. Saskatchewan R.

1818 49th Parallel

UNITED STATES OF AMERICA

THE NORTH-WESTERN TERRITORY

1820 Leased to Hudson's Bay Co.

Mackenzie R.

Peace R.

Fort Edmonton

Rocky Mountain House

Fraser R.

Columbia R.

OREGON TERRITORY

Open to British and American citizens

1819

42°

MEXICO 1821

ALASKA

Pacific Ocean

54° 40'

800 km

400

0

N

INTERNATIONAL BOUNDARIES
—— Definite
---- Indefinite

OTHER BOUNDARIES
—— Definite
---- Indefinite

British
American
Russian

The Staple Resources

The fishery was the oldest and most rewarding of British North America's resource commodities. It had been successfully exploited since the early years of the sixteenth century. Traditionally associated with Newfoundland, it continued to dominate that colony's economic picture throughout the nineteenth century. By the end of the War of 1812, the actual production of fish was almost entirely in the hands of Newfoundland residents. Although after 1815 the market for Newfoundland cod remained stagnant for decades, the fishing economy experienced considerable change. Smaller buyers of fish in the outports were squeezed out by the larger merchants of Water Street in St John's. The fishery expanded into Labrador, and sealing became far more important, representing over one-third of the value of the fishery's exports by 1831. Newfoundland was unable to gain ground in the lucrative Caribbean trade. Nova Scotia merchants now had their own local suppliers of fish, and were able to carry more diversified cargoes to the West Indies. The Lower Canadian fishery of the Gaspé region was the object of the agricultural interests' disdain. While the industry was not a particularly buoyant one after 1815, it did employ

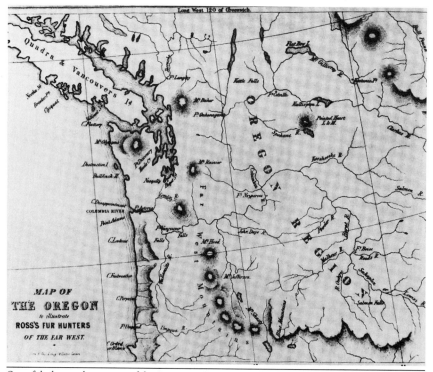

One of the best early accounts of the Oregon territory was written by retired fur trader Alexander Ross, who lived with his Okanagan 'princess' wife and their mixed-blood children in Red River. *Fur Hunters of the Far West* was first published in 1853. This map of the territory is from the 1855 edition.

a considerable workforce. It produced a significant export trade, and it required a large number of sailing vessels both large and small. These characteristics contributed both to the shipbuilding industry and to the carrying-trade capacity of British North America.

The fur trade was the other traditional resource industry. By the nineteenth century, the fur trade's economic value was very small in comparison with that of other resources. In a non-economic sense the fur trade was of enormous importance. It provided the means by which Great Britain retained its claim to sovereignty over much of the northern half of the continent. It also supplied the administration of the British relationship with the indigenous peoples of that region. With the merger of the two great rivals in 1821, the fur trade stabilized under the aegis of the Hudson's Bay Company. The Pacific coast became increasingly important to the HBC. It deliberately overtrapped in the far west since it assumed that it would eventually lose out to the Americans. Indeed, the company was able to hold its own against fur competitors, but not against the constant stream of American settlers into the Willamette Valley. The fur trade had a remarkable influence in the west, chiefly because furs were its only export

After the amalgamation of the Hudson's Bay Company and the North West Company into a single Hudson's Bay Company in 1821, the fur trade spread rapidly across western and northern Canada. Its earliest centre remained, however, at the 'foot of the Bay'. This sketch map, taken from *The Letters of Letitia Hargrave*, edited by Margaret Arnett MacLeod, shows the major trading posts in this region (Metropolitan Toronto Reference Library).

These two photographs from the New Brunswick lumber camps, originally reproduced in *Canada and Its Provinces*, volume 14, edited by Adam Shortt and A.G. Doughty, obviously postdate the pre-1840 period, but there is no reason to think that conditions in the timber trade had altered much over the course of the nineteenth century (Metropolitan Toronto Reference Library).

commodity. The entire region was organized politically and economically around the trade.

The old staples of fish and fur were replaced by timber and grain in primary economic importance in the nineteenth century. Both these commodities benefited from imperial preference, which gave them considerable advantage in the large and lucrative British market during their start-up years. Not until the 1840s did Britain begin seriously to eliminate the differential duty scales that the Corn Laws and the Timber Laws had created during the Napoleonic Wars. Every hint of change in imperial regulations brought a chorus of fears of economic disaster from the colonial mercantile community. While colonials may have been chained economically to the mother country, they revelled in the chains and were loath to break them.

Every province of British North America except Newfoundland quickly became involved in the timber trade after Napoleon closed the Baltic (the traditional source of British supply) in 1807. Even tiny Prince Edward Island enjoyed a considerable boom from cutting down its trees, most of which were relatively accessible to open water. Primary-growth forest was cut as quickly as possible with no thought for either conservation or oversupplying the market. In no province was the industry more important than in New Brunswick. Its dependence on timber as an export commodity had become almost complete by the mid-1820s. The needs of the industry controlled every aspect of the province's life. Settlement was closely connected to the opening of new timber territory. It was no accident that the handful of timber princes who controlled the licences to cut on Crown land were also the leading politicians of the province. Under the large entrepreneurs was a variety of local businessmen— storekeepers, brokers, and sawmill operators—who actually organized and dealt with the hundreds of small parties that wintered in the woods. The industry preferred to do as much processing of the timber on the spot as possible, moving inexorably in that direction. As early as 1837 the sawmills of Samuel Cunard, on the Miramichi River in northeastern New Brunswick, were capable of cutting 42,471 ft (12,945 m) of boards per day, 'the produce of 320 logs and 50 workmen' (quoted in Wynn 1980). Much timber was also processed into wooden sailing-ships.

In the extensive agricultural lands of the St Lawrence Valley and Upper Canada, wheat quickly became the dominant crop. It met a growing demand abroad and it transported well either as grain or flour. Wheat quickly turned farmers into agricultural specialists, who exploited their soil much as did the timbermen the forest. Lower Canada's wheat yields on rapidly exhausted soil often cropped for decades were frequently inadequate for home consumption. While Upper Canada was able to transform its wheat profits from great surpluses into non-agricultural investment, by the 1850s it too had exhausted

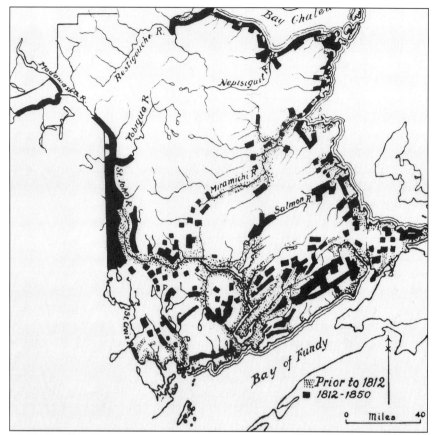

New Brunswick's territorial expansion after the War of 1812 was the result of the demands of the timber trade and the needs of the Acadians. As this map (originally in *Canada and Its Provinces*, volume 14, edited by Adam Shortt and A.G. Doughty) suggests, settlement was confined almost entirely to the river valleys and the seacoast (Metropolitan Toronto Reference Library).

its best soils and was looking westward. Most farmers also produced for their own consumption, of course, and some (such as those on Prince Edward Island) produced livestock and potatoes for export or supplied a local market with produce. Even Maritime farmers grew more wheat than was good for them, however.

The Mercantile System

The resource economy worked only because of its capacity to deal with the international market. The merchant capitalist looked after transportation and marketing in a world of totally unsophisticated credit and banking. Merchants operated at all levels of volume and capital investment. Some placed goods in a number of vessels and invested small amounts in other ships and voyages, as had been done in the colonies since the earliest days. The growing extent of the resource trade demanded larger entrepreneurs, however. Whether the merchant was large or small, international mercantile activity in the first half of the nineteenth century was extremely dangerous. Financial disaster lurked everywhere. Ships could be lost at sea, markets could be miscalculated, debtors could be unable to pay. Communications were incredibly slow. Because of the difficulties in finding trustworthy partners and agents abroad, the extensive family network was still the international basis of much mercantile activity. Few of the large merchant princes of this period avoided at least one bankruptcy, and fewer still left fortunes to their heirs. The sailing-ship, filled with outgoing cargoes of resource commodities and incoming ones of manufactured goods and new immigrants, remained the backbone of British North America's economic system in this period.

Some manufacturing activity did exist in British North America. It involved relatively small establishments that engaged in two kinds of production. One was by artisans producing goods and services that either could not be imported profitably or could not imported at all. Every town had its saddler, every village its blacksmith. As well as producing specialized goods and services for a local market, there was an increasing amount of the processing of resource commodities. Grain was distilled into whisky, brewed into beer, and milled into flour. Wood from land being cleared by farmers was burnt into potash, and timber was cut at sawmills into deals. Among many specialized manufacturing enterprises, shipyards that transformed timber into sailing vessels were the most extensive. The small shipyard was to be found wherever there was timber and open water; the commerce of the Great Lakes required as many sailing vessels as the transatlantic trade.

Shipbuilding was the ideal colonial processing industry. It relied primarily on a rich natural resource—timber—that British North America had in abundance. It did not require excessive capital outlay for physical plant or materials, and its end product provided its own transportation to market. On the other hand, even during its heyday it was not an industry with either a future or a capacity to generate industrial development. As early as 1840 wood and sail were already being overtaken by iron and steam. These technologies required an entirely different form of industrial organization than a handful of craftsmen employing hand tools, carefully assembling a wooden ship on the edge of open water. Neither the technology nor the industrial organization flowed logically out of the nature of colonial shipbuilding, which became instead the symbol of the mercantile resource economy's limitations.

Providing the infrastructure for trade and commerce was a gradual business. Banks were slow to develop because most colonials were suspicious of institutions that could, in effect, manufacture money. The Bank of Montreal was founded in 1817, and the Bank of Canada was chartered in 1821, opening at York in 1822. Early banks did not cooperate together and their services were limited. An expanding internal economic system required roads, bridges, and canals to connect the population with their markets and sources of supply. Most people wanted such facilities, but did not want to pay for them out of taxes. Much road building was done by labour levies upon the local population. After the American success with the Erie Canal, canal building became the craze in the Canadas. The early Canadian canals—the Lachine Canal, the Welland Canal, the Rideau Canal, and the Chambly Canal—either opened water access into Lake Ontario or improved the St Lawrence River system. Their thrust was to enable the economy to shift from a transatlantic focus to an internal one. This process would really take hold with the introduction of the railroads in the 1850s.

Trade and commerce were the basis of urban growth, although the major cities of the British colonies in North America were also the centres of political activity as well as of its commerce. It was easier to flourish, however, without being a capital (Montreal or Hamilton) than without trade (Fredericton). No city dominated more than its immediate region and none was very large. Nonetheless, most urban centres in British North America were growing rapidly. York in 1795 contained twelve cottages. By the time it was incorporated and renamed Toronto in 1834 it had over 1,000 houses, 100 shops, and its population was 9,252. The cities were small in area as well as population, many being collections of tightly packed buildings radiating out from a port facility. In such

View in King Street [Toronto], Looking East, 1835, by Thomas Young. The buildings on the left (north) are the jail, the courthouse, and St James Church at Church Street (National Archives of Canada C-1669).

a city there was little concept of zoning and not many amenities, although by the 1830s matters were improving. Toronto was fairly typical for 1830 in lacking sidewalks, drains, sewers, water supply, and street lighting, all developments of the 1830s and 1840s. Policing consisted at best of a few ward constables and a night watch. For most urban centres in British North America, 1840 marked the break between remaining an eighteenth-century town and becoming a nineteenth-century city.

IMMIGRATION

After 1815 circumstances combined to alter patterns of immigration, especially from the British Isles. Resistance to emigration from both the British government and the British ruling classes was quickly broken down by unemployment and a new round of industrialization and agricultural rationalization. Pressures on Britain's poor relief system increased, and among those who governed the nation it became common wisdom that Britain was once again overpopulated. The burgeoning of the North American timber trade provided the shipping capacity for the transatlantic movement of immigrants at low cost. Immigrants came to British North America chiefly to obtain access to land, something that was becoming increasingly difficult to obtain in the British Isles. Many Britons had an extremely idealized picture of the wilderness. The essayist Thomas Carlyle wrote in 1839 of the vastness of North America, 'nine-tenths of it yet vacant or tenanted by nomads, . . . still crying, Come and till me, come and reap me!' Despite the best efforts of a number of writers of immigration manuals, many newcomers failed to appreciate the need for capital or the difficulties involved in clearing much of this vacant land of trees and brush.

This illustration of Irish emigrants leaving Cork *en route* to North America first appeared in *The Illustrated London News* on 10 May 1851 (National Archives of Canada C-3904).

Table 4.1

The Quantity of Crown Lands Granted and the Conditions on Which the Grants Were Given from 1823–1833

LOWER CANADA

Year	Number of acres granted to militia claimants	Number of acres granted to discharged soldiers and pensioners	Number of acres granted to officers	Number of acres granted, not coming within the previous descriptions	Total number of acres granted
1824	51,810	—	4,100	34,859	90,769
1825	32,620	—	1,000	16,274	49,894
1826	3,525	5,500	—	48,224	57,249
1827	7,640	6,300	800	38,378	53,118
1828	7,300	—	4,504	9,036	20,840
1829	3,200	—	—	5,282	8,482
1830	81,425	—	2,000	10,670	94,095
1831	9,400	8,273	3,408	9,900	30,981
1832	10,116	19,000	4,000	4,000	37,116
1833	5,200	22,500	1,200	—	28,900
Total	**212,236**	**61,573**	**21,012**	**176,623**	**471,444**

Settler's Conditions: That he do clear twenty feet of road on his lot within the space of ninety days.
Military and Militia Conditions: That he do, within the space of three years, clear and cultivate four acres of his lot, and build a dwelling-house thereon.

UPPER CANADA

Year	Number of acres granted to militia claimants	Number of acres granted to discharged soldiers and pensioners	Number of acres granted to officers	Number of acres granted, not coming within the previous descriptions	Number of acres granted to UE Loyalists*	Total number of acres granted
1824	11,800	5,800	5,500	134,500	30,200	187,800
1825	20,300	5,700	8,100	149,060	45,000	228,160
1826	16,600	3,100	4,700	19,390	24,800	68,590
1827	10,900	4,200	7,200	33,600	20,200	76,100
1828	10,800	900	3,000	4,304	30,800	49,804
1829	5,300	7,500	8,400	3,230	22,600	47,030
1830	6,400	12,500	12,600	9,336	27,400	68,236
1831	5,500	58,400	7,200	8,000	34,200	113,300
1832	19,300	97,800	7,600	6,100	62,600	193,400
1833	35,200	46,000	—	9,100	135,600	225,900
Total	**142,100**	**241,900**	**64,300**	**376,620**	**433,400**	**1,258,320**

Condition: Actual settlement
*UE Loyalists means United English Loyalists—individuals who fled from the United States on the breaking out of the American war of independence. The grants in the above column are mostly to the children of these individuals.

Source: C.P. Traill, *The Backwoods of Canada* (London: M.A. Nattali, 1846).

Catharine Parr Traill's *The Backwoods of Canada* provided 'some official information' 'to render this Work of more practical value to persons desiring to emigrate'. Among the statistics were these charts on the sale of Crown land in Upper and Lower Canada, 'abstracted from Parliamentary documents'. How might this data have assisted a prospective emigrant? What could a prospective emigrant have concluded from these charts?

Four patterns of organized emigration and settlement developed after 1815. The first pattern involved government assistance, which was often a combination of British official recruitment of emigrants and settlement, with public aid, on land made available by the several colonial governments. Such schemes, frequently involving either soldiers disbanded after the wars or excess Irish population, continued sporadically until 1830. What the various schemes best demonstrated was that the financial cost of establishing British emigrants in British North America was high. Even those who argued that the existing operations were unnecessarily profligate estimated £60 for a family of five. In the late 1820s the British government rejected a proposal for a major government resettlement scheme to be financed by local authorities as an alternative to poor relief. It was brought forward by the parliamentary undersecretary at the Colonial Office, Robert John Wilmot-Horton. Thereafter government policy abandoned public assistance for emigration.

The other three patterns were not mutually exclusive. Some emigrants could even combine all three. The second pattern emphasized settlement on the land. It involved private proprietors of land, usually large land companies. These occasionally offered financial assistance, but most frequently they made land available to emigrants on affordable terms. This process was intended to appeal to emigrants with some financial resources. There were three large land companies: the Canada Company, the British American Land Company (in the Eastern Townships of Quebec), and the New Brunswick and Nova Scotia Land Company. In 1826 the Canada Company had purchased most of the Crown

Bush Clearing with Log House is an illustration in *The British Farmer's Guide to Ontario* (1880) (National Archives of Canada C-44633).

reserves and half of the clergy reserves of Upper Canada, thus providing a colonial revenue. It settled large number of emigrants on its lands.

A third pattern emphasized transport to North America but not settlement on the land. Private emigrant contractors would offer passage to North America in sailing vessels. The ships involved were usually in the timber trade, temporarily converted to provide accommodation on the outward passage. The contractor provided low rates of passage but as few services as possible. His passengers were frequently deposited at seaports in British North America and left to their own devices. The lucky ones managed to make their way to some destination.

The vast majority of emigrants, whatever their transport and settlement arrangements, fitted into the fourth pattern. They had arranged their own passage, frequently coming to British North America without fixed plans or destination. Sometimes they intended to join relatives or friends who had preceded them. If they had capital, they found land. It was generally estimated that at least £100 (beyond the cost of passage) was required to establish a farm from wilderness land, and even more was required to purchase one already improved. Those who could not afford this expense joined the ranks of the labouring class or, in the case of unattached females, went into domestic service. The transatlantic passage in sailing-ships lasted from six to eight weeks, and was long and arduous even for those who could afford cabin accommodation. For those in steerage (the vast majority), the discomfort and health hazards were high. After 1825 the British government abandoned attempts to regulate the traffic in any serious way.

Aside from the assisted settlement schemes, public policy was never really mobilized to settle British North America. The major shift in policy after the mid-1820s, in addition to the ending of assisted settlement, was the abandonment of giving colonial land away in favour of charging a 'sufficient price' that would ensure a revenue for colonial improvement, as well as guaranteeing that those acquiring land had some capital. In the end, settlement was achieved out of the trials and tribulations of those who tried their luck. Apart from their physical energy, the immigrants were also a great source of wealth for the colonies they entered. If every immigrant brought on average only £10, between 1815 and 1845 that amount would have injected £10 million into the local economies.

THE RESOURCE SOCIETY

The resource society of the early nineteenth century was dominated by two overlapping élites. One governed, the other controlled international commerce. In most colonies their separate identities were easily confused when they battled politically, employing imported rhetoric that suggested deeper divisions than actually existed. By far the majority of the population was composed of the non-élite: small shopkeepers, artisans, minor civil servants; owners of small industries such as gristmills, tanneries, soap factories, and breweries; and resource workers and farmers. In the British context of distinguishing between those who held land and those who did not, few 'landholders' in British North America possessed anything but land that was in the process of becoming farms. Most landowners were forced to hold multiple employments, often working side by side with the landless. Women in this society acquired the status of their husbands. Those without spouses had some autonomy, but were severely limited in any upward mobility. Finally, the indigenous peoples lived outside the social structure, although the missionaries constantly tried to bring them into it.

The governing élite included the leading appointed colonial officials of government, military officers, church leaders, and the merchants who lived in the capital city. The first three enjoyed the enormous advantage of a substantial guaranteed annual salary, usually paid in London in pounds sterling. This income, the access to credit, and the style of living it encouraged, all enabled colonial officials to emulate the British values of the landed gentry. Their houses reflected their aspirations. The magnificent house of John Strachan (1778–1867) on Front Street in Toronto was popularly known as 'The Palace' even before he became bishop of Toronto in 1839. In 1819, the year after it was built, his brother visiting from Scotland is alleged to have commented, 'I hope it's a' come by honestly, John' (quoted in Arthur 1986:44). Not surprisingly, colonial officials believed in the balance of interests and order, the maintenance of which John Beverley Robinson (1791–1863) once described as 'the foundation of good government in the social state' (quoted in Brode 1984:175). Such men were well educated and very able. They governed British North America with an extremely limited vision, usually without soiling themselves in sordid graft and corruption.

The most successful merchants (and a few professional men) shared the lifestyle of the major colonial office-holders, usually without their status. What really limited the social positions of the merchants was the impermanence of their incomes, which could be greatly affected by conditions in the market. The British associated status with land because an income from landed estates was rightly regarded as far more permanent and inheritable than income from trade or industry. British North America was never able to generate a landed aristocracy. The colonial official's income was only for life, although a few offices passed on from father to son. The typical seigneur in Lower Canada did not have enough income to cut much of a figure. The trouble with land in North America was its sheer availability. An Upper Canadian backwoods farm consisted of a larger acreage than many an English landed estate. Most land was held for speculation rather than status. Lacking an aristocracy based on land, British North America instead began developing a social structure based on wealth and conspicuous consumption. Money might be temporary, but it could be made visible. British North America also had considerable regard for education, professional training, and the life of the mind. The concentrations of leading professional men in the larger towns were admitted to the ranks of élite society, though in a subordinate position.

While the governing élite and its merchant partners lived mainly in the political capitals that were also the great commercial centres of British North America, a sprinkling of others in the hinterlands also assumed the functions of leadership. Such regional leaders included local merchants and professional men, prominent farmers, and retired half-pay officers. These were the men who were elected to the provincial houses of assembly from the countryside, where they inevitably came to contend with the governing élites for political control of the province. Regional prominence was recognized by election to the assembly and appointment to local civic office. Thus these were also the men who served as local justices of the peace. They tended to be the militia officers as well. Before 1840 most would have described themselves as farmers, although they usually engaged in a variety of diversified occupations, hoping to succeed and survive. One of the most striking feature of the lives of most British North Americans was their lack of occupational specialization. Over the course of a lifetime most colonials would hold many different jobs, both in succession and simultaneously.

Coming to terms with the remainder of society in British North America is more complicated than dealing with the élite. Despite the vaunted availability of land, not everyone was a landholder, that British (and American) ideal, the yeoman farmer. In some places (Newfoundland, Prince Edward Island, and Lower Canada), freehold land was not easily available. Moreover, what really mattered was not the holding of wilderness land but of an improved market farm. Cultivating land carved out of primary-growth forest was a tedious process. Such 'improvement' was hampered by the difficulties of finding a market for surplus agricultural products. Farmers inevitably embraced crops such as wheat, which could be transported into a regular market system. Improvement was further hampered by the availability of alternate employment in fishing, timbering, shipbuilding, and construction—which could sustain a farming family before it was plugged into the market—but would also slow down the clearance of land so essential to agrarian success.

At the bottom of colonial society were the poor. They fell into three categories: permanent, immigrant, and casual; and into two major groups: those who had relations or friends to look after them and those who did not. While British North America was often spoken of on both sides of the Atlantic as a

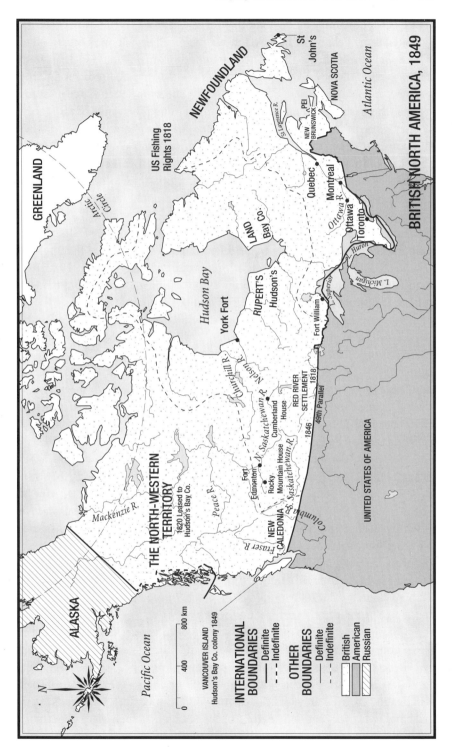

BRITISH NORTH AMERICA, 1849

GREENLAND

NEWFOUNDLAND

St John's

NOVA SCOTIA

PEI

NEW BRUNSWICK

St. Lawrence R.

Atlantic Ocean

US Fishing Rights 1818

Quebec

Montreal

Ottawa R.

Ottawa

Toronto

L. Huron

L. Michigan

L. Superior

Arctic Circle

Hudson Bay

York Fort

LAND

Bay Co.

RUPERT'S

Hudson's

Fort William

Churchill R.

Nelson R.

N. Saskatchewan R.

Cumberland House

S. Saskatchewan R.

RED RIVER SETTLEMENT

1818

1846

49th Parallel

THE NORTH-WESTERN TERRITORY

1820 Leased to Hudson's Bay Co.

Mackenzie R.

Peace R.

Fort Edmonton

Rocky Mountain House

NEW CALEDONIA

Fraser R.

Columbia R.

UNITED STATES OF AMERICA

ALASKA

Pacific Ocean

N

800 km

400

0

VANCOUVER ISLAND
Hudson's Bay Co. colony 1849

INTERNATIONAL
BOUNDARIES
—— Definite
---- Indefinite

OTHER
BOUNDARIES
—— Definite
---- Indefinite

British
American
Russian

'land of opportunity' and a 'good poor man's country', it was absolutely essential to be healthy, or to have kinfolk prepared to help with one's welfare. Those who through disability, incompetence, or misfortune (such as young orphans) could not look after themselves and had no one to do it for them became the objects of charity or lived permanently in squalor. Recent immigrants who arrived without capital resources joined the ranks of the poor in whatever port they disembarked. Unable to move onto the land, these newcomers merged into the third category, the casually employed. Because of the seasonal nature of most Canadian employment, winter saw the largest number of unemployed. Winter was also the worst time to be poor, for food costs increased and the need to keep warm in a Canadian winter was inescapable. Malnutrition and inadequate clothing, combined with under-heating, provided a ready-made recipe for the spread of illness and contagious disease. The poor were 'relieved' chiefly to prevent their turning 'by despair to commit depredations' (quoted in Fingard 1988:197). Contemporary society tended to identify poverty with the city and personal failure. It saw poverty as a moral rather than an economic problem.

Between the poor and the prosperous was a variety of numerous occupational and social groups that defy rational ordering by almost any scheme. An examination of the Newfoundland fishing-boat owner suggests some of the difficulties. A property owner and an employer, the boat owner was probably landless except for a small house lot for which he held no deed. He was usually deeply in debt to the merchant who bought his fish and supplied him with essentials. Forced to contract debt, the fisherman soon found himself in slavish servitude. The fishery's truck system also operated in the timber districts and the fur trade. In another guise it also worked in farming communities, which accumulated large debts to local storekeepers who supplied goods that could not be made at home. Moreover, huge portions of British North America consisted of uneconomic farms that were kept operating on a subsistence level, often by women and children, while the male landholder was off elsewhere working for wages. As with the élites, houses told the tale. Settlers hoped to progress from log hut (or shanty) to log-house to permanent dwelling built of stone or brick or finished lumber in accordance with their prosperity. In 1831 Upper Canada had 36,000 dwellings, of which 75 per cent were constructed of logs and less than 1,000 were built of brick and stone.

Colonial society also included a number of categories of people who were quite outside the social structure as it was then understood. One such group was women. Politically disenfranchised—several provinces even passed legislation in this period depriving widows of the vote—they were especially disadvantaged by marriage. All real property passed into the hands of the husband, who was entitled to control his spouse. Women were expected to

Building a Log-House in Upper Canada

[Catharine Parr Traill (1802–99) was the youngest of nine Strickland children, seven of whom (including Susanna Strickland Moodie) became published authors. Catharine married a retired army officer in 1832, and the couple headed off to Canada to settle. Catharine's pioneering experiences, originally told in letters sent home, were published anonymously in England. *Source*: C.P. Traill, *The Backwoods of Canada* (London: M.A. Nattali, 1846):135–43.]

It was the latter end of October before even the walls of our house were up. To effect this we called 'a bee.' Sixteen of our neighbours cheerfully obeyed our summons; and though the day was far from favourable, so faithfully did our hive perform their tasks, that by night the outer walls were raised. . . . The following day I went to survey the newly raised edifice, but was sorely puzzled, as it presented very little appearance of a house. It was merely an oblong square of logs raised one above the other, with open spaces between every row of logs. The spaces for the doors and windows were not then sawn out, and the rafters were not up. . . . A day or two after this I again visited it. The *sleepers* were laid to support the floors, and the places for the doors and windows cut out of the solid timbers, so that it had not quite so much the look of a bird-cage as before. After the roof was shingled, we were again at a stand, as no boards could be procured nearer than Peterborough, a long day's journey through horrible roads. . . . Well, the boards were at length down, but of course of unseasoned timber: . . . we console ourselves with the prospect that by next summer the boards will all be seasoned, and then the house is to be turned topsy-turvy by having the floors all relaid, joined and smoothed. The next misfortune that happened was that the mixture of clay and lime that was to plaster the inside and outside of the house between the chinks of the logs was one night frozen to stone. Just as the work was about half completed, the frost suddenly setting in, put a stop to our proceeding for some time, as the frozen plaster yielded neither to fire nor to hot water, the latter freezing before it had any effect on the mass, and rather making bad worse. Then the workman that was hewing the inside walls to smooth them wounded himself with the broad axe, and was unable to resume his work for some time. . . . We have now got quite comfortably settled, and I shall give you a description of our little dwelling. . . . A nice small sitting-room with a store closet, a kitchen, pantry, and bed-chamber form the ground floor; there is a good upper floor that will make three sleeping rooms. . . . Our parlour is warmed by a handsome Franklin stove with brass gallery and fender. Our furniture consists of a brass-railed sofa, which serves upon occasion for a bed; Canadian painted chairs; a stained pine table; green and white muslin curtains; and a handsome Indian mat which covers the floor. One side of the room is filled up with our books. Some large maps and a few good prints nearly conceal the rough walls, and form the decoration of our little dwelling. Our bed-chamber is furnished with equal simplicity. We do not, however, lack comfort in our humble home; and though it is not exactly such as we could wish, it is as good as, under existing circumstances, we could have.

Marriage Customs on the Moving Frontier

[Susanna Moodie (1803–85) was one of several sisters who immigrated to Upper Canada and described their experiences in print. Although the following extract was published in 1852, it describes earlier experiences. *Source*: S. Moodie, *Roughing It in the Bush, or, Life in Canada*, vol. 1 (London: Richmond Bentley, 1852):225–8.]

It was towards the close of the summer of 1833, which had been unusually cold and wet for Canada, while Moodie was absent at D——, inspecting a portion of his government grant of land, that I was startled one night, just before retiring to rest, by the sudden firing of guns in our near vicinity, accompanied by shouts and yells, the braying of horns, the beating of drums, and the barking of all the dogs in the neighbourhood. I never heard a more stunning uproar of discordant and hideous sounds.

What could it all mean? The maid-servant, as much alarmed as myself, opened the door and listened.

'The goodness defend us!' She exclaimed, quickly closing it and drawing a bolt seldom used. 'We shall be murdered. The Yankees must have taken Canada, and are marching hither.'

'Nonsense! That cannot be. Besides, they would never leave the main road to attack a poor place like this. Yet the noise is very near. Hark! They are firing again. Bring me the hammer and some nails, and let us secure the windows.'

The next moment I laughed at my folly in attempting to secure a log hut, when the application of a match to its rotten walls would consume it in a few minutes. . . . Just at this critical moment . . . , Mrs O—— tapped at the door, and although generally a most unwelcome visitor, from her gossiping, mischievous propensities, I gladly let her in.

'Do tell me,' I cried, 'the meaning of this strange uproar.'

'Oh, 'tis nothing,' she replied, laughing. . . . 'A set of wild fellows have met to charivari Old Satan, who has married his fourth wife to-night, a young girl of sixteen.' . . .

'What is a charivari?' said I. 'Do, pray, enlighten me.'

'Have you been nine months in Canada, and ask that question? Why, I thought you knew everything! Well, I will tell you what it is. The charivari is a custom that the Canadians got from the French, in the Lower Province, and a queer custom it is. When an old man marries a young wife, or an old woman a young husband, or two old people, who ought to be thinking of their graves, enter

produce many children in an age when maternal mortality ran very high. Despite the drawbacks, most women preferred marriage to the alternatives. At least among the élite and the very prosperous, there was the beginning of a process of converting the home into the central social unit for cultural transmission and the pursuit of happiness. Women were placed on a pedestal as keepers of culture and as civilizing influences.

Other groups almost completely marginalized by colonial society included indigenous peoples and Blacks. In much of the eastern region of British North

for the second or third time into the holy estate of wedlock, as the priest calls it, all the idle young fellows in the neighbourhood meet together to charivari them. For this purpose they disguise themselves, blackening their faces, putting their clothes on hind part before, and wearing horrible masks, with grotesque caps on their heads, adorned with cocks' feathers and bells. They then form in a regular body, and proceed to the bridegroom's house, to the sound of tin kettles, horns and drums, cracked fiddles, and all the discordant instruments they can collect together. Thus equipped, they surround the house where the wedding is held, just at the hour when the happy couple are supposed to be about to retire to rest—beating upon the door with clubs and staves, and demanding of the bridegroom admittance to drink the bride's health, or in lieu thereof to receive a certain sum of money to treat the band at the nearest tavern. . . . Sometimes they break open the doors, and seize upon the bridegroom; and he may esteem himself a very fortunate man, if he escapes being ridden upon a rail, tarred and feathered, and otherwise maltreated. . . . tis the custom of the country, and 'tis not so easy to put it down.'

America, settlement had eliminated hunting grounds and there was no place for the indigenous peoples to go. They were offered the choice of provisions of land in unsurveyed local reserves or general integration into the farming community. Those who remained beyond the pale continued to have some independence and autonomy, although the reverberations of extensive settlement could be felt at long distances from the actual European presence, and settlement was inexorably coming to the west as well as to the east. As for the Blacks, thousands flocked to Upper Canada between 1820 and 1860. Most were slaves seeking freedom, for it was well known in the United States that slavery was illegal in British North America. By and large, the Upper Canadian authorities protected slaves who made their way into the province. But the now-free Blacks faced considerable prejudice and social disadvantage in their new land. They were never really made to feel at home, and most returned to the United States after the Emancipation Proclamation of 1863.

RELIGION AND EDUCATION

The privileged élites were supported by the clergy of the established church, the Church of England, as well as by the Church of Scotland and the Roman Catholic Church. These churches taught doctrines of subordination to rightful authority. Those not associated with these churches found the pretensions of the ecclesiastical establishment, particularly in maintaining such traditional monopolies as marriage rites and education, constant irritants that could be associated with the oligarchic constitutional system. Dissenters chafed under arrangements that granted 'liberty of conscience' to all Christians while denying them full powers to act in such matters as the solemnization of marriage. The Church of England fought an unsuccessful rearguard action to maintain its pretence to monopoly.

In Lower Canada, the Catholic Church solidified its position within the political structure, especially under Bishop Joseph-Octave Plessis (1763–1825, bishop and archbishop, 1806–25), who was appointed to the province's legislative council in 1817. Plessis presided over the devolution of the Church in British North America. In 1819 Rome elevated him to an archbishopric at the same time that it created new dioceses in Upper Canada and Prince Edward Island, both headed by Highland Scots. Plessis was not himself an ultramontanist. He did not believe that the Church, although the guardian of moral law, must be heeded in all matters relating to politics. But he did attempt, with some success, to strengthen the structure of his Church by educating more clergy, by obtaining government recognition of its legal position (especially in Lower Canada), and by reforming its far-flung governance.

Dissenters in every colony not only chafed at the conservative social vision of the established churches and their support of hierarchy and privilege but also objected to the view of God they promulgated. The most numerous dissenters were Methodists and their itinerant preachers, although the Baptists also had a considerable following. Most dissenters were evangelicals who believed that God had to be felt emotionally rather than comprehended rationally. These feelings were 'awakened' in revivals in the Methodists' 'camp meetings' which were so common in Upper Canada. The evangelicals were not only passionate and irrational but also populist in their attitude. For many in the establishment, passionate populism was tantamount to revolution.

Education was another area of conflict between establishment privileges and the needs of an expanding population. The Church of England attempted to insist that it alone was entitled to the revenue from Crown lands set aside for the support of a Protestant clergy. It also tried to maintain a close control over the institutions of higher education—universities, colleges, and academies— on the grounds that such education had to involve moral as well as technical knowledge. Only a relative handful of students had places at these institutions. For the authorities, education was seen as necessary for social order. For the common folk, it represented a means of mobility and liberation. Systems of education brought to the colonies after 1815 were based on teaching the older children, who in turn passed their lessons by rote to the younger. Only towards the end of the period was there much demand for broadly based public education. The curricula of such schools as existed was extremely eclectic. Despite the absence of regular schooling in most provinces, the population was surprisingly literate. Immigrants brought with them their educational experiences in England, Ireland, Scotland, or America. These experiences were often coloured by a substantial class bias as well as ethnic and denominational ones.

A Complaint About America

[Along with their families, the highland Scots brought their bards, who recited and composed stories and songs as part of the oral tradition. In the following lines, an unknown bard describes Prince Edward Island in the 1830s. The translation from the Gaelic, by Sister Margaret MacDonell, is taken from her *The Emigrant Experience: Songs of Highland Emigrants in North America* (Toronto: University of Toronto Press, 1982):119–25.]

I am lonely here
in Murray Harbour not knowing English;
it is not what I have been accustomed to,
for I always spoke Gaelic.

My neighbours and I
used to chat at length together;
here I see only scoundrels,
and I do not understand their language.

I am offended at my relatives
who came before me;
they did not tell me about this place
and how it has tried them.
Going through the wilderness
there is nothing but a blazed trail;
this is truly a lonesome place
for one who lives by himself.

A matter of grave concern,
as you may surmise,
is the want of footwear and clothing
for each one who needs them.
No one can procure anything
unless he wrests it from the forest
The length of winter is depressing;
it is fully half one's lifetime.

I'll never send word
to ask friends or relatives
to come to this place
with no other resident but myself.

. . . .

You will not come to live here
if you are in your right mind.
If I knew how to write
so that I could tell my story,
the truth would suffice
to condemn the place; one need not
        dissemble.
Though one might do one's best here
when the weather is favourable,
the winter cold is fearsome;
men and beasts freeze [to death].

Far better to be in Scotland
even though lands there be rugged too;
no matter which direction I went
along the calm sea.
I would roam a while in the dusk there,
and go about alone
without fear of being killed
by wild beasts in the forests.

Even when it was a dark day,
misty, the wind from the north and no
        sun in sight,
it was not in swampy woods
that we took a stroll,
but by water-cresses and springs
and the blue rushes on the mountain
        slope.
It was fun for me to be there then
herding the cattle.

What a beautiful place it was,
with pasture for the herd;
there was dew on the grass
quickening the seed in May.
The cuckoo and the mavis
harmonized in the treetops;
here I'll never see
even those again. . . .

'Sam Slick' Compares Americans and Nova Scotians

[Thomas Chandler Haliburton (1796–1865), born in Windsor, Nova Scotia, was a Tory in the eighteenth-century tradition of the squirarchy. He worked as a lawyer and then served as a judge, first of the Inferior Court of Common Pleas from 1829, then of the Supreme Court of Nova Scotia from 1841 to his retirement to England in 1856. He nevertheless made time for a prodigious writing output, including, in 1835–6, twenty-one sketches about Sam Slick, a wise-cracking Yankee clockmaker from Connecticut who toured Nova Scotia and commented on Nova Scotia society. They became so popular that Haliburton enlarged them into *The Clockmaker; or The Sayings and Doings of Samuel Slick, of Slickville. Source*: T.C. Haliburton, *The Clockmaker: or The Sayings and Doings of Samuel Slick, of Slickville* (London: Richard Bentley, 1838):41–6.]

Thomas Chandler Haliburton, a lithograph by E.V. Eddie (National Archives of Canada C-6087).

When we resumed our conversation, the Clockmaker said, 'I guess we are the greatest nation on the face of the airth, and the most enlightened too.'

This was rather too arrogant to pass unnoticed, and I was about replying, that whatever doubts there might be on that subject, there could be none whatever that they were the most modest, when he continued, 'We "go ahead"; the Nova Scotians "go astarn." Our ships go ahead of the ships of other folks, our steamboats beat the British in speed, and so do our stage-coaches, and I reckon a real right down New York trotter might stump the univarse for going ahead. . . . If they

COLONIAL CULTURE

The schools were not yet the bearers of the cultural aspirations of the resource society of British North America. While a common stereotype identifies this period as one of extremely limited and primitive cultural and artistic production—particularly by European or American standards—such a view reflects a particular set of assumptions about culture. Indigenous high culture was understandably rare. Foreign models were usually employed. There was, however, a substantial folk culture, which included a well-established oral tradition, in the form of tales and songs, handed down from generation to generation from group to group. There was also a tradition of craftsmanship. The simple pine furniture of clean, uncluttered functional lines produced by

only had education here, they might learn to do so too, but they don't know nothin.'

'You undervalue them,' said I; 'they have their college and academies, their grammar schools and primary institutions, and I believe there are few among them who cannot read and write.'

'I guess all that's nothin',' said he. 'As for Latin and Greek, we don't vally it a cent; we teach it, and so we do painting and music, because the English do, and we like to go ahead on 'em, even in them 'ere things. As for reading, it's well enough for them that has nothing to do; and writing is plaguy apt to bring a man to states-prison, particularly if he writes his name so like another man as to have it mistaken for his'n. Ciphering is the thing. If a man knows how to cipher, he is sure to grow rich. We are a "calculating" people; we all cipher. . . . If we had this Province we'd go to work and "cipher" right off. Halifax is nothing without a river or back country; add nothing to nothing, and I guess you have nothing still; add a railroad to the Bay of Fundy, and how much do you git? That requires ciphering. It will cost three hundred thousand dollars, or seventy-five pounds your money. . . . Can you count in your head?'

'Not to any extent,' said I.

'Well, that's an etarnal pity,' said the Clockmaker, 'for I should like to show you Yankee ciphering. What is the entire real estate of Halifax worth, at a valeation?'

'I really cannot say.'

'Ah,' said he, 'I see you don't cipher, and Latin and Greek won't do; them 'ere people had no railroad. Well, find out, and then only add ten per cent to it for increased value, and if it don't give the cost of a railroad, then my name is not Sam Slick. . . . Put this railroad into operation, and the activity it will inspire into business, the new life it will give the place will surprise you. . . . [T]his 'ere railroad will not, perhaps, beget other railroads, but it will beget a spirit of enterprise, that will beget other useful improvements. It will enlarge the sphere and the means of trade, open new sources of traffic and supply, develop resources, and what is of more value perhaps than all, beget motion.'

hundreds of anonymous craftsmen during the colonial period found little favour in succeeding generations, which regarded heavy ornamentation and the use of highly polished wood veneers as exemplary. But today we recognize that the aesthetic values of those anonymous furniture makers were on a level with their high craftsmanship.

Most high culture was produced by people who made their living in some other way, and who often regarded their artistic activity as diversion or by-product rather than as either conscious art or professional activity. Most of the producers of élite culture —like most of the élite of this period—were born abroad. Of the 538 people given entries in Volume VII of the *Dictionary of Canadian Biography*, covering those who died between 1835 and 1850, fewer

Thomas McCulloch

Born in Scotland, Thomas McCulloch (1776–1843) was a Presbyterian minister who came to Pictou, Nova Scotia, in 1803. He accepted a call to a church there, and led the Presbyterians in their fight to establish an interdenominational institution of higher learning at Pictou. He became the first principal of Pictou Academy, founded in 1809. McCulloch was constantly embroiled in public controversy over such things as religious and educational matters, usually in opposition to the Halifax establishment and its defence of privilege. Despite his public involvements, McCulloch wrote extensively, including some fiction. His major literary success was in the form of some short sketches, *The Letters of Mephibosheth Stepsure*, originally printed in the pages of the *Acadian Recorder* in 1821, 1822, and 1823. (They were not published in book form until 1960.) McCulloch created a fictional observer, the decidedly self-righteous and distinctly Scots Presbyterian Stepsure, to comment on the affairs of 'our town'. The resulting satire was double-edged in that the reader learned of the foibles of both the community and the narrator. The subtle humour, which requires a thorough understanding of the

pretensions of the time, is difficult for modern readers to appreciate. McCulloch made a social and didactic point of mocking the materialism, upward mobility, and immorality (especially through the consumption of alcohol) of Nova Scotians who forsook agrarian values—usually without success—in their search for the presumed greater wealth of commercial enterprise. This pastel portrait was made in 1845, two years after McCulloch died, by Sir Daniel Macnee, presumably by copying an earlier portrait (Nova Scotia Museum).

than 200 were born in the colonies, and most of these were born in Lower Canada. Young people educated in British North America were usually trained by seniors who were educated abroad, usually with emphasis on slavish reproduction of both form and content. There was some respectable work.

In literature, John Richardson (1796–1852) produced one unusual novel in *Wacousta, or, The Prophecy*, published anonymously in London and Edinburgh in 1832. Thomas McCulloch (1776–1843) had a literary success with short sketches, *The Letters of Mephibosheth Stepsure*, originally published in a newspaper and not collected in book form until 1960. Thomas Chandler Haliburton (1796–1865) wrote twenty-one sketches about Sam Slick in 1835–6, which became *The Clockmaker; or The Sayings and Doings of Samuel Slick, of Slickville*. Haliburton went on to become an international best-selling writer. Both McCulloch and Haliburton produced their best work for a local colonial audience. When they wrote for international markets, they were less imaginative and inventive.

In the non-literary arts, the official culture of British North America was derivative and unadventurous. Painters inevitably emphasized European styles and techniques, which were sometimes acquired from working with established masters, and the market had little interest in anything else. Within this tradition a few fine painters emerged, such as William Berczy (1744–1813), Louis Dulongpré (1759–1843), and Joseph Légaré (1796–1855). In architecture, Late Georgian style predominated. It was not only what architects and craftsmen knew, it symbolized British authority and epitomized British standards.

Rather more interesting things were happening in the vernacular culture of the common people, which tended to be oral rather than written, traditional rather than imitative, and often connected either with artisan conventions or religious energy. For all inhabitants of British North America, singing religious

The Woolsey Family, 1809, by William Berczy. The curiously detached appearance of each member of the family is explained by the fact that Berczy first drew each figure separately in pencil, then traced it onto the canvas. Once they were all painted, the background—the mirror, the window opening onto the St Lawrence beyond, the classical mantel, and the painted canvas floor-covering—was filled in around them (National Gallery of Canada, Ottawa; gift of Major Edgar C. Woolsey, Ottawa, 1952).

hymns and secular songs was an important part of their lives. People sang as they worked in the fields, the voyageurs sang as they paddled their canoes, and fishermen sang as they pulled up their nets. Most of what was sung was inherited from Europe, although both music and lyrics were frequently altered by time and new circumstances. Many pioneers sprang from ethnic backgrounds in which the bard, a combination poet and songster, represented an important folk memory. Gaelic-speaking bards from the highlands of Scotland not only carried on the tradition in British North America but extended it. A rich heritage of crafting in wood produced not only furniture and useful ornamentation (such as the weather vane), but the sailing-ship itself, a monument to the skills of carpenters and builders. Popular culture suggested some of the rich possibilities for creative adaptation. By 1840, for example, Scottish settlers familiar with the sport of curling had not only imported the game into a climate ideally suited for it but had made great strides forward in its popularization and regularization. So successful was the game that around 1840 the world's first indoor curling facility was constructed in Montreal.

THE POLITICS OF THE ÉLITE

Like culture, the politics of the resource society were in flux. By 1820 the governments of the various provinces of British North America were becoming well ensconced in power. The pattern was a fairly standard one, even for Newfoundland, which still did not have representative government and would not acquire it until 1832. Each colonial government was headed by a governor (or lieutenant-governor). Appointed in England, he was often a military man. No figureheads, governors of this period had considerable power and autonomy. The governor administered the province in association with the principal office holders—also English appointments, although sometimes colonials were appointed—who, with the prominent merchants, comprised his council or councils. The resultant oligarchy was variously derisively labelled. In Upper Canada it was called the 'Family Compact', in Lower Canada the 'Château Clique', in Nova Scotia the 'System', and in Prince Edward Island 'the Cabal'. As administrations, these groups were not necessarily unenlightened Tories. They believed in the need to increase the prosperity of their colonies, and usually attempted to mediate among the conflicting interests that emerged, provided they remained well ordered. Most of the oligarchies favoured government intervention in the economy, particularly through the creation of new infrastructure such as banks, roads, and canals. The popularly elected assembly, which comprised one part of the legislative system that also included the council (or in some provinces, a separate legislative council), had a very limited role in the process of government. In 1820 the assemblies did not yet have

William Lyon Mackenzie

William Lyon Mackenzie (1795–1861) was born north of Dundee. His father died a few weeks after his birth, and he was brought up in straitened circumstances. The urge for self-improvement was great, however, and he read 958 books (which he meticulously listed and categorized) before 1820 when he departed for Canada.

In 1824 he began his newspaper, the *Colonial Advocate*, soon moving with it to York, the tiny capital of Upper Canada. From the outset the paper was characterized by failing finances and editorial attacks on the Tory establishment. In 1826 a mob of young Tories, dressed as Natives, trashed his press for scurrilous editorial remarks he had made. A jury awarded Mackenzie a large sum in compensation, and the paper was saved. For a time Mackenzie led the reform forces in constitutional (if contentious and acrimonious) directions. Like most reformers of his time, he sought to overturn the corrupt oligarchy of his province, the 'Family Compact', and to replace it with a government sympathetic to agrarian and antimercantile policies that would reduce its involvement in the economy and society of the day. Then in 1837 he

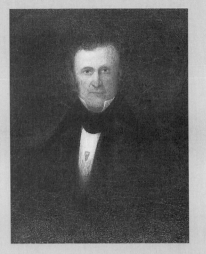

attempted to organize the populace to overthrow the government. When the uprising was easily put down by the authorities, he escaped to the United States, spending some months in a New York jail for violation of the American neutrality laws. He returned to Canada in 1850, spending the remainder of his life as an independent supporter of reform. This oil portrait from Mackenzie House, Toronto, was painted in 1834 after he became mayor of Toronto (Toronto Historical Board Collection, Toronto, Canada).

control of the revenue or finances of the provinces, much less any real involvement in their administration.

Under this constitutional arrangement, political conflict could take a number of forms. One involved disagreement between the governor and the oligarchy that comprised the provincial administration. This could come about either because the governor was expected to implement unpopular instructions from the mother country, or because he sought to limit the self-perpetuating power of the oligarchs. More frequently after 1820, the conflict involved a fierce struggle between the ensconced administration and leaders of an assembly eager to expand its prerogatives and authority. A new generation of political

Joseph Howe

Joseph Howe (1804–73) was the son of a Halifax Loyalist printer, largely self-educated, who had entered the family firm and then began publishing his own newspaper, the *Novascotian*, in 1828. His paper increasingly pressed for political reform, and Howe was acquitted of criminal libel in 1835. This persecution encouraged him to enter politics in 1836 as a Reformer, and it was his government in 1847 that achieved responsible government. In 1855 he helped recruit in the United States for the Crimean War, making comments that cost him the Catholic vote in his province in 1857. He became premier again from 1860–3, then imperial fishery commissioner from 1863–6.

Although the young Howe had visions of a unified British North America, the mature politician did not want Nova Scotia to become absorbed into Canadian expansion. Thus Howe led the anticonfederate forces in Nova Scotia, focusing in 1866 particularly on the failure of the Tupper government to submit the question to an election. He led an anticonfederate party to success in the first dominion elections, but was unable to effect repeal in Ottawa and entered the federal cabinet in 1869. Howe was famed as one of the great orators of nineteenth-century Canada. The portrait of Howe in 1851 is by C.S. Crehen (Public Archives of Nova Scotia).

leaders emerged who were willing to invoke popular support on behalf of their attacks on the prevailing governments. Four reformers stand out in this period: William Lyon Mackenzie (1795–1861) of Upper Canada, Louis-Joseph Papineau (1786–1871) of Lower Canada, Joseph Howe (1804–73) of Nova Scotia, and William Cooper (1786–1867) of Prince Edward Island. None of these men actually overturned the political system, but they did make some inroads against it, anticipating in a variety of ways a gradual democratization of politics in British North America.

All four reformers (and others) sounded radical in their rhetoric. All believed in the importance of the 'independent cultivator of the soil', displaying profound hostility to commerce, the merchant classes, and expensive economic development by the public sector (quoted in Halpenny 1976:156). Equality of conditions and opportunity was what mattered. William Cooper sought this equality through escheat, a process by which the large landholders of Prince Edward Island would be stripped of their ill-gotten holdings and the land redistributed to those who actually tilled the soil. In the 1830s both Papineau and Mackenzie turned to the American ideas of Jacksonian democracy when they found themselves unable either to persuade the British government of the inadequacy of existing constitutional arrangements or to alter the system by political activity. These reformers wanted to overturn the corrupt oligarchies that ran their respective provinces, replacing them with administrations that were responsible to the province as represented in the House of Assembly. They could also agree, as a result of their agrarian and anticommercial assumptions, that public 'improvements' paid for by the public purse or sponsored by the

Louis-Joseph Papineau

Louis-Joseph Papineau (1786–1871) was the son of a Montreal notary who purchased the seigneury of Petite-Nation from the Quebec seminary in 1802. He was educated at the Petit Séminaire of Quebec and then trained as a lawyer.

In 1809 Papineau was first elected to the legislative assembly of Lower Canada, beginning an association of nearly fifty years with that body. He joined the *Parti Canadien* at the outset, and was chosen speaker of the House in 1815. As leader of that party and its successor, the Patriote party after 1826, he advocated political reform that would leave the traditional social system intact. Papineau was simultaneously a democrat and a social conservative suspicious of the economic and social transformations occurring in his province.

Over the years his commitment to British institutions decreased, and he became more attracted to the American model of Jacksonian democracy, which sought to eliminate political privilege without radical social change. Papineau's commitment to the survival of beleaguered French Canada also increased. He did not produce the popular rebellion

of 1837, but he did try (with limited success) to become its leader. His inability to lead the rebellion was intimately connected with his inability to understand the aspirations of the rebels. When threatened with arrest, he fled to the United States and played little part in the renewal of insurrection in 1838. He spent some years in exile in France, returning to Canada in 1845 and to politics in 1848. This portrait is by Antoine Maurin (National Archives of Canada C-5435).

government (such as canals and banks) represented an unnecessary financial burden on the taxpayer, being in effect 'class legislation'. As Mackenzie argued, the 'true source of a country's wealth' was 'labour usefully and prudently applied' (quoted in Fairley 1960:217). For Papineau in Lower Canada, an active economic state was being dominated not only by a mercantile class but by a British mercantile class, which promoted capitalism.

It is in the context of the struggle between commercial capitalism and agrarian idealism that we must understand both the Tory commitment to public involvement in economic activity and the reform opposition. These political reformers had no conception that public economic development could be executed on behalf of the people, any more than they had a general conception of any positive role for the state in ensuring the social well-being of its citizenry. They were instead typical nineteenth-century liberal democrats who sought to reduce (rather than increase) the influence of government on the lives of the population, as well as to limit the temptation of special privilege. As Mackenzie put it in a broadside entitled 'Independence' in late November 1837, 'We contend, that in all laws made, or to be made, every person shall be bound

William Lyon Mackenzie Describes an Upper Canadian Election Campaign

[*Source*: M. Fairley, ed., *The Selected Writings of William Lyon Mackenzie* (Toronto: Oxford University Press, 1960):20–2].

On Monday morning we arrived at St Thomas, the place appointed for holding the election for the county of Middlesex, of which I will now give a brief account. The hustings were placed near the church, on a high and well-chosen spot of ground. The village was crowded with people, and the result of a contested election, not yet begun, was joyfully anticipated by the friends of all three of the candidates, though, of course, only two could succeed. Groups stood in every direction, some wearing an oak-tree leaf in their hats, which signified 'Mathews and Liberty;' others, ribbons as favours. On one man's hat was tied a broad orange ribbon: the inscription, 'Rolph and

Mathews', showed his party; three-fourths of the people had no party emblems about them at all. A little after ten o'clock, Mr Warren, the returning officer, Colonel Talbot, Mr Rolph, Colonel Burwell, Captain Mathews, and Mr Bostwick, mounted the hustings. Mr Warren was dressed in blue, had his sword appended to his side, and cut a fine figure as returning officer. He read the writ, and five or six hundred persons, who were bystanders, were hushed, when the tall figure of Colonel Burwell was extended to its full length, as he arose to address the multitude. He commenced pleading in justification of his past conduct, and parried admirably the thrusts of some teasing electors who were perpetually demanding why he had acted so and so, why did this, and said that? He spoke of the milk of human kindness, of location tickets, of flogging bills,

alike—neither should any tenure, estate, charter, degree, birth or place, confer any exemption from the ordinary course of legal proceedings and responsibilities whereunto others are subjected' (quoted in Fairley 1960:223).

REFORM AND REBELLION

Eventually in 1837 the frustration of the reformers in the Canadas led to rebellion. Political violence was hardly anything new in 1837, but was instead endemic throughout this era. Though sometimes spontaneous, it could also be carefully calculated for partisan purposes. The mob was the political expression of the ordinary inhabitant, who was not usually at the centre of politics in this period. What was different in 1837 was the attempt to coordinate large-scale violence to overthrow the governments of the Canadas by force. The uprisings can be viewed in a variety of ways: as political events, as cultural manifestations, as examples of subterranean pressures resulting from agrarian discontent, or, in Lower Canada, as an expression of Anglo-French animosity. They were a combination of all these things. Had the rebellions not been so quickly and brutally suppressed, similar uprisings might well have broken out

of asking no votes, and read part of the Upper Canada Gazette for the edification of those present. . . . The next speaker after Colonel Burwell, was Captain Mathews, of the half-pay (or rather retired allowance) royal artillery; he met a joyful, kind reception. His manly, athletic form and courteous demeanour, added to the independent English principles he professored to espouse, secured to him a distinguished place in the good graces of many a worthy yeoman. . . . This wealthy intelligent, and patriotic Englishman made an excellent speech, remarkable for its brevity, considering the variety of subjects he embraced; as he concluded the people rent the air with their acclamations. . . . His well-wishers have only one fear, namely that he will [act] *too independent* a part. Mr Rolph (who spoke last) promised to act with independence, and to defend the people's rights; spoke with considerable animation of the fine country in which he that day had the honour to be a candidate; expressed a warm interest in its prosperity and that of the province at large; adverted to the time when it was a desert; reminded them of what had been effected in twenty-one years, and augured well of the future fate of the country, its agriculture, and its infant manufactures. Getting warm, he forgot that he was at a country election, and commenced a sentence in his professional way, 'Gentlemen of the Jury'. . . . It was a cheering spectacle to a friend of Canada to see the happy groups of horsemen from every quarter ride up to the hustings, shouting blithely, 'Rolph and Mathews!'—'Mathews and Liberty!' Even the newly-elected members of Oxford came with their bands of yeoman to vote for the men of the people's choice. Mr Burwell had represented the county for twelve years, and his votes and conduct had so incensed the farmers that they determined to put him out. That precious political selection, the local magistracy, supported him almost to a man.

in the lower provinces, particularly in Prince Edward Island, where agrarian and political discontents were also strong.

On one level the rebellions of 1837 were unsuccessful challenges to the stability of the élite political cultures of the Canadas. The ostensible leaders, William Lyon Mackenzie and Louis-Joseph Papineau, had become totally frustrated in their attempts to wrest control of the government from the hands of the powerful cliques of Toronto and Quebec and put it in the hands of the popularly elected assemblies. Part of the frustration, particularly for Mackenzie, was that the assemblies themselves could be manipulated by the oligarchy. The so-called 'popular parties' in the assemblies of the colonies were in large part dominated by regional élites representing more the grassroots countryside than did the oligarchs. The regional élites wanted a more open political culture. If home rule was one ambition of the reformers, the expansion of politics beyond the ranks and kin of the governing élite was another. In this sense the rebellions marked the first of a series of movements in Canadian history to decentralize authority and political power.

In Lower Canada, the *Parti Canadien* and its successor, the *Parti Patriot*, more consistently dominated the lower house than had the reformers in Upper Canada. This was because the party conflict in Lower Canada had long since taken on racial overtones. The *Parti Canadien* was dominated by French-Canadian professionals who represented the regional élites and who had no hope of gaining admission to the ranks of the ruling *Château Clique*. In February 1834, the Ninety-Two Resolutions, prepared by Papineau and three others, were adopted by the assembly of Lower Canada and submitted to London. They catalogued grievances and requests, among them the legislature's control of revenue, the executive's responsibility to the electorate, and the election of legislative councillors. These resolutions were in effect rejected by the British Parliament in March 1837, and the way was opened for rebellion.

Beyond their political and constitutional significance, the rebellions were also manifestations of popular, especially agrarian, discontent. Part of the reason for the ineffectuality of the rebellions was that there was little relationship between the reform leaders—who were operating within the élite system even while trying to change it—and popular opinion, which was responding to the collapse of the international wheat market in the mid-1830s. Both Mackenzie and Papineau persistently denied that they had planned insurrection, although they were prepared to lead one when it emerged. Rural districts had been restive for several years in both provinces, and some protest meetings held in 1837 were attended by armed farmers. A rural uprising near Brantford, Upper Canada, led by Dr Charles Duncombe (1792–1867), dispersed on 13 December when he heard of the easy defeat of Mackenzie's motley crew of rebels at Montgomery's Tavern north of Toronto. Certainly the rural districts in

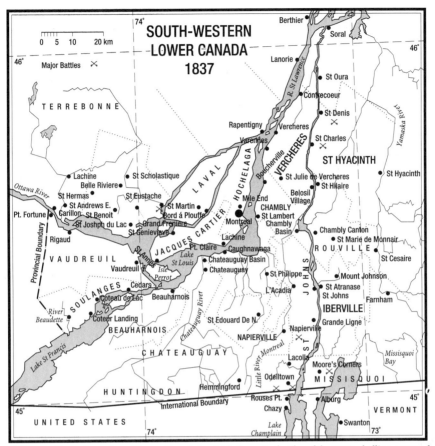

This map shows the region of Lower Canada in which the major battles of the 1837 rebellion occurred. The battles, mainly the result of local rural uprisings, are marked with crossed swords on the map, which is based on a map from A.D. Decelles's *The 'Patriotes' of '37: A Chronicle of the Lower Canadian Rebellion* (1916).

Lower Canada provided their own rationale and impetus for rising in arms against the government. When political agitation turned to insurrection, many moderate members of the élite leadership of the reformers fell away, to be replaced by armed farmers.

Unfortunately for the rebels in both the Canadas, their self-declared leaders had a fairly narrow agenda of political change and no notion of how to turn a spontaneous uprising into an organized rebellion. Mackenzie, Papineau, and Duncombe all became caught up in their own hysteria, panicked, and fled to leave others to face the music. There was considerable music to face, especially after a second uprising in Lower Canada in November 1838, which was brutally suppressed by the authorities. As in the earlier rebellion, the government allowed the leaders to escape and went instead after the rank and file. This time

Lord Durham on Responsible Government

[John George Lambton, Lord Durham, was a maverick Whig whom the ministry of Lord Melbourne was pleased to send to North America. Born in 1792, he was known as 'Radical Jack' and was a principal advocate of the Reform Bill of 1830. Constantly in ill health, he had served briefly as British ambassador to Russia, but was back in England in 1837. Had Durham returned to Parliament, he would have become a lightning-rod for the Radical opposition to the prime minister, Lord Melbourne. He arrived in Quebec in May 1838 and left a few months later when the ministry refused to support his order to send the leading prisoners from the 1837 rebellion into exile in Bermuda. His recommendation for constitutional reform in Canada was connected to his recommendation for the union of the two Canadas; he assumed that there would be an English-speaking majority in the reformed legislature. The following passage is reprinted from C.P. Lucas, ed., *Lord Durham's Report,* vol. 1 (Oxford: Clarendon Press 1912):276–81.]

I rely on the efficacy of reform in the constitutional system by which these Colonies are governed, for the removal of every abuse in their administration which defective institutions have engendered. If a system can be devised which shall lay in these countries the foundation of an efficient and popular government and ensure harmony, in place of collision, between the various powers of the State, and bring the influence of a vigorous public opinion to bear on every detail of public affairs, we may rely on sufficient remedies being found for the present vices of the administrative system. . . . It is not by weakening, but strengthening the influence of the people on its Government, by confining within much narrower bounds than those hitherto allotted to it, and not by extending the interference of the imperial authorities in the details of colonial affairs, that I believe that harmony is to be restored, where dissension has so long prevailed; and a regularity and vigour hitherto unknown, introduced into the administration of these Provinces. It needs no change in the principles of government, no invention of a new constitutional theory, to supply the remedy which would, in my opinion, completely remove the existing political disorders. It needs but to follow consistently the principles of the British Constitution, and introduce into the Government of these great Colonies those wise provisions, by which alone the working of the representative system can in any country be rendered harmonious and efficient. We are not now to consider the policy of establishing representative government in the North American Colonies. That has been irrevocably done; and the experiment of depriving the people of their present constitutional power, is not to be thought of. To conduct their Government harmoniously, in accordance with its established principles, is now the business of its rulers; and I know not how it is possible to secure that harmony in any other way, than by administering the Government on those principles which have been found perfectly efficacious in Great Britain. I would not impair a single prerogative of the Crown; on the contrary, I believe that the interests of the people of these Colonies require the protection of prerogatives, which have not hitherto been exercised. But the Crown must, on the other hand, submit to the necessary consequences of representative institutions; and if it has to carry on the Government in unison with a representative body, it must consent to carry it on by means of those in whom that representative body has confidence. . . . When a ministry ceases to command a majority in Parliament on great questions of policy, its doom is immediately sealed; and it would appear to us as strange to attempt, for any time, to carry on a Government by means of ministers perpetually in a minority, as it would be to pass laws with a majority of votes against them. . . . If colonial legislatures have frequently stopped the supplies, if they have harassed public servants by unjust or harsh impeachments, it was because the removal of an unpopular administration could not be effected in the Colonies by those milder indications of a want of confidence, which have always sufficed to attain the end in the mother country. . . . Every purpose of popular control might be combined with every advantage of vesting the immediate choice of advisers in the Crown, were the Colonial Governor to be instructed to secure the co-operation of the Assembly in his policy, by entrusting its administration to such men as could command a majority; and if he were given to understand that he need count on no aid from home in any difference with the Assembly, that should not directly involve the relations between the mother country and the Colony. This change might be effected by a single dispatch containing such instructions; or if any legal enactment were requisite, it would only be one that would render it necessary that the official acts of the Governor should be countersigned by some public functionary. This would induce responsibility for every act of the Government, and as a natural consequence, it would necessitate the substitution of a system of administration, by means of competent heads of departments, for the present rude machinery of an Executive Council. . . . I admit that the system which I propose would, in fact, place the internal government of the Colony in the hands of the colonists themselves; and that we should thus leave to them the execution of the laws, of which we have long entrusted the making solely to them.

753 men were captured and 108 brought to court martial, resulting in ninety-nine death sentences. In the end, twelve were executed and fifty-eight banished to Australia. In both Canadas the ruling élite was still very much in charge. The militia, which prided itself on having fought off the Americans in 1815, had another mark of its loyalty.

After reports of the first rebellions had reached Britain, the authorities dispatched a fact-finding commission headed by John Charles Lambton, Lord Durham (1792–1840). Although he did not remain long in Canada, his famous 'Report on the Affairs in British North America', filed in January 1839, was a thorough and eloquent examination of the problems in Canada. Durham recommended two political solutions: the introduction of responsible government and the unification of the two Canadas. He also wanted changes in land policy, including a general system for the sale of Crown land at sufficient price and the elimination of the proprietorial system in Prince Edward Island.

While the rebellions accomplished little more in the short run than to focus Great Britain's attention on the need for change in her American colonies, Durham's recommendations for the union of the Canadas and for responsible government were adopted over the next few years. Nevertheless, other forces would help remake British North America. Free trade, railroads, economic expansion, and industrialization were, in the end, more powerful engines of change than either political uprisings or constitutional reform.

Major Events 1841–1867

1841 Union of Upper and Lower Canada proclaimed.

1842 Webster-Ashburton Treaty resolves the New Brunswick border. Great Britain experiments with partially elected, partially appointed legislature for Newfoundland.

1843 Fort Victoria established on Vancouver Island.

1846 Oregon Boundary Treaty settles the western boundary. Corn Laws and Timber duties are repealed by British Parliament. St John's, Newfoundland, is destroyed by fire.

1848 Nova Scotia gets responsible government. Lord Elgin concedes responsible government to Canada. Newfoundland reverts to an elected assembly.

1849 Vancouver Island is leased by the British to the Hudson's Bay Company and becomes a Crown colony. Rebellion Losses Bill is enacted, leading to riots in Montreal. Annexation movement flourishes.

1851 James Douglas becomes governor of Vancouver Island. Cable is laid from New Brunswick to Prince Edward Island. Prince Edward Island receives responsible government.

1852 Grand Trunk Railway is incorporated.

1854 Reciprocity Treaty with United States is signed for ten years.

1855 Petroleum is discovered in southwestern Canada. Newfoundland receives responsible government.

1856 The first legislature meets on Vancouver Island.

1857 British Parliament holds enquiry over the future of the Canadian northwest. Palliser and Canadian Exploring Expeditions are sent west to investigate the region. Gold is discovered on the Thompson and Fraser rivers. Ottawa is chosen by Queen Victoria as the site for capital of Canada. Canadian legislature passes the Act for the Gradual Civilization of the Indian Tribes in the Canadas.

1858 British Columbia is embodied as a colony.

1859 The first steamer is launched on Red River. First newspaper (*Nor'wester*) is established in Red River.

1860 Cariboo Gold Rush begins in British Columbia.

1861 American Civil War begins. Montreal and Toronto introduce horse-drawn cars for public transportation.

1862 Cariboo Road is begun in British Columbia. Asbestos is discovered in Quebec.

1863 First salmon fishery on the Fraser River is established.

1864 Reciprocity Treaty is terminated by a vote of the US Senate, to take effect in 1866. Charlottetown and Quebec conferences are held to discuss union.

1866 Transatlantic cable is laid from Newfoundland to Europe. Union of British Columbia and Vancouver Island, with Victoria as capital.

1867 The British North America Act is passed by British Parliament, to take effect 1 July 1867. Emily Howard Stowe obtains a medical degree in the United States.

5
Becoming a Nation

❧

A seamless web of political and economic expansion, beginning somewhere around 1840, ended in Canadian Confederation. Because the province of Canada took the lead in national unification, the beginning of the process can be said to have begun from the Act of Union, which joined Upper and Lower Canada in July 1840. The era of political unification witnessed some substantial technological advances—particularly associated with the steam engine on sea and land—that radically altered perceptions of distance in a vast domain separated from Europe by thousands of miles of ocean. Travel not only sped up, it acquired a predictable timetable. The discovery of telegraphy, and the eventual laying of a transatlantic cable from Newfoundland in 1866, affected the perception of time as well as distance. The ability to operate to a schedule completely altered the world. These changes were not a necessary prerequisite for union, but they were clearly part of the facilitating background.

FROM IMPERIALISM TO FREE TRADE

By 1840 the mercantile economy of British North America had reached its apex and began to undergo considerable change. That alteration resulted from a number of factors. The most important was clearly the British government's demolition of the imperial trading system, which had prevailed since the seventeenth century. Instead of mercantilism, Britain moved to free trade. In the process the mother country wiped out protectionist advantages for her colonies. As a result, in place of a transatlantic economy based on the sailing-ship, some of British North America began to think in terms of a continental economy. Fortunately, the railway came along at exactly this time, providing possibilities for internal development and internal markets. Equally fortunately, Britain resolved long-standing differences with the Americans, making possible the negotiation of a trade treaty, which provided some access for British North America into the lucrative American market. Inherent in the reorganization of the commercial economy was the rise of industrialization. Internal markets within the continent required not raw materials but finished goods. Colonial business sought to oblige.

British economists, beginning with Adam Smith's *Wealth of Nations* in 1776, provided a thoroughly reasoned theoretical critique of the old mercantile

Table 5.1

Trade Statistics 1850–1866

TRADE OF THE PROVINCE OF CANADA WITH THE UNITED STATES

Year	Imports from the United States $	Exports to the United States $	Year cont.	Imports from the United States $	Exports to the United States $
1850	6,594,860	4,951,156	1859	17,592,916	13,922,314
1851	8,365,764	4,071,544	1860	17,273,029	18,427,918
1852	8,477,693	6,284,520	1861	20,206,080	14,261,427
1853	11,782,144	8,936,380	1862	22,642,860	15,063,730
1854	15,533,096	8,649,000	1863	18,457,683	18,426,891
1855	20,828,676	16,737,276	1865	14,820,577	21,340,350
1856	22,704,508	17,979,752	1866	15,242,834	32,587,643
1857	20,224,648	13,206,436			
1858	15,635,565	11,930,094			

TRADE OF THE UNITED STATES WITH THE BRITISH NORTH AMERICAN PROVINCES

Year Ending June 30	Exports from the United States $	Imports by the United States $	Year Ending June 30 cont.	Exports from the United States $	Imports by the United States $
1850	9,515,991	5,179,500	1863	27,619,814	17,484,786
1851	11,770,092	5,279,718	1864	26,574,624	29,608,736
1852	10,229,608	5,469,445	1865	28,829,402	33,264,403
1853	12,432,597	6,527,559	1866	24,828,880	48,528,628
1854	24,073,408	8,784,412	1867	21,020,302	25,044,005
1855	27,741,808	15,118,289	1868	24,080,777	26,261,379
1856	29,025,349	21,276,614	1869	23,381,471	29,293,766
1857	24,138,482	22,108,916	1870	25,339,254	36,265,328
1858	23,604,526	15,784,836	1875	36,225,735	28,271,926
1859	28,109,494	19,287,565	1880	30,775,871	33,214,340
1860	22,695,928	23,572,796	1885	40,124,907	36,960,541
1861	21,676,513	22,724,489	1890	41,503,812	39,396,980
1862	20,573,070	18,511,025			

system. They offered an alternate vision of international expansion based upon free trade. In the years following Smith, a number of classical political economists in Britain—Malthus, Chambers, Ricardo, and Mill—expanded on earlier critiques of mercantilism, always insisting that freedom worked best, especially in the market-place. Despite the intellectual demolition of protectionism in the first quarter of the nineteenth century, British governments found it hard to give up; it artificially assisted influential sectors of the economy, particularly agriculture. Eventually the free traders won out, chiefly because of Britain's industrial successes after 1815. By the 1840s, the British industrial economy could no longer afford the luxury of protectionism, which limited its access to foreign raw materials and protected markets. The ministry, led by Sir Robert Peel, gritted its teeth and systematically removed protection for corn and other

Table 5.1

Trade Statistics 1850–1866 continued

TRADE OF THE LOWER COLONIES WITH THE UNITED STATES

(Unit £1,000)

	New Brunswick Imp. from the US	Exp. to US	Nova Scotia Imp. from US	Exp. to US	Prince Edward Island Imp. from US	Exp. to US	Newfoundland Imp. from US	Exp. to US
1850	262	77	322	197	8	11	153	20
1851	330	83	283	151	16	20	201	20
1853	574	121	415	277	37	24	177	41
1854	711	97	575	318	39	16	237	28
1855	782	123	738	481	43	33	354	79
1856	714	173	678	413	52	27	388	109
1858	564	163	583	408	42	63	323	113
1859	675	236	576	456	62	87	361	106
1860	688	248	651	446	56	78	364	81
1862	616	185	605	362	46	43	345	47
1863	739	259	771	373	71	105	344	60
1864	691	263	860	489	83	77	306	41
1865	636	361	865	723	90	120	348	109
1866	779	386	808	645	74	21	291	88

	Imports by the Province of Canada from the United States Dutiable $	Free $	Imports by the United States from the Province of Canada Free $	Dutiable $
1850	5,803,732	791,128	636,454	3,649,016
1851	6,981,735	1,384,030	1,529,685	3,426,786
1852	7,613,003	864,690	761,571	3,828,398
1853	10,656,582	1,125,565	1,179,682	4,098,434
1854	13,449,341	2,083,757	380,041	6,341,498
1855	11,449,472	9,379,204	6,876,496	5,305,818
1856	12,770,923	9,933,586	16,487,822	640,375
1857	9,966,430	10,258,221	17,600,737	691,097
1858	8,473,607	7,161,958	11,267,618	313,953
1859	9,032,861	8,560,055	13,703,748	504,969
1860	8,526,230	8,746,799	18,427,141	434,532
1861	8,338,620	11,867,460	18,287,217	358,240
1862	6,128,783	16,514,077	15,026,093	227,059
1863	3,974,396	14,483,287	13,358,127	567,677

Source: D.C. Masters, *The Reciprocity Treaty of 1854* (London: Longmans Green & Company, 1936): Appendix B.

raw materials, including timber. The British still sought to emphasize import-ing cheap raw materials and exporting finished goods overseas. Instead of trading with colonies, however, they sought to trade with the entire world. British free-trade policies had a tremendous psychological impact on colonial merchants. Britain's industrial needs also contributed to the need for interna-tional peace and bilateral understandings.

One of the understandings came with the United States. Since 1815 Britain had sought entente with the Americans, a process that gained impetus during the period of free trade. By 1846 most of the outstanding boundary questions between the two nations had been resolved. In 1842 the Webster-Ashburton Treaty had sorted out the complex eastern boundary issues along the Maine-New Brunswick border. The western boundary west of the Rocky Mountains was settled in 1846. Under the Oregon Boundary Treaty the border across the Rockies to the Pacific continued from the Great Lakes at the 49th parallel to the Pacific (excluding Vancouver Island). This 'compromise' allowed the Americans to possess the state of Washington, in which they had virtually no nationals and which had been occupied chiefly by the Hudson's Bay Company. While the geographical interests of British North America may have been sacrificed by the Oregon settlement, entente was good for business.

In the short run, the British North American rush to export wheat and timber under the old system, before the repeal of the Corn Laws and Timber duties of 1846 took effect, resulted in a collapse of prices in 1847 that would last for the remainder of the decade. Further complicating matters for colonial governments was the arrival of thousands of impoverished Irish immigrants, refugees from the Great Famine of the 1840s. They brought sickness and expense to the colonies along with their anguish. The result of these blows was a conviction that the mother country had subverted the old empire. The crisis seemed much worse in the united Province of Canada because of its reliance on wheat exports. Canadian mercantile policy in the later 1840s was to attempt to come to terms with the Americans. The Canadians continued to improve their canal system. They argued for reciprocal free trade between British North America and the United States in the natural products of each.

Along the way to reciprocity, arguments for annexation temporarily seduced Canadians to the United States. Annexationism was a movement that gained support after an intense political debate over compensation for Lower Canadians who had not rebelled but had lost property in 1837. It was a far less important movement than that of reciprocity. Both flourished in the economic and political uncertainties of the late 1840s. Many British North Americans saw annexation as the inevitable result of the failure to achieve reciprocity rather than as a desirable end in itself.

Canadians, especially those dependent on the wheat economy, viewed internal markets—which to them meant the United States—as the only alternative to those lost in Britain. The eastern provinces also saw advantages to gaining access to the American market. The Americans displayed no interest until 1852 when the British government decided to toughen its fishery policy. The resultant Reciprocity Treaty of 1854 was hardly a very broad-reaching free trade agreement. It removed tariff and other barriers on a variety of enumerated goods, chiefly raw materials common to both countries. It did not remove barriers on finished goods, although the Americans hoped that a more prosperous British North America would buy more American manufactures. The treaty was potentially much more beneficial to British North America than to the United States. This helps explain why the Americans were so eager to end it at the expiration of its initial ten-year term. It does not appear to have greatly increased trade in either direction during its lifetime. The Reciprocity Treaty of 1854, nevertheless, was of enormous psychological value to British North America.

THE RISE OF INDUSTRIALISM

The Reciprocity Treaty encouraged merchants, entrepreneurs, and politicians (mainly in the Province of Canada) to continue reconceptualizing their economic orientation. They moved from an imperial context, in which the British market was critical, to a continental context, in which internal markets were dominant. Once turned from its traditional transatlantic economy to a continental one, Canada began to industrialize. Indeed, one of the principal reasons why American trade in dutiable items did not expand during the ten years of the agreement was that the manufacturing capacity of British North America—again, particularly in the Province of Canada—grew substantially as well in this period. The internal market permitted agriculture in Canada West to shift partially out of grain cultivation into mixed farming. The concern for modernization led to the elimination of the seigneurial system in the St Lawrence Valley by legislative fiat. A bill replaced traditional seigneurial obligations with a quitrent, which gave tenants the opportunity to purchase their lands.

The process of economic reorientation was not a uniform one. Canada and the Atlantic region moved in somewhat different directions. While the Canadians became immersed in internal development—even territorial expansion into the prairie west—the Atlantic provinces continued to find the older transatlantic economy quite comfortable. They based their prosperity on a shipping industry committed to the wooden sailing-ship, which the region was still successfully producing. The period from 1840 to the early 1870s was the 'Golden Age of Sail' in the Atlantic region. With hindsight, it is possible to recognize the long-term technological weaknesses of the wooden sailing-ship. So long as vessels that cost less than half as much to produce as iron steamers were more than half as profitable, however, they would flourish. The carrying trade provided employment for thousands. It also produced an outward-looking international orientation rather than one that focused on internal continental development. The Atlantic provinces sought to expand transportation links with Canada (mainly railways) in terms of transatlantic linkages.

The Province of Canada saw railways as a means to continental rather than transatlantic linkages. Canadian railway expansion would not occur in earnest

Table 5.2 Railways of Canada

STATEMENT SHOWING THE COST, STOCK, BONDS, LOANS, FLOATING DEBT, AND DIVIDEND ACCOUNTS, OF CANADIAN RAILWAYS IN 1860 (COMPILED FROM THE REPORT OF THE INSPECTOR OF RAILWAYS)

Corporate name of railway	Cost of road and equipment	Capital stock paid in	Funded Debt.			Government loan	Floating debt	Interest paid on debt in 1860	Dividends paid in 1800
			1st preference bonds	2d preference bonds	3d preference bonds				
Great Western and its branches	23,000,104.00	16,158,641.00	6,327,640.00	Included in 1st pref. Bds.		2,791,947.00*	—	528,254.00	3 per cent for six months
Grand Trunk and its branches	55,690,039.92	13,524,803.48	9,733,333.33	4,066,262.23	17,096,450.60	15,142,633.33	12,163,213.07	1,039,685.72	—
Northern (Toronto to L. Huron)	3,890,778.68	823,818.50	491,046.67	1,092,566.68	287,481.35	2,311,666.67	—	55,545.21	
Buffalo and Lake Huron	6,403,045.86	4,345,701.26	2,433,333.33	811,111.11	—		145,999.99	—	
London and Port Stanley	1,017,220.00	939,542.00	399,400.00	120,000.00	—		77,770.00	—	
Welland	1,309,209.92	710,299.60	486,666.67	243,333.33	—		211,851.93	—	
Erie and Ontario	—	—	—	—	—		—	—	
Port Hope, Lindsay and Beaverton, and branch	—	—	—	—	608,333.33		—	—	
Cobourg and Peterborough	—	—	—	—	—		—	—	
Brockville and Ottawa, and branch	1,901,000.00	207,000.00	—	648,000.00	—		280,000.00	4,968.00	
Ottawa and Prescott	1,432,647.21	300,630.35	486,666.67	300,000.00	243,333.34		179,332.37	2,321.90	
Montreal and Champlain, and branch	2,485,425.16	1,226,250.00	777,186.66	192,200.00	84,400.00		285,525.51	92,451.69	
Carillon and Grenville	50,171.00	42,300.00	—	—	—		—	—	
St Lawrence and Industry							909.00	48.00	2 per cent
Stanstead, Shefford, & Chambly	—	—	—	—	—		—	—	
Peterboro & Chemung Lake	—	—	—	—	—		—	—	
	97,179,641.75	38,278,986.19	21,743,605.66	7,473,473.35	17,711,165.29	20,246,247.00	13,344,600.87	1,869,224.52	

*The total amount borrowed from the Province by the Great Western Railway, on account of the Guarantee Law, was, $3,755,555.18. In July 1858, this company repaid $957,114.45 of this amount.

Note: The length of roads for which there are no returns of cost in the above table is 172 1/4 miles, including eleven miles of Preston and Berlin, not running. The cost of these roads cannot be far from $5,000,000, and the total cost of Canadian Railways is over $100,000,000. The expenditure 'on capital account', is much greater than the 'cost of road and equipments'. In the case of the Grand Trunk Railway, the total expenditure is about $70,000,000—the difference representing interest and discount accounts, loss in working, etc. Of the Grand Trunk cost, $1,621,231.69 was on the Portland Division, and therefore not in Canada.

STATEMENT SHOWING THE EARNINGS, EXPENSES, INCOME, MILEAGE, NO. OF EMPLOYEES, AND NO. OF LOCOMOTIVES AND CARS ON CANADIAN RAILWAYS IN 1860 (COMPILED FROM REPORT OF INSPECTOR OF RAILWAYS)

Corporate name of railway	Total earnings in 1860	Total expenses in 1860	Net income for 1860	Earnings per mile per week	Expenses per mile per week	% of expenses to earn's	Total miles run exclusive of piloting, shunting & c.	Total persons employed on line	No. of locomotives	Passengers	Freight
Great Western and its branches	2,197,943.34	1,993,806.00	204,043.00	122.51	111.13	91	1,261,604	2,049	89	127	1,269
Grand Trunk and its branches	3,349,658.18	2,806,583.17	533,075.01	58.72	49.20	84	8,195,064	3,118	217	135	2,538
Northern	332,967.01	260,466.56	72,500.45	67.40	52.72	78	280,035	370	17	20	801
Buffalo and Lake Huron	315,763.99	264,191.29	51,572.70	37.48	31.36	83	334,457	458	28	24	255
London and Port Stanley	29,385.57	23,256.02	6,129.75	23.55	18.62	78	41,300	38	2	2	50
Welland	64,554.40	51,274.35	13,280.06	49.64	39.44	79	47,810	104	4	4	87
Erie and Ontario	—	—	—	—	—	—	11,220	—	1	4	10
Port Hope, Lindsay and Beaverton, and branch	53,694.04	40,111.01	13,583.08	18.28	18.64	75	73,806	66	5	3	65
Cobourg and Peterborough	—	—	—	—	—	—	—	—	4	2	66
Brockville and Ottawa, and branch	53,801.10	34,427.25	19,373.85	16.30	10.42	64	53,715	74	3	8	79
Ottawa and Prescott	75,362.16	51,465.11	23,897.05	26.83	18.33	68	67,911	92	5	8	79
Montreal and Champlain	232,803.44	136,349.62	105,708.82	53.45	31.31	59	185,633	202	16	15	173
Carillon and Grenville	7,937.25	5,762.18	2,175.06	11.77	8.54	72	6,000	11	2	5	5
St Lawrence and Industry	8,796.00	7,819.00	978.00	14.08	12.50	88	12,440	24	2	5	5
Stanstead, Shefford, & Chambly	—	—	—	—	—	—	43,720		Leased by the Montreal & Champ.		
Peterboro & Chemung Lake	—	—	—	—	—	—			Worked by Cobourg & Peterboro.		
	6,722,666.48	5,675,511.56	1,046,316.78	63.65	53.73	84	5,614,715	6,606	395	862	4,982

The improvement in the gross receipts of the first three roads since 1860, is as follows:

1861

	Gross earnings	Earnings per mile
Great Western	$ 2,266,684	$ 6,570
Grand Trunk	3,517,829	3,226
Northern	414,100	4,359

1862

	Gross earnings	Earnings per mile
Great Western	$ 2,686,060	$ 7,786
Grand Trunk	3,975,071	3,647
Northern	409,899	4,309

Source: H.Y. Hind, *The Dominion of Canada* (Toronto: L. Stebbins, 1869).

The Philosophy of Railways

[In 1849 the Canadian engineer, Thomas Coltrin Keefer, published, on behalf of the directors of the Montreal and Lachine Railroad, a pamphlet entitled 'The Philosophy of Railroads'. It was obviously a promotional effort. The author waxed poetic about the advantages railways could bring to a backward Canada. Within a few years many others in Canada agreed. The following excerpt is taken from the fourth edition. *Source*: T.C. Keefer, 'Philosophy of Railroads, Published by Order of the Directors of the St Lawrence and Ottawa Grand Junction Railway Company', 4th ed. (Montreal: J. Lovell, 1853):3–11.]

Old winter is once more upon us, and our inland seas are 'dreary and inhospitable wastes' to the merchant and to the traveller;—our rivers are sealed fountains—and an embargo which no human power can remove is laid on all our ports. . . . Far to the South is heard the daily scream of the steam-whistle— but from Canada there is no escape: blockaded and imprisoned by Ice and Apathy, we have at least ample time for reflection—and if there be comfort in Philosophy may we not profitably consider the PHILOSOPHY OF RAILROADS. . . .

Railway stocks, unlike most others, are a species of real estate immoveably attached to the soil, and have therefore become of late years favourite channels for investment with all classes of capitalists. Banks may fail—commerce may languish or be partially diverted—manufactures be rendered unprofitable— even the earth may for a time refuse to many a return for the capital invested in it; but as long as there are men to profit or to lose by speculations, there will be people to sustain a Railway; and if universal ruin be inevitable, *they* will be the last public works to succumb to the general prostration. The cart road is succeeded by the turnpike, this again by the macadam or plank roads, and these last by the Railway. The latter is the perfected system and admits of no competition—and this characteristic pre-eminently marks it out as the most desirable object for investment in the midst of an enterprising and increasing population. . . .

until after 1850, after the complete demolition of the old imperial trade system. By 1850 only 60 mi. (97 km) of track were in operation in Canada. The obstacles had not been technological; the technology had been available since the 1820s. Finance and psychology were the barriers. Railways were expensive capital investments, few routes in British North America promised to be immediately profitable, and investors shied away, at least until the railway boom of the 1850s. In that decade a mania for internal development totally captured the imaginations of Canadian politicians and investors, encouraged by exaggerated promises of profits resulting from railway expansion. Canadian railway trackage had to be well built because of the climate. By 1867 the total cost to Canada of 2,188.25 mi. (3,520 km) of track was $145,794,853, or roughly $66,000 per mile. In order to pay for this construction, the railways borrowed on the British

Let us take a case of which Canada (we are proud and sad to say) presents more than one instance. A well cultivated district, in which all the lands are occupied (perhaps by the second generation) with or without water power, but situated twenty to fifty miles from the chief towns upon our great highway, the St Lawrence, and without navigable water transportation with it. . . . There is no stimulus for increased production—there are less facilities for it: the redundant population have all been accustomed to agriculture, and as the field for this is unrestricted, they move Westward to prevent a subdivision of the homesteads, and to become greater landowners than their fathers. . . . We will now suppose (we would we could more than suppose), that two of our cities should be moved to unite by the iron bond of a Railway, which in its course will traverse the district just described. . . . And now some of the 'city folks' come out and take up a water privilege, or erect steam power, and commence manufacturing. . . . A town has been built and peopled by the operatives—land rises rapidly in value—the neglected swamp is cleared and the timber is converted into all sorts of wooden 'notions'—tons of vegetables, grains, or grasses, are grown where none grew before—the patient click of the loom, the rushing of the shuttle, the busy hum of the spindle, the thundering of the tri-hammer, and the roaring of steam, are mingled in one continuous sound of active industry. While the physical features of our little hamlet are undergoing such a wonderful transformation, the moral influence of the iron civilizer upon the old inhabitants is bringing a rapid 'change over the spirit of their dreams'. . . . The civilizing tendency of the locomotive is one of the modern anomalies, which however inexplicable it may appear to some, is yet so fortunately patent to all, that it is admitted as readily as the action of steam, though the substance be invisible and its secret ways unknown to man. Poverty, indifference, the bigotry or jealousy of religious denominations, local dissensions or political demagogueism may stifle or neutralize the influence of the best intended efforts of an educational system, but that invisible power which has waged successful war with the material elements, will assuredly overcome the prejudices of mental weakness or the designs of mental tyrants.

exchanges. Governments had to guarantee the loans and contribute themselves. The Canadian government itself, by 1867, had incurred a provincial debt on railway construction of over $33 million, and its municipalities added considerably more.

Vast expenditures brought out the worst in businessmen and politicians, who commonly served together on interlocking directorates and engaged in the various aspects of railway construction. Allan MacNab (1798–1862), who was seven times chairman of the Canadian assembly's railway committee between 1848 and 1857 and served the province as copremier in 1854–6, was at various times president of three railway companies, chairman of another, and director of two more. Small wonder he once commented, 'All my politics are railroads.' Bribes to politicians were common. Construction overruns were a

The Great Western Railway Station in Toronto, facing southwest on Yonge Street at The Esplanade. Designed by William G. Storm in the Romanesque style, this wooden building was completed in March 1866. In 1882, when the Great Western amalgamated with the Grand Trunk Railway, the station became a depot for freight, then for wholesale produce. It was in use as recently as May 1952, when it was destroyed by fire. This engraving of a Notman and Fraser photograph appeared in the *Canadian Illustrated News* on 2 April 1870 (Metropolitan Toronto Reference Library).

way of life. Corruption ran rampant. The most serious problem, however, was that too much construction occurred in advance of a settled population that could sustain a profitable level of traffic. This would always be the Canadian dilemma: trading off development against sustainability.

All railway promoters insisted that their lines would promote manufacturing by reducing transportation costs. Railways not only closed the distance between markets, they also served as a major market for industrial goods, often becoming industrial manufacturers themselves. The Grand Trunk Railway, incorporated in 1852 to build a railway from Toronto to Montreal, began by building its own rolling stock. By 1857 it decided to produce its own rails as well, constructing an iron foundry and rolling mill in Hamilton. This was the heavy-industry section of the economy. As manufacturing grew and required increasing amounts of capital investment, most of the large firms were relatively recent creations. Some of the old entrepreneurs successfully made the shift from the commercial economy. Many others did not.

The growth of industrialization—the introduction of manufacturing and related commerce on a large scale—inevitably made labour relations an increasingly important issue in British North America. The resource economy had employed large numbers of men on a seasonal basis, offering little opportunity for organization. Industrialization rationalized and stabilized the labour market. Manufacturing tended to be more continuous, and much of it was conducted indoors. Overhead costs encouraged employers to seek a stable and experienced labour force. The rise of a capitalistic labour market stabilized and settled the workers, but did little for their bargaining position. Those with highly developed skills were in the strongest position, and labour organization first developed in industries employing such workers, such as printing. Early trade unions emerged in certain skilled industries in various cities. Such unions almost never had any contact with one another. They could achieve only immediate and localized gains.

Like organization, labour militancy was local and extremely limited. Most industrial action consisted of unsystematic rioting. Employers responded to industrial action of any kind by calling in the police or the military. Before the 1850s there was a tendency for unions to identify with the trade rather than with fellow workers in other trades in other places. The development of industry and the rise of factories employing mechanization brought considerable change to the incipient labour movement. A handful of international unions appeared, either British or American in origin. Unions with several local chapters also organized. Although mechanization encouraged unionization, the impersonality of the factory system created problems for labour, particularly when juveniles and women were drawn into the labour market. These were hard to organize.

WESTWARD

By mid-century there were signs that the vast territory west of the Lakehead would not forever remain the monopoly of the fur trade. There were also signs of Canadian interest in the west, beginning with editorials in the Toronto *Globe* in 1850. One key development in western settlement was the establishment in 1848 of Vancouver Island as a British colony. Until then, Britain had been content to allow the Hudson's Bay Company to act as custodian of all British interests in the west. Earlier the HBC had sent James Douglas (1803–77) from Fort Vancouver (now in the state of Washington) to establish Fort Victoria on Vancouver Island. This was a fall-back position if the Oregon Territory were lost, as it was in 1846. In 1849 Vancouver Island was leased to the company for an annual payment of seven shillings. The HBC would organize the colony there. James Douglas returned to Fort Victoria as chief factor of the company, subsequently becoming its governor in 1851. Settlement on the West Coast was slow. Most newcomers came from the British Isles. They sought to reproduce British gentry conditions on the Pacific Slope.

In 1838 the British government had extended the Hudson's Bay Company monopoly over the west for twenty-one years. A major parliamentary enquiry

Robert Ballantyne Describes Christmas at York Factory

[Robert Ballantyne (1825–94) was born in Edinburgh. In 1841 he joined the service of the Hudson's Bay Company, living and working in Rupert's Land for six years before returning to Scotland. The first of his more than 100 books, mostly for young readers, was the autobiographical *Hudson's Bay; or, Life in the Wilds of North America*. Allowances should be made for what we would now see as his racist language and attitudes; they were common throughout the nineteenth century. *Source*: R. Ballantyne, *Hudson's Bay: or, Everyday Life in the Wilds of North America* (London: T. Nelson and Sons, 1879):192–200.]

I . . . sat down with Mr Wilson to discuss our intended proceedings during the day. These were—firstly, that we should go and pay a ceremonious visit to the men; secondly, that we should breakfast; thirdly, that we should go out to shoot partridges; fourthly, that we should return to dinner at five; and fifthly, that we should give a ball in Bachelors' Hall in the evening, to which were to be invited all the men at the fort, and *all* the Indians, men, women, and children, inhabiting the country for thirty miles around. . . .

Our Christmas dinner was a good one, in a substantial point of view; and a very pleasant one, in a social point of view. We ate it in the winter mess-room; and really (for Hudson Bay) this was quite a snug and highly decorated apartment. True, there was no carpet on the floor, and the chairs were home-made; but then the table was mahogany, and the walls were hung round with several large engravings in bird's-eye maple frames. . . .On the present grand occasion the mess-room was illuminated by an argand lamp, and the table covered with a snow-white cloth, whereon reposed a platter containing a beautiful, fat, plump wild-goose, which had a sort of come-eat-me-up-quick-else-I'll-melt expression about it that was painfully delicious. Opposite to this smoked a huge roast of beef, to procure which one of our most useless draught oxen had been sacrificed. This, with a dozen of white partridges, and a large piece of salt pork, composed our dinner. But the greatest rarities on the board were two large decanters of port wine, and two smaller ones of Madeira. These were flanked by tumblers and glasses; and truly, upon the whole, our dinner made a goodly show.

Just as we had reached the . . . climax, the sound of a fiddle struck upon our ears, and reminded us that our guests who had been invited to the ball were ready; so, emptying our glasses, we

took place in 1857 before the government decided its policy. The enquiry's report was not very favourable to the HBC. It acknowledged 'the desire of our Canadian fellow-subjects that the means of extension and regular settlement should be afforded to them over a portion of this territory' (quoted in Bumsted 1969:220). It recommended that the HBC cease to control Vancouver Island. It also encouraged the annexation to Canada of the districts on the Red River and the Saskatchewan River. At the same time, the report maintained that for much

left the dining-room, and adjourned to the hall. Here a scene of the oddest description presented itself. The room was lit up by means of a number of tallow candles, stuck in tin sconces round the walls. On benches and chairs sat the Orkneymen and Canadian half-breeds of the establishment, in their Sunday jackets and capotes; while here and there the dark visage of an Indian peered out from among their white ones. But round the stove—which had been removed to one side to leave space for the dancers—the strangest group was collected. Squatting down on the floor, in every ungraceful attitude imaginable, sat about a dozen Indian women, dressed in printed calico gowns, the chief peculiarity of which was the immense size of the balloon-shaped sleeves, and the extreme scantiness, both in length and width, of the skirts. . . . On a chair, in a corner near the stove, sat a young, good-looking Indian, with a fiddle of his own making beside him. This was our Paganini; and beside him sat an Indian boy with a kettle-drum, on which he tapped occasionally, as if anxious that the ball should begin.

. . . .[W]e each chose partners, the fiddle struck up, and the ball began. Scotch reels were the only dances known by the majority of the guests, so we confined ourselves entirely to them. . . . Between eleven and twelve o'clock our two tables were put together, and spread with several towels; thus forming a pretty respectable supper-table, which would have been perfect, had not the one part been three inches higher than the other. On it was placed a huge dish of cold venison, and a monstrous iron kettle of tea. This, with sugar, bread, and a lump of salt butter, completed the entertainment. . . . After all were satisfied, the guests departed in a state of great happiness. . . .

In consequence of the breathing of so many people in so small a room for such a length of time, the walls had become quite damp, and ere the guests departed, moisture was trickling down in many places. During the night this moisture was frozen, and on rising the following morning, I found, to my astonishment, that Bachelors' Hall was apparently converted into a palace of crystal. The walls and ceilings were thickly coated with beautiful minute crystallized flowers, not sticking flat upon them, but projecting outwards in various directions, thus giving the whole apartment a cheerful, light appearance, quite indescribable. The moment our stove was heated, however, the crystals became fluid, and ere long evaporated, leaving the walls exposed in all their original dinginess.

of the west, the continuation of the trading monopoly of the company was desirable and appropriate. While the British Parliament was considering the future of the west, two scientific expeditions (one British and one Canadian) set out in 1857 to investigate the region first-hand. The leader of the British expedition was an Irishman, Captain John Palliser (1817–87). The Canadian Exploring Expedition was under the titular command of George Gladman (1800–63), assisted by Simon James Dawson (1820–1902) and Henry Youle

A Letter from the Cariboo Gold Fields

[Anson Armstrong, in Williams Lake, BC, wrote to James Thomson on 24 February 1863. *Source*: R.A. Preston, ed., *For Friends at Home: A Scottish Emigrant's Letters from Canada, California and the Cariboo 1844–1864* (Montreal and London: McGill-Queen's University Press, 1974):328–31.]

Lake Valley Ranch Feb 24th 1863
Dear Thomson,

I received your kind letter you sent me from Victoria Nov 21st by Frank the dutchman that sawed here last summer, and I was almost over joyed in receiving it as I had not heard anything from you or any of the Boys since I got the letter you sent me from Spences Camp. I received it about 10th Dec. The one from Victoria 10th Feb. You stated that you intended leaving for home the first vessel & I suppose it is well you did for there has been very hard times there this winter. There has a few men come up already and they say there is about 2000 Strapt men there now & how they are going to get to the mines I cannot tell unless by begging like some that have come up already. I suppose you hear some most fearful exciting accounts about the mines by this time for there has very exciting accounts gone down & have been printed in the Colonist & of course they have reached Canada ere this and will no doubt cause another great excitement like last year. It is true there has been a great amount of gold taken down this winter, but it has all come out of three or four claims & those Claims have been working all winter. The Claims that have paid so well is the Black Jack Tunnel the Canadian Claim & one or two more. There has different parties gone down this winter with from two or three hundred lbs weight of gold that came out of those rich Claims. Now these stories will be published all through Canada & people will think of course that the whole of Cariboo is just as rich. It is true that Williams Creek is supposed to be the richest creek ever

Hind (1823–1908). The findings of both these expeditions helped to end the public perception of this vast region as utterly unfit for human habitation. Both published reports acknowledged the great agricultural potentiality of the west, once opened by a railway.

Meanwhile on the West Coast, sheer serendipity brought the region to the attention of the world. In 1857 the discovery of gold on the mainland, along the Thompson and Fraser rivers, brought fortune-hunters scurrying from around the world. The amount of gold easily available was quite small by earlier California standards. The ensuing rush was a pale imitation of the American one. Nevertheless, hundreds of miners, mainly from California, made their way to the Fraser River in the interior of British Columbia in the spring of 1858. The quiet village of Victoria was transformed overnight into a major port. South of

discovered in the world but that is not going to help those that have not Claims there for it is all claimed now & there will be a great many who has claims there that will be much disappointed next season, who think they have struck it just as big as those others, but they or no person else can tell what is under the ground.... Provisions is just as high this winter as last, and it is supposed that they will be just as high next summer as they were last. Flour is selling in the mines now for $1 per lb. bacon 1.50 Beans c90 & other things in proportion. Well, Thomson, I have put in a very lonesome time of it this winter, here all alone from morning till noon & from noon until night in this great big house & I have not been more than fifty rods away from it for over two months. Whilst here alone I often get thinking about the boys and wish some of them would come along and I often go to the window at the lower end of the house to see if some of them are coming, but I have looked & looked again in vain. I can see nothing but mountains on every side but still winter will soon be gone and summer will come again. And though I am here all alone

through the day, I can enjoy myself much better than in the evenings when the other Boys are here for it is very unpleasant to sit & talk or listen to them talking when every other word is an oath. You know what the people in this country are for swareing. There is only two stopping here besides Bill & myself & they were both strangers to me. They are clever enough men only very wicked & sware. I think I could enjoy myself if I could have the priviledge of sitting and chatting with my old friends, for an hour or two once in a while or the chance of hearing a good sermon.... I hope you had a pleasant passage home, found Mary and your little pets all well and all the rest of the folks at home & may you long live to enjoy the Comforts of home friends & society which I am deprived of. May God bless us all & if we are never permitted to meet again at home, May we all meet in a home in Glory.

Ever pray for me, From your Affect. Brother

Anson

the 49th parallel, talk of American annexation spread rapidly. The British government rushed legislation putting New Caledonia under the direct jurisdiction of the Crown. The mainland colony of British Columbia came into formal existence on 2 August 1858, with James Douglas as governor. The two colonies were initially administratively separate. The miners, however rough in appearance, were not really badly behaved and accepted British authority readily enough.

Most of the gold required proper machinery and capital expenditure to extract. Many of the gold seekers found employment in other ways, taking advantage of the developmental spin-off from the rush. The discovery of gold irreversibly altered life for the indigenous peoples of the Pacific Slope. Even remote regions could contain great mineral wealth. The settlers and the government

The Aurora Gold Mine, Williams Creek, BC, 15 August 1867, photographed by Frederick Dally. Dally arrived in Victoria in 1862 and became a photographer in 1866, documenting the Native peoples and life in the goldfields. He left Victoria in 1870 and eventually returned to England (Metropolitan Toronto Reference Library T14321).

ignored the land claims of indigenous peoples in the rush to exploit the land itself. Few settlers disagreed with the view that the 'indolent, contented savage, must give place to the busteling [*sic*] sons of civilization & Toil' (quoted in Fisher 1977:105). For Native peoples the result was a very serious cultural disruption, recovery from which would be extraordinarily difficult, if not even impossible.

The Fraser River gold rush presaged a new element in the resource economy of British North America: exploitation of the rich mineral wealth of the northern part of the continent. New technologies provided a constantly expanding market for British North America's mineral wealth. They also brought new means of extracting it from the ground. By the 1850s copper ore was being mined along Lake Superior, and petroleum was discovered in southwestern Ontario in 1855. Production of crude oil in Canada by 1863 ran to 100,000 barrels a year. Unlike timbering, mineral production tended to be extremely capital intensive, requiring specialized scientific knowledge. Until the twentieth century, production involved only a few minerals well located for outward transportation in bulk. Coal seams on both coasts were obvious targets. The continent's burgeoning industrialization would demand ever larger quantities of minerals, and the future potential was indisputable.

RESPONSIBLE GOVERNMENT AND THE REORIENTATION OF POLITICS

The British government gradually resolved the constitutional problems of the commercial period in British North America over the decade following the unification of Upper and Lower Canada in July 1840. Legislative union did not by itself satisfy Lord Durham's other major recommendation for Canada, the right of the assembly to decide policy and its implementation through control of 'the persons by whom that policy was to be administered' (quoted in Craig 1963:141). Part of the problem was that nobody at the time understood the importance of political parties or how they could work in responsible government. Colonial governors served as party brokers rather than conceding responsible government. Finally in 1848 the governor of Canada, Lord Elgin (1811–63), called upon the leaders of the Reform parties, recently successful at the polls, to form a ministry. Louis La Fontaine (1807–64) and Robert Baldwin (1804–58) had allied their respective parties in 1842 on a Reform platform. In placing himself, as a representative of the Crown, above party politics and leaving government in the hands of leaders selected by their parties, Lord Elgin inaugurated responsible government in the Province of Canada.

The victory of responsible government in Canada did not begin the story nor end it, however. Nova Scotia—where Joseph Howe had been agitating for responsible government as a Reformer since 1836—finally achieved it after an election on 5 August 1847, which focused on that single issue. The Reformers were victorious, and when a Reform administration took office in late January 1848, the province became the first colony to achieve responsible government. Prince Edward Island acquired responsible government in 1851 and New Brunswick in 1854. A British attempt at alternative constitutional arrangements complicated the situation in Newfoundland. In 1842 Britain gave the colony a legislature composed partly of elected and partly of appointed members, thus amalgamating the old council and assembly into one body. The experiment was not popular and never had a proper chance to work. The older Constitution returned in 1848. Newfoundlanders immediately began agitating for 'a form of Government. . . with a departmental Government and Executive Responsibility similar in character to that form lately yielded to. . . Nova Scotia' (quoted in Gunn 1966:315). The British reluctantly gave in to this demand in 1855.

The lower provinces, even including Newfoundland, were sufficiently homogeneous to be able to live with a two-party system. Canada was not so fortunate. It could and did create four parties. The Reform alliance of Baldwin and La Fontaine was largely illusory. It quickly transpired that Canada East (the unofficial designation for the former Lower Canada) had slipped back into old voting patterns removed from Reform. The principle of governing by a coalition from each of the two sections of the united province, was inherently unstable. By the mid-1840s the French had become enamoured of the principle

George Brown

George Brown (1818–80) was born in Clackmannan, Scotland, and attended school in Edinburgh. He accompanied his father to the United States in 1837 and to Canada in 1843. They established the Toronto *Globe* in 1844. By 1853 the paper, the semiofficial mouthpiece for the Liberal Party, became a daily with the greatest circulation in British North America.

Brown first ran for Parliament in 1851, losing to William Lyon Mackenzie. By this time, he was the leader of the Clear Grit faction of the Liberals, committed to democratic political reform, voluntary churches unconnected with the state, reciprocal trade, and non-sectarian public education. He soon added 'rep by pop' to the platform, and, after 1856, the expansion of Canada by annexing the northwest.

In 1864 he joined the Great Coalition committed to a British North

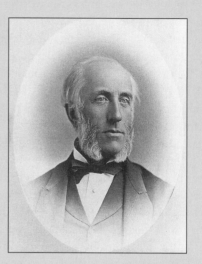

American federal union. He took little part in the government of the new country after 1867. In 1880 he was shot in the leg by an irate employee and died of an infection from the wound (National Archives of Canada C-6165).

of the 'double majority', in which the province would be governed by an assembly majority in each of its two main sections. Such an arrangement naturally appealed to French Canada's growing sense of nationality. It also required the parallel growth of political parties in the two sections. Two factors emerged to complicate matters for the Province of Canada.

One was the rise of a new political movement in Canada West at the end of the 1840s. A radical Reform group known as the Clear Grits, with whom the moderate Reformers gradually merged, appeared under the leadership of George Brown (1818–80). Centred in the western districts, the Grits were the heirs of William Lyon Mackenzie rather than Robert Baldwin. They were democrats, populists, geographical expansionists, and opponents of close connections between church and state in a Protestant rather than a true secularist sense. Furthermore—and ominously—they were hostile to French Canada in traditional anglophone ways. In 1840, when the population of Canada East had been greater than that of Canada West, each section of united

Canada got forty seats in Parliament. When the census of 1851 showed that the population of the anglophone section was growing more rapidly, George Brown adopted 'representation by population'—'rep by pop'—as a campaign slogan when he stood as an independent Reformer in the general election of that year. He won easily. 'Rep by pop' came to epitomize the brassy reformism of the Clear Grits.

The growing pressures of the Grits contributed to, but did not by themselves produce, the second development of the 1850s. This was the gradual withdrawal of French Canada into its own agenda, centred on the development of nationalist pretensions and the preservation of French-Canadian culture and society. The leaders of the Catholic Church took upon themselves the mantle of nationalism. They used the Grits to separate nationalism from reform. In the context of Canada West, the Grit espousal of 'voluntaryism'—the separation of church and state—was directed chiefly against the Anglican Church. Such ultra-Protestantism had even more implications for the Catholic Church. Voluntaryism was not quite the same as secularism. The voluntaryists sought to free the state from 'religious privilege', but could contemplate with equanimity the passage of legislation controlling the availability of alcoholic beverages during the sabbath (which they held sacrosanct). While God might not be eligible to hold land and or be exempt from taxation, he could be used to justify state intrusions in matters of morality. Such principles were very much at odds with French-Canadian religious nationalists. The result was an alliance between them and the Upper Canadian opponents of the Grits.

The rise of denominational divisions as major factors in politics was not confined to the Canadas, although the sectional situation—Roman Catholicism in Canada East and evangelical Protestantism in Canada West— gave such matters a special edge in that province. To a considerable extent, denominational politics reflected the growing democratization of the political process. As the interest, involvement, and size of the electorate grew, politicians turned to issues that appealed to the voter. Denominations also reflected ethnic background and regional strengths. Infighting among religious denominations constantly tussling for advantage transferred easily into the political arena. In Nova Scotia such struggles had occurred for years over the creation of institutions of higher learning. No denomination could allow another an educational edge, and the result was a series of college and university creations, one for each major denomination (and one for each ethnic branch of Catholicism in the province). By the 1850s the venue for denominational disagreements had shifted to public education. In Prince Edward Island the question began over Bible reading in the schools, a practice pressed by the evangelical Protestants and opposed by the Roman Catholics. The 'Bible Question' helped realign island politics as Catholics and liberal Protestants, backed by the old Tories,

The Victorian era was quite fond of graphic illustrations of progress. These woodcuts of improvement in schoolhouses, as illustrated in H.Y. Hind's *The Dominion of Canada: Containing a Historical Sketch of the Preliminaries and Organization of Confederation* (1869), are typical of the approach.

John A. Macdonald

John A. Macdonald (1815–91) was another Scots-born politician, perhaps the most famous Canadian of the nineteenth century. Born near Glasgow, he came with his family to Upper Canada in 1820, where they settled first at Kingston and then at Hay Bay, Adolphustown. At age fifteen he was articled to a Kingston lawyer, and opened a branch office of the firm at Napanee in 1832. He soon became a prominent Kingston lawyer, involved mainly in commercial law.

In 1844 he was elected to the Parliament of Canada, and ten years later emerged from a new political coalition—the Liberal-Progressives—as one of its leaders. In 1856 he became copremier of the province with Etienne-Paschal Taché. He led the Canadian drive for a union of British North America, preparing the first draft of the system he defended on various occasions in 1864 and thereafter. He became the new nation's first prime minister, leading a coalition government that gradually returned to its old divisions. He lost office in 1873 through political scandal, but returned in 1878 to lead the nation until his death.

Macdonald's political success could be attributed to his capacity for working with French Canada and to his simultaneous ability to associate himself and his

party with the aspirations and development of the Canadian nation. His enemies charged that he had no principles beyond political survival. His friends told him and themselves that 'You'll never die, John A.' In later years, Macdonald became a legendary figure, noted for his heavy drinking and his wit. This photograph was taken in 1856 (National Archives of Canada C-6512).

joined against evangelical Protestants. By 1858 the principal issue in that year's election was between Protestantism and Romanism, and the result was a Protestant and a Catholic party. In Newfoundland as well, the contending political parties wore denominational as well as ethnic faces, the Liberals backed by the Irish Roman Catholics and the Tories supported by the English Protestants.

In Canada, John A. Macdonald (1815–91), the Scots-born lawyer from Kingston, came gradually to dominate the anglophone Conservatives. Macdonald was not a man to allow abstract principle, such as the double majority, to stand in the way of power. In 1856 he was able to forge a new coalition among the moderate (some said very pragmatic) Tories whom he led and the *Bleus* of French Canada, led after 1859 by George-Étienne Cartier (1814–73). This alliance enabled the Tories to remain in power despite Grit victories in Canada West. It also led George Brown's *Globe* to comment in August of 1856 that 'If Upper and Lower Canada cannot be made to agree, a federal union of all the provinces will probably be the result.' By 1863 most of Canada's leading politicians had come to concur with the need for some other form of union.

VICTORIAN SOCIETY

The relationship between political unification and social change was a complicated one. There were some obvious connections, however. Two major themes dominated the society of these years. First, there was an unmistakable sense of geographical movement, mainly out of the older and more settled rural districts. Secondly, the class structure of society began to take shape and even solidify. The chief changes were the appearance of a new business class, the emergence of a working class associated with urbanization and industrialization, and the rapid professionalization of certain educated and skilled segments of the middle class. Along with the development of social classes went a concurrent strengthening of certain caste lines associated with class but not identical with it.

Throughout the 1840s and 1850s British immigration to North America continued at high levels. Driving immigration were the potato famines in Ireland, which peaked in 1846. Between 1840 and 1860 well over 600,000 British immigrants arrived in British North America, most of them seeking land on which to build a new life. Combined with the natural population increase within the colonies, the arrival of this horde of new settlers put enormous pressure on available agricultural land, particularly land suitable for staple crop farming for the market. Second-generation farmers accepted less desirable land or moved to the United States, where a more rapid industrialization than in British North America had created new employment and where the west was open to settlement. Thus, at the same time that thousands of land-hungry immigrants were moving in, thousands of disillusioned members of the younger generation within the colonies were moving out.

The first sign of serious out-migration had come from the seigneurial districts of French Canada, the heartland of French-Canadian culture, language, and religion. Almost any opportunity was superior to a future on a farm of less than 100 acres (40 ha) of worn-out land. As early as the 1830s more than 40,000 left Lower Canada for the United States, and that figure jumped to 90,000 in the 1840s and 190,000 in the 1850s. One clergyman called this population loss the cemetery of the race. The visitor to New England can still see

Choosing a Career in Lower Canada in the 1860s

[In the mid-1860s, Quebec novelist Antoine Gérin-Lajoie (1824–82) published his two-volume novel, *Jean Rivard*, the volumes subtitled *Le Défricheur* (1862) and *L'Economiste* (1864). One of the most popular French-Canadian novels of the nineteenth century, it was reprinted seven times before the close of the century. Its theme was the virtue of agricultural settlement in the uninhabited regions of Quebec. In the following excerpt, his *curé* advises Jean Rivard on a career. The priest begins by commenting on Rivard's preference for the law. *Source*: A. Gérin-Lajoie, *Jean Rivard*, translated by Vida Bruce (Toronto: McClelland and Stewart, 1977):23–5.]

'. . . You admit that in taking up this career, like all your colleagues you have hopes of making money. You may be right. You could be one of the privileged few, even though you yourself admit you possess neither the assurance nor the facility of expression which make outstanding lawyers. But there is an easy way to enlighten yourself on the subject. Take a list of the lawyers admitted to the various bars of Lower Canada in the last twenty years and see what proportion of them live exclusively from the exercise of their profession. I don't think I am mistaken in saying you will find that barely a quarter of them do. The other three quarters, after waiting for several years for a clientele that never appears, withdraw in discouragement. Some throw themselves into journalism, others into business or speculations of a more or less legal character. Some look for jobs in a public office, others hide their disappointment abroad. Large numbers remain as burdens to their relatives or their friends. Others, steeped in disgust and boredom, slide into habits of dissipation and come to a bad end. . . . [It] is scarcely possible for a young man without funds to study the profession adequately or to acquire a clientele afterwards, unless he has patrons. . . . '

'And finally my child,' added the good priest, 'there is another point that doesn't concern you much at your age

standing, usually empty and forlorn, the extensive brick buildings that housed the nineteenth-century factories employing these migrants. Thousands of French Canadians also moved into the Eastern Townships of Canada East, originally intended as anglophone enclaves. In the Upper St Francis district of the Eastern Townships, for example, the francophone population grew from 9.7 per cent of the district in 1844 to 64.1 per cent by 1871. Others continued to fill up unpopulated regions in the Laurentians and around Lac St-Jean. State and church both promoted colonization of these regions as an alternative to migration to the United States. As well as moving out of the country or into new districts, thousands of French Canadians moved into the cities and expanding towns of the province where they often found employment as manufacturing workers. In Montreal especially, many of the newcomers were female. Some found employment as domestic servants, but most worked in a few burgeoning

but that seems to me more important than all the others, and that is that life in the city exposes you to all sorts of dangers. Of the great numbers of young people who go there to study the professions or to learn business, very few can save themselves from the contagion of vice. They let themselves be influenced by the flood of bad example. In big cities, you see, men are separated, so to speak, from nature. Living surrounded by their own works distances them from the thought of God. If they could, like us, admire each day the wonders of creation, perhaps they would be lifted up in spite of themselves toward the Author of all things; and cupidity, vanity, ambition, all the vices that torment them would no longer have such a hold on their hearts. . . .

'However, after long deliberation and after having made this question the subject of my meditations for many years, I have come to the conclusion that the most natural and effective way to neutralize the evil, if not to stop it completely, is to encourage our educated youth, in any and every way, to take up an agricultural career.

'In my opinion that is the surest way to increase our general prosperity while assuring the welfare of individuals, and the best way to call attention to the high regard this class of people, the most numerous in our population, should enjoy in every land. I don't need to repeat to you all that has been said on the nobility and usefulness of this profession. But just consult for a moment the experts who have been busy searching for the causes of the prosperity of nations. You will see that they all agree in saying that agriculture is the primary source of enduring wealth. It offers more advantages than any other employment. It favours the development of the intellect more than any other industry. It gives rise to manufactures of all kinds. It is, in short, the mother of national prosperity and the only truly independent occupation for individuals. The farmer who lives from his work can right say that "he knows only God for master."'

industries, particularly clothing manufacture, textile production, and the making of tobacco products.

In Canada West, most of the movement into the United States before 1870 was into the rich agricultural districts of the American Midwest, and beyond. A constant stream of Canadians made their way across Ohio, Indiana, and Illinois onto the American prairies, contributing to the rapid settlement of states such as Minnesota and the Dakotas. A key factor driving the migrants was the ultimate inability of the family farm to accommodate the needs of all family members. Successful farming required numbers of children, but the resultant large families created pressures for the expansion of landholdings and eventually led to the removal of some of the younger generation. In this male-dominated society, only males normally had expectations of inheritance, hence the tendency in all British North American rural society to throw off a disproportionate number of

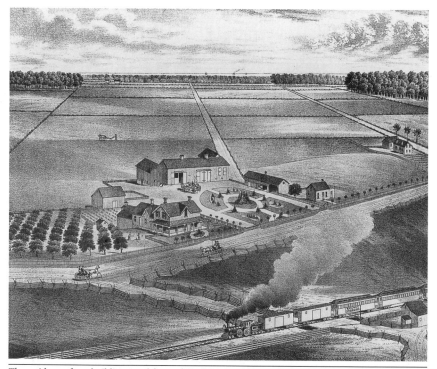

The residence, farm buildings, and farm of Hugh McQuoid in Durham County, near the Bay of Quinte on the north shore of Lake Ontario, 1878. The drawing appeared in one of twenty-nine county atlases (on Northumberland and Durham), published in Ontario between 1875 and 1881, containing maps, biographies of residents, and illustrations of their properties (for which they presumably paid), and offering a vivid, if idealized, glimpse of rural life at the time. The railway is the Great Western (Metropolitan Toronto Reference Library).

females (usually between the ages of fifteen and twenty-one) into the cities and non-agricultural employment. Some farms in some districts were more divisible than others, but the pressures on the younger members of the next generation to seek their fortunes elsewhere was always strong. Elder sons (and the women they married) could look forward to becoming pillars of and local leaders in their community. For most of the children of most farmers, however, coming of age meant moving on. Some new land within Canada West was available to the north. Settlement after mid-century moved rapidly up to Georgian Bay and into the Muskoka country, heedless of the prominent outcroppings of the Canadian Shield. For most who chose to remain in Canada West, however, cities and towns were the obvious destination.

The years before 1860 were ones of considerable internal expansion in the Atlantic region. Settlers moved onto less desirable and more remote lands, while others moved into the major urban centres. Population growth rates continued to be extremely high despite decreasing immigration, although they had ominously begun to decline for Nova Scotia as early as the 1850s. By the end of that decade, very few of the older settled districts could support their natural increases in population, much less sustain incoming immigrants. In Newfoundland, for example, there was considerable movement into the largely unsettled western part of the island, and a vast increase in a seasonal migration into the Labrador fisheries; in some outports over two-thirds of the working males became seasonal workers in Labrador. Neither expansion nor seasonal migration could, in the end, accommodate the growing population. Many began to turn to out-migration, often to the United States. By the 1860s over one-third of the counties in the Maritime provinces were experiencing population losses. The correlation between rural counties (with economies largely dependent on fishing and farming) and depopulation was very high. While out-migration was a general phenomenon, Scots and Irish were overrepresented in the exodus and Acadians underrepresented. Most of those departing were between the ages of fifteen and twenty-five.

Most British North Americans uprooted themselves at least once. Many a British North American was constantly on the move. Wilson Benson, an immigrant of the 1830s, tells the story in his autobiography. Beginning in Ireland at age fifteen, Benson changed his district of residence eleven times (six times in Ireland and Scotland between 1836 and 1838 and five times in Canada West between 1838 and 1851) before finally settling on a farm in Grey County in 1851 at age thirty. He bought the farm not with his savings but with an inheritance from Ireland. Benson had changed jobs twenty-nine times in those years, and apprenticed to at least six different trades in the 1830s and 1840s before finally settling down to farming. In his later years, he also kept a store in his community. On the whole, transients like Wilson Benson were not economically successful. In both urban Hamilton and in rural Peel County, Upper Canada, there was a remarkable correlation between transiency and poverty. Whether such people failed because they were continually on the move, or constantly moved in search of a better life they never found, is debatable. So too is the question of whether their failure was so deep-rooted as to be transmittable to their children. In any case, the success stories (at least measured in terms of wealth) usually involved those who remained more or less permanently in one place.

Rural overpopulation produced migrants who would settle and tame undeveloped regions, as well as those who would provide a labour force for industrialization. While the farming pioneers remained small-scale commodity producers indeterminately related to the class structure, the urbanized workforce swiftly turned into a landless working class. At the other end of the scale, merchants turned into bankers, financiers, and industrialists, and became far wealthier. Over the middle decades of the nineteenth century, the older

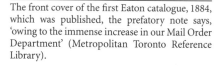

The front cover of the first Eaton catalogue, 1884, which was published, the prefatory note says, 'owing to the immense increase in our Mail Order Department' (Metropolitan Toronto Reference Library).

social structure of élites and non-élites disappeared, to be replaced by one far more clearly stratified.

Successful businessmen were highly esteemed in the era of economic transformation, achieving their high status partly by self-ascription and partly by their acknowledged economic and political power. Nowhere was the power more evident than at the municipal level, where businessmen formed a mutually supportive coterie that took the lead in all aspects of life in the city, including its development and land market. Most business leaders in this period were self-made men, not in the sense that they had risen from rags to riches, but in that they had achieved their position in the community by their own efforts. Scots were overrepresented in business ranks, where Protestantism predominated. The new wealth was in finance and manufacturing. The wealthier business leaders of Montreal and Toronto began to adopt extravagant lifestyles that were in many respects comparable to those of their American counterparts.

As Canadian cities began the shift from commercial entrepôts to industrial and financial centres, they already contained significant inequalities in terms of wealth and income. In Hamilton, for example, the most affluent 10 per cent of the city held 88 per cent of its propertied wealth, drew nearly half its income, and controlled about 60 per cent of its wealth. On the other hand, the poorest 40 per cent earned only about 1 per cent of the city's total income and controlled about 6 per cent of its total wealth. Nevertheless, rich and poor in Hamilton lived in close proximity to each other. Only as cities grew larger and developed an expanding middle class that could afford to move out of the

Table 5.3

Schedule of the Course of Study, University of Toronto, 1868

Matriculation:
Xenophon's Anabasis, book i.
Sallust's Catilina
Virgil's Aeneid, book ii.
Latin Prose Composition

Arithmetic, to end of square root
Algebra, first four rules
Euclid, book i.
English Grammar
Outlines of English History

Not including the honour course, which includes option, etc.

Outlines of Roman History, to death of Nero
Grecian History, to death of Alexander
Ancient and Modern Geography

First year
Homer's Iliad, book vi
Lucian's Vita and Charon
Virgil's Aeneid, book vi
Cicero, de Amicitia
Latin Prose Composition
Arithmetic
Algebra
Euclid, books i–vi
Plane Trigonometry
English Composition
English Language and Literature
French Grammar
Montesquieu's Grandeur et Decadence des
    Romaines
Ancient History
British History
Elements of Chemistry
Elements of Physiology
Elements of Botany
Paley's Natural Theology
Paley's Evidences
Second year
Homer's Odyssey, book xi
Demosthenes' Olynthiacs
Horace, Odes
Cicero, two orations
Latin Prose Composition
Statics, Dynamics
English Composition
English Literature
French Composition
La Bruyère Caractères
French Literature
German Grammar
Adler's German Reader
German Literature
German Composition
Schiller's William Tell, etc.
German Literature
Medieval History
British History
Chemistry and Chemical Physics

Mineralogy and Geology
Murray's Logic
Wayland's Moral Philosophy
Locke, books ii, iii, and iv
Third year
Sophocles, Oedipus Rex
Herodotus, book ii
Horace, Satires and Epistles
Livy, book v
Latin Prose Composition
Hydrostatics, Optics
French Composition
Racine's Phédre and Athalie
Bossuet's Oraisons Funèbres
French Literature
German Grammar, etc.
German Composition
Lessing's Minna von Barnhelm
German Literature
Modern History
British History
Chemistry
Comparative Physiology
Vegetable Physiology, etc.
Reid's Intellectual Powers
Stewart's Moral and Active Powers
Whately's Political Economy
Final examination
Euripides, Medea
Thucydides, book vii
Juvenal, sat. iii, vii, viii, and x
Tacitus, Germania and Agricola
Latin Prose Composition
Acoustics, Astronomy
English Composition
English Language and Literature
French Composition
Corneille's Le Cid
De Staël's De l'Allemagne
French Literature
Chemistry, Minerology, Geology, Physical
    Geography, and Meteorology
Smith's Wealth of Nations

Source: H.Y. Hind, *The Dominion of Canada* (Toronto: L. Stebbins, 1868): 463–5.

urban centre and a working class desperate for housing would the industrial city emerge with its clear divisions between rich and poor, and between one economic function and another. In the preindustrial city the role of women and children in the labour force was fairly limited. Industry could and did employ both women and children for some of the simple repetitive tasks that supplemented the machines. Factory owners found that children worked for low wages. Families often insisted that employers take on the entire family, so they would earn enough to live. In the last analysis, the major characteristic of families on the unskilled side of industrialization was their vulnerability to poverty. Not all the working-class poor worked in factories. Opportunities for women were strong at the lower end of the labour force in domestic service, as well as in business and clerical occupations. The mid-Victorian Age saw changes in the retail trade as well as in manufacturing. In 1840 retail establishments were relatively small. By 1870 general merchandising had begun to spawn the department store. The T. Eaton Company was founded in Toronto in 1869.

Between rich and poor, the middle class—although it ranged from small urban merchants to small-town industrialists to well-to-do rural farmers—came increasingly to be anchored by members of the educated professional occupations. Professionals' relative dependability of income tended to set them apart. Guaranteeing that dependability through professionalization was the chief development with the middle classes in this period. The trend was both to increase the number of qualified practitioners through formal education, and then to limit professional practice to those who had met stringent licensing requirements, often set by the occupation itself. The doctors took the lead. An attempt in 1839 to create by legislative enactment a College of Physicians and Surgeons of Upper Canada failed in 1840, although another similar attempt in Canada East in 1847 was more successful. Perhaps significantly, doctors were one of the first groups to organize nationally: the Canadian Medical Association formed in the very year of Confederation. Lawyers engaged in a similar policy, with most provincial law societies formed between 1846 and 1877.

Outside the class structure entirely were the castes, which included women, indigenous peoples, people from Asia, and Blacks (or Negroes, as they were then called). In Victorian Canada women were regarded as the bearers and nurturers of children. Their proper place was to be in the home as wife, helpmate, and mother. Women had few legal rights. A woman could not expect automatically to inherit a deceased husband's property. In most provinces, a husband could sue a wife for divorce on grounds of adultery, but a wife could sue a husband only if he were adulterous and had committed some other heinous offence. The courts expected women to reform violent husbands rather than prosecute them. Mothers had a better chance to rights of guardianship over children if they were unwed. Despite the ideal, many women worked.

The most invisible women workers were the domestic servants. The typical domestic servant in the census of 1871 was female, lived in the house, was young (in her twenties), single, and could both read and write. The highest occupation to which most women could aspire was that of schoolteacher. Actively recruited into the teaching ranks, they then remained at the lower end in terms of both salary and responsibility. There was little opportunity for entrance into the professions. Emily Howard Stowe (1831–1903) obtained a medical degree from the New York Medical College for Women in 1867, but she could not achieve proper accreditation until 1880. The first woman lawyer would not appear until the next century.

Blacks and Chinese joined the indigenous peoples in suffering from widespread racial prejudice and discrimination in British North America. After 1840 governments pressured the indigenous peoples of the settled provinces to become freehold farmers. While governments recognized some Native rights, that alone did not lead to much protection. In 1850 the Canadian Parliament passed legislation that operationally defined who was and who was not an 'Indian' within the meaning of the acts involved. The process of legislating for Natives rapidly escalated after 1850. In 1857 the legislature of Canada passed the Act for the Gradual Civilization of the Indian Tribes in the Canadas. It contained many provisions that ran against the expressed wishes of the Natives.

Chinese construction workers on the CPR in their camp at Kamloops, BC (National Archives of Canada C-2880C).

Canadian policy became not only devoted to removing Natives from the paths of settlement, but doing so by coercion and compulsion if necessary. Most of these policies—which defined Indians, made them citizens when properly educated, and provided for land grants—passed on to the Dominion of Canada from the Province of Canada in 1867.

Few British North Americans believed that the state might ever come to their assistance in times of trouble. For some, politics and government were a source of employment or patronage, but for the average person the government (whether local, provincial, or federal) existed mainly to act as an impartial and somewhat distant umpire. Government mostly affected events outside the citizen's personal experience. Nevertheless, the exodus from older settled districts, with traditional agrarian and resource-oriented economies, into towns and cities demonstrated two points. First, it showed the extent to which the older mercantile economy was unable to support the rate of population growth. Second, it showed the extent to which new economic development was essential. By the 1860s politicians were extremely conscious of the movement of depopulation, particularly to the United States. Territorial expansion westward was one solution. A more sophisticated economy was another. Both seemed to many political leaders across British North America to require new political arrangements.

THE ROAD TO CONFEDERATION

The political problems of the Canadas were the immediate prod for Canadian politicians to begin to explore the possibility of a larger union with the eastern provinces, beginning at the famous Charlottetown Conference of September 1864. Such a solution did not come from midair, however. Politicians had discussed the political unification of the provinces of British North America on and off since the days of the Loyalists. Few of the early proposals were very elaborate. Most gave no consideration to whether the union proposed would result in an independent national state. Most came from Tories concerned with enhancing the power of the Crown or providing a basis for economic development. By the 1850s, however, there was emerging, particularly in the Canadas, some sense of the existence of 'a true Canadian feeling—a feeling of what might be termed Canadian nationality, in contradistinction to a feeling of mere colonial or annexation vassalage', as the Montreal *Pilot* put it on 6 April 1850. Sometimes high-flown rhetoric couched these sentiments. Often economic or cultural protectionism dominated the phraseology, but a new Canadian feeling was growing in power after mid-century. It flourished partly on changing communications technology that made it possible to transmit fast-breaking news across the provinces in moments.

Neither the bind of the double majority nor the beginnings of national sentiment was alone sufficient to propel British North Americans to national

The Charlottetown Conference, September 1864. On the left, Charles Tupper is standing against the first pillar and D'Arcy McGee against the second, with George-Étienne Cartier in front of him; next to Cartier, seated, is John A. Macdonald (National Archives of Canada C-733).

unification. As so often was the case, events in the United States provided the catalyst. The American federal union broke apart with surprising suddenness in 1861. The southern states seceded into their own Confederacy. The American Civil War began. Many Canadians quietly rooted for the Confederacy despite its maintenance of slavery. Britain adopted an official policy of neutrality. The British watched warily while public opinion in the northern states, whipped up by American newspapers, talked openly of finding compensation for the lost Confederacy by annexing British North America.

Britain could hardly leave her North American colonies unprotected. Defending them at great expense was not something the British faced with relish, however. By the 1860s the British ruling classes believed that colonies like British North America would inevitably separate from the mother country. Why not hasten the process and save money? An independent British North America could organize its own defences. In 1864 the military situation in the United States turned more dangerous for British North America, as the Union forces gained clear victories over the Confederacy. In several respects the efforts of the Canadians to create a larger union fitted very well with British desires for reduced colonial responsibility and expense. The full weight of the still-considerable influence of the British colonial system came down on the side of unification.

In Canada the difficulty of agreeing to military mobilization was one of the many factors that led George Brown to propose a political coalition with

Social Life at the Quebec Conference, 1864

[Frances Monck, the wife of Canadian Governor-General Lord Monck's brother Dick, kept a journal during her time in Canada. What follows is her journal account of a ball given on 20 October 1864, in the midst of the Quebec Conference. It offers a somewhat different perspective on some of the delegates. *Source*: W.L. Morton, ed., *Monck Letters and Journals 1863–1868: Canada from Government House at Confederation* (Toronto: McClelland and Stewart, 1970):157–9. Deletions from earlier published versions have been restored within the(/).]

We drove after lunch yesterday to hear the 25th band play on the Esplanade. After dinner, Dick, Captain Pem., and I drove to Madame Tessier's ball in the open waggon. Mr Tessier is the 'orateur' of the Upper House. I opened the ball with him, opposite to Madame and Dick. At French parties there are no fast dances, all quadrilles and lancers; it seems so odd. The R.C. Bishop won't allow 'round' dances. Six of the 25th string band played so well. So many old people I don't think I ever saw, and the older they were the more they danced. No officers but Captain G.D. Webber, 17th and Colonel Hassard, R.E.—they were in uniform, because this is considered an official week. Amongst others I danced with Dr Tupper, Premier of Nova Scotia, and with Honourable Mr Coles, leader of the Opposition in the Parliament of Prince Edward's Island. /I never suffered so in my life from subdued laughing as at this party. The swarms of old people dancing, with white heads!/ Colonel Grey is gentlemanly. I like Dr Tupper. Old Coles /is, I believe a retired butcher, and oh! So vulgar I could not describe him. He is grey haired and red faced, and looks as if his legs were fastened on after the rest of his body, to support his fat. He /asked to be introduced to me, and when I said we were going away, he got introduced to Dick, and said to me, 'Silence means assent, so come and dance.' He does steps, and gives you his hand with a bow of the head and a shake of the

his enemies. The understanding rested on a commitment to a British American federal union. This Great Coalition—a ministry formed by a union of the Conservatives under Macdonald and the *Bleus* under Cartier, with the Grits led by Brown, announced in the Canadian Parliament on 22 June 1864—broke the political deadlock. The new government moved on a variety of fronts over the summer of 1864. Most important was to prepare the outlines of federal union for a conference of Maritime delegates called at Charlottetown in September to discuss Maritime union. The maritime region contained a good deal of abstract support for unification with Canada, tempered by two realities: any Maritime participation in a larger union must not work to the disadvantage of the provinces, and a strong feeling that the Maritimes were doing pretty well within the existing imperial structure.

body. /I shall not cry when these delegates are gone; it is a bore dancing with them./ He said to me, 'I'm a sort of fellow who talks away and forgets to dance.' /Then he told me 'has'ow my daughter is ill. What with the ship, and going to see an Indian encampment, she has diptheria.' He said 'as 'ow' so often, and 'harrd' for hard./ He said, 'We *gentlemen* don't know how to decide between Mrs Dundas and Lady M.— they are both so pretty and nice.' /I bore him pretty well, till I spied Capt. Pem. Staring at me with a broad grin on his face, and then I broke down and laughed aloud. He never seemed to think I was laughing at him. The new M.P.P.'s wife, Madame Gingras, amused me not a little. Her husband is going to make our sleigh: he is a coachmaker. She looks so vulgar; she wore a feather *in* her eye, and held her very short dress (when she danced) with her first finger and thumb, her other fingers held apart from each other. I could not at first find out who she was, and I asked all Coles, who said, 'I can't remember these Canadian ladies' names, what with their gingrans and gingrasses; but I'll remember *your* name, for it's well known of course.' I had a broad smile all night long on my face, by the way of being so happy, but really to hide my sufferings of restrained laughter. John A. Macdonald is always drunk now, I am sorry to say, and when some one went to his room the other night, they found him in his night shirt, with a railway rug thrown over him, practising Hamlet before a looking-glass. At the drawing room he said to Mrs Godley he should like to blow up Sir Robert Macdonnell with gunpowder; very unfortunate for this week and last; they wanted all Canadians to appear their best before the delegates. The G.-G. has had a telegram that has fussed him, and he is gone on now the moment after breakfast to Quebec; it is about Confederates and Yankees I believe [the St Albans raid]. The K.O.B. soldiers' theatricals come off tonight for the Canadian Military Asylum (for widows or orphans of soldiers out here). Tomorrow night is the Bachelor's ball, given by six rich bachelors in the Parliament house; they are lumberers and merchants. It is to be 'select'. Their invitation looks like a shop *affiche,* and they have on it 'Quadrilles 9,' which does *not* mean only quadrilles.

Canadian historians have always tended to view the Maritime defence of local interests as parochial. Such an interpretation misses the point. One problem with the Canadian initiative was that Canada was so much bigger and more powerful than the other provinces that almost any union would seem more like annexation than confederation. The Maritimes, moreover, were already part of a larger political and economic system known as the British empire. Having travelled on sailing-ships to the far corners of the world, in many ways the Maritime electorate was far more cosmopolitan than the Canadians themselves. In its own day the case against Confederation was quite reasonable. Unification seemed an impracticable visionary scheme, proposed by politicians in the Province of Canada to meet their needs. It was not necessarily in the best interests of the other colonies.

Considerable ingenuity was required in 1864 to explain to delegates from smaller constituencies how the Canadian proposal really worked to their benefit. The union as finally developed was somewhat different than the one initially proposed. The biggest difference was in the place of the provinces. The Canadians originally intended to create a strong central government by consolidating all the provincial legislatures (and their powers) into one grand Parliament. This procedure of legislative union was how Great Britain had earlier unified Scotland and Ireland. The Canadians granted the need for local governments to deal with local matters. They did not intend those local governments to be fully articulated provincial governments, certainly not provincial governments capable of forming a counterweight to the central federal one. Neither Scotland nor Ireland (after union) had separate political administrations based upon legislatures, although both still had local governments. The Maritime delegates at Charlottetown responded to visions of greatness, fuelled by food, drink, and much convivial conversation. They agreed to the Canadian

John A. Macdonald on Federal Union

[On 11 October 1864 the Quebec Conference opened at the Conference Chamber of Parliament House, Quebec. A month previously the Charlottetown Conference had agreed to the outlines of a union of the provinces. Now the details had to be sorted out. Delegates from Newfoundland, Prince Edward Island, Nova Scotia, and New Brunswick joined delegates from Canada for the sessions. After procedural motions, John A. Macdonald moved 'That the best interests and present and future prosperity of British North America will be promoted by a Federal Union under the Crown of Great Britain, provided such union can be effected on principles just to the several Provinces.' He then spoke to the motion. *Source*: Sir J. Pope, *Memoirs of the Rt Hon. Sir John A. Macdonald*, vol. 1 (Toronto: Oxford University Press 1930):284–6.]

The various States of the adjoining Republic had always acted as separate sovereignties. The New England States, New York State and the Southern States had no sympathies in common. They were thirteen individual sovereignties, quite distinct the one from the other. The primary error at the formation of their constitution was that each state reserved to itself all sovereign rights, save the small portion delegated. We must reverse this process by strengthening the General Government and conferring on the Provincial bodies only such powers as may be required for local purposes. All sectional prejudices and interests can be legislated for by local legislatures. Thus we shall have a strong and lasting government under which we can work out constitutional liberty as opposed to democracy, and be able to protect the minority by having a powerful central government. Great caution, however, is necessary. The people of every section must feel that they are protected, and by no overstraining of central authority should such guarantees

scheme. At the Quebec Conference a month later, many had experienced sober second thoughts.

Prince Edward Island took the lead at Quebec against the Canadian steamroller. The smallest province of British North America, the island had fought annexation to Nova Scotia for almost a century. It found it hard to give up its autonomy to proposals that reflected Canadian dominance. When John A. Macdonald moved that the three sections of British North America—Canada West, Canada East, and the four Atlantic provinces—each have twenty-four members in the Senate, he gave away the game. In the American Senate, each state had two senators regardless of population; in the Canadian Senate, the four smaller provinces would have only one-third of the senators among them. Eventually the Quebec Conference accepted this arrangement, offering Newfoundland an additional four senators. Prince Edward Island also made a big issue—without any success—over getting one more member of the House of Commons (six instead of five) than its population allowed. A further and

be overridden. Our constitution must be based on an Act of the Imperial Parliament, and any question as to overriding sectional matters determined by 'Is it legal or not?' The judicial tribunals of Great Britain would settle any such difficulties should they occur. . . .

A great evil in the United States is that the President is a despot for four years. He is never considered as being the father of his people. It was otherwise with Washington, who did not escape slander. Every President is the leader of a party, and obliged to consider himself as bound to protect the rights of a majority. Under the British Constitution, with the people having always the power in their own hands and with the responsibility of a Ministry to Parliament, we are free from such despotism. These weaknesses in the United States Constitution have not only attracted our attention, but also that of Confederate States, who endeavour to avoid them by having lengthened terms for their President. With them great questions are not settled in committees as in the United States, but they allow Ministers to

appear on the floor of the House to defend their measures. They have cut the wings of the President as leader of a party by providing that no Government employee shall be dismissed without cause—that is, that the right shall not be capriciously exercised. . . .

With respect to the mode of appointments to the Upper House, some of us are in favour of the elective principle. More are in favour of appointment by the Crown. I will keep my own mind open on that point as if it were a new question to me altogether. At present I am in favour of appointment by the Crown. While I do not admit that the elective principle has been a failure in Canada, I think we had better return to the original principle and in the words of Governor Simcoe endeavour to make ours 'an image and transcript of the British Constitution.'

telling debate came over the power of the local governments. The majority case was that Canada's fundamental principle had always been that 'all the powers not given to Local should be reserved to the Federal Government' (quoted in Waite 1962:95). But a number of Atlantic delegates were not happy. The subsequent debate over the Quebec resolution was not over the principle of union but over its terms. While it would be convenient to see the matter of terms as a petty haggling over details, some of the details were fairly important.

Another Canadian principle was legislative sovereignty. 'We the People' would not create this union, as in the United States. Instead, an act of the British Parliament would create Canada. Conveniently enough, this denial of popular sovereignty meant that Confederation did not go before the public in the form of an election, a ratification convention, or a referendum/plebiscite. The public debate did not always understand the niceties of political theory, but critics understood the basic thrust of the proposals well enough. The debate over the Quebec resolutions did affect their interpretation and ultimate implementation, however. While the Canadians had initially intended to reduce the provincial governments to municipal proportions, both French Canada and the Maritimes made clear that the provinces would have to survive relatively intact. The proponents of union in Canada East emphasized that Confederation meant giving French Canadians their own province, with—as the *Courrier de St-Hyacinth* put it in September 1864—the two levels of government both 'sovereign, each within its jurisdiction as clearly defined by the constitution'. An informal adjustment addressed this matter. On the other hand, the opposition fulminated unsuccessfully to the end over the refusal of the proponents of Confederation to take the scheme to the people.

Newspapers, pamphlets, and debates held in the legislatures of each of the provinces discussed the Quebec resolutions. What these demonstrated most of all was the success of the proponents of union in capturing most of the positive ground. Critics could reduce the proposals to rubble, but had little to put in their place. For Canada, the absence of alternatives was particularly striking. The debates also demonstrated that the Quebec resolutions were, on the whole, far more acceptable to Tories than they were to Reformers. Although the debates in the Canadian Parliament were long and long-winded, the ultimate result was approval. The eastern provinces could stand pat, however, and some did. Newfoundland—convinced it would be little more than 'the contemptible fag-end of such a compact' with Canada after an election fought on the question in 1869—remained outside Confederation until 1949. Prince Edward Island felt insufficiently compensated for 'the surrender of a separate Government, with the independent powers it now enjoys'. It would not join until 1873.

The situation in New Brunswick and Nova Scotia was more complex. In the former province, a coalition of opponents to union headed by A.J. Smith (1822–83) blew away the pro-Confederation government of Samuel Leonard Tilley (1818–96) in an 1865 election. A year later another election was held against the background of threatened invasion by thousands of Irish nationalists (the Fenians), many of them veterans of the American Union army who had kept their arms when disbanded. The threat was sufficient to return Tilley to office. The new administration moved an address favouring Confederation, not, it must be noted, as embodied in the Quebec resolutions but 'upon such terms as will secure the just rights and interests of New Brunswick, accompanied with provision for the immediate construction of the Intercolonial Railway'. When this motion carried, opposition disappeared.

In Nova Scotia, which owned 1 ton of sailing ship for each of its 350,000 inhabitants, there was much concerted opposition to union. Joseph Howe led the opponents of Confederation. He attacked the union's Canadian origins from the vantage point of someone perfectly content with the British empire. Confederation smacked too much of Canadian self-interest. It gave Upper Canada rep by pop, Lower Canada provincial autonomy, and offered nothing to Nova Scotia. The Nova Scotia legislature never did approve the Quebec resolutions. The government, led by Charles Tupper (1821–1915), introduced a motion calling for a 'scheme of union' in which 'the rights and interests of Nova Scotia' would be ensured (quoted in Pryke 1979:27). It passed thirty-one to nineteen. Unlike the situation in New Brunswick, the opponents of Confederation in Nova Scotia did not melt away. They eventually went on to elect full slates of candidates provincially and federally that promised to take Nova Scotia out of the union in which it had become involved.

Although neither Nova Scotia nor New Brunswick ever actually approved the Quebec resolutions, which all but the most ardent unionists recognized would consign the smaller provinces to national impotence, the basic fundamentals of Quebec were what became the new Constitution. Small wonder that the region later complained about the deal it had made. In November 1866 delegates from Canada, Nova Scotia, and New Brunswick met in London to work out the final details, essentially the Quebec resolutions with more money for the Maritimes and the Intercolonial Railway. All agreed the name of the new country should be that of its principal progenitor, thus openly declaring the primacy of Canada in the arrangement and causing confusion ever afterwards for students of Canadian history. The resulting legislation, the British North America Act, passed quickly through the British Parliament in 1867. The MPs barely looked up from the order paper as they voted. The Queen signed the bill into law on 29 March 1867, with the date of proclamation 1 July. Governor-

General Lord Monck (1819–94) called upon John A. Macdonald, the man everyone most closely associated with the union, to be the first prime minister.

On the morning of 1 July—a day of celebration and military parades in all four provinces—the new country was proclaimed in the recently completed Parliament buildings in Ottawa. Macdonald received a knighthood. The ceremonial launching of the new nation did not, however, guarantee its success. Much work was still needed to make Canada work.

Major Events, 1867–1885

1867 British Columbia's legislative council resolves that the province be allowed eventual admission into Canada, which officially comes into existence on 1 July 1867 under an all-party government headed by Sir John A. Macdonald. Resolutions for territorial expansion are passed by Canadian Parliament in December. Americans purchase Alaska from Russia.

1868 Canada First is founded in Ottawa. Five hundred and seven Zouaves are recruited in Quebec for papal army.

1869 Resistance to Canada, led by Louis Riel, begins in Red River. Newfoundland election produces an anticonfederate assembly.

1870 Louis Riel executes Thomas Scott. The Manitoba Act is passed by Canadian Parliament. The Wolseley Expedition is sent to Red River. Negotiations are begun with British Columbia for admission to Canada. Dominion Notes Act of 1870 is passed.

1871 British Columbia enters Confederation on 20 July 1871. The Washington Treaty is signed with the United States. The Bank Act of 1871 is passed.

1872 In a federal election, Conservatives win 103 to ninety-seven Liberals. Ontario Society of Artists is formed.

1873 Prince Edward Island enters Confederation. The Macdonald government resigns over the Pacific Scandal. Liberals under Alexander Mackenzie take over.

1874 Liberals win a clear majority in Parliament (133 to seventy-three) over Conservatives.

1875 Woman's Christian Temperance Union is founded in Picton, Ontario. Joseph Guibord is finally buried in Roman Catholic cemetery in Montreal.

1876 Intercolonial Railway is completed, linking Saint John, Halifax, and Montreal. Alexander Graham Bell invents a workable telephone. The first wheat is exported from Manitoba.

1877 Saint John fire leaves 13,000 homeless.

1878 Conservatives elected, 137 to sixty-nine Liberals. Sir John A. Macdonald returns as prime minister.

1880 Royal Canadian Academy of Arts is formed. Canadian government signs a contract with Canadian Pacific Railway.

1881 CPR reaches Winnipeg. The boundaries of Manitoba are expanded.

1882 Royal Society of Canada is formed. Conservatives are re-elected, 139 to seventy-one Liberals, now led by Edward Blake. Macdonald remains prime minister.

1883 CPR construction crews discover nickel near Sudbury, Ontario. Canadian Labour Congress is founded.

1884 Louis Riel returns to Canada.

1885 The second Riel resistance (the North West Rebellion) is crushed. Riel is executed. The last spike is driven in the Canadian Pacific Railway.

6
Expanding the Nation, 1867–1885

✿

Although 1 July 1867 would be celebrated a century later as the date for Canada's 100th birthday, it was in the larger sense only an interim point. The new union consisted of four provinces—Ontario, Quebec, Nova Scotia, and New Brunswick—carved from the three that had created it. Sir John A. Macdonald's government was conscious that a lot of British territory on the continent had been excluded. The new government was also quite obviously the old Canadian coalition, with a few Maritime faces. Its organization was the old Canadian departments. It used buildings erected in Ottawa for the old Province of Canada. If the new administration seemed familiar, so did many of its policies. It bought off the malcontents in Nova Scotia with better terms that were entirely financial. It started building the Intercolonial Railway along the eastern coast of New Brunswick. With the prodding of the British, the Hudson's Bay Company would sell Rupert's Land and the Northwest Territory to the new nation. Canada devoted much energy to rounding up the strays and expanding coast to coast.

In many respects, the two decades from 1867 to 1885 would focus on elaborating the myriad loose ends created by unification. There was the need to create new policies for the new Canada. In the end, too many policies continued from the older Canada, occasionally writ larger to accommodate the other provinces. The creation of new identities was even more difficult. The easiest identities to accept were the old provincial ones. Collectively, these provincial identities grew to provide one alternate vision to the national one envisioned by the founding fathers.

ADDING NEW TERRITORY

One of the earliest legislative actions of the new Canadian government in December 1867 was the passage of resolutions calling for transcontinental expansion. Most of the legislators regarded such expansion as the nation's inevitable right, a sort of Canadian version of manifest destiny. As a result, in 1868 a ministerial delegation went to London to arrange the Hudson's Bay Company's transfer of the northwest to Canada. While complex negotiations continued, the Canadian government began building a road from Fort Garry to Lake of the Woods. This was part of a proposed road and water system linking

Sitting Bull Rejects American Overtures

[In June 1876, American General George Armstrong Custer led a frontal cavalry charge against a Sioux encampment at Little Bighorn, Montana. All the 250 soldiers involved, including Custer, were killed. The Sioux—both those involved in the battle and others—led by Chief Sitting Bull (c. 1834–90), withdrew north of the 49th parallel under the protection of Great Britain and the recently formed Royal North-West Mounted Police. This portrait of Sitting Bull was taken in 1892 (National Archives of Canada C-20038). In his memoirs, *Forty Years in Canada: Reminiscences of the Great North-West*, Colonel Sam Steele described the visit in October of 1878 to Fort Macleod by an American commission seeking to get Sitting Bull and his people to return to the United States. *Source*: S. Steele, *Forty Years in Canada: Reminiscences of the Great North-West* (Toronto: McClelland, Goodchild & Stewart, 1915):127–9.]

The day after his arrival, General Terry and General Lawrence, who accompanied him, were met at the officers' mess-room by Colonel Macleod and his officers, and received Sitting Bull and his chiefs in council. A number of American and Canadian newspapers were represented. . . . The proceedings began by Colonel Macleod stating that General Terry and his staff were present by invitation, and that the Sioux chiefs had been summoned to meet them. General Terry then addressed the chiefs, through an interpreter who, it is to be regretted, did not know even his own language and was in no manner to be compared with those who did duty at the great Blackfeet and Cree treaties. Few men of good education had opportunities of learning Sioux, consequently the fine display of oratory of some of the chiefs was cut down to laconic remarks even coarser than one sometimes heard in the magistrate's court at Fort Macleod.

The general told the chiefs that their band was the only one that had not

Red River with Canada. The road builders established informal connections with Dr John Christian Schultz (1840–96), the influential leader of the local faction that had been agitating for Canadian annexation for years. Nobody bothered to pay any attention to the mixed bloods who constituted the bulk of the local population of the settlement. The Canadian delegation in London finally worked out a deal for the transfer. The British government received the territory from the Hudson's Bay Company (the Canadians put up £300,000 and

surrendered to the United States, and that it was the desire of his government that they should return to their reservations, give up their arms and horses, and receive cattle in exchange for the money realized by the sale. In reply Sitting Bull said:

For 64 years you have kept me and my people and treated us badly. What have we done that you should want us to stop? We have done nothing. It is the people on your side who have started us to do these depredations. We could not go anywhere else, so we took refuge in this country. It was on this side of the country that we learnt to shoot, and that was the reason I came back to it again. I should like to know why you came here. In the first place I did not give you the country, but you followed me from one place to another, so that I had to leave and come over to this country. I was born and raised in this country with the Red River half-breeds, and I intend to stop with them. I was raised hand-in-hand with the Red River half-breeds, and we are going over to that part of the country, and that is the reason I have come over here. Here Sitting Bull shook hands with Colonel Macleod and Major Walsh. *That is the way I was raised, in the hands of the people here, and that is the way I intend to be with them. You have got ears and you have got eyes to see with, and to see how I live with these people. You see me, here I am. If you think I am a fool, you are a bigger fool than I am. This house is a medicine house. You come here to tell us lies, but we do not want to hear them. I do not wish any such language used to me, that is, to tell me such lies in my Great Mother's house. Do not say two more words. Go back to where you came from. The country is mine, and I intend to stay here, and to raise this country full of grown people. See these people here, we were raised with them.* Again he shook hands with the Mounted Police Officers. *That is enough, so no more. You see me shaking hands with these people. The part of the country you gave me you ran me out of. I have now come to stay with these people, and I intend to stay here. . . .*

The Indians . . . arose and were about to depart when the interpreter was directed by General Terry to ask: 'Shall I say to the President of the United States that you have refused the offer he has made to you? Are we to understand from what you have said that you refuse those offers?' to which Sitting Bull replied: *I could tell you more, but that is all I have to tell you. If we told you more, why, you would not pay attention to it; that is all I have to say. This part of the country does not belong to your people. You belong to the other side. This side belongs to us.*

agreed to substantial land grants for the company) and subsequently transferred it intact to Canada.

Since the arrangements for the west were made without bothering to inform the Red River people of their import, it was hardly surprising that the locals were suspicious and easily roused to protest. The Métis were concerned on several counts. A number of racist incidents involved the road-building party. There was transparent haste on the part of the Canadian government to

Louis Riel, leader of the Métis, was hanged for treason after leading a revolt in 1885 in Saskatchewan (National Archives of Canada C-7625).

build a road and to send in men to survey land. This rush suggested that Canadian settlement would inundate the existing population without regard for its 'rights'. Canada made clear that it intended to treat the new territory as a colony. Furthermore, some of the road builders bought land cheaply from the indigenous peoples—land that the Métis thought was theirs. The Métis quickly perceived the Canadians as a threat to their way of life, perhaps even to their very existence. The Canadian government received a number of warnings in 1869 that trouble was brewing. The warnings came from the Anglican archbishop of Rupert's Land, Robert Machray (1831–1904); from the governor of the Hudson's Bay Company, William Mactavish (1815–70); and from Bishop Alexandre Taché (1823–94), the Catholic bishop of St Boniface. Ottawa received all such reports with little or no interest. Subsequent events were largely a consequence of avoidable Canadian blunders and insensitivities. In colonial thralldom itself until only a few years previously, Canada had little experience in managing imperial expansion. It handled it very clumsily, and the entire nation would pay dearly for the mistakes.

In October 1869 a leader of the Métis appeared in the person of Louis Riel (1844–85), a member of a leading family in the community. His father, for whom he was named, had successfully led a Métis protest in 1849 against the Hudson's Bay Company, which had won the right to trade freely in furs. The young Riel spoke out publicly against the surveys. He then led a party that stood on the surveyors' chains and ordered them to stop. In the meantime, William McDougall (1822–1905) was on his way from Canada to assume office as lieutenant-governor of the northwest. A newly formed National Committee of the Métis resolved that McDougall should not be allowed to enter the country. The Métis made it clear that they would oppose him by force if necessary. Canada responded to the unrest by refusing to take over the territory until it was pacified. Riel escalated the conflict. In early November he and a large band of armed Métis took possession of Upper Fort Garry, the Hudson's Bay Company central headquarters. The Métis then invited the anglophone inhabitants of the settlement, most of whom were mixed bloods themselves, to send delegates to meet and coordinate policy. Riel managed to get tacit consent for the establishment of a provisional government and approval of a 'list of rights'. On 7 December he and his men surrounded Dr Schultz's store, taking Schultz and forty-eight Canadians to Fort Garry as prisoners. The next day Riel issued a 'Declaration of the People', announcing a provisional government. He declared that the people of Red River wanted to be allowed to negotiate their own entry into Confederation on the basis of the 'rights' already agreed to by the residents. William McDougall made a fool of himself with an illegal proclamation of his government—Canada having refused to take possession of the territory—and then returned home.

Louis Riel marshalled his forces brilliantly. A convention of forty representatives, equally divided between the two language groups, debated and approved another 'list of rights'. The convention endorsed Riel's provisional government. It appointed three delegates to go to Ottawa to negotiate with the Macdonald government. So far, so good. But in early March, Thomas Scott, a prisoner who was an Orangeman, got into trouble with Riel and his guards. A Métis court martial condemned Scott to death without offering him a chance to be heard. Riel accepted the sentence, commenting, 'We must make Canada respect us.' The 'murder' of Scott would have enormous repercussions in Orange Ontario, which was looking desperately for an excuse to condemn the Red River uprising. The three-man delegation from Red River, headed by Abbé Noel Ritchot (1825–1905), gained substantial concessions from the Canadian government. If honoured, they would guarantee some protection for the original inhabitants of Red River against the expected later influx of settlers and land speculators. At what the Canadians always regarded as the point of a gun, the Métis extorted the Manitoba Act of 1870. This legislation granted provincial status to a Manitoba roughly equivalent to the old Red River settlement, with 1,400,000 acres (566,580 ha) set aside for the Métis and bilingual services guaranteed. The remainder of the northwest became a territory of Canada. One of its government's principal tasks was to extinguish

Louis Riel and His Councillors

This photograph shows Louis Riel at the centre of his provisional government sometime in early 1870 (National Archives of Canada C12854). In the top row, left to right, are: Bonnet Tromage, Pierre de Lorme, Thomas Bunn, Xavier Page, Baptiste Beauchemin, Baptiste Tournond, and Thomas Spence. In the middle row are Pierre Poitras, John Bruce, Louis Riel, John O'Donoghue, and François Dauphenais. In the front row are Robert O'Lone and Paul Proux.

Although Canada had not annexed Red River in December 1869 as planned, it never admitted that this government was legal. Riel (1844–85) brilliantly led the Métis resistance to Canada in 1869–70. He began as secretary of the Métis National Committee, with John Bruce as president. He took over from Bruce as president of the committee in late December 1870, and was formally elected president of the provisional government in early February. His only blunder was the execution of Thomas Scott. That mistake enabled the Macdonald government to bypass Riel and his provisional government, however, and occupy the territory by force. Scott's death also stood in the way of an amnesty for Riel and his lieutenants. The amnesty question was finally resolved in 1875 when Riel was sent into exile for five years. In the wake of this decision, he spent some time in a mental institution. He eventually ended up in North Dakota as a schoolteacher and an American citizen.

In 1885 he led a second resistance to Canada, and was eventually convicted of treason and hanged for the offence. Riel's lawyers tried to plead insanity, but Riel himself eloquently told the six-man jury that he was not insane. The jury found him guilty, but requested clemency. The Macdonald government ignored the request.

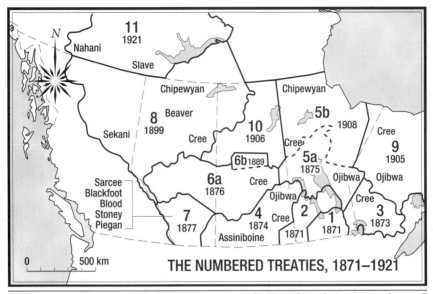

THE NUMBERED TREATIES, 1871–1921

Source: J.R. Miller, *Skyscrapers Hide the Heavens: A History of Indian-White Relations in Canada*, rev. ed. (Toronto: University of Toronto Press, 1991):166.

Aboriginal title through the negotiation of treaties with the indigenous peoples. These agreements would prepare for settlement by people of European origin.

In May 1870 the Canadian government sent a so-called peaceful military expedition to Red River. The troops occupied the province for Canada in late August, forcing Riel and his associates to flee for their lives. The Scott execution provided the Canadian government with the excuse to deny Riel and his lieutenants an official amnesty for all acts committed during the 'uprising'. Those who negotiated with Canada always insisted that such an amnesty had been unofficially promised. The result was that Louis Riel went into long-term exile instead of becoming premier of the province he had created. (An amnesty was granted Riel in 1875, on the condition that he be banished from the country for five years.) Whether the government would keep better faith over its land guarantees to the Métis was another matter.

While the question of Rupert's Land dragged slowly to its conclusion, the Canadian government was presented with an unexpected (although not totally unsolicited) gift. It consisted of a request from British Columbia—to which Vancouver Island had been annexed in 1866—for admission into the new union. The initiative from the Pacific colony had originated with the Nova Scotia-born journalist, Amor De Cosmos (William Alexander Smith, 1825–97), a member of the colony's legislative council. As early as March 1867 he had introduced a motion that the British North America Act, then about to be passed by the British Parliament, allow for the eventual admission of British

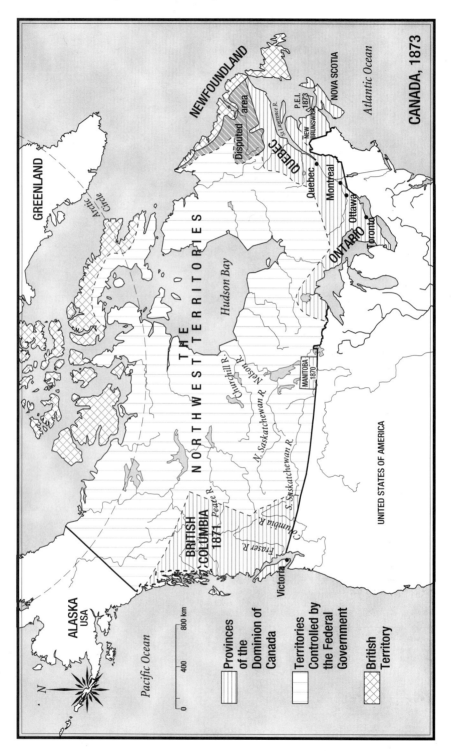

CANADA, 1873

GREENLAND

NEWFOUNDLAND

Disputed area

QUEBEC

St. Lawrence R.

P.E.I.
1873

NEW
BRUNSWICK

NOVA SCOTIA

Atlantic Ocean

Arctic Circle

Quebec

Montreal

Ottawa

Toronto

ONTARIO

THE NORTHWEST TERRITORIES

Hudson Bay

Churchill R.

Nelson R.

N. Saskatchewan R.

S. Saskatchewan R.

MANITOBA
1870

UNITED STATES OF AMERICA

BRITISH
COLUMBIA
1871

Peace R.

Columbia R.

Fraser R.

Victoria

ALASKA
USA

Pacific Ocean

N

0   400   800 km

Provinces of the Dominion of Canada

Territories Controlled by the Federal Government

British Territory

Columbia. Entry into Confederation would introduce responsible government, as well as resolving the colony's serious financial difficulties, which resulted partly from the interest on debts incurred for road building during the gold rushes. Union with Canada received an additional impetus when—coterminously with the passage of the British North America Act but quite independent of it—the American government purchased Alaska from the Russians. The purchase touched off demands in the American press for the annexation of British Columbia as well. Officially the British notified the colony in November 1867 that no action would occur on its relationship with Canada until Rupert's Land had been duly incorporated into the new nation.

Negotiations between British Columbia and Canada took place in the late spring of 1870. The Canadians were generous to a fault. Of course British Columbia could have responsible government. Of course the debt would be wiped out. Of course there would be subsidies and grants, as well as federal support for the naval station at Esquimalt. And of course British Columbia could have a rail link with Canada, to be begun within two years and completed within fifteen. The terms were far better than expected, and on 20 July 1871 British Columbia entered Confederation as the sixth province. While in most respects the new province remained isolated until the completion of the rail link in 1885, Confederation encouraged the development of a new land policy for the province. The provincial government opened its Crown lands to massive pre-emption and free land grants, by which the largesse of British Columbia would far exceed that of the federal government.

Prince Edward Island's acceptance of terms in 1873 was almost anticlimactic. The tiny province had tried to survive without much support from the British. Both the Americans and the Canadians actively wooed it. In the end, the island entered Confederation in the wake of a profligate policy of railway construction, which many saw as a scheme to force it into union. As well as offering to take over the debt and the railway, Canada agreed to guarantee continuous communication with the mainland and to help buy out the last of the old landed proprietors. Only one island MLA, the crusty farmer Cornelius Howatt, refused to vote for the Canadian offer.

Unlike Prince Edward Island, Newfoundland was not persuaded to join the union at all. In 1869 Newfoundland held an election fought on the issue of Confederation with Canada. The economy improved, while the opponents of Confederation employed every argument in their rhetorical arsenal. These included rumours that Canada would use Newfoundland children as wadding for their cannons. The 1869 election went decisively against the pro-Confederates. Both the British and Canadian governments acquiesced in Newfoundland's continued autonomy—despite sporadic union discussions as in 1887 and 1895—until 1949.

THE DEVELOPMENT OF NATIONAL POLICIES

As well as completing the creation of a transcontinental nation, the Macdonald government gradually improvised some national policies with which to govern the new Dominion. Confederation was encouraging to foreign investment. From its inception, Canada was able to import large amounts of capital to help create its infrastructure. Between 1865 and 1869 Canada raised $16.5 million in Great Britain, a figure that rose to $96.4 million in 1870–4, $74.7 million in 1875–9, and $69.8 million in 1880–4.

The government obtained some recognition of Canadian diplomatic autonomy by its acquiescence to the Treaty of Washington in 1871. Outstanding issues with the Americans included the *Alabama* claims. The *Alabama* was a Confederate raider built in Britain for the southern states. The Americans, half-seriously, demanded the cession of British-American territory in compensation for the losses it inflicted on northern shipping. In 1871 the British government made Macdonald a member of an international joint commission set up in 1870 to deal with the fisheries question. The British made clear they were willing to surrender Canadian interests to settle outstanding Anglo-American differences. Macdonald signed the resulting treaty.

On the domestic front, the banking system of the new nation grew rapidly from 123 chartered bank branches in 1869 to 279 in 1879 and 426 by 1890. Two major pieces of national legislation were the Dominion Notes Act of 1870 and the Bank Act of 1871. The former allowed the government to issue circulating notes of small denominations, only partly backed by specie. The latter exerted control over the banking system. The Bank Act specified capital requirements for banks, prohibited new foreign-owned banks, and supplied general regulation. Canada accepted the international gold standard, but the government would share the issuance of currency (and the control of the creation of money) with the banks until well into the twentieth century.

The opportunity for railway expansion was one of the principal arguments for Confederation. Railways were a prime target of foreign investors. The Macdonald government was slow to move on a transcontinental line, chiefly because of the enormous expense involved in building so far ahead of population needs. To some extent, the offer to British Columbia cast the die. There followed an unseemly scuffling over a charter, awarded in 1873 by Parliament to the Canada Pacific Railway Company of Sir Hugh Allan (1810–82). Then the Pacific Scandal broke. Allan had provided the government with money for its 1872 election campaign. Macdonald was unable to step totally clear of the corrupt dealings. In November 1873 the government resigned. Replacing it was a Liberal government headed by a Scottish-born former stonemason, Alexander Mackenzie (1822–92). He sought to build a transcontinental line

Sir John A. Macdonald on the National Policy, 1882

[Canadian political parties did not adopt official platforms until late in the nineteenth century. In earlier elections, the voter could glean some notion of party policy from the speeches of its leaders, which were widely reported in the press of the day. The following excerpt is from various campaign speeches by Sir John A. Macdonald, reported in the Toronto *Mail* in May and June 1882.]

WHY THE GOVERNMENT GOES TO THE COUNTRY

Because we thought it was of the greatest consequence to Canada, and to the future prosperity of the manufacturers of Canada, that the people should have an opportunity of expressing their opinion whether our policy is wise or not. A good many manufactures have been commenced, but they would have been quadrupled, four times as many manufactures would have been started in Canada, if it were not for the dread that the policy of 1878 would be destroyed and upset by a free trade Parliament in 1883.

THE ISSUE

We desire that the people may at once declare whether they wish to have fair trade, plenty of work, and prosperity, or free trade, want of labour, and poverty. We place that fairly before the people and say:—If you want to reverse that policy, do; if you want a continuance of prosperity, declare so at the polls, and you will have five years ahead during which that policy cannot be reversed. We have had three years now and at the end of five years more the manufacturing interest will be so strong that, as in the United States, it will be able to fight its own battles, and there is no fear of that policy being reversed to ruin the manufacturer who has put his money, his means, his credit, and his capital into such enterprises.

Why, sir, the true National Policy is this—to find, at all events, a home market for as much as we can, and if in consequence of our industry and of good seasons we raise more in the country than we can consume ourselves, to send the surplus abroad.

more gradually, using public funds. He also encouraged private interests to hook up with American western lines. Trains began running from Minnesota to Winnipeg late in 1878.

Mackenzie's government was also largely responsible for the initial funding of western railway construction. It gave the railway companies large land grants along the right of way. Although Canada developed a seemingly generous homestead policy by which pioneers could receive free land grants in return for developing the land, the generosity was deceptive. Almost no homestead land was available within easy access to the rail lines. Most early settlers ended up purchasing their land, either from the railways or from the Hudson's Bay Company.

The probity of his government did not save Alexander Mackenzie in 1878. Sir John A. Macdonald returned to power. Recognizing the temper of the times, Macdonald worked hard to restore in the public mind a sense of identification between his party and the process of nation building. Decisiveness and flamboyance were part of the image. Even before the election was called, Macdonald had his platform. He introduced into the House of Commons a resolution 'That this House is of the opinion that the welfare of Canada requires the adoption of a National Policy, which, by a judicious readjustment of the Tariff, will benefit and foster the agricultural, the mining, the manufacturing, and other interests of this Dominion' (quoted in Easterbrook and Watkins 1962:238). The Tory leader invented neither the policy nor the term used to describe it. Both went well back into the history of the Province of Canada, which had begun using a tariff as an instrument of both protection and revenue in the late 1840s. Nor did John A. Macdonald ever articulate the version of the national policy as it was later lovingly described by economic historians and textbook writers. But he certainly recognized some relationship involving tariffs, manufacturing, employment, and national prosperity. He also wanted a transcontinental railway and the accompanying western settlement necessary to make it a reality. All these features had been and remained a traditional part of Canadian economic expansionism.

What Macdonald achieved was masterful in its own way. He succeeded in persuading a large number of Canadians in all provinces that policies strongly driven by the economic self-interest of some of the people in some of its constituent parts were in the best interest of the nation as a whole. He then persuaded the electorate that his party was the one that had successfully built the nation and would continue to do so. The fact that the opposition party took the lead in developing a different version of nation building helped in this identification.

THE QUEST FOR IDENTITY, REGIONAL AND NATIONAL

The British North America Act had no guarantees that political unification would necessarily create a nation. After 1867 Canadians made various attempts to locate themselves in their world. Some of these attempts were political and constitutional. Others were cultural, with intellectuals and artists playing their part with rhetorical flourishes and the creation of national institutions in which the arts could operate.

The development of nationhood in the years after 1867 should not obscure the fact that not all Canadians shared in the same vision (or version) of the meaning of the nation. One of the major questions was whether Canada was an indissoluble new creation or the product of a compact among the provinces that they could either modify or even leave. Since the time of the debate over

Confederation in the 1860s, people had disagreed over the nature of the union. While most Canadians in 1867 saw the British North America Act as creating a strong central government, provincial legislatures still existed. They would quickly assert more than the mere local power accorded them by the Quebec resolutions. One of the arch-critics of Confederation, Christopher Dunkin (1812–81), had prophesied in 1865 that 'In the times to come, when men shall begin to feel strongly on those questions that appeal to national preferences, prejudices and passions, all talk of your new nationality will sound but strangely. Some older nationality will then be found to hold the first place in most people's hearts' (quoted in Waite 1963:511). Even Sir John A. Macdonald had admitted in Parliament in 1868 that 'a conflict may, ere long, arise between the Dominion and the States Rights people' (quoted in Cook 1969a:10).

Ontario initially spearheaded the provincial rights interpretation of the new union. Such a movement was inherent in the constitutional arrangements and could have begun anywhere. As early as 1869 Ontario became distressed at 'the assumption by the Parliament of Canada of the power to disturb the financial relations established by the British North America Act (1867), as between Canada and the several provinces' (quoted in Cook 1969a:11). Not surprisingly, it was the old Reform Party of Canada West, in the persons of George Brown, Edward Blake (1833–1912), and Oliver Mowat (1820–1903) who took the lead. It demanded—in Blake's phrase of 1871—'that each government [Dominion and provincial] shall be absolutely independent of the other in its management of its own affairs' (quoted in Cook 1969a:13). The *Rouges* of Quebec soon joined in the same call, adding the identification of French-Canadian 'national' rights to Ontario's 'provincial' ones. Before long, Liberals in most provinces—many of whom had either opposed Confederation or been lukewarm about it—had embraced provincial rights.

Provincial rights often seemed interchangeable with Ottawa-bashing for local political advantage, lacking in any other principle than the desire to pressure Ottawa into fiscal concessions. In its early years, Quebec did not dominate the movement. There was little insistence upon Confederation as a cultural deal between two distinct societies. In 1884, for example, the Honourable Honoré Mercier (1840–94) tabled resolutions in the Quebec legislature that insisted merely that 'the frequent encroachments of the Federal Parliament upon the prerogatives of the Provinces are a permanent menace to the latter' (quoted in Cook 1969a:31). The ensuing debate involved no more cultural nationalism than one back-bencher's assertion that 'le Quebec n'est pas une province comme les autres' (quoted in Cook 1969a:33). Although the Riel business of 1885 (discussed later) pushed Quebec towards the brink of arguments of cultural distinctiveness when Mercier (by this time premier of Quebec) invited the provinces to the Interprovincial Conference in 1887 to re-examine the federal compact, broad agreement could be reached on demands for better terms and constitutional change by the five provinces attending without the need for such concepts.

Provincial rights involved on one level a political-constitutional struggle over revenue and power. On another level they were a reflection of the continued identification of the people of Canada with their province of residence, as much or more than with their nation. The educational structure of Canada certainly encouraged this identification. In all provinces education showed a pattern of passage from private to public financial support at the same time that schooling became increasingly universal. However, section 92 of the British North America Act left education completely in the hands of the provinces. It is almost impossible to talk about any integrated national movements. Indeed, education would become one of the most divisive issues in the new nation. A major question was whether provinces would have a single public school system for all students, or would support separate religious (and linguistic) ecucation as well. Educational diversity was still the norm after Confederation. There were, at best, provincial educational systems and norms, not national ones.

Difficulties of the movements of emerging nationalism also aided the continuation of strong provincial loyalties. The movement calling itself Canada First, for example, did not have a program that was particularly attractive outside Protestant circles in Ontario. Canada First was an exclusive secret society rather than a broad-based organization. It did not help that its vision of Canada was really that of Canada West writ larger. Despite the presence in its ranks of the Nova Scotian Robert G. Haliburton (1831–1901), the son of T.C. Haliburton, most of Canada First's membership, including Charles Mair (1838–1927) and George Denison (1839–1925), were from Canada West. The movement's chief accomplishment was turning the Ontario public against the Métis of Red River by arousing sentiment over the 'murder' of Thomas Scott. Indeed, Canada First's nationalism was, in several senses, racist. Haliburton was one of the earliest exponents of the notion that Canadians were the heirs of the Aryan northmen of the Old World. He told the Montreal Literary Club in March 1869 that the new Canadian nationality comprised 'the Celtic, the Teutonic, and the Scandinavian elements', and embraced 'the Celt, the Norman French, the Saxon and the Swede' (quoted in Berger 1986:154–60). Canada Firsters looked down their noses at Aboriginal peoples and the Métis. They saw the French as the great 'bar to progress, and to the extension of a great Anglo-Saxon Dominion across the Continent', as the Toronto *Globe* put it in 4 March 1870.

While Canada First's notions fit together, to some extent, with the westward thrust of Canada West, they were, fortunately, not totally typical of the conscious development of Canadian nationalism. The French-Canadian poet, Octave Crémazie (1827–79), for example, lamented ironically that Canada's major literary languages were entirely of European origin. He continued, 'if we spoke Huron or Iroquois, the works of our writers would attract the attention of the old world. . . . One would be overwhelmed by a novel or a poem translated from the Iroquois, while one does not take the trouble to read a book written in French by a native of Quebec or Montreal' (quoted in Raspovich 1969:225). The search for an essential 'Canadian-ness' went on in many corners of the new Dominion. It was nowhere so successful as in that somewhat remote New Brunswick town, Fredericton, home of the University of New Brunswick. There the rectory of St Anne's Parish (Anglican) produced Charles G.D. Roberts (1860–1943), while not far down the road lived his cousin, Bliss Carman (1861–1929). Along with Ottawa's Archibald Lampman (1861–99) and Duncan Campbell Scott (1862–1947), these men comprised the Confederation Poets. Modern literary critics have invented this designation for this first school of Canadian poets who wrestled with Canadian themes, notably the local or regional landscape, with any degree of skill and sensitivity. As Crémazie had suggested, however, the European origins of their language limited their efforts.

While many intellectuals and artists sought ways to articulate Canadian-ness in their work, others took a more prosaic route towards the realization of a Canadian national identity. Curiously enough, it was the painters, not normally known for their political acuity, who took the lead in organizing national groups to maintain professional standards and publicize Canadian achievement. The Ontario Society of Artists, formed in 1872 and incorporated in 1877, took the lead in this effort. It was instrumental in the formation of the Royal Canadian Academy of Arts in 1880—in collaboration with the governor-general, Lord Lorne (1845–1914)—and in the establishment that same year of the National Gallery of Canada. One of the founders of this organization wrote, 'We are bound to try to civilize the Dominion a little' (quoted in Williamson 1970:64). The year 1880 was doubly important in art circles, for in that year the Canadian Society of Graphic Art was also founded.

The Royal Society of Canada was founded in 1882 to promote research and learning in the arts and sciences. Lord Lorne again provided much of the impetus, replicating a British institution to establish the importance of cultural accomplishments in creating a sense of national pride and self-confidence. The first president, J.W. Dawson (1820–99), principal of McGill University (another Nova Scotian transported to central Canada) emphasized in his presidential address a sense of national purpose. Dawson stressed especially 'the establishment of a bond of union between the scattered workers now widely separated in different parts of the Dominion' (quoted in The Royal

Society of Canada 1932:91–2). Thomas Sterry Hunt (1826–92), a charter member and later president, observed that 'The occasion which brings us together is one which should mark a new departure in the intellectual history of Canada' (The Royal Society of Canada 1932:91–2). He added that 'the brightest glories and the most enduring honours of a country are those which come from its thinkers and its scholars' (The Royal Society of Canada 1932:91–2). However romantic that state might sound, what mattered was Hunt's emphasis on the country as a whole. Like the Royal Canadian Academy, the Royal Society had its headquarters in Ottawa.

The first president of the Royal Canadian Academy, the painter Lucius O'Brien (1832–99), was art director of an elaborate literary and artistic celebration of the young nation. George Monro Grant (1835–1902), principal of Queen's University, edited *Picturesque Canada* (1882). He stated in the preface: 'I believed that a work that would represent its characteristic scenery and the history and life of its people would not only make us better known to ourselves and to strangers, but would also stimulate national sentiment and contribute to the rightful development of the nation' (Grant 1876). The two large volumes of *Picturesque Canada* contained some 540 illustrations—wood-engravings based on paintings and, for the West, photo-engravings of photographs—of serene vistas that fulfilled the promise of the title. The descriptive texts by Grant, Charles G.D. Roberts, and others presented an idealized, complacent view of the cities, towns, and countryside of Canada, praising the present and pointing to their glorious future. *Picturesque Canada* was a perfect symbol of the convergence of culture and national sentiment.

OTHER IDENTITIES

We can easily make too much of the political arena. The elaboration of a number of competing and occasionally incompatible identities by and for its citizens characterized the Victorian Age. As well as their national and provincial loyalties, most Canadians had firm allegiances to their ethnic origins, whether these were French Canadian, Acadian, or British. French Canada further elaborated its cultural identity in this period, and the Acadians began consciously to develop one. As for those people whose origins were in the British Isles, they simultaneously thought of themselves as British as well as Welsh, Scotch, Irish, or English. Indeed, British Canadians may well have thought of themselves as more British (as opposed to Welsh or Scottish) than did their compatriots at home.

The state did not weigh heavily on the daily lives of most Canadians in this era. Taxation had not yet become ubiquitous and occurred mainly as tariffs and duties. Moreover, the state—as represented by province, nation, or city—did not normally provide social benefits or solace when one got sick, lost a job, retired, or died. For some, politics and government were a source of employment or patronage. For the average Canadian, however, the government was an impartial and somewhat distant umpire, affecting mostly events outside his or her personal experience. For many people, political allegiance to the state was therefore not as important as loyalty to the caring institutions: family, ethnic group, religion, and fraternal organization. Churches and religion were most important. Canada was a Christian country and few of its citizens openly defied Christian norms and values. By the 1880s the mobility of many Canadians contributed to the tendency to belong to a good many other voluntary organizations beyond the church. In an earlier period, voluntary organizations supplemented or provided municipal services such as water, light, fire, and libraries as well as charity. By the 1880s some organizations had begun providing entertainment and companionship for their members.

The mid-Victorian period was a crucial era for Roman Catholicism in Canada. Within French Canada the period witnessed the emergence of the Church as the leading voice of French Canada's national aspirations and the assumption of local leadership by the *curé*. It also saw the Church take on the ultramontane character that would remain with it for many years. In Quebec, the man who symbolized the ultramontane Church in the mid-Victorian period was Bishop Ignace Bourget (1799–1885). Bourget was consecrated coadjutor to the bishop of Montreal in early 1837, on the very eve of rebellion, and succeeded to the see in 1840. He died in June 1885, on the eve of the second Riel uprising, although he had retired a few years earlier. Bourget was always an active defender of both the papacy and the position of the Church in Canada. He introduced the Roman liturgy and fervently opposed the principles of the European revolutions of 1848. Gradually he became the leading opponent of liberal thinking in the province, particularly as it was represented by the *Institut Canadien* in Montreal. Bourget carried on a lengthy battle against the *Institut* and especially its library, which contained many prohibited books. Equally important was his expansion of the ecclesiastical administration of his diocese, so that nearly every parish had a priest and nearly half the priests had an assistant. The clergy were now able to mobilize public opinion, as they did in 1868 when they helped raise 507 Zouaves in Quebec (and over $100,000 to support them) to serve in the papal army. Quebec bishops strongly supported the doctrine of papal infallibility at the Vatican Council.

English-speaking Catholicism had succeeded by 1840 in separating itself from francophone control. At about the same time, the hierarchy had also re-established its control over the laity, which had previously assumed considerable autonomy in the absence of local bishops and clergy. Anglophone bishops from the Maritime region were among those who attempted unsuccessfully to prevent the issue of papal infallibility from being decided at the Vatican Council of 1869–70. Contemporaries often overlooked the importance of anglophone Catholicism in the nineteenth century. Only in Canada West/Ontario were Protestants in such a clear numerical ascendency and position of power that the regional culture assumed obvious Protestant dimensions. This Ontario culture, especially as it expanded westward onto the prairies, began in some circles to be confused with Canadian culture.

By 1840 Protestantism everywhere in British North America had largely cut itself free from its foreign origins in either Great Britain or the United States. The major development of the mid-Victorian period, notably in an Ontario where Protestantism emerged as a distinct and all-embracing culture, was the construction of a broad alliance among the major denominations: Anglican, Presbyterian, and Methodist. The gradual elimination of the major points of public friction between the established churches and the dissenters made this possible. The result was a Victorian Protestant culture in Ontario that emphasized the relationship between social stability and Protestant morality. A firm belief in God and his millennium formed the basis for the latter. Gradual social change was progressive, offering a way of understanding the events and changes that swirled around the individual in the Victorian era. The moral code was strict, but chiefly voluntary and individualistic.

The churches, especially the Protestant ones, were a key to the growth of a vast network of clubs, societies, and charities. By the mid-nineteenth century women members were implicitly challenging the male governance of the churches. Evangelically oriented churches frequently employed their ladies' aid or women's auxiliary groups to sponsor missionary activity. By 1885 there were over 120 Baptist Women's Missionary Aid Societies scatttered across the Maritimes. Women usually used their own money to support their religious organizations, which kept separate accounts and offered many women their first opportunity at independent administration.

Technically independent of the churches, but closely connected in overlapping membership and social goals, were reform organizations like the Women's Christian Temperance Union (WCTU). Letitia Youmans (1827–96), a public school and Sunday school teacher in the Methodist Church, founded the first Canadian local of the WCTU in Picton, Ontario. The WCTU spread rapidly across Canada in the 1880s, preaching that alcohol abuse was responsible for many of the social problems of contemporary Canada and campaigning for public prohibition of the sale of alcoholic beverages.

The WCTU measured its membership in the thousands. That most characteristic Canadian society, the Orange Order, could count participants in the tens of thousands. Founded in Ulster in 1795 with the twin aims of defending Protestantism and maintaining loyalty to the British monarchy, the order's appeal was non-sectarian within a Protestant matrix. Religion was important, however, and the final qualification for membership in the early order called for 'the strictest attention to a religious observance of the Sabbath, and also of temperance sobriety'. In Canada the order added a strong fraternal aspect to its politico-religious aims, providing social activity and ritual for its local members. Although Orangism came to British North America with the Irish, it became very popular with Scots in some places, gradually taking on an air of WASPishness rather than Irishness. At its height, the Orange Order probably had as many as 50,000 actual members, scattered across the Dominion and across social classes. One estimate suggests that as many as one in three Protestant Canadians in the Victorian period had strong Orangist links.

Canadians have tended to associate Orangism with political matters— organizing parades on 12 July, opposing Roman Catholics, objecting to the 1870 execution of Thomas Scott—and with the Irish. The order's real importance and influence, however, rested on the twin facts that its membership united British Protestants of all origins and that it served as a focal point on the local level for social intercourse and conviviality. As a 'secret' society, it had elaborate initiation rites and a ritual that appealed to men who spent most of their lives in drudgery. Lodges provided a variety of services for members, including an elaborate funeral. But if local fraternity was the key to Orangism's success, its public influence was enormous.

The Orange Order was hardly the only fraternal organization that grew and flourished in Canada. Because most of these societies were semisecret, with rites based on Freemasonry, they appealed mainly to Protestants. The Masons themselves expanded enormously during the mid-nineteenth century. They were joined by a number of other orders, such as the Independent Order of Oddfellows (founded in England in 1813 and brought to Canada by 1845), the Independent Order of Foresters (founded in the United States in 1874 and brought to Canada in 1881), and the Order of Knights of Pythias (founded in Washington, DC, in the early 1860s and brought to Canada in 1870). The Knights of Labour was an all-embracing labour organization that owed much to the lodges. Fellowship and mutual support were the keys to the success of all of these societies. Their success led to the formation in 1882 of the Knights of Columbus as a similar fraternal benefit society for Roman Catholic men, although the first chapters in Canada were probably not founded until the early 1890s. While few of these societies admitted women directly, most had adjunct or parallel organizations for women. By the 1880s many Canadians belonged to one or more of these societies. Membership offered a means of social introduction into a new community, provided status and entertainment to members, and increasingly supplied assurance of assistance in times of economic or emotional crisis.

CULTURAL LIFE

The creation of the nation did not directly affect all aspects of cultural life. Indeed, most culture in Canada existed quite apart from political considerations entirely. Despite their new self-consciousness about the need for cultural achievements to match their political accomplishments, Canadians would probably have ignored some of the most interesting developments in documenting progress, particularly in the area of popular culture. Only a brief sampling of cultural activity in Victorian Canada—focusing on music and organized sports—can be included here.

Although only the occasional trained musician existed in British North America, the mid-Victorian era saw the development of a widespread musical life. Garrison bands and choral groups were the chief components. In British Columbia the band of the Royal Engineers brought new standards of musical performance when it arrived in the colony in 1859. From that year until 1863 (when it was reposted to Britain) it entertained as militia band, fire-brigade band, brass band, and even a dance band. In British Columbia, as elsewhere, brass bands were the most common and popular forms of instrumental ensembles throughout the nineteenth century. Few band musicians were professional or professionally trained. A number of brass bands were organized in the province in Aboriginal communities and residential schools. At least thirty-three sprung to life between 1864 (when the Oblates founded the St Mary's Mission Band near Mission City) and the end of the century. In Red River, a brass band from St Boniface played as the Métis provisional government raised its new flag in December 1869.

By the time of Confederation, larger cities were producing substantial numbers of musical societies, chiefly choral in their orientation. In 1864, for example, the Mendelssohn Choir and the *Société Musicale des Montagnards Canadiens*, as well as *Les Orphéonistes de Montréal*, joined the Montreal Oratorio Society. Montreal also helped produce the first well-known Canadian composer, Calixa Lavallée (1842–91), best known today for the music to 'O Canada'. He made his debut at the piano in Montreal at age thirteen, spending much time in the United States until he went to Paris in 1873. Returning to settle in Quebec, Lavallée wrote a grand cantata for the reception of Governor-General Lord Lorne and his wife. It concluded with a stirring contrapuntal intramixture of 'God Save the Queen' and 'Comin' thro' the Rye'. Unable to make a living in Canada, the composer spent the last years of his life in exile in the United States. Although Canada was not often generous to its professional musicians, it embraced amateur musical performance with gusto. Most music making occurred in the home, with people gathering around the piano to sing hymns and popular songs of the day.

A composite photograph of a baseball game in Tecumseh Park, London, Ontario, between the London Tecumsehs and Syracuse in 1871. The Middlesex County Court House can be seen in the background (National Archives of Canada PA-31482).

The mid-Victorian period in Canada saw a continued development of organized sports and games. Most were imported, although some (like lacrosse) had local origins. Lacrosse had begun life as an Aboriginal game called variously *baggataway* or *tewaarathon*, and was played by many tribes under various rules. In 1833 the First Nations near Montreal played lacrosse, and in 1856 the Montreal Lacrosse Club was organized, joined by two others before 1860. A Montreal dentist, William George Beers (1843–1900), codified the game in Montreal and promoted it across the country. By October 1867 Beers had established eighty lacrosse clubs with 2,000 members across the new Dominion. The game flourished between 1868 and 1885, achieving great success as a spectator sport until overtaken by baseball and hockey. Snowshoeing, which became very popular as an organized winter activity in the 1860s (often among the summer lacrosse crowd) was another obviously Native development. The Montreal Snow Shoe Club was organized in 1843, and in Winnipeg a snowshoe club, begun in 1878, was the major winter diversion for members of the city's élite by the early 1880s.

The formulation of rules for these and other sports occurred in most cases between 1840 and 1880, which was the great era of codification of sports. Precise dates are very contentious, with many communities advancing their own claims for 'firsts'. Certainly by 1880 most sports and games familiar to us today had reached a stage of rule development that would have made them comprehensible to a modern Canadian. What is important about the development of sports is not simply the introduction of standardized rules, techniques, and equipment, but the sheer scope and ubiquity of sporting activity on the part of both participants and spectators. While many Canadians participated, many more gathered to watch sporting activity. The development of any of the major games followed roughly the same path of regularization, which made it possible for teams from one place to play teams from another.

By 1885 two aspects of sports in Canada had evolved: participation and spectacle. Sports still had not achieved an overt political meaning. There was not yet the creation of either national leagues or national teams to play in international competitions. Expansion, sophistication, and growing organization matched the development of the nation. The mobility of the population moved various sports and games around the country and made the standardization of rules both possible and necessary. Both the development of official rules and growing hierarchies of teams and players pointed to the future.

THE STRUGGLE FOR THE WEST

Sincere efforts on the part of many in the new Dominion attempted to encourage a sense of nationhood transcending the linguistic barriers between French and English and the geographical barriers of the provinces and the regions. Nevertheless, the new Canadian nationality remained fragile, more than a bit artificial, and very racist. In addition, at least outside French Canada, it tended to express the prejudices and values of British Ontario writ large. The crucible for the new Canada, many believed, was in the vast expanse of territory west of the Great Lakes. Here its limitations were most clearly evident.

The interests of the Canadian government in the Northwest Territory, especially under Sir John A. Macdonald, were focused on agricultural settlement. This would provide both an outlet for excess eastern population and the means of encouraging the development of a truly transcontinental nation. The process of settlement pushed the Aboriginal inhabitants of the region out of the way as quickly as possible. The Canadian government negotiated a number of treaties with the First Nations. They extinguished Aboriginal titles in exchange for reserves on the most marginal and least attractive land. In August 1876, for example, the Indians of central Saskatchewan forgathered at Fort Carlton to consider the terms of the government's Treaty no. 6. The Plains Cree chief Poundmaker (Pitikwahanapiwiyin, c. 1842–86) objected to the arrangement, saying that the government should be prepared to train his people as farmers and assist them in other ways after the buffalo disappeared. Nevertheless, Poundmaker signed the treaty, and three years later accepted a reserve on the Battle River. Another important Plains Cree chief, Big Bear (Mistahimaskwa, c. 1825–88), refused to sign for six years. He capitulated on 8 December 1882 when his people were starving and needed food. The following July, his small band was moved north to a reservation near Fort Pitt.

The Canadian government established the North-West Mounted Police in 1873 to act as its quasi-military agent in the west. It modelled the NWMP on the

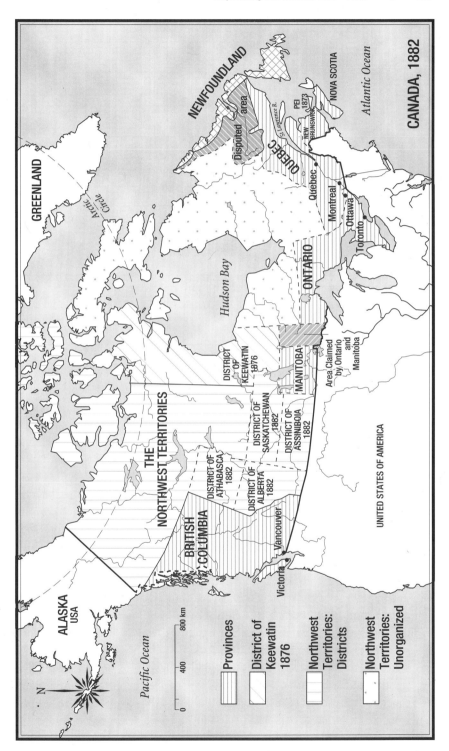

CANADA, 1882

GREENLAND

NEWFOUNDLAND

Disputed area

QUEBEC

St. Lawrence R.

Québec

Montreal

Ottawa

Toronto

ONTARIO

PEI 1873

NEW BRUNSWICK

NOVA SCOTIA

Atlantic Ocean

Arctic Circle

Hudson Bay

DISTRICT OF KEEWATIN 1876

DISTRICT OF SASKATCHEWAN 1882

DISTRICT OF ASSINIBOIA 1882

MANITOBA

Area Claimed by Ontario and Manitoba

THE NORTHWEST TERRITORIES

DISTRICT OF ATHABASCA 1882

DISTRICT OF ALBERTA 1882

BRITISH COLUMBIA

Vancouver

Victoria

UNITED STATES OF AMERICA

ALASKA USA

Pacific Ocean

N

800 km

400

0

Provinces

District of Keewatin 1876

Northwest Territories: Districts

Northwest Territories: Unorganized

Big Bear trading at Fort Pitt, a Hudson's Bay Company post on the North Saskatchewan River until 1884 when it was taken over by the North-West Mounted Police. In April 1885 Big Bear and his band attacked it; it was evacuated and then burned by Big Bear's Cree followers (National Archives of Canada PA-118768).

Irish constabulary. Its officers, drawn from the élites of eastern Canada, believed in a notion of public stability that associated crime and violence with the 'lower orders' and the Aboriginal peoples. The Mounties kept ahead of settlement and have always been seen as the chief instruments of a more peaceful western expansion than was true in the neighbouring United States. Certainly in Canada there was less overt violence, but this was often owing to the early exertion of state power and control.

Settlement drove the Métis, like the First Nations, to the margins. By 1885 Ontario-born settlers outnumbered the Métis five to one in Manitoba, and only 7 per cent of the population of the province was of mixed-blood origin. Many Métis drifted farther west, to the Saskatchewan Valley, where they formed small mission settlements including Qu'Appelle, Batoche, and Duck Lake. The buffalo were becoming scarce everywhere. Government surveyors caused uncertainty and fear, as they had in Red River a decade earlier. The winter of 1883–4 was particularly severe, and many Métis and Indians starved. In June 1884 Big Bear and his followers, with many others, travelled to Poundmaker's reserve to hold a big meeting. They discussed the serious state of affairs, after which some 2,000 Indians put on a thirst dance, a religious ritual. For their part, the Métis turned in despair to Louis Riel. He had apparently put his life back together after years of exile in the United States and hospitalization in 1876–8 for mental disturbance at Longue Pointe, Quebec. He became an American citizen and was teaching in St Peter's,

Montana (where he had married), when a delegation from the Saskatchewan country visited him on 4 June 1884. They told him of the grievances that were burdening the peoples of the region, explained that agitation was developing against the Canadian government, and pleaded with him to return to Canada to lead them. Why Riel agreed to do so is one of the many mysteries surrounding his life. However, within a month he and his family were in Batoche. By December 1884, Riel and W.H. Jackson (secretary of the Settler's Union) had finished drafting a long petition (with twenty-five sections), which they sent to Ottawa. It concluded by requesting that the petitioners 'be allowed as in [1870] to send Delegates to Ottawa with their Bill of rights; whereby an understanding may be arrived at as to their entry into confederation, with the constitution of a free province'. Ottawa acknowledged the petition, but gave no other response.

In March 1885 events took a menacing turn. Riel's military leader, Gabriel Dumont (1836–1906), intercepted a small NWMP detachment near Duck Lake. The engagement turned into a full-fledged battle in which fatalities occurred on both sides. Riel called upon the Indians to assist him, which they did. Poundmaker's people broke into buildings in Battleford, terrifying settlers. The Cree warrior, Wandering Spirit (Kapapamahchakwew, c. 1845–85), led a band that attacked Frog Lake, killing nine. Prime Minister Macdonald determined to crush this rebellion quickly, sending an armed force under Major-General Frederick Middleton (1825–98) by way of the new Canadian Pacific Railway. The Canadian force of 800 men arrived at Batoche on 9 May. They quickly defeated Riel and about 200 Métis. The uprising was over by 12 May. Dumont and others fled to the United States. The government arrested Riel.

A formal charge of high treason, carrying the death penalty, was laid against Riel on 6 July. (Despite the fact that Riel was an American citizen, the Canadian government held with the British government that he was also a British subject, since British citizenship acquired through birth could never be renounced.) The trial began on 28 July in Regina, where feelings ran high. It was a political trial, infamously coloured in many ways by Macdonald's determination to have Riel found guilty and executed. Riel passionately denied a plea of insanity introduced by his lawyers. The jury found him guilty, but recommended mercy. Ottawa dismissed two appeals, and hanged Riel on 16 November. Poundmaker stood trial for treason and was sentenced to three years in prison. Released after a year, he died four months later. Big Bear received a similar sentence, but was released after a year and a half. Wandering Spirit was hanged.

The execution of Louis Riel had a lasting impact on Canada. In Quebec it strengthened French-Canadian nationalism and helped turn voters away from

Poundmaker

Poundmaker was a Plains Cree chief who objected to the terms of the Canadian government's Treaty no. 6 with the Natives of central Saskatchewan. Although his mother was Métis, he had acquired much status when he was adopted into the Blackfoot tribe as the son of a head chief. He insisted that the government should be prepared to train the Native peoples as farmers and offer them more assistance as the buffalo herds disappeared. The suggestion was not well received by the Canadian negotiators. Poundmaker signed the treaty and accepted a reserve on the Battle River three years later. The Natives met in June 1884 on this reserve to discuss their relations with Canada, ending with a huge thirst dance in which over 1,000 dancers participated. Poundmaker tried to protect one of those involved in the ceremony from North-West Mounted Police arrest, offering himself as a hostage, but was forced to surrender the fugitive.

Poundmaker did not participate in the summons to Louis Riel, and he was unable to prevent his younger warriors from joining the Métis uprising. He eventually surrendered unconditionally and was tried for treason with Riel at Regina. He told the court that he had done everything possible to prevent bloodshed and was in custody 'because I wanted justice'. His health was broken at Stony Mountain Penitentiary after only one year of a three-year sentence, and he died soon after his release. This painting shows the surrender of Poundmaker (National Archives of Canada).

Riel in the prisoner's box. He addressed the court twice during his trial, once after all the evidence had been presented (when he spoke for over an hour), and once before sentence was pronounced (National Archives of Canada C-1879).

the Conservative Party, which they had supported since Confederation. On 22 November 1885, at a huge gathering in the public square in Montreal called the Champ de Mars, Honoré Mercier, the Liberal leader in Quebec, joined Wilfrid Laurier in denouncing the government action. Mercier insisted: 'In killing Riel, Sir John has not only struck at the heart of our race but especially at the cause of justice and humanity which... demanded mercy for the prisoner of Regina, our poor friend of the North-West.' Laurier added: 'Had I been born on the banks of the Saskatchewan... I would myself have shouldered a musket to fight against the neglect of governments and the shameless greed of specula-tors.' The two leaders disagreed over Mercier's proposal that French Canadians leave the two major parties and form one of their own. Laurier insisted that Mercier's proposal would destroy Confederation. Symbolically, French Canada took the execution of Riel to represent the final exclusion of the francophone from the west. Few spoke of the symbolic meaning of the execution of Wandering Spirit for the Aboriginal peoples.

The military defeat of the Métis and the public execution of Louis Riel in November 1885 were only part of the reason why that year (and that month) were so significant, not only in the history of the west but in the history of Canada. In November 1885 workers drove the last spike at Craigellachie in east-ern British Columbia, marking the completion of the Canadian Pacific Railway. The CPR had been resurrected in 1881 as a hybrid corporation controlled by

A CPR construction crew at Malakwa, BC (National Archives of Canada C-1602).

Arrival of the first transcontinental passenger train at the foot of Howe Street in Vancouver, 23 May 1887 (City of Vancouver Archives, CAN.P.78,N.52).

private capitalists and financed largely by the state, which, along with public subsidies, gave it about 25 million acres (10,117,500 ha) of land along its right of way. Contemporaries actively debated the question of building in advance of settlement, particularly given the inducements needed to persuade hard-headed businessmen to proceed with construction. The Macdonald government defended the railway on the grounds of national interest. Since this concept is not measurable in dollar amounts, it is impossible to know whether the price was too high. Even before the line was completed, Macdonald used it to send troops west to help suppress the Métis uprising of 1885. The construction of the CPR was a spectacular feat of engineering, partly thanks to the managerial skills of William Van Horne (1843–1915). The CPR was built chiefly on the backs of 6,500 Chinese coolie labourers especially imported for the job. Many died, and those who survived were summarily discharged when the work was completed. With the CPR finished, the Canadian government moved swiftly to limit Chinese immigration. With the Plains Indians and their allies, the Métis, totally subjugated, Canada was open for settlement from coast to coast.

The west was to be an anglophone colony of Canada. Not only were First Nations, Métis, and Chinese cast aside as quickly as possible, but French Canadians were not expected to settle there in any substantial numbers. National consolidation was arguably complete in 1885, but much Canadian 'nationalism' still bore the distinctive mark of the Ontario WASP. Two cultures, French and English, were in firm opposition to each other, and other cultures were thoroughly marginalized. Trying to satisfy the nation's two main components would continue to be the most challenging task facing the Canadian government.

Major Events, 1886–1918

1886   W.S. Fielding introduces legislation in Nova Scotia calling for secession from the union. The first CPR transcontinental arrives in Manitoba.

1887   Honoré Mercier leads *nationaliste* Liberals to victory in Quebec. St Catharines opens electric street railway.

1890   Manitoba government abolishes public funding for Catholic schools. CPR builds rail line through Maine to connect Moncton with Montreal.

1891   Sir John A. Macdonald dies.

1892   A great fire destroys St John's, Newfoundland.

1896   Sir Wilfrid Laurier leads the Liberal Party to a national electoral victory. Gold is discovered in the Klondike. The Manitoba Schools Question becomes a national issue.

1898   A national referendum is held on prohibition of alcoholic beverages. Newfoundland completes a railway across the island.

1899   Canadian Northern Railway is incorporated. Alaska Boundary Dispute is referred to an international tribunal. Canada agrees to send volunteer troops to South Africa.

1900   Art Museum of Toronto is founded. Prohibition legislation is passed in Prince Edward Island.

1901   The first wireless message transmitted across the Atlantic is received on Signal Hill near St John's, Newfoundland.

1902   Ernest Thompson Seton founds Woodcraft Indians.

1905   Saskatchewan and Alberta are created out of the Northwest Territories. Ontario Conservatives finally win political control of the province.

1906   Ontario Hydro-Electric Commission is created.

1907   Development of Marquis wheat. Canadian Department of the Interior begins paying bonuses to European immigration agents for labourers. Canadian Art Club is founded in Toronto.

1910   Steel Company of Canada is created by an amalgamation of smaller firms.

1911   Robert Borden's Conservatives take over federal government in the Reciprocity election. Marius Barbeau is appointed as anthropologist in the Museum Branch of the Geological Survey of Canada. Noranda gold-copper mine opens in Quebec.

1912   Social Services Council of Canada is organized. Quebec's boundaries are extended to Hudson Bay.

1914   Canada and Newfoundland enter the Great War.

1915   Canadian Expeditionary Force fights in the first Battle of Ypres. Ontario introduces Regulation 15.

1916   Canada introduces a business profits tax. The Newfoundland regiment is decimated at the Battle of Beaumont Hamel.

1917   Canadian Expeditionary Force suffers heavy losses at Vimy in April. Canada introduces income tax. Conscription Crisis emerges over introduction of Military Service Act, followed by the Wartime Elections Act. Much of Halifax is destroyed in an explosion.

1918   The First World War ends. Spanish influenza epidemic begins.

Becoming Modern, 1885–1918

✢

In the years after Confederation, Canada became one of the richest nations in the world in terms of gross national product and per capita income. Given the vantage point of hindsight, historians from comparably sized countries—such as Mexico, Brazil, or Argentina—can only envy Canada's privileged position of wealth, if not power, in this critical period. From the late 1870s to the end of the First World War, Canada was in the top ten of the world table of industrial development. Though the country possessed rich agricultural and natural resources, much of the key to its success lay in the exploitation of these advantages by a burgeoning industrial sector. Canadians often saw the weaknesses of the Canadian economy. From the vantage point of most of the world, however, Canada was rich, powerful, highly industrialized, and 'progressive'. It possessed a vibrant labour movement. Before the Great War, Canada had created a self-sustaining internal economy and a dynamic foreign trade. While the nation was transforming its economy, it was also altering its society and culture. There was another round of immigration, much of it drawn from outside the British Isles. Canada became an increasingly urbanized country. This was also the great era of reform, both political and social. As well, there was a great national debate over Canada's place within the British empire. The political system that made all these developments possible operated through the mediating influence of political parties.

THE DEVELOPING POLITICAL AND CONSTITUTIONAL SYSTEM

The Fathers of Confederation had not written political parties into the Canadian Constitution. Nevertheless, by the mid-1880s a two-party system had evolved at both the federal and provincial levels that would remain unchanged until the First World War. Indeed, this period was in many respects the golden age of Canadian party politics. Party affiliations were serious matters. Being a Liberal or a Conservative was a commitment passed on from father to son; small towns had parallel Liberal and Conservative business establishments, including undertaking parlours. The seeming vitality of the two-party system disguised, to some degree, the underlying tensions of Canadian federalism. Before 1914, however, the parties seemed flexible enough to contain various currents of conflict and disagreement. Both national parties developed consensual systems capable of holding differing ideologies, sections, and interest groups.

The key to the successful functioning of the national parties—and the allegiances of their adherents—was in large part in the power of patronage. Both parties, in office, distributed honours and jobs to their leading supporters, employing careful systems of apportionment to individuals whose qualifications were judged solely in terms of political service and loyalty. The patronage system rewarded chiefly those members of the Canadian professional and business élites (mainly from the so-called middle class) who ran the two parties. The system diminished ideological and regional differences, offering French Canadians their own opportunities for advancement. Patronage thus encouraged a stable party system in which matters of principle were less important than the division of the spoils of victory.

Despite their consensual utility, Canadian political parties had considerable difficulty in mediating the relationships between the federal and provincial levels of government. The rise of a strong movement for provincial rights, initiated by Ontario, joined by Quebec, and supported on occasion by all provinces, was almost inevitable. The chief, although not sole, bone of contention would be economic development. Provinces insisted that they, not the federal government, should control development within their boundaries. What was unexpected was the support for provincial rights provided by the Judicial Committee of the British Privy Council, the court of last resort for federal-provincial disagreement. In a series of landmark decisions stretching from the 1880s to the Great War, the Judicial Committee consistently reduced the power of the federal government and enhanced that of the provinces. Both anglophone and francophone voters tended to support this readjustment of Confederation. They saw the provinces as a check on the federal government's power, and they consistently supported provincial parties that wanted to confront Ottawa. Thus there was nothing unique about the 1887 victory in Quebec of the *nationaliste* Liberal government of Honoré Mercier (1840–94). W.S. Fielding (1848–1929) had won for the Liberals in Nova Scotia in 1884 on a platform of provincial rights. In 1886 Fielding introduced legislation calling for the secession of Nova Scotia from the union. Obviously provincial parties could not afford too close an identification with their federal counterparts, particularly while the latter were in power. Only with the success of Laurier's Liberals in 1896 did the Ontario Tories escape the incubus of a federal Conservative party, for example. By 1905 they won a control of the province that they would seldom relinquish over the next ninety years.

A great irony of Confederation was that French Canada continued as the region upon which national political success had to be built. Until the death of Sir John A. Macdonald in 1891, the Conservatives had successfully appealed to

Quebec with a judicious combination of local political patronage and national political policies. The execution of Louis Riel late in 1885 threatened that appeal, but the government's Quebec ministers held firm. The Grand Old Man's successors, including J.J. Abbott (1821–93), John S. Thompson (1844–94), and

John A. Macdonald in 1867 (National Archives of Canada C-6513).

Wilfrid Laurier

Wilfrid Laurier (1841–1919) was born at St-Lin, Canada, and studied law at McGill. He was an opponent of Confederation and served briefly in the Quebec legislature before being elected to the House of Commons as a Liberal in 1874. He would remain in the House until his death.

Laurier opposed the execution of Louis Riel in 1885, and became leader of the Liberal Party two years later. Ironically, given his earlier opposition to the union of British North America, he became a principal supporter of national unity, especially after he became Canada's first French-Canadian prime minister in 1896.

Laurier continually accepted the 'lesser evil' rather than divide the coun-try along any of the fault lines that existed. He compromised on the fate of Manitoba's Catholic minority, allowed only volunteers to go to South Africa, and again sacrificed cultural dualism for the North West Territories when they were made provinces in 1905.

During the First World War, he supported Canadian participation and voluntary enlistment, but opposed conscription. His efforts at compromise failed, and he remained at the head of a Liberal Party much weakened by defections to the Union government. Whether Laurier made too many or not enough concessions to Quebec remains an open question. This photograph of Laurier was taken around 1882 (National Archives PA-13133).

Charles Tupper (1821–1915), simply did not have the magic. In 1896 Wilfrid Laurier (1841–1919) became the national *chef*. He had put together a coalition of provincial Liberal parties by softening the potential issues of division. Laurier's agonizing over the Manitoba Schools Question of the early 1890s, when his distaste for a unilingual policy for Manitoba schools was matched only by his refusal to prevent provinces from running affairs within their own general mandate, was a pure reflection of his approach. Laurier saw national unity and national harmony as identical and, not surprisingly, viewed a biracial state as essential. He was able to survive politically on the strength of Quebec support and a period of great national prosperity until 1911. In that year the Liberal program of establishing a Canadian navy and limited free trade with the United States brought defeat. Through his compromises, Laurier had managed to blunt to some considerable extent the growing sectional division between Quebec and the remaining provinces of Canada.

The Conservatives of Robert Borden (1854–1937) replaced Laurier's Liberals in 1911. The Tories split the Quebec vote while sweeping Ontario, thanks in large measure to the support of the Ontario provincial party. Key issues in the 1911 election were American reciprocity and imperial naval defence. Borden's victory was a triumph for Canadian imperial sentiment, anti-continentalism, and middle-class reform. Borden had set out his Halifax Platform in 1907, calling for civil service reform, public ownership of telephones and telegraphs, a reformed Senate, and free mail delivery in rural areas. Borden spoke for the 'progressive' forces of Anglo-Canadian society and reform, which had been marshalling strength since the mid-1880s. Laurier had enacted some of Borden's planks, including civil service reform in 1908, but the Conservatives still claimed the imperial mantle. Borden achieved some of his imperial vision only with the beginning of the Great War. The Conscription Crisis of 1917 completed the process, which began in 1911 with the defeat of Laurier, of the political isolation of French Canada. At the same time, neither the west nor the Maritimes were content, as events after the war's end soon demonstrated.

THE ECONOMIC INFRASTRUCTURE

Control of capital through chartered banks headquartered chiefly in central Canada was one of that region's great advantages. Unlike the United States, Canadian banking was always highly centralized. In 1914 in Canada there were only twenty-six banks operating 2,888 branches. Some of the larger banks (the Royal Bank, the Bank of Commerce) had more than 300 branches each. From the beginning, Canadian chartered banks served local customers less than they facilitated the transfer of commodities and funds. Their credit facilities, especially for outlying districts of the nation, were quite limited. The banking

The Canadian Bank of Commerce building at 25 King Street West, Toronto—designed by R.A. Waite and erected in 1889–90—was one of several new office buildings in the city that had some claim to architectural distinction and even grandeur. At seven-and-a-half storeys—soaring over neighbouring three- and four-storey buildings—it was influenced by the first skyscrapers in New York and Chicago. Demolished in 1928, it was replaced in 1929–31 by the building that—with thirty-four office floors above a seven-storey base—was for some years the tallest in the British empire (City of Toronto Archives, Micklethwaite Collection SC 497 #21).

industry itself wrote Canadian banking legislation. The Canadian Bankers' Association was an organization of a few powerful men. The president of *La Banque Provinciale* complained that it was 'a tool in the hands of three or four men who today control the whole of the finance of the country'.

Although in 1913 Montreal-headquartered banks held almost half of the assets of all Canadian banks ($788 million of $1,551,000,000), Quebec contained considerably fewer branch banks per capita than the remainder of the nation. The result was the founding by Alphonse Desjardins (1854–1920) of the *caisses populaires*, often run by *curés* in association with Catholic parishes. Financial institutions to compete locally with the chartered banks did develop, not only in the form of *caisses populaires* but as government savings banks, local savings banks, and credit unions. Their economic power was limited, however, and the chartered banks continued to grow. Banks with head offices in central Canada refused to make local loans and set local interest rates at high levels. Sir Edmund Walker (1848–1924), president of the Bank of Commerce, labelled regional complaints as 'local grievances against what we regard as the interests of the country as a whole' (quoted in Naylor 1975, I:103).

Transportation continued to be an essential ingredient of development. As in the age of the first railway boom of the 1850s, railways were both a means of development and a field of investment. Substantial railway construction involved considerable public subsidies, often in the form of land grants along the right of way, as well as other boons. The CPR received from the government the completed line from Fort William to Selkirk, as well as the line from Kamloops to Port Moody. Moreover it received a cash payment of $25 million, plus 25 million acres (10,117,500 ha) 'fairly fit for settlement', and various tax exemptions on its land. In addition, it had a monopoly position. Nor was the Canadian Pacific the only railway so favoured. Dozens of railways incorporated in Canada during these years. Local communities fought desperately for railways, seeing them as links to a prosperous future. Sir William Mackenzie (1849–1923) and Sir Donald Mann (1853–1934) constructed a second transcontinental line, the Canadian Northern Railway, which passed considerably to the north of the CPR. Everyone outside central Canada complained about the high costs of freight, but all Canadians relied on the railway. Passenger travel was swift and relatively inexpensive.

Energy was another essential. Canada always possessed rich potential energy resources. Coal never provided much advantage, but abundant water

The interior of a CPR colonist railway car, as drawn by Melton Prior for the *Illustrated London News*, 24 November 1888 (Glenbow Archives NA-978-4).

power did. Changing technology at the close of the nineteenth century enabled major natural waterfalls to be harnessed and others to be created through dams. Development for hydroelectric power was substantial in the early years of the twentieth century. No province had greater potential for hydroelectricity generation than Quebec. Unlike Ontario, which established the Ontario Hydro-Electric Commission in 1906, under the chairmanship of Sir Adam Beck (1857–1925), Quebec permitted its hydroelectric development to be carried out by private enterprise. The process of exploiting electricity, both for light and for power, was one of the great unsung technological developments of the age. Industry could use water-power as an alternative to fossil fuel. Cheap hydroelectric power became an advantage for Canadian industry. The manufacturing community saw cheap power as essential to its growth and development. Hydroelectricity lit Canadian homes at relatively low cost. It fostered the growth of electric-powered public transportation, such as the tram and the trolley.

Charles E. Saunders (National Archives of Canada C-9071).

The period between 1880 and 1919 was a great age of science and technology throughout the Western world. Most fields of scientific endeavour transformed out of all recognition the basic theoretical assumptions that had dominated humankind for generations. The number of inventions that altered in practical ways how people lived and worked was astounding. Canada played little role at the frontiers of pure science. Its record in the technical application of science was somewhat better, as the record of the Dominion Experimental Farms system (created by Ottawa in 1886) demonstrated. The great achievement of Canadian agricultural research in this period was Charles Edward Saunders's (1867–1937) creation of Marquis wheat in 1907. In both science and technology, however, Canada was fortunate to be able to borrow heavily from Great Britain and the United States. Most Canadian technical accomplishment came through adapting imported technology to Canadian conditions.

Population growth was also necessary for economic development. Immigration provided much of that growth for Canada in this period, as in others. Between 1880 and 1920 nearly 4.5 million immigrants arrived in Canada,

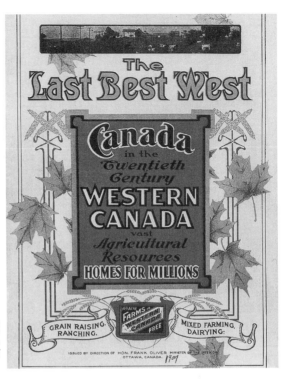

This 1907 poster exhorted immigrants to settle in western Canada (National Archives of Canada C-30621).

mainly from Europe and the United States. Beginning in the mid-1890s, the origins of the newcomers shifted perceptibly. Most of the earlier immigrants came from the British Isles, while after 1896 large numbers came from eastern and southern Europe. In addition, Americans again began arriving in Canada in large numbers, their destinations the 'Last Best West' in Alberta and Saskatchewan. By 1901, 34 per cent of the newcomers came from other countries, with 33 per cent from the United States and 22 per cent from Britain. During the peak decade of immigration (1905–14), nearly 2,800,000 immigrated to Canada, with the numbers about equally divided among central and eastern Europe, the United States, and the British Isles. Between 1901 and 1911 alone, the Canadian population grew by 43 per cent. In the 1911 census, over 20 per cent of all Canadians enumerated had been born abroad. While many of the newcomers settled on farms, fully 70 per cent joined the labour force in industry and trans-portation. Canadian business and government specifically recruited many of the newcomers, often on a contract basis, to provide an industrial workforce. In 1907 the Canadian Department of the Interior began paying bonuses to European immigration agents for people who had labour experience, such as farmers, navvies, or miners. Many other workers arrived as contract labourers. Much of this industrial workforce ended up in Canada's cities.

Workers at looms (*c.* 1908) (City of Toronto Archives, James Collection 137).

ANOTHER ROUND OF INDUSTRIALIZATION

The growth in financial centralization and industrial capacity, particularly the shift from the processing of primary goods into the secondary manufacturing of finished goods, were both major economic developments in Canada in the years 1880–1919. Continued industrialization always involved more than the construction of new and larger factories. Canadians needed to extend and rationalize transportation facilities. They had to mobilize investment, exploit resources, and recruit a labour force. Despite the national policy, Canada did not maintain control over, or ownership in, its economy. Its emergence on the international scene increased its vulnerability to world economic conditions and economic cycles. Moreover, its industrial development was distinctly uneven, with industrial growth well above the national average in Ontario, on the national average in Quebec, and well below the national average in the Maritime and western provinces. Larger urban centres, such as Montreal and Toronto, expanded constantly, while smaller communities fell steadily behind.

One of the keys to Canadian economic growth between 1885 and the Great War was an influx of foreign investment. Few nations depended so heavily on foreign capital in order to fuel economic growth as has Canada throughout its history. Investment in this era—particularly in the boom years 1900–13—was significant. Like other countries, Canada used most of its imported capital to

finance large development projects, such as railways and hydroelectric generation. Canada's imports of capital came in the two forms of indirect (portfolio)
investment and direct investment. These two types of investment reflected the
respective activity of Canada's two largest financial partners. Much of the portfolio investment came from Great Britain. Much of the indirect investment came
from the United States. In terms of the foreign domination of the economy that
resulted, the two types of investment were quite different. Direct investment
resulted in far greater control. At the time few Canadians agonized over-much
about the extent or the origin of foreign ownership. Foreign control did not
become a serious issue in Canadian economic theory or public life until the late
1950s. Throughout this period, almost all Canadians might have agreed with
American entrepreneur Frank Clergue, who declared in 1901 that 'foreign money
injected into the circulating medium of Canada' would 'remain forever to the
everlasting blessing of thousands of its inhabitants' (quoted in Bliss 1972:38).

As students now learn routinely in introductory courses in economics,
portfolio investment represents money borrowed against securities, in this
period mainly bonds. Bonds are a relatively safe investment. They do not carry
management implications. The British preferred portfolio investment in
Canada because their prosperous citizens wanted to clip coupons in their old
age. Government (federal, provincial, municipal) and the railways did most of
Canada's borrowing in Britain. The money went to finance transportation
networks and public works. Little was available for private enterprise, almost
none for venture capital. In the first years of the twentieth century, Canadian
entrepreneurs exploited the British investment market in new ways. The chief
innovation was the promotion of bond issues for giant industrial operations
created from the merger of smaller companies. Nobody was more successful at
merging than William Maxwell Aitken (1879–1964, later Lord Beaverbrook),
son of a New Brunswick Presbyterian minister. His great triumph came in 1910
with the creation of the Steel Company of Canada, the bonds for which his
Royal Securities firm sold in London. 'I created all the big trusts in Canada',
Aitken boasted after he had moved to England in search of greater challenges.
He was the most visible and sharpest operator in a movement that saw fifty-
eight giant corporations created in Canada between 1909 and 1912.

The United States was an importer of British capital before the First World
War and had little available for overseas portfolio investment. The Americans
invested directly in Canada to gain access to Canadian raw materials and the
Canadian market. They went heavily into the resource sector. They also invested
in Canadian manufacturing to gain maximum access to the Canadian market.
Less than half of American direct investment was in manufacturing, but the total
amount involved was over $100 million by 1910. The protective tariff played an
important role in encouraging American branch-plant investment. Early

An Employer Describes Industrial Working Conditions in the 1880s

[In 1886 the government of Sir John A. Macdonald appointed a royal commission 'for the purpose of enquiring into and reporting on all questions arising out of the conflict of labor and capital'. The commission heard almost 1,800 witnesses in the course of seven months of hearings. The following testimony is by George T. Tuckett of Hamilton, a junior member of the tobacco manufacturing firm of G.E. Tuckett & Son. *Source*: G. Kealey, ed., *Canada Investigates Industrialism [The Royal Commission on the Relations of Labour and Capital, 1889*, abridged (Toronto: University of Toronto Press, 1973):143–7.]

Q. Do you employ many hands? *A.* About 300. . . .

Q. Of what ages? *A.* From fourteen up to about forty.

Q. Have you a considerable number of young persons working for you? *A.* I should say about 120 to 150, boys and girls; they are changed from time to time. Of course we have more in winter time than in summer time.

Q. Do you think any of them are under fourteen? *A.* Well, we have a rule that firms have to be guided by, that no one shall be employed less than fourteen. We had some factory inspectors going through the factory, and I told them we had a great deal of trouble in finding out the age, and they told me they were going to get out certificates which parents would sign.

Q. What rates of wages can these people earn? *A.* They average about $1.25 a day; that is what we pay ourselves. The children are paid by the 'rollers,' and when I said 300 hands I was counting only the grown up people—those we pay ourselves. . . .

Q. Is it necessary to employ young persons in this business? *A.* Yes; in order to strip the tobacco; the older hands would not be so nimble.

Canadian protectionism sought to foster employment. Canadians did not worry much about the outflow of profits or the influx of foreign managers. Canadians generally accepted that Canadian businessmen and investors were not very adventurous, preferring familiar fields and allowing the Yankees to take the chances. Far from endangering the Canadian identity, American investment fostered it. The alternative was immigration to the United States.

The Americans preferred to locate their branch plants in southern Ontario. This choice came for a variety of reasons. Americans were active in the heavy industries of Ontario, partly because Ontario was so close to the industrial heartland of the United States south of the Great Lakes. Moreover, Ontario deliberately encouraged Americans to invest in the processing of raw materials through virtually free access to the province's natural resources. Ontarians believed that they had all the requirements for self-sufficiency within their own

Q. Are these children living with their parents generally? *A.* Generally they are mechanics' families and poor people. Some are the children of widows.

Q. Would it not be better for them to go to school than to work for you? *A.* Well, the mothers come to me and say that their children will not go to school, and in order to keep them off the streets, they send them to me.

Q. Have you reason to know that many of them are the children of such mothers? *A.* I could not say. At times we have children of that sort. As a rule, we have the parents come to the factory, and have a bargain made between the 'roller' and the mother or father, in our presence, the first time, and we see that the children go with the proper man and get properly paid for their work. The wages of children from fourteen to sixteen are from $3 to $4.50 a week. . . .

Q. Is the work in your factory a trade, so that those who have learned it will be called mechanics? *A.* Yes. If the stemmer goes along and gets to be smart he gets to be a 'roller'; then he gets on to be a

wrapper, and then the foreman mentions it to us, and when they are at eighteen or nineteen, and fit to become apprentices, they are given benches. He serves for three years, for the first two years at ordinary work and the last year in fine work, and after the last year they become journeymen, and get journeymen's wages.

Q. Can you tell us anything about the experiment made a few years ago in your factory by reducing the hours of labor? *A.* We found that by starting in the summer time at 7 o'clock and working until 6, and giving them a half holiday on Saturday, so that they could get off and enjoy themselves, they worked steadier and with more vigor. In the winter time we start at 7:30 in the morning and work until 6 o'clock, allowing them one hour at dinner, and giving them from 4 o'clock. This allows the mothers to do the marketing in the daylight, and we find that they can do the same amount of work in the nine hours, and then they appear more healthy and strong than when working the longer hours.

borders. The province required that resources taken on Crown land be processed in Canada. 'Debarred from the opportunity of cutting logs for export, it is an absolute certainty that the American lumberman, in default of other sources of supply, will transfer his sawmill enterprises to Canadian soil' (quoted in Nelles 1974:217). American preference both contributed to and reflected the industrial development of Ontario.

After 1885 manufacturing replaced commerce as the chief propellant of urban growth in Ontario. Much of the new industrial plant involved sophisticated technological applications, often imported from the United States. Ontario became the centre of the Canadian iron and steel industry. The transformation of the older iron industry into the steel industry was symptomatic of the process that was occurring. Coal replaced charcoal as the source of heat. The refining process turned into two steps, first involving open-hearth furnaces and then a steam-driven rolling mill. The result was a product with a slightly higher carbon content. Its name was steel. Mechanization occurred at every step in the manufacturing process. 'Gigantic automation' was the watchword at huge installations like Stelco's Hamilton plant or Algoma's Sault Ste Marie operation. Steel rails were the most common standard product. Ontario's manufacturing grew in a number of smaller urban centres.

Quebec manufacturing relied far less heavily on heavy industry (and vast capitalization) than did Ontario. It depended far more on an industry based on labour and fussy mechanization, such as clothing, wood products, textiles, and food processing. Part of the explanation for the difference may reside in labour availability. Part may have been the availability of cheap hydroelectric power in Quebec after 1900. Quebec had eliminated Ontario's early advantage in secondary over primary manufacturing by 1915. Montreal provided the greatest concentration of Quebec's manufacturing sector. By 1900 workers in that city represented about half the manufacturing labour in the province. It is easy to overemphasize the notorious lag between the two central Canadian provinces. They were more like one another than they were like the remainder of the nation. The industrial disparity between the central provinces and the others grew continually in the years before 1914.

While the absence of industrialization in the Canadian west was a consequence of the recentness of its settlement, this did not apply to the Maritime region. Here rural stagnation joined a crisis in the shipbuilding industry. The growth of new technologies was partly to blame, but the problem was mainly a failure of the Maritime shippers' nerve. The shippers always viewed their ships as instruments of trade. Instead of reinvesting their capital in a modern shipbuilding industry, they and the business community of the region made a desperate effort to exploit the internal market. It accepted the national policy and tried to work within it. The attempts at continentalism seemed initially successful in the 1880s, but rapidly turned to failure.

The reasons for the ultimate Maritime failure remain uncertain. Most Maritime entrepreneurs seemed to lack the financial resources to withstand the ups and downs of the economic cycles. They tended to blame many of their problems on high railway freight rates. At about the same time that the region's business community was moaning about railway rates, outside capital moved in and began buying up locally based companies. Montreal capitalists did most of the damage. They bought up and dismantled many burgeoning industries still servicing the local market. Maritime entrepreneurs, convinced that they were at a substantial geographical disadvantage in competing with central Canada, ceased trying in most sectors after 1895. Instead, the region turned to the panacea of iron and steel. Surely the presence of local raw materials would make this industry a competitive one. Unfortunately, central Canadian interests soon took over the Maritime steel industry. By 1911 Montreal controlled much of the region's industrial enterprise. Toronto, on the other hand, moved into the region's wholesale and retail marketing sector. Between 1901 and 1921 the number of regional businesses that were branches of central Canadian firms more than doubled, from 416 to 950. The net result of both sorts of take-overs was a regional loss of economic autonomy. Outsiders siphoned capital away from the Maritimes, and when times got tough, they closed stores and factories. The region was systematically deindustrialized and decommercialized. It would never recover its economic vitality.

Most of the businessmen who operated the industrializing economy were immigrants or sons of immigrants, with Scots farmers overrepresented in both categories. Few had begun at the bottom of the social scale. French Canadians were seriously underrepresented among large-scale entrepreneurs and industrialists, even within their own province. Most French-Canadian businesses remained small in scale, family controlled, and confined chiefly to the province of Quebec. These businessmen did share an overall philosophy. They insisted on government involvement in large schemes of public development, such as railways. They accepted government power to grant monopolies of public service through charters or access to Crown lands through advantageous leases. They sought to minimize competition wherever possible, even if public regulation was the price paid for the reduction. Small businessmen who could not combine institutionally to control trade, such as the small retailers, fought hard for early closings and price-fixing. Business rhetoric about competition extolled less about the virtues of free enterprise than complained about unfair competition. The business community insisted that what it wanted was a 'living profit', a reasonable return on investment of time and capital.

While few business leaders believed in policies of *laissez-faire* in the relationship between the state and business, the situation was quite different when it came to labour organizations. Labour organization was an illegitimate combination designed to erode the right of the individual to run his business as he saw fit. Nevertheless, the growth of industrialization was conducive to an expanding worker militancy. The Canadian state proved relatively receptive to the rights of labour to organize. Whereas in the United States public policy was almost universally hostile to labour organization, in Canada laws that legalized union activity were put on the books beginning in the 1880s. Many of the late nineteenth-century labour organizations in Canada were foreign imports, chiefly from the United States. If Canadian labour got much of its structure from the Americans, it drew much of its practical experience from Great Britain. For Canada as a whole, the Canadian Labour Congress formed in 1883 as a holding body for local trade councils, and in 1892 became the Trades and Labor Congress of Canada.

In this period most labour conflict revolved around the right to organize and the recognition of unions. Government acceptance of union activity in some ways increased the frequency of conflict. Moreover, the civil authorities frequently intervened in labour conflicts, usually in the name of public order and often on the side of management. Such intervention often produced violence. Strikes were certainly common everywhere in Canada, especially after 1900. In Ontario's ten largest cities between 1901 and 1914 there were 421 strikes and lockouts involving 60,000 workers. In the Maritimes, 324 strikes occurred between 1901 and 1914. Except in the far west, the majority of the workers involved in these confrontations were skilled rather than unskilled. By 1914 approximately 155,000 Canadians belonged to organized labour unions, many of them affiliated with American internationals.

NATURAL RESOURCES

If Canada were to avoid eternal international balance-of-payment deficits, which so plague Third World countries in our own era, it obviously needed commodities to export. It found many of these in the natural resources sector. To a considerable extent Canada's resources were the old mainstays of the colonial staple economy, now produced under different guises. Resources not only earned money abroad, they encouraged manufacturing at home.

Agriculture

As if on some master schedule, the Canadian wheat economy continued to expand without pause. Fields of operation moved from central Canada to Manitoba and slightly later to the Northwest Territories (which became the provinces of Saskatchewan and Alberta in 1905). Between 1870 and 1890 thou-

A Ukrainian family harvesting wheat in 1918 (National Archives of Canada PA-88504).

Equipping a Homestead

[In 1905 English writer Georgina Binnie-Clark came to Canada to establish a farm on the Canadian prairies, ultimately using the experience to write a book entitled *Wheat and Woman,* published in 1914. *Source*: G. Binnie-Clark, *Wheat and Woman* (Toronto: Bell & Cockburn, 1914):36–8.]

My general ignorance of agriculture proved deplorable in the matter of the selection of implements. I made a good start with the Massey-Harris up-to-date six-foot binder reaper; but the principal implement on a farm, especially where there remains much land to be broken, is a plough; and into this booby-trap I fell headlong. Mr McGusty was the Massey-Harris agent at Fort Qu'Appelle, and is duty bound to sell their implements when possible. I bought the Sulkey model he recommended at fifty-six dollars in good faith—later in these pages it may tell its own tale. The disc cost forty-five dollars. The mower and rake had been purchased, but not paid for, by the first buyer, and Mr McGusty let me have them for fifty dollars. The mower still does good work; the rake was not satisfactory. The seeder, a 'Kentucky,' I bought of a neighbour, who was also its agent, for the sum of one hundred and thirty dollars; but it is wisdom to buy an implement of a direct agent, and that he should be within reach, because of the frequently urgent matter of repairs. The hay-rack was made to order at a cost of twenty three dollars seventy, which included lumber, bolts, &c., and carpenter's charges. It was much too heavy and clumsy for its purpose, and has been succeeded by two—one was sold to me for ten dollars by the sharp son of a really clever father, and finally I had a Yankee model copied at the inclusive cost of seventeen dollars seventy-five. A hay-rack is deserving of thought, labour, and money, as it is one of the most useful of farm chattels; but most Canadians make their own, and the average collection of racks on a threshing gang is characteristic of Canada, in expressing the individuality of its particular owner untrammelled by the law of order or any sense of loyalty to form. . . .

The total cost of my original outlay in implements and chattels amounted to nearly one hundred and fifty pounds [about $750]. This included the cost of buggy and harness which my brother had purchased for his homestead at about nineteen pounds, and also the second wagon, which was useful but not indispensable. There was also the cost of binder-twine, thirty-six dollars, and an account from the local iron stores for such items as brooms and buckets, grain-shovel, spades, forks, rakes, barrels, halters, and those items of stable equipment which are absolutely indispensable, and the cost of which always seems inconsiderable; but its sum demands a distinct place in the consideration of capital adequate to secure the success of agricultural experiment within reasonable time.

sands of farmers, chiefly from Ontario, poured into the west. The number of acres of occupied land went from 2.5 million to over 6 million (1,011,750 to 2,428,200 ha) in the years 1881–91, while the acres of land under cultivation exploded from 279,000 to 1,429,000 (112,911 to 578,316 ha) in the same ten-year period. The opening of the CPR was critical for the production of western wheat. So too was the appearance of new wheat strains suitable for maturation in the short prairie growing season.

Before the mid-1890s the typical prairie settler was an Ontario-born farmer who came west to make a new start. Despite the passage of the Dominion Land Act of 1872, which made considerable homestead land available, most farmers preferred to purchase land from companies set up by the great corporate benefactors of government land grants, especially the railways. Farmers believed (with some legitimacy) that homestead land was less likely to acquire rail transportation than was land owned by the railway itself. Although homestead land was free to the male settler (married women could not apply for homesteads), successful farming still required considerable capital investment. Conservative estimates of the costs of 'farm-making' ranged from a minimum of $300 (the annual wage for an unskilled labourer) to $1,000. Most farmers brought money with them from the sale of land back east. The western farmer was a market farmer. Although the family grew as much foodstuffs as possible for personal consumption, the farmer's instinct was to increase constantly his acreage under production. Before the First World War, mechanization was limited mainly to harvesting. Animals (horses and oxen) did most of the ploughing and cultivation. Nevertheless, the individual farmer managed to cultivate considerable quantities of land, limited mainly by the size of his labour force. In 1898 Ontario-born A.J. Cotton (1857–1942) harvested a crop of over 17,000 bushels of top-grade wheat in Treherne, Manitoba.

Beginning in the 1890s an open and aggressive Canadian immigration policy, conducted by both the federal and provincial governments, brought new settlers to the prairies. Many came from the United States, which no longer had an unsettled frontier of its own. Others came from eastern Europe, where a long tradition of grain culture existed. The new immigrants moved onto the great dry-belt area of Saskatchewan and southern Alberta, where they initially experienced some very good luck with rain and moisture. By 1921 over 44 mil-lion acres (17,806,800 ha) of the prairies were under cultivation. According to one set of calculations, the wheat economy in 1901–11 contributed over 20 per cent of the growth in per capita income in Canada.

While wheat was the big prairie crop, others were possible. Before the arrival of farmers, much of southern Alberta and southwestern Saskatchewan was the domain of ranchers, who grazed their cattle on open range leased from the federal government. At the height of the cattle boom in 1898, Canadian ranchers exported 213,000 live head. Although ranchers insisted that much of the range land was unsuitable for farming because of water shortages, their obvious self-interest in an open range negated the force of much of their argument. Nevertheless, water was a major potential problem in much of the west.

Mines and Timber

In 1890 Nova Scotia was the leading mining province in Canada, chiefly because of its rich coal resources. After that year, three factors hastened a great shift in Canadian mineral extraction. One was the development of new technologies to extract ore. Another was the increasing availability of railway transportation to remote areas. Most important of all, the international market created a new demand for metal that Canada had in abundance: copper, nickel, and silver. Almost overnight, Ontario and British Columbia became the leading mineral producers.

Although the most famous mining rush of the period was to the Yukon's Klondike district for gold, the Klondike was hardly typical of the mining industry. More representative were the series of mining towns that suddenly sprang up and equally rapidly closed down in the mountains of British Columbia and Alberta. Like most Canadian mines, these required considerable machinery and expertise to exploit, well beyond the resources of the individual miner. Well-capitalized corporations opened such mines, employing money and technology often imported from the United States. In Quebec, the most buoyant segment of the mineral industry from 1900–20 was in asbestos fibre, used chiefly in construction material consumed in the United States. The Canadian mining industry greatly benefited from the military requirements of the Great War.

In the forest industry, the decline through permanent depletion of the white pine forests of eastern Canada pushed the centre of the timbering industry to the west. British Columbia had millions of acres of Douglas fir and cedar. The province started harvesting in the coastal regions close to water, but soon pushed inland. Most of its production went to American markets. The remaining forests of eastern Canada proved valuable for their softwood. The pulp and paper industry expanded rapidly, driven by an insatiable American demand for inexpensive newsprint. By 1915 wood pulp and paper represented one-third of the value of Canadian exports, virtually equal to wheat and grain in the overseas market. Quebec produced nearly one-half of Canada's wood pulp and paper.

The resource sector produced its own version of labour militancy. The sector was difficult to organize by traditional means. In mines and lumber camps, the categories of skilled and unskilled had little meaning. Nevertheless, worker alienation was often extreme. In British Columbia, labour unrest was particularly strong among miners, who worked for large absentee corporations under difficult conditions. In this kind of environment, syndicalists and radicals (such as the Wobblies or the Impossibilists) did very well. They preached the need for the destruction of capitalism and the organization of all workers into general unions.

URBAN AND RURAL CANADA

In 1881 Canada had a population of 4,325,000, of whom 3,349,000 lived outside urban centres. Forty years later, of the nation's 8,788,000 inhabitants, only 4,811,000 resided in non-urban areas, and 1,659,000 lived in cities with a population over 100,000. While the non-urban population had grown over these years from 3,349,000 to 4,811,000, the number of city dwellers had burgeoned from 974,000 to 3,977,000. Urban growth was obviously a major trend of the period 1880–1918. Canada developed some very large metropolitan centres, but their residents did not constitute the entire urban population. If 1,659,000 Canadians lived in cities over 100,000 in 1921, another 2.2 million lived in smaller centres, with 1,058,000 in towns of 5,000 to 29,999 people and 765,000 in towns of 1,000 to 4,999. Canadian urban growth in this era produced all sorts of new problems for the nation. At the same time, urban development was hardly the entire story for these years. As the statistics well demonstrate, before 1921 more Canadians continued to reside in rural rather than urban areas. Rural Canada, although its earlier dominance was gradually eroding away, was nevertheless still very important to the national ethos. Moreover, the very sense of the gradual loss of traditional rural values was critical for the Canadian psyche.

A prosperous farmstead near Darlingford, Manitoba, established before the First World War. The large house and barn are screened by trees on the north and west and are open to the sun on the southeast (Eberhard Otto).

The City

As with most other aspects of Canadian development in this period, urban growth was not even across the regions. Maritime cities grew fairly sluggishly. None could establish regional dominance. Indeed, Halifax lost ground as central Canada siphoned off its financial institutions. In Quebec, Montreal continued its path to the status of the Dominion's premier city, with Quebec City and other towns lagging far behind. In Ontario, Toronto was plainly the 'Queen City', although a number of smaller cities (Hamilton, London, and Kingston) were vibrant. Ottawa inhabited a world of its own as the nation's capital, as it always would. The most spectacular urban growth rates were in the west, which in this era spawned two major cities, Winnipeg and Vancouver, and two contenders for such a rank in Edmonton and Calgary. While western settlement usually suggests farms and agriculture, urban development in the west was strong from the outset. Land speculation drove local pretensions, and many communities aspired to be regional entrepôts. In the prairie provinces the urban population grew from 103,000 to 606,000 between 1900 and 1916. City dwellers, who represented 25 per cent of the region's population in 1901, had increased to 35 per cent only ten years later. By 1921 in British Columbia,

Torontonians celebrating the fall of Pretoria during the Boer War, 5 June 1900, on Yonge Street near Adelaide in Toronto (City of Toronto Archives, James Collection 524).

Vancouver (117,217) and Victoria (38,727) contained 25 per cent of the population of that Pacific province.

The larger cities of Canada most clearly exposed the social problems of the later Victorian and subsequent Edwardian eras. The greatest problem was poverty. Existing evidence suggests that up to half of the Canadian urban working class lived below, or at best around, the poverty line. Most working-class families were glad to supplement the father's income with the earnings of wife and children in menial occupations. Given the grinding conditions of their lives, it is not surprising that many sought refuge in alcohol. Unbalanced diets and malnutrition were only the start of the problems of the poor. Their housing conditions involved overcrowding, poor sanitation, and a lack of open yards and spaces. Home-ownership was difficult, even for the middle classes, because mortgages were hard to obtain and were only of short duration, often no more than three or four years. Malnutrition and deplorable housing conditions combined to produce high overall death rates and high infant mortality rates in Canada's largest cities. The mortality differentials between the poor and the prosperous were substantial, ranging from 35.51 deaths per 1,000 in 1895 in one working-class ward in Montreal to less than thirteen per 1,000 'above the hill'. Infant mortality rates in Canadian cities were little different from those in

A slum interior in October 1913, with a nursing mother (whose husband is presumably at work or looking for work), her many children, and their grandmother, all living in a small space (City of Toronto Archives, DPW 32-243).

places like Calcutta and Bombay. The children of the urban poor often got little schooling. Moreover, the poor resisted pressures for compulsory education.

If the city had social problems, it also made possible a rich and varied cultural life. Before 1918 cultural life maintained an amateur tradition of considerable vitality. The major development of Canadian urban culture in this era meant not so much the appearance of first-rate artists as the creation of an institutional infrastructure that might eventually make possible their emergence. The city made possible the creation of cultural institutions in the form of both organizations and buildings to house them. The construction of museums, for example, was characteristic of the age. The Art Museum of Toronto appeared in 1900, the Royal Ontario Museum in 1912 (it opened in 1914). Equally characteristic of the era was the formation of artistic organizations. The Canadian Art Club (1907) was organized in Toronto, although its founders had no idea how to achieve their goal of introducing new Canadian painting to the entire nation. Formal art and music schools were organized in most of the larger urban centres, offering regularized instruction to neophyte painters and musicians. Theatrical buildings became a measure of a city's status. As early as 1891 Vancouver had a 1,200-seat opera house. Toronto's Royal Alexandra Theatre (1906–7) seated 1,525, and Winnipeg's Walker Theatre (1907, recently renovated as a theatrical venue) seated 2,000 in splendid comfort. These buildings operated continuously, housing mainly professional touring companies and local amateurs. Indigenous professional theatre emerged first in Montreal. There were ten different professional companies at work in Montreal in the 1890s. In 1899 alone these companies gave 618 performances of 109 plays.

The extent of the growth of urban Canada between 1880 and 1919 was largely unanticipated. The large city cut against most of the dominant ideologies of the time, which were traditional and rural. The institutions of urban government were not well integrated into the overall Canadian political system. The British North America Act did not leave much room for the governance of cities that would have budgets and revenues as large as those of the provinces in which they were located. Urban government and urban politics operated outside the structures of Confederation, with their own agendas and distinct party labels. Most cities were slow to abandon property qualifications for voting. Local merchants and real estate promoters tended to dominate city councils, even in cities with a relatively democratic franchise. The ward system produced municipal politicians who curried favour with the electorate by various corrupt practices ranging from the purchasing of votes to 'jobs for the boys'.

No urban centre could expect to prosper in this era if it was not on a mainline railway. Contemporaries clearly recognized this reality. During the several outbursts of railway expansion—particularly between 1906 and 1915, when

Teenagers in 'Toronto the Good' at the End of the Nineteenth Century

[C.S. Clark's *Of Toronto the Good*, published in Montreal in 1898, was subtitled *A Social Study. The Queen City of Canada as It Is*, and carried the motto 'Not necessarily Toronto alone but every city in America'. Imitative of both American muckraking and British urban investigative journalism, Clark's book sought to get behind the city's smug self-image to present the 'dark side of life' in an urban community that was rapidly expanding in both area and population. Despite some attempt at realism and moral neutrality, the entire book reeked of ill-concealed moral outrage. *Source*: C.S. Clark, *Of Toronto the Good: A Social Study* (Montreal: Toronto Publishing Co., 1898):127–34.]

I assert . . . that the present day theorists are entirely behind the times. Boys and girls of tender years are as well aware of the artificial means by which conception can be prevented as old men of a gener-

ation ago. I saw a druggist's advertisement a short time ago in a Toronto paper, with this significant black line: **Rubber Goods of** ALL KINDS **for Sale.** There is not a boy in Toronto, I dare say, who does not know what that means. . . . A lad of sixteen, a druggist's apprentice informed me that it was incredible the quantity of 'rubber goods' they sold. 'We sold more of them than anything else,' he laughed.

It may be remarked by those ladies who talk of passing laws restricting this thing and that thing that it is against the law to sell rubber articles such as are advertised. In reply to any such observations, I might say that there is not a boy in the city of Toronto who could not get any such article if he wanted it. The druggist might and very possibly would refuse to sell to him, if he did not know him, but the boy could easily get what he wanted from the druggist's apprentice as I happen to know is done. A young fellow of sixteen once handed me a pasteboard

more than 14,000 new miles (22,530 km) of railway track were laid in Canada—efforts by aspiring communities to become depots and junction points were prodigious. Conversely, rumours of new railway construction were sufficient to create a village where none had existed previously. The extremes to which communities would go to publicize themselves in order to attract railways were occasionally ludicrous and often expensive. Agricultural fairs, as well as the presence of town bands and sports teams, publicized communities. A marching brass band and a baseball team were two of the best advertisements an 'up-and-at-'em' town could enjoy. 'Bonusing'—financial inducements for railways and business entrepreneurs alike—was a way of life in this period.

If urban growth relied upon railway networks, it operated in a context of fairly blatant and open land speculation. The attempted creation of every new city in western Canada began with a land boom. This stage of development usually ended with a collapse in land prices that required years of recovery. Many small businessmen in the west made a decent living selling out in one

coin, silvered over. When I mentioned to him that I saw nothing in the possession of such a coin, he laughed and told me to tear off the outside layer. I did so, and discovered one of the articles I have endeavoured to describe. I have it in my possession yet, and regard it as a valuable piece of evidence. . . . The use of such articles opens the way for the commission of sin by girls of highest respectability, who fear the results that may ensue from breaking the seventh commandment. . . .

One evening immediately after one of the band concerts in Clarence Square a friend of mine and I walked along Front street west. We did not meet a single pair of the opposite sexes, but fully half a dozen. Boys of 16 or 17 years old age, wearing short pants, and girls certainly not older and in short dresses. What were they doing there? Well, when you see boys with their arms around girls waists as the majority of these were, and in other positions equally suggestive, I do not think it can be contended that their friendship was purely Platonic.

I happen to know who some of these boys were. One of them was the descendant of a well-known United Empire Loyalist, whose family is known all over Canada, another was the son of a lawyer, who though not a prominent man is still well known in Toronto, and the youth himself has been mentioned in the newspapers as a prize winner in one of the city schools, while a third is the son of a prominent King street merchant. The girls I have not the honour of knowing, but presumed them to be misses in the middle walks of life. I do not say that they had committed any act of wrong, but it is a reasonable presumption that boys of assured social position do not usually go with girls so much their inferior socially for any good purpose, and it might also be mentioned that Front street west is not a thoroughfare frequented by respectable people at nights, to any great extent.

community just ahead of the bust, and moving to a new town site further down the rail line. The false fronts on western small-town stores were symbolic of the transitory nature of commitment. Speculation in land involved not merely businessmen—or the west. Almost all segments of local communities across Canada joined a real estate speculation whenever they could. Indeed, the attempt to turn a profit by investing in undeveloped land must surely be one of the most enduring features of Canadian life. Speculation was different from development. The former involved the holding of land for future profit, the latter the translation of land—often acquired at bargain prices—into immediate profit as sites for houses or factories.

Town and Suburb

In the larger urban centres land speculation and development were inseparable from the process of suburbanization. This trend combined with urban expansion away from the commercial core of most cities. There were three distinct motives for suburban expansion. Different types of suburbs were the result. The first motive dominated among the prospering business and professional classes, who moved to new residential suburbs to escape the noise, odours, and bustle of the central city. Horse droppings on busy city streets, for example, were a major problem before the Great War. Some of these suburbanites were attempting to separate themselves from the growing slums of the industrializing city. The architectural style most closely associated with the new suburban élites grew out of the English Arts and Crafts movement and became known as the English Domestic Revival. A second motive for suburban growth was the quest for lower land costs and lower taxes outside the central city. The result was the development of a number of industrial suburbs, such as Maisonneuve in Montreal, which flourished outside the city but was within its orbit. The third motive was proximity to work. As industrial development moved into the cheaper outskirts, workers were forced to follow their jobs into often inadequate new housing. During in this period, most large cities in Canada grew by a continuous process of absorbing outlying communities.

The genuine Canadian small town tended to fit one of two models. It was either a community serving a surrounding rural area, or a single-resource community, often remotely located, that had formed around a mine or mining/smelter operation. Many resource towns, though not all, were company towns. The service community was the centre of economic, social, and recreational life for its district. Before the advent of radio and television, the social life of small-town Canada bustled impressively. Organizations of all kinds proliferated and flourished. Most towns had a variety of lodges and an endless round of meetings, dances, and 'occasions'. The last ranged from concerts to plays to sermons by visiting evangelical preachers to lectures on temperance or travel to exotic places. By the end of the Great War, most towns had a 'movie house' or a hall that exhibited motion pictures on a regular basis. Many small towns had exercised the local option permitted by liquor legislation and 'gone dry'. The resource town consisted almost exclusively of single males and a handful of women. There were precious few sources of entertainment other than booze and gambling. Such communities were both violent and restive.

Rural Canada

A number of major changes occurred in Canadian agriculture during the period from 1880 to 1914. The most obvious was the enormous expansion of farming in the prairie west, concentrating singlemindedly on grain cultivation. Elsewhere, the era saw a major shift in eastern Canada into specialized farming. In central Canada, farmers moved into specialized high-quality consumer production, becoming increasingly dependent on off-farm processing, particularly of cheese, butter, and meat. By 1900 Ontario had over 1,200 cheese factories that had captured over half of the British market. Ontario cheese makers were renowned around the world. Quebec farmers had greater difficulty in making the change because of the marginality of much of their land. Specialty farming was very remunerative for those able to engage in it. The aristocrats of farming were the dairy farmers and the fruit farmers. Along with specialized farming came new technology, although the ubiquitous tractor did not replace the horse until after the Great War. More important were mechanical harvesters, centrifugal cream separators, and the introduction of refrigeration. Technology was essential to specialization. It was also capital intensive. Not all farmers could make the shift. Those who could not often stagnated or failed absolutely. Between 1891 and 1921 the Maritime region lost 22,000 farms and 1,556,709 acres (630,000 ha) of farm land under cultivation. Unmodernized farms could not continue to support the entire family. By 1911 the *Farmer's Advocate* could refer to the 'perennial debates as to "Why the Boys Leave the Farm"'. While urban migration was one response, one alternative was the entrance of farmers—and farm women—into the traditional resource industries of the nation. Males went to sea to fish or into the woods to cut timber. Females worked seasonally in factories, processing farm products or fish.

Contemporaries often blamed the growing rural exodus on the social and cultural attractions of the city. While it might thus be tempting to visualize rural Canada as a vast wasteland of isolated and unlettered country bumpkins, such a view would be most inaccurate. Isolation did exist, as did educational limitations. On the other hand, a relatively efficient and inexpensive postal service provided contact with the wider world. People read books and discussed them at clubs that met in local churches. Clergymen often talked about controversial books and topics from their pulpits. Rural Canadians voraciously devoured newspapers and magazines that often required far more of readers than do their modern counterparts. Many farm families received at least one daily newspaper through the mail, seldom on the day of publication, but usually only a day or two later. Canadian dailies in this era provided more substantial fare than today. International coverage was much fuller, and many papers saw themselves as 'papers of record', often reproducing verbatim accounts of court trials and important meetings. In the spring of 1919, for example, the *Winnipeg Tribune* carried a full stenographer's report of the debates at the labour convention in Calgary, which agreed to 'an Industrial Organization of all workers'. Most rural folk also relied heavily for their edification on farm journals such as the *Grain Growers' Guide* (1908–28) and more general magazines like the *Christian Guardian*, the voice of the Methodist Church, which was begun in 1829 by Egerton Ryerson and continued under

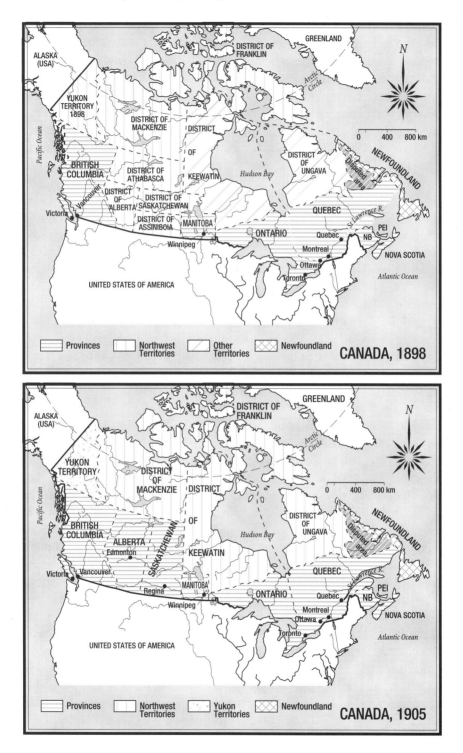

Provinces | **Northwest Territories** | **Other Territories** | **Newfoundland**

CANADA, 1898

Provinces | **Northwest Territories** | **Yukon Territories** | **Newfoundland**

CANADA, 1905

this name until 1925. The wide range of letters to the editor included in most of these periodicals suggest both their circulation and vitality.

If rural Canadians had access to considerable information, they were also surprisingly able to get together socially with each other. The school and the church were both local institutions that served other functions besides providing formal education and worship services. School districts were usually the only sign of public organization in vast regions of rural Canada that were otherwise politically unorganized. The community jealously guarded its schoolhouse, which was from coast to coast typically of one room. The most common Quebec school in the 1913 census had one room, built at a cost of $1,200. Whether Protestant or Catholic, francophone or anglophone, rural Canadians took their religion seriously. Sermons served as topics for daily conversation. The activities of various auxiliary groups connected with any church, particularly the picnics and socials, were very popular. Winter did not so much shut down social life in rural areas as provide the venue for its flowering. The demands of the farm were much lighter in winter, while snow and ice provided a decent surface for horse-drawn sleighs and carrioles to travel about the countryside. 'A working day. . . was from about 4:30 a.m. to 11 o'clock at night', reported one western farmer, 'but this was only in seeding and harvesting time. In the winter we used to really have fun' (quoted in Voisey 1988:158). A number of diaries and journals kept by rural Canadians in this period have recently appeared in print. They provide two revelations for the modern reader. The first is the sheer volume of social interchange, especially among the young, that was not only possible but actually occurred. The second is the extent to which Canadians of this era actively participated in their own entertainment rather than being amused as passive spectators by the activities of others. Canadians of both sexes and all ages routinely spent a social evening in singing hymns and other songs. They created and performed their own skits and joined together in active games such as charades.

Rural life was not all bucolic pleasure, of course. The real reasons for the rural exodus were not isolation but exploitation and lack of economic opportunity. The underside of life on the family farm was the considerable exploitation of those who would not in the end inherit a substantial share in the property. The system was particularly hard on women, who usually did not share in the ownership of the farm and who seldom received remuneration for their labour. Western farmers especially were hostile to 'anachronistic' legal concepts such as dower rights. The homesteading system was generally unsympathetic to the rights of women to set up as independent farmers. For many women everywhere in Canada, the daily routine was even more continually demanding than it was for men. Women's responsibilities included not only the kitchen garden and the small livestock but care of the family itself. One of the

A Girlhood in New Brunswick, 1892

[Sarah (Sadie) Estelle Harper was born in Shediac in 1875 and grew up with six siblings in a large Victorian house on Sackville Street. Father Harper was a partner in a shoe factory, and the Harper family was thus relatively well-off economically. For Sadie, growing up was a pleasant and happy experience. This excerpt is from her diary. *Source*: S.E. Harper, *A Full House and Fine Singing: Diaries and Letters of Sadie Harper Allen*, edited by Mary Biggar Peck (Fredericton: Goose Lane, 1992):66-7.

Wed. June 29 [1892]: Well here it is just a beautiful day, fine and just warm enough to be pleasant. This is the third day of our holidays and I can't say I have enjoyed them very much so far. Yesterday it poured from dinner time until tea time, but still I was not very lonely because there is such a houseful of us. Besides, Aunt Rose (who came over a week ago tomorrow) came up and stayed all day, and she is just splendid company. In the morning I did my housework up and then trimmed May's sailor hat, and after dinner I got Winnie's ready for trimming and then made lemon filling for my Washington pie which I made yesterday and made frosting for it also. And I practised some and read some of a book called *Little Journey in the World* by the same author of *Baddeck and That Sort of Thing*. Mr Bailey and Eddie White, Fred Henderson and Leonard Webster came up and spent the evening. We had lots of fun as usual over those Tiddlywinks. We had two tables, and when one side missed they had to go to the other table, and the best players kept their same places. There were Mr B. and Nell, Win and Fred, Leonard and Blois, and Eddie and I. After playing we had a lot of music. Leonard sang 'They are After Me' and some other songs, and Mr Bailey gave us a solo, then we had some Charades. We also made up an orchestra just for fun. Mr B. played on the mouth organ (he plays just beautifully on it), and Leonard had the tambourine, Blois a tin whistle, Eddie another, and May the table bell, and Winnie played one piano and Nell accompanied her on the other,

side consequences of the shift into specialized farming was that parts previously consigned to women—'egg money', which often provided them with a small income independent of their husbands—were taken over by the males. Canadian rural society continued to be inherently patriarchal in its organization. Men owned the land and usually made the decisions, including when to uproot and resettle, often against the wishes of their wives. The rural patriarch, an intensely self-righteous but essentially a land-hungry, materialistic tyrant, became a common motif in Canadian fiction of this and a slightly later period.

Despite the darker side, a vast majority of Canadians continued to hold rural values and to think of the nation largely in pastoral terms. Those who read Canadian poetry or looked at Canadian art found little but Canadian nature. Foreigners inevitably saw Canada as a completely undeveloped country and Canadians as an agricultural people. In the hands of the poets, Canadian nature

whilst I had the zither. Oh but we had fun over that.

Monday morning (day before yesterday) was fine but the afternoon was wet. I wrote a long letter to Ted before dinner. She wrote Nell and I while she was on her journey when they had stopped for a while at a little place a hundred miles from Port Arthur. Her mother told me yesterday that they both liked it in Winnipeg very much and Lottie was feeling very well only tired and sleepy. It is just three weeks I think from Monday since they left. For the last month back, part of the Lodge members were getting up a drama for the Lodge called *The Social Glass*. Nettie Evans, Mrs Lodge and Floss White and Eddie McDonald, Mr Russell, Mr Butler, Mr Colwell and Mr Belyea and Es Hamilton are the ones that took part in it. So they gave it to the public last Monday evening. It was just fine. They had a full house and the band played between every act, some very pretty selections. They all took their parts splendidly. Hardly anybody knew Flo, when the curtain rose, as she was dressed in a light blue dress and her hair done up and flowers in it and she looked just sweet but so womanly. Es Hamilton was too comical for anything as Bob Brittle. Oh he was grand. Nettie Evans as Nettie Nettlebee could not have been better. It just suited her to a tee. 'She did love to make folks happy.' Will Butler was splendid as Fairly. He acted the delirium tremens fine and also the rest were good too. Though it was ridiculous and comical in places, yet it was sad when you thought it was just real life. This social glass at first and then it gets to more and more until your own life is ruined by it and many many others.

Soon after Mama's birthday, which was the twelfth of May, Papa got us a large lovely double-seated carriage. So now we go out almost every time we want to. Last Friday evening we all went over to Pully Dickie's to a company she had. There were: Flo and Ed, Jennie and Leonard, Fred H. and Nell, Blois and I, and Will Sprague and his mother and Mrs Clayton Dickie and Mrs Brae. We had a fine time, not one stiff five minutes. I guess I laughed from the time I reached there until I left, and I think the rest did their share at it too.

was chiefly benign. Writers of prose sometimes depicted nature differently, often in terms of the victory of hardy settlers over the harsh landscape and climate. Many Canadian writers and painters of this period romanticized the farm and farming, none more so than Lucy Maud Montgomery. *Anne of Green Gables* summed up a major conflict of the era: the problem of reconciling the bucolic beauty and tranquillity of the rural landscape with the need to leave it in order to fulfil one's ambitions. For large numbers of Canadians of this era, growing up meant leaving the farm.

Another form of the romanticization of rural life flourished in the collection of its folklore and folk songs. Marius Barbeau (1883–1969) was the first great Canadian collector of folk traditions, beginning in 1911 when he was appointed an anthropologist at the Museum Branch of the Geological Survey of Canada (now the National Museum of Canada). There were thousands of

A Farmer's Wife in British Columbia

[In 1912 the English journalist Ella C. Sykes published *A Home-Help in Canada,* a report of a tour of Canada she had taken 'to investigate what openings there might be in the Dominion for educated women'. For part of the visit, she had posed as a home helper. One of the places she visited was a chicken farm near Vancouver, British Columbia. Sykes describes the role of her host's wife and offers an assessment of her prospects. This book was one of many accounts published before the First World War of prospects for British immigrants in Canada. *Source*: E.C. Sykes, *A Home-Help in Canada* (London: G. Bell & Sons Ltd, 1912):168–9.]

Mrs Bent was almost as fully occupied as her husband. Her house was beautifully clean and well kept, her stove brightly polished, and she had to prepare four meals a day, afternoon-tea being included in their menu, and also make her own bread. Once a week she scrubbed out her large kitchen and pantry (probably she will have recourse to covering the floor with linoleum later on, or painting it), on Monday she did the household wash, and Tuesday was ironing-day.

Most women would consider that her house gave her occupation and to spare, especially as she was dainty in her table appointments and always had flowers in the pretty living room, but she did almost as much on the ranch as her husband. The stock had to be fed, and needed water at frequent intervals, this being mixed with a few grains of permanganate of potash as a disinfectant, and clover had to be gathered daily at some little distance from the house to provide green food for the hens which were shut up in runs. The fowls were fed three times a day, twice with grain, and their 'balanced ration' (a mixture of grain, meal, powdered green food and ground-up bone) was given them in the evening, while the chickens required five meals. She also washed and packed the eggs for market, put the chickens into 'brooders' for the night, and lit the lamps to keep their shelters up to the right temperature, and on occasion she would chop up logs to feed the insa-

publications, texts, and songs that Barbeau recorded and preserved in archives that document not only the folk traditions of rural Quebec but also those of the Tsimshian Indians of British Columbia. The folkways and songs that Barbeau and others collected were part of the traditional rural experience of Canada. They preserved almost nothing of urban origin. The collectors desperately gathered up dialects, riddles, tall tales, children's rhymes, all of which told more of the daily life of the people than most other historical evidence. Underlying the desperation was the fear that these traditions would disappear in the rapidly changing society of the period.

The dominance in Canada of the myth of agriculture carried over into the various efforts of the period to turn Aboriginal peoples into 'peaceable agricultural labourers'. Agrarian ideology had the advantage of both justifying the

tiable stove, wielding an axe with skill, and making me feel ashamed that I never got much beyond splitting up kindling with this weapon, so dangerous to unaccustomed hands.

Though she never grumbled, yet to me her life seemed lacking in relaxation. She and her husband could not leave the ranch together, unluckily she had no congenial neighbours close at hand (they were of the English labouring type), and as her chief friends lived at a distance, she did not care to go and see them by herself—in fact, I believe that during my visit she went farther afield than she had done since her marriage.

To balance this, she was young and full of hope, there was the possibility that people of her own class might settle near them later on, and more than all, the encouraging sense that she and her husband were making their way in the world together, and that their efforts had every prospect of being crowned with success. . . .

I was very sorry when the time came for me to leave the Bents, and as I got into the waggon beside Mr Bent, and drove off to an accompaniment of squeaks and squeals from a couple of small pigs confined in a packing-case behind us, I felt that this was the close of a pleasant episode in my Canadian tour. It had left me with the conviction that poultry-farming would be a profitable undertaking for active women with a little capital, who would work in partnership. They must be capable, all-round girls, accustomed to make the best of things, and, of course, properly trained for the work. Let no elderly woman, who has looked after the fowls in England with a boy under her to do all the rough work, think that she will 'make good' in the Dominion, unless she is exceptionally vigorous and adaptable. Canada is the Land of Youth and Hope. Everyone seems to have a sense of the great openings and possibilities there are in the country, and this helps the newcomers to tide over many a rough bit; but the life is not an easy one in many ways, and the hardships would be intolerable to a middle-aged woman wedded to English comforts. The work on a chicken ranch is constant, and outside distractions would be few, for girls must be prepared to do everything themselves, as hired help is most expensive and would eat up all their profits.

dispossession of the Native peoples of their hunting grounds and providing them with an alternate way of life. Before the Great War most Canadians regarded agriculture as 'the mainspring of national greatness' and farming as a way of life that uplifted one 'morally and emotionally' (Carter 1990:20). Scientists saw agriculture as a crucial step in the ladder of progress. They perceived other ways of using the land, such as mining or lumbering, as tainted and inferior. The government displaced Aboriginals by treaties, then removed them to reserves and encouraged them to farm. Exhortation was not the same as useful practical assistance. Native Canadians needed a good deal of help to shift from a nomadic hunting/gathering existence to a settled agricultural one, and they did not consistently receive assistance. Government aid was sporadic, cheese paring, and patronizing. After 1885 coercion replaced subsidization as the federal government's major weapon to impose agriculturalism on the reserves. Not surprisingly, the policy failed.

A final illustration of nature's appeal for Canadians came in the various back-to-nature movements. One form involved mounting crusades to preserve Canada's natural environment in the face of encroaching civilization. The fight for the conservation of Canadian wildlife involved the establishment of game reserves and legislation to curb indiscriminate hunting. The crusade's major victories came with the establishment of large numbers of national and provincial parks across Canada in the years before the Great War. Another form of the back-to-nature movement was the summer cottage, which flourished among urbanites who could afford one by the early years of the twentieth century. Still another variation was the growth of outdoor recreation, particularly wilderness travel. Thousands of Canadians headed off every summer from the city to canoe on the nation's more remote waterways. Ernest Thompson Seton (1860–1946), who founded an organization called Woodcraft Indians in 1902, promoted a junior version of this outdoor activity. Some of the best publicists for the canoe and the wilderness were painters, especially those who eventually formed the Group of Seven in 1920. Its

The Imperialist

[In 1904 Canadian novelist Sara Jeannette Duncan (1861–1922) published *The Imperialist*. Duncan was one of the first generation of female journalists in Canada, serving as a parliamentary correspondent for the Montreal *Star* in 1888. Although most of her novels were set in India, this one was located in an Elgin, Ontario, clearly modelled on her native Brantford. The theme of the work is Imperial Federation, giving Duncan an opportunity to espouse her own political views, as in the following excerpt, where her protagonist Lorne Murchison discusses his impending visit to England with a young lady friend. *Source*: S.J. Duncan, *The Imperialist* (Toronto: McClelland and Stewart, 1990):109–10.]

'Oh, of course, I'm glad you're going, really,' [Dora Milburn] assured him. 'And we'll all be proud to be acquainted with such a distinguished gentleman when you get back. Do you think you'll see the King? You might, you know, in London.'

'I'll see him if he's visible,' laughed Lorne. 'That would be something to tell your mother, wouldn't it? But I'm afraid we won't be doing business with His Majesty.'

'I expect you'll have the loveliest time you ever had in all your life. Do you think you'll be asked out much, Lorne?'

'I can't imagine who would ask me. We'll get off easy if the street boys don't shout: "What price Canucks?" at us! But I'll see England, Dora; I'll feel England, eat and drink and sleep and live in England, for a little while. Isn't the very name great? I'll be a better man for going, till I die. We're all right out here, but we're young and thin and weedy.

members, mainly English-born Torontonians making a living as commercial artists, had begun travelling north into the Georgian Bay and Algonquin wildernesses as early as 1911. This group captured the iconographic essence of wilderness Canada: a bleak and sombre but nonetheless curiously beautiful landscape of jack pines, rock outcroppings, and storm-driven lakes, totally uninhabited by people.

IMPERIALISM, RACISM, AND REFORM

Contemporaries often characterized Canadian political life in this era in terms of its lack of ideology, as well as its predilection for what the French observer Andre Siegfried called the 'question of collective or individual interests for the candidates to exploit to their own advantage' (Siegfried 1907:142). Lurking only just beneath the surface, however, were some serious and profound issues. First was the so-called Canadian question, which bore in various ways upon the very future of the new nation. It often appeared to be a debate between those who sought to keep Canada within the British empire and those who wanted it to assume full sovereignty. Into this discussion other matters merged subtly,

They didn't grow so fast in England, to begin with, and now they're rich with character and strong with conduct and hoary with ideals. I've been reading up the history of our political relations with England. It's astonishing what we've stuck to her through, but you can't help seeing why—it's for the moral advantage. Way down at the bottom, that's what it is. We have the sense to want all we can get of that sort of thing. They've developed the finest human product there is, the cleanest, the most disinterested, and we want to keep up the relationship—it's important. Their talk about the value of their protection doesn't take in the situation as it is now. Who would touch us if we were running our own show?'

'I don't believe they are a bit better than we are,' replied Miss Milburn. 'I'm sure I haven't much opinion of the Englishmen that come out here. They don't think anything of getting into debt, and as often as not they drink, and they never know enough to—to come in out of the rain. But, Lorne—'

'Yes, but we're very apt to get the failures. The fellows their folks give five or six hundred pounds to and tell them they're not expected back till they're making a living. The best men find their level somewhere else, along recognized channels. Lord knows we don't want them—this country's for immigrants. We're manufacturing our own gentlemen quite fast enough for the demand.'

'I should think we were. Why Lorne, Canadians—nice Canadians—are just as gentlemanly as they can be! They'll compare with anybody. Perhaps Americans have got more style;' she weighed the matter; 'but Canadians are much better form, I think.'

including the race question and the reform question. The former involved the future of French Canada within an evolving Anglo-American nation. The latter concerned the institution of political and social change through public policy. Debate and disagreement over imperialism, Anglo-French antagonisms, and reform—the three strands loosely linked—kept political Canada bubbling with scarcely suppressed excitement from the 1880s to the beginning of the Great War. Canada's involvement in the military conflict of Europe would certainly bring these strands together, even if it did not resolve them.

Imperialism

The period from 1880 to 1914 saw a resurgence of imperial development around the world. The French, the Germans, even the Americans, took up what Rudolph Kipling called the 'White man's burden' in underdeveloped sectors of the world. About the same time, Great Britain began to shed its 'Little England' free trade sentiments. The world's shopkeeper discovered that substantial windfall profits came from exploiting the economies of Asia, Latin America, and Africa, especially the last. Canada first faced the implications of the resurgence of Britain's imperial pretensions in 1884 when the mother country asked it to contribute to an expedition to relieve General Charles Gordon, besieged by thousands of Muslim religious fanatics at Khartoum in the Egyptian Sudan. Sir John A. Macdonald's immediate response was negative, but he ultimately found it politic to allow Canadian civilian volunteers to assist the British army. By the end of the century Joseph Chamberlain at the Colonial Office was advocating that Britain's old settlement colonies be joined together in some political and economic union, the so-called Imperial Federation.

Encouraged by a new infusion of immigrants from Britain—nearly half a million between 1870 and 1896 and a million between 1896 and 1914—many anglophone Canadians began openly advocating Canada's active participation in the new British empire. Their sense of imperial destiny was not necessarily antinationalistic. They saw no inconsistency between the promotion of a sense of Canadian unity and a larger British empire. 'I am an Imperialist', argued Stephen Leacock (1869–1944) in 1907, 'because I will not be a Colonial.' Leacock sought 'something other than mere colonial stagnation, something sounder than independence, nobler than annexation, greater in purpose than a Little Canada' (quoted in Bumsted 1969, II:78). Such pan-Britannic nationalism came to express itself concretely in demands for Imperial Federation. It was most prevalent in the province of Ontario.

Unfortunately for the imperialists, not all Canadians agreed with their arguments. Several strands of anti-imperial sentiment had emerged by the turn of the century. One strand, most closely identified with the political journalist Goldwin Smith (1823–1910), insisted that the geography of North America

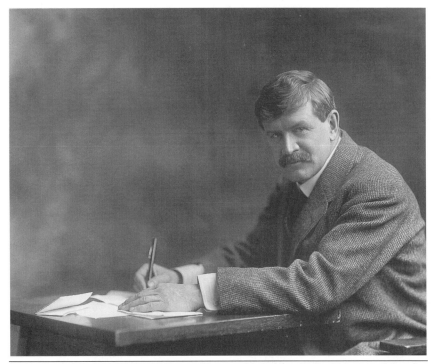

Stephen Leacock in 1914 (11-202933 Notman Photographic Archives, McCord Museum of Canadian History, Montreal).

worked against Canadian nationalism. Smith advocated Canadian absorption into the United States. Fear of this development led many Canadians to oppose a new reciprocity agreement with the United States in 1911. Another strand, led by John S. Ewart (1849–1933) insisted on federal Canada's assumption of full sovereignty. Ewart argued that 'Colony implies inferiority—inferiority in culture, inferiority in wealth, inferiority in government, inferiority in foreign relations, inferiority and subordination' (Ewart 1908:6). Yet another perspective was enunciated by Henri Bourassa (1868–1912), who advocated a fully articulated bicultural Canadian nationalism. He wrote, 'My native land is all of Canada, a federation of separate races and autonomous provinces. The nation I wish to see grow up is the Canadian nation, made up of French Canadians and English Canadians' (quoted in Monière 1981:190). This Bourassa version of nationalism was considerably larger than the still prevalent traditional nationalism of French Canada. As the newspaper *La Vérité* put it in 1904, 'what we want to see flourish is French-Canadian patriotism; our people are the French-Canadian people; we will not say that our homeland is limited to the Province of Quebec, but it is French Canada. . . .'

On Imperialism and Nationalism

[One of the leading opponents of Canadian imperialism was Henri Bourassa (1868–1952). In 1912 he explained his position in a Canadian Club address. *Source*: H. Bourassa, *Canadian Club Addresses 1912* (Toronto: Warwick Bros & Rutter Ltd, 1912):78–80.]

We speak of 'our Empire.' Have you ever considered how little we Canadians count in that Empire, the most wonderful fabric of human organization that has ever existed. Of course, as far as land is concerned, and water, and rocks, and mines, and forests, we occupy a large portion of the Empire. As to population we are only seven millions out of over four hundred millions. As the imperial powers, we have none. The people of the British Kingdom, forty millions in number, possess as their sole property the rest of that Empire. Suppose you except Canada with her seven millions, Australia with her four millions and a half, New Zealand with one million, and South Africa, with a little over one million of white people: apart from those semi-free states, the whole empire of India, the hundreds of Crown colonies, and those immense protectorates in Africa or Asia, no more belong to us than they belong to the Emperor of Germany, or to the President of the French Republic. We have no more to say as regards the government, the legislation, the administration, the revenue and the expenditure, and the defence of that territory, comprising four-fifths of the total population of the Empire, than have the coolies of India or the Zulus of Matabeleland! I am not saying this in disparagement of the system; I am simply putting our position as it is. At the present time, the seven millions of people in Canada have less voice, in law and in fact, in the ruling of that Empire, than one single sweeper in the streets of Liverpool, or one cab-driver on Fleet Street in London; he at least has one vote to give for or against the administration of that Empire, but we, the seven million Canadians, have no vote and no say whatever.

When I hear splendid phrases, magnificent orations, sounding sentences, about that 'Empire of ours,' I am forcibly reminded of the pretension

The most common confrontations over the role of Canada within the empire occurred in the context of imperial defence. At Queen Victoria's Jubilee celebration in June 1897, Laurier had fended off a regularization of colonial contributions to the British military. The question arose again in July 1899 when the mother country requested Canadian troops for the forthcoming war in South Africa against the Boers. When the shooting began on 11 October 1899, the popular press of English Canada responded with enthusiasm to the idea of an official Canadian contingent. Newspapers in French Canada opposed involvement. As *La Presse* editorialized, 'We French Canadians belong to one country, Canada: Canada is for us the whole world, but the English Canadians have two countries, one here and one across the sea.' The government compromised by sending volunteers, nearly 5,000 before the conflict was

of a good fellow whom I had hired to look after the furnace of a building of which I had the management in Montreal. Every year, when the time came to purchase the coal for the winter, he used to exclaim, with a deep sense of his responsibilities: 'How dear it costs us to keep up our building!' Our right of ownership, of tutelage, of legislation, in the British Empire is exactly what the right of partnership of that stoker was in that building.

. . . [A]t the sixth Imperial Conference, the delegates from Australia, representing a courageous, intelligent, progressive British community, with a high sea trade amounting in imports and exports to $650,000,000 a year, asked the representatives of the British Government why the British authorities, without even thinking of asking the opinion of Canada, of Australia, of South Africa, and of New Zealand, had concluded with the great maritime powers the international treaty known as the Declaration of London, which may affect beneficially or otherwise the trade of the world in future naval wars. They enquired also if it would be possible to have at least one representative from the self-governing British colonies on the Board of Arbitration, eventually to be constituted, under the terms of that treaty, to adjudicate upon the seizures of trade and ships in times of war. Sir Edward Grey, undoubtedly one of the ablest men in British public life to-day, showed there, I think, his great tact and his extraordinary command of words and of diplomatic means. But, when all the courteous terms and all the frills were taken off, his answer amounted to this: On that board the negro President of Hayti could sit, the negro President of Liberia could sit, but the Prime Minister of Canada or of Australia could not sit, simply because Hayti and Liberia are nations, whilst Canada or Australia are not nations. He explained that the colonies were not consulted because they exist only through Great Britain, and that the moment Great Britain accepted that treaty it applied to us as to her. Undoubtedly true and another evidence, I think, to show that in the 'imperial partnership,' in the enjoyment of that imperial citizenship of which we hear so much, there still remains a *slight* difference between the British citizen in England, Scotland and Ireland, and the British citizen of Canada: one is a member of a sovereign community, the other is the inhabitant of a subjected colony.

over. The defence issue emerged again in 1909, this time over naval policy. Under imperial pressure, Canada finally agreed to produce a naval unit of five cruisers and six destroyers. Both sides attacked Laurier's compromise Naval Service Bill of January 1910. The anglophone Tories insisted it did not provide enough assistance for the British, while in Quebec a coalition of nationalists and Conservatives joined forces to fight for its repeal.

Racism

The link between outward-looking imperial sentiment and domestically oriented reform was provided by racial sentiments, which were at their height during this period. Part of the 'race question in Canada' was not really about race at all but about the conflict between French and English Canada. While there was no racial barrier between French and English, contemporaries accepted racial arguments and analyses of various kinds as part of the scientific advancement of the age. Many imperialists regarded the historical progress of the United States, Great Britain, and Canada as evidence of the special genius of the 'Anglo-Saxon race'. The French were acceptable partners because they too were a northern people. Out of the scientific theories of Charles Darwin came the conviction that inheritance was the key to evolution. Races were formed by natural selection, exhibiting quite unequal characteristics. In almost everyone's hierarchy, the present Canadian population was at the progressive top of the racial scale. Newcomers who could or would not assimilate would inevitably lower the Canadian 'standard of civilization'.

Canadians saw the new immigration after 1896 as particularly troubling. Even that secular saint, J.S. Woodsworth, associated criminality with the newcomers. Many feared the potential degeneracy of the 'great northern race' through comingling with lesser stocks. Others concentrated on the campaigns for social purity, mixing restrictions on the consumption of alcoholic beverages with hostility to prostitution, venereal disease, and sexual exploitation. The first serious efforts at large-scale immigration restriction, designed mainly to keep out the degenerates, began in the early years of the century. Campaigns for social purity, immigration restriction, and Asiatic exclusion all came out of the same stock of assumptions about heredity and environment that informed many reform movements of the period. The reformers often emphasized social and moral aspects, directing their efforts chiefly against newcomers.

Reform

The reform movement of this period was rich and varied in its interests. It ranged from the women's suffrage movement to various efforts at social and humanitarian change. Mainstream Canadian reform movements had some features in common, however. Their leaders were members of the middle and professional classes who shared assumptions of the age about regeneration and social purity. Those of Protestant backgrounds tended to predominate, particularly in temperance/prohibition, public health, education, and women's suffrage. Women, because of their general nurturing role in society, played a major role in most reform movements. These women were often less concerned with restructuring gender roles in society than with the need for instituting middle-class virtues or with helping the poor. French-Canadian women were significantly underrepresented in most national reform movements, partly because of the political isolation of Quebec, and partly because the antifeminist ideology of the traditional society greatly limited the place of women in that province.

The suffrage movement did emphasize the gender question. It addressed women's political powerlessness by attempting to win for them the right to vote. The movement was chiefly an urban one, dominated by well-educated women who saw political power as necessary to bring about other legislative change. The suffragist leadership was almost exclusively Canadian or British-born and belonged to the main-line Protestant churches. Well over half of the female leaders were gainfully employed, mostly in journalism and writing. The movement gradually lost contact with working-class women, who were suspicious of the class biases of both suffrage and reform. It also failed to gain the support of farm women because it did not understand rural issues, especially the concern over rural depopulation. Many rural women became involved in their own organizations designed to deal with their own problems, such as the Women's Institutes. Adelaide Hoodless (1857–1910) founded the first Institute at Stoney Creek, Ontario in 1897. (In Henry James Morgan's biographical compilation *The Canadian Men and Women of the Time*, 2nd ed., 1912, she is listed under the entry for her husband John, who was an obscure furniture manufacturer in Hamilton.) Women's Institutes promoted appreciation of rural living, as well as encouraging better education for all women for motherhood and home-making. In 1919 the Federated Women's Institutes of Canada organized with its motto 'For Home and Country.'

One female reform organization, the Woman's Christian Temperance Union (WCTU) had both rural and urban memberships. Founded in 1874 in Owen Sound, Ontario, the WCTU claimed 10,000 members by 1900, and had an influence far beyond that number. Despite its name, the WCTU wanted prohibition, soon seeing the elimination of alcoholic beverages as a panacea for many of the ills currently besetting Canadian society, such as crime, the abuse of women and children, political corruption, and general immorality. The WCTU was only one of several members of the Dominion Alliance for the Total Suppression of the Liquor Traffic. Like most Canadian reform movements, prohibition required state intervention to be effective. This factor eventually led some of its supporters to women's suffrage. Laurier held a national referendum on prohibition in 1898. Although its supporters won a narrow victory, the prime minister refused to implement national legislation because only 20 per cent of the total electorate had supported the principle. The prohibitionists turned to the provinces, succeeding in getting legislation passed in Prince Edward Island in 1900 and in Nova Scotia in 1910. Local option was even more effective, since it involved local communities where prohibitionist sentiment could be strong. Prohibitionism exemplified both the best and worst features of reform. It had little Catholic or urban working-class support. Moreover, it tended to clothe its single-minded arguments with intense moral fervour, often of the social purity variety.

Humanitarian reform, usually of urban abuses, often focused on the human victims of disastrous industrial social conditions. One of the main spearheads of such reform was the Social Gospel. Beginning in the Methodist Church and expanding to all Protestant denominations in Canada, the Social Gospel saw Christ as a social reformer and the institution of the Kingdom of God on earth as its (and his) mission. A wave of city missions and church settlement houses produced the establishment of the Social Services Council of Canada in 1912. The most prominent Social Gospeller was James Shaver Woodsworth (1874–1942). Another branch of humanitarian reform involved various professionals who became concerned with social problems through their professional practices. Thus doctors, for example, were active in promoting a public health system and in recommending ways of improving public health care. Among the medical professional's public health recommendations was compulsory medical inspection of schoolchildren.

Schools and members of the teaching profession were also in the front lines of humanitarian reform. In this period educators pushed not only for improved schooling but for the schools to assume much of the burden of social services for the young by acting *in loco parentis* for the children of slum and ghetto dwellers. The pressure for compulsory school attendance legislation, extended on a province-by-province basis across the nation by 1914, was partly reformist in nature. Regular school attendance would provide a more suitable environment for children than roaming the streets or working in factories. The children might learn skills that would lift them out of their poverty, and (in the case of the immigrant) would become assimilated to the values of Canadian society. Educators clearly believed that using schools for reform purposes was in the best interests of Canadian society. It was also in their own best interest. Compulsory education opened more employment and introduced the educator as social expert, a professional who knew more about what was important for children than parents, particularly the parents of the disadvantaged. Compulsory education, medical examinations, school nurses, lunch programs, all were part of a new form of social engineering that would only increase in emphasis over the century.

Over the course of time many of the private agencies of reform became conscripted as quasi-public ones under provincial legislation. They served as arms of the state in the intermediate period before the establishment of permanent government bureaucracies. Thus private child welfare programs became officially responsible for abandoned, abused, and delinquent children. Despite this trend towards a public approach, the framework remained that of individual morality. The humanitarian reformers commonly linked vice, crime, and poverty. Even those who focused on poverty tended to attribute it to almost every other cause than the failure of the economic system to distribute wealth equitably.

A classroom in School District No. 3, Glenelg, Ontario, 1910. The teacher is J.L. MacDonald (National Archives of Canada C-15490).

The concept of a basic minimum standard of living as the right of all members of society was slow to develop in Canada. Attacks on poverty of this period retained a certain class overtone, with a 'superior' class helping an 'inferior' one.

Another whole category of reformers sought structural alteration within the Canadian system. Their model was often sound business practice, for the leaders of this movement were usually successful businessmen. They sought the elimination of wasteful graft and corruption through political reform, the creation of publicly operated (and profitable) utilities to reduce unnecessary taxation, and the introduction of public planning. They tended to focus on the big city, although they spilled over in various directions. These reforms, which in the United States were associated with the Progressive movement, all found allies within associated middle-class and professional groups. The City Beautiful Movement, for example, received much of its support from an expanding community of professional architects, who combined an urge to plan the city as a whole with aesthetic considerations of coherence, visual variety, and civic grandeur. Like Americans, many Canadians saw cities as the culmination of civilization, and many grand plans made their appearance on paper. Cities settled for a few monumental new buildings, such as the imposing legislative structures completed in many provinces before the war. Political reform of municipal government concentrated on 'throwing the rascals out', combined with structural changes to reduce the damage they could do when they were in. The changes often included the replacement of elective councils with more professional government by commission. Businessmen reformers also fought fierce battles over the question of the ownership of utilities. While the utilities barons complained of the attack on private enterprise, the corporate reformers countered by arguing that utilities were intrinsic monopolies that should be operated in the public interest.

Much of the impulse behind reform of all sorts consisted of fears of class warfare and moral degeneration. The reformers did *for* the poor rather than *with* the poor. The result was a vast increase in the public concerns of the state, and the beginnings of the growth of a public bureaucracy to deal with social matters. As with many other aspects of Canadian life, the Great War would have a profound impact on reform.

THE GREAT WAR

The entrance of Canada into the First World War marked a triumph of sorts for Canadian imperialism. Canada did not make its own declaration of war, but simply joined the British war effort. Before it ended, the war had inflicted extremely heavy Canadian casualties: 60,661 killed in action and 172,000 wounded out of some 620,000 Canadians in uniform drawn from a population of only 8 million. The war gradually isolated French Canada and made possible sweeping national reforms on several fronts. Reform had always implied an interventionist state, and wartime conditions encouraged the Canadian government's intrusion into many new areas of life and work. The government's expenditures were enormous, but it managed to find the money to keep going, mainly through extensive borrowing. One of the new developments was a business profits tax, retroactive to the beginning of the war, introduced in 1916. Another was an income tax, first levied in 1917. Yet another was the nationalization of the railways. The war also accelerated and distorted virtually every economic development that Canada had experienced during the previous forty years.

Canadians entered the war with no idea of its ultimate length, intensity, or futile savagery. The initial enthusiasm of English-speaking Canadians assumed a short and swift defeat of Germany and its allies. By 1917 support for the war effort emphasized the extent of the sacrifices already made. Canada's military contribution was substantial. Nevertheless, Canadians who fought in Europe were almost exclusively volunteers. Serving as the shock troops of the British empire, Canadians achieved an enviable reputation for bravery and fierceness. Their commanders continually placed them in the most difficult situations, and they performed well. The list of battles at which they fought heroically (and at heavy cost) was a long one, beginning at Ypres in 1915 and continuing through to the Belgian town of Mons, where fighting ended for the Canadians at 11 a.m. on 11 November 1918.

The Canadian government had to fight hard for a voice in imperial war policy. It also worked hard to maintain separate Canadian unit and command structures. The arguments for autonomy—and the manpower necessary to sustain them—dragged the government ever deeper into the quagmire. By the time of Vimy in April 1917, Canada could no longer recruit new volunteers to replace the mounting casualties. The government saw conscription as the only solution. Conscription was a policy intensely opposed by many French Canadians. From the standpoint of Anglo-Canadians, French Canada had not borne its fair share of the burden of war. English Canada argued that less than 5 per cent of the Canadian volunteers had come from French Canada. On the other hand, French Canadians came to feel increasingly under attack by English Canada. They focused on the plight of francophones in Ontario as a symbol of their position. Regulation 17 of 1915 had seemingly imposed unilingualism on Ontario's elementary school system. Virtually all French-Canadian members of Parliament opposed the Military Service Act, which became law in August 1917. In its wake, and with a federal election upcoming, a Union

A Canadian battalion going 'over the top', October 1916 (National Archives of Canada PA-648).

Torontonians celebrating Armistice Day, 11 November 1918 (City of Toronto Archives, James Collection 891).

government formed out of the Conservatives and those Anglo members of the Liberal party who had broken with Laurier over his opposition to conscription.

French Canada was not alone in becoming isolated by the war. Members of Canada's other ethnic minorities, many of them originating in parts of Germany and the Austro-Hungarian empire, found themselves under attack. The government became increasingly repressive as the war continued. It interned 'aliens' by Order in Council and suppressed much of the foreign-language press. The Wartime Elections Act of September 1917 ruthlessly disenfranchised Canadians of enemy origin. Organized labour found itself shackled. The government introduced compulsory arbitration into all war industries in 1916. In the crisis year of 1917, the government announced its intention to outlaw all strikes and lockouts.

The Union government was simultaneously bipartisan and sectional. It was able to implement several national reforms favoured by its Anglo-Canadian supporters. Many provinces had allowed women the vote earlier in the war. The Wartime Elections Act in 1917 granted the federal electoral franchise to women with close relatives in the war. In 1918 all women got the vote federally. Prohibition also triumphed nationally in 1918, not only to keep the soldiers pure and to ensure that the country to which they returned would be a better place to live but also to prevent waste and inefficiency. Previous arguments about infringing personal liberty lost their cogency during wartime.

Canadian industry—at least in central Canada and industrial Nova Scotia—benefited directly from the war. By March 1915 over 200 firms had converted to munitions manufacture. Later in 1915 the government set up the Imperial Munitions Board, chaired by businessman Joseph Flavelle (1858–1939). Canadian munitions production rose dramatically, raising the export of iron and steel products from $68.5 million in 1915 to $441.1 million only two years later. The Canadian munitions industry employed 200,000 workers in 673 factories. By 1917 the Imperial Munitions Board alone had an annual budget three times that of the federal government in 1914. In the latter years of the war nearly 40 per cent of Canadian manufacturing products found export markets. The high point came in 1918 when Canadian manufacturing exports reached $636 million, and total exports peaked at $1,540,000.

As for Canadian agriculture, it could not produce enough in the short run. From 1914 to 1919 in Canada as a whole, agricultural acreage under cultivation doubled. Wheat prices trebled, and western farmers expanded the size and number of their farms. The federal government created a national Wheat Board in 1917 to facilitate marketing. The number of prairie farms actually increased by 28 per cent between 1911 and 1921. Although the sons of Canadian farmers could gain exemption from conscription, by the time it appeared there were few young men left on the farms. Rural Canada, especially in the west, had outdone the remainder of the country in volunteer enlistment. The result was an increase in labour costs, forcing farmers to buy more agricultural equipment. Increased production also pushed up the price of land. Farmers therefore increased production by borrowing money at high rates of interest. Farm debt increased substantially. High prices also encouraged farmers to move cultivation onto marginal land while abandoning most of the tested techniques of soil and moisture conservation hitherto practised. The result of all this expansion would be an inevitable disaster when the price of grain and other crops ultimately fell on the international market.

The Great War thus had a profound impact on Canada in almost all aspects of life. Its rhetorical side was one of present sacrifice for future benefits. This war-to-end-all-wars would make the world safe for democracy. An era of full social justice would follow the great victory. That the Canadian government had ignored democratic civil liberties in fighting the war was an irony that escaped most contemporaries. The war's conclusion amounted to a triumph for Protestant Anglo-Canada, with little thought given to the tomorrows that would follow the coming of peace. A nation that had drawn heavily on its resources was really not ready to deal with the negative legacies of its efforts.

Lucy Maud Montgomery Casts Her First Vote, 17 December 1917

[Women who had husbands, sons, and brothers fighting in the war were enfranchised for the 1917 election, and fought over the issue of conscription and the question of Canada's continued active participation in the war. One of those who voted was noted author Lucy Maud Montgomery, who recorded her thoughts in her journal. *Source*: M. Rubio and E. Waterston, eds, *The Selected Journals of L.M. Montgomery: volume II: 1910-1921* (Toronto: Oxford University Press 1987):234-5.]

Wednesday, Dec. 19, 1917
The Manse, Leaskdale, Ont.

On Monday, Dec. 17, I polled my first vote!

I have never, I admit, felt any particular interest in politics. Perhaps this was because a woman could take only a theoretical interest anyhow. But I never felt any especial desire to vote. I thought, as a merely academic question, that women certainly should vote. It seemed ridiculous, for example that an educated, intelligent woman should not vote when any illiterate, half or wholly disloyal foreigner could. But it did not worry me in the least. And now that women have, or are soon to have, the vote I do not at all expect a new heaven or a new earth as the result. I hope and believe that certain reforms will be brought appreciably nearer by the women's vote. But I suspect that matters will jog on in pretty much the same way for a good while yet—or if they do not, it will be owing to the war and conditions arising from it and not to the franchise.

It is rather too bad that I, who have called myself a Liberal all my life should have to cast my first vote against Wilfrid Laurier—whom at one time I thought little lower than the angels. This was simply because I was brought up that way. In P.E. Island in the old days—and even yet for that matter—one was born Grit or Tory and so remained. My earliest political recollections are of anathemas hurled at old 'Sir John A.' whom Grandfather Macneill seemed to regard as a demon in human form. Wilfrid Laurier was Grandfather's political idol and I, who was nothing if not loyal to my clan, worshipped him also. . . .

Well, Wilfrid Laurier is an old man now and he has outlived his glory and betrayed his country. Why? Senility—superstition—base political cunning? It is vain to ask. Perhaps even Laurier himself does not know. But on Monday I voted, with a queer little qualm of regret and a queer feeling of disloyalty to my old traditions, for the Government which is Union but which is headed by Laurier's long rival, the Conservative chief, Borden.

The poll was held in a most disreputable old vacant store next to the manse. . . . The candidate I voted for was Major Sam Sharpe who has always been a rank 'Tory.' If Hogg, his opponent, had not been an equally rank anti-conscriptionist I would have found it much harder.

Having voted, there was nothing to do but wait. After supper Ewan [her husband] went to Uxbridge to hear the returns and I hied me to the church where a practice of kiddies for our Sunday School concert was being held. In this occupation I contrived to pass the time with outward calmness until ten when I came home to find that Edith [the serving girl] had been listening in on the phone and had this 'news'.

Sam Sharpe was in with a big majority and Ontario was almost solid for the Gov't.—*but they had done nothing in the west.*

I went to bits. If the West had gone against us, all hope had vanished. Edith went to bed. I could not work or read or sit still. So I began to walk the floor. I walked it until half past eleven when my legs gave out and I sat down perforce. I do think 'politics' is too strenuous for women.

At twelve Ewan came home. I met him in the kitchen and looked at him but I did not speak. I was quite past speaking and I was as cold as ice from head to foot. When he told me that it was Laurier who had 'done nothing in the West' and that the Gov't was in with a majority that was already fair and would probably be a large one, I could have sat down and cried with relief.

For the first night for a week I had a sleep untroubled by three o'clock visions of a rejoicing Kaiser and a Quebec-bossed Canada. Yesterday the full returns came in and gave the Union Gov't a majority of from 45 to 50. My prediction was about as correct as predictions usually are so I think I may count myself in Class C of the prophets. British Columbia instead of breaking even went almost solid for Union, whereas the Maritimes gave a small majority for Laurier. The rest was by the book,—Ontario matched Quebec and the West turned the scale lavishly.

It is over—and well over. I hope such an election need never be fought in Canada again.

Major Events, 1919–1944

1919 'Red Scare' begins. Winnipeg General Strike occurs. First Congress of the League of Indians meets in Sault Ste Marie. *Canadian Bookman* is founded.

1920 Progressive Party is formed. First issues of *Canadian Forum*, *Canadian Historical Review*, and *The Dalhousie Review* appear. The Group of Seven hold their first exhibition of paintings.

1921 In a federal election, the Progressive Party wins sixty-four seats. William Lyon Mackenzie King's Liberals form the government. Maritime Rights Movement is organized.

1923 Famous Players' Canadian Corporation takes over Allen Theatres.

1924 William Aberhart begins the Prophetic Bible Institute broadcasts over Calgary's CFCN.

1925 United Church of Canada is formed. Pacific Coast Hockey League folds.

1929 Stock market collapses. Aird Commission reports on public broadcasting; favours nationalization of radio.

1930 Great Depression begins. R.B. Bennett's Conservatives are elected to power in Ottawa.

1931 Ottawa government arrests and imprisons eight leaders of the Communist Party.

1932 Co-operative Commonwealth Federation is founded at Calgary. Bennett government forms the Canadian Radio Broadcasting Commission.

1933 Depression sees huge unemployment rolls. Regina Manifesto is adopted by the CCF. Maurice Duplessis becomes leader of the Conservative Party of Quebec. T. Dufferin Pattullo wins election in British Columbia.

1935 R.B. Bennett announces a 'New Deal' for Canada, but is defeated by King in the election. Social Credit under Aberhart sweeps to power in Alberta. Duplessis forms Union Nationale. The On-to-Ottawa Trek is suppressed in Regina.

1936 Canadian Broadcasting Corporation is formed.

1937 General Motors strike in Oshawa. Royal Commission on Dominion-Provincial Relations is appointed. Lord Tweedsmuir creates the Governor-General's awards.

1939 Canada declares war on Germany. British Commonwealth Air Training Plan is founded.

1940 Royal Commission on Dominion-Provincial Relations recommends restructuring of public finances.

1941 Emily Carr wins the Governor-General's award for *Klee Wyck*. Hong Kong surrenders.

1942 Dieppe raid sees 2,700 Canadians killed or captured. National plebiscite votes to release government from non-conscription pledge.

1943 Marsh report on social security is tabled in House of Commons.

1944 Family Allowances Act and National Housing Act are passed.

Deferring Expectations, 1919–1945

❀

Once the Great War had ended, Canadians did their best to put the conflict behind them. Many hoped for the emergence of a more just society. Stephen Leacock well expressed the ambivalence of the postwar period in *The Unsolved Riddle of Social Justice* (1919). Recognizing that industrial society did not normally employ its full potential, Leacock could only hope that the destructive energy of war could be harnessed for peacetime reform. The unsolved riddle was simply stated. 'With all our wealth, we are still poor,' he wrote. Every child, Leacock insisted, should have 'adequate food, clothing, education and an opportunity in life'. Unemployment should become a 'social crime' (Bowker 1973:74–80). Leacock did not offer specific solutions. Such a collective transformation would not be easy to accomplish. There were too many unresolved economic, constitutional, and social problems. The development of Canada over the next quarter-century demonstrated that at least in peacetime, Canadians still had great trouble in coming to terms with the paradox Leacock had identified in 1919. During the Great Depression especially, the state seemed impotent to improve conditions. The politicians blamed the Constitution. Beginning in 1939, however, Canada would again demonstrate its capacity for waging total war.

RETURNING TO 'NORMALCY'

During demobilization Canada experienced one of the most devastating epidemics of modern times, the Spanish flu outbreak of 1918–19. The situation was so desperate in November 1918 that the government actually attempted, without success, to postpone public celebration of the Armistice for fear of spreading infection. Canadian deaths from the flu ultimately ran to 50,000, only some 10,000 thousand fewer than the number of Canadians who had died in battle. Fatalities had shifted from the trenches to the home front.

Yet another form of infectious epidemic made its appearance in 1919 with the great 'Red Scare'. The Bolshevik Revolution of 1917–18 in Russia provided the Canadian government and businessmen with an example of what might happen if popular unrest got out of hand. The Canadian authorities were quite ready to believe that large segments of Canadian society had been infiltrated by radical agitators, mostly of foreign origin. Political paranoia was as catching as

Influenza, Armistice, Daylight Savings, and General Strike

[Edith Durand was born in Pennsylvania in 1883. In 1912 she married Gilbert Beebe McColl and moved to Winnipeg. For many years Edith wrote regular letters home to her family, and from these the following passages were extracted in 1981 and presented in diary form by F.V. McColl. They offer a housewife's view of late 1918 and 1919. *Source*: E. Durand, *Vignettes of Early Winnipeg* (Winnipeg: Frances McColl, 1981):25–30.]

Sun. Eve. Oct. 13, 1918: We have 30 cases of Spanish Influenza here, mostly soldiers who have come from Quebec, but a few civilian cases have developed in the last few days. All public meetings are banned indefinitely.

Fri. Eve. Oct. 17, 1918: 80 some new cases of Flu today—very few deaths so far. Six cases in the house next to R's—a new one every day. Mrs R. Came this aft. I told her to come on—I'd chance her carrying the Flu—I wanted to see her so badly. They are all well—but everyone is afraid of the [street] cars.

Tues. a.m. Nov. 12, 1918: I don't feel like settling down to write much—there's just a constant refrain in my mind 'The war is over—the war is over.' I just can't grasp it all at once. Today closes the last Victory loan. I'd give a good deal to have a few hundred to invest in that. But you can't invest in what you haven't got, or buy on installment plan unless the regular income is assured. Probably things will pick up in the spring, with the war over. We have enough to live on this year anyway—& have fuel & vegetables & apples in the cellar enough to last a good while. So we're not so bad off. The flu kitchen is doing excellent work. Food is sent to anyone in need on application of Dr or nurse, to rich as well as poor. Those who can pay do. The situation is pretty bad for lack of nursing. Slightly smaller no. of cases, but good many deaths.

Sun. Jan. 19, 1919: . . . S. Is back in Canada. G's last letter from him came Wed. In it he said the adjutant asked him how much warning he needed to get ready to come home and he said 'Just about 15 min.' That same evening (Wed.) F. Had a wire from him that he was in Quebec. There were three boats reached Canada last week, and another docks tomorrow. The Olympic bro't 5500 men. The others not *quite* so many, but they are surely coming back fast.

Tues. Apr. 15, 1919: . . . .H. took the crowd to 'The Princess' . . . & treated us to 'Banana Split'—two balls of ice cream—one vanilla & one maple—pineapple—raspberry—cherry

the flu. Both the government and the business community became hysterical over the possibility that the revolution was nigh. The immediate focus of their concern was the Winnipeg General Strike of 1919. Behind that strike lurked the organization of the One Big Union, formed in Calgary in February amidst considerable anticapitalistic rhetoric. As usual, the Canadian government responded to anything smacking of popular uprising with repression.

Most of the conditions and issues that initially produced labour unrest in Winnipeg in the spring of 1919 were traditional ones exacerbated by the war:

nuts—whipped cream & a banana split lengthwise at each side.

Tues. Apr. 22, 1919: We are in the biggest mess in Canada over Daylight Saving. The Dominion Parliament turned it down. Some cities have taken it up, but Wpg. hasn't yet. But all the railroads have it so as to keep their connections with U.S. trains & the Grain Exchange & certain other places have to use it if the railroads do. It is very confusing. The early trains leave at 6 a.m. now instead of 7 and the street cars don't start running till 6—people who want them have to walk or hire a taxi. We go on one time, Mrs H. next door on the other. It is confusing when I ask her in for tea.

Sun. May 4, 1919: Taking baths here means heating water in the boiler & carrying the water upstairs by the pailful—so it's not the small item it sounds. As soon as we get rich we'll connect the boiler with the kitchen stove and have warm water in summer too.

Tues. May 13, 1919: Big strike called for tomorrow. Every union and public utility in city is to go out. May last *weeks.*

Sun. June 8, 1919: I understand letters will go out if posted in the main P.O. The bread and milk drivers were called out again. The city took over the milk & one goes to the nearest school to get it. Bread is supposed to go to the stores, but Mr. G. could only get 100 loaves in the morn. & another 100 in the

aft.—sold out in 1/2 hr. I baked bread and buns—delicious. Maybe the [street] cars will start. The mayor says they will as soon as he gets enough special constables sworn in. They took on about 500 a day Fri. and Sat. & want that many more. We get a letter delivery every aft. Now, today also had a paper postie. They are not delivering on all routes, only the *safe* ones. A good many people are refusing to accept mail—can you imagine it—& all such is being returned to the senders. One postie handed a woman the paper as he went in & she threw it at him and called him 'Scab'. So he said 'All right madam, I'll take your letters back to the office.' She pled in vain for them too. No cars yet & little hope of them. All the police are out & have been dismissed—also their Chief. The Deputy Chief has been made his successor & is organizing the new force. There are about 3000 special constables paid by the city. The police force is provincial, besides the Mounties. P.O., telephone, etc. Are building up out of new material—absolutely refusing to take any back who did not come back when the ultimatum was issued. Oh it's the limit.

recognition of union rights to organize, higher wages, better working conditions. A walk-out by workers in the city's metal trades and building industries was quickly joined by other malcontents (as many as 50,000) in a general sympathy strike. On 15 May the strikers voted to close down the city's services. Much of the rhetoric of the strike sounded extremely radical. Some labour leaders certainly hoped to use the general strike as a weapon to bring capitalism to its knees. Many demobilized servicemen supported the strikers. Worried businessmen certainly saw the general strike as a breakdown of public author-

The Winnipeg General Strike, 21 June 1919 (Provincial Archives of Manitoba N2771, Foote Collection 1705).

ity. Workers in other cities, such as Toronto and Vancouver, responded with declarations of support and threats of their own strikes. The Canadian government, represented locally by acting Minister of Justice Arthur Meighen (1874–1960), responded decisively. He supplemented the army with local militia, the Royal North-West Mounted Police, and 1,800 special constables. The Canadian Naturalization Act was hastily amended in early June 1919 to allow for the instant deportation of any foreign-born radicals who advocated revolution or who belonged to 'any organization entertaining or teaching disbelief in or opposition to organized government' (quoted in Avery 1986:222).

Meighen effectively broke the strike on 17 June when he ordered the arrest of ten strike leaders on charges of sedition. A few days later, a public demonstration of strikers and returned soldiers, marching towards the Winnipeg city hall, was met by a charge of Mounties on horseback. The result was a violent *mêlée* that injured many, killed two strikers, and led to the arrest of a number of 'foreign rioters'. 'Black Saturday' (21 June) occurred despite the best efforts of the strike leaders to prevent the demonstration from going forward. The Strike Committee subsequently agreed to call off the strike if a royal commission investigated it and its underlying causes. The royal commission, called by the province of Manitoba, found that much of the labour unrest in Winnipeg was justified and that the strike's principal goal was to effect the introduction of collective bargaining. On the other hand, the Manitoba Court of Queen's Bench convicted most of the arrested leaders (who were either British or Canadian-born) on charges of sedition. The Department of Immigration held deportation hearings for the 'foreigners' in camera. The use of the civil arm to suppress radicalism, long a part of the Canadian tradition, was given a new meaning in postwar Winnipeg. Perhaps most significantly, the strike and its handling by the government demonstrated the fragility of the postwar readjustment. The next decade would further emphasize the problems.

REGIONAL PROTEST IN THE 1920S

The decade of the 1920s is usually associated with prosperity, but in truth the period saw great economic difficulties. The boom did not begin in 1924 and it was quite limited in its influence. The depression of 1920–3 had seen world prices for resource products fall abruptly, while costs fell much more gradually. Prosperity finally came from a substantial growth in new housing construction and a great wave of consumer spending, both understandable after the war and subsequent depression. There was a major expansion of consumer credit facilities to finance the new spending. An advertising industry quickly developed to promote consumerism. Speculative activities—in real estate, in the stock market, and in commodity futures—all flourished. So did gambling. However, much of the boom was at best internal, at worst artificial. International markets, except in the United States, were very soft. The traditional resource sectors of the economy had suffered most from the worldwide fall in prices, although they recovered somewhat in the latter years of the decade. Only Ontario's economy really prospered, chiefly on the strength of the manufacture of the motor car, both for domestic consumption and for export into a British empire protecting itself against the Americans. The economy of the Maritime provinces continued to decline precipitously, since both the power revolution and the new industrialization bypassed them while foreign markets (especially for fish) continued to decline.

Despite the government's brutal suppression of the Winnipeg General Strike, industrial unrest remained high through 1925. The One Big Union, a radical and militant industrial union, flourished briefly in western Canada. In 1921 labour representatives sat in seven of nine provincial legislatures. In the election of that year, labour candidates contested over thirty federal constituencies, although only four were actually elected. Labour unrest after Winnipeg was most prevalent in the geographical extremes of the country. There were a number of notable strikes in Cape Breton, in Alberta, and in British Columbia. In the coalfields, 22,000 miners were on strike in August 1922. Several unions were broken in some of the most bitter labour violence that Canada had ever

The 'dust bowl', the Prairies in the 1930s (Agriculture Canada, Research Branch, Research Station, Lethbridge).

seen. Tactics in the mining communities made Winnipeg seem like a Sunday school picnic. A number of movements, mainly regionally based, sprang up to protest inequalities in the national system. Their collective inability—from a variety of different approaches—to effect much change was, and is, instructive.

Certainly nobody felt harder done by after the Great War than the farmer. The movement of farm protest reached its height in the 1921 election, before the wheat market collapse and the spread of drought conditions. Farmers in Anglo-Canada disliked inflation and had two specific economic grievances beyond the wheat price collapse of 1920. First, the national wheat marketing system of the war had been abandoned by the government in 1919. Secondly, the government had failed to introduce serious tariff reform to lower the costs of farming. Behind these complaints was a long-standing farmer conviction that the political system operated to the advantage of profiteering central Canadian capitalists. Farmer discontent was national in scope, although western farmers were the most alienated. The new Progressive Party, formed in 1920, won sixty-four seats in the 1921 election in Parliament in six provinces: thirty-seven on the prairies, twenty-four in Ontario, one in New Brunswick, and two in British Columbia. Joining fifty Conservatives and 117 Liberals, the Progressives broke the established two-party tradition.

Though they were entitled to become the official opposition, the Progressives were badly divided. Former Liberals wanted free trade, while the farm protesters sought more radical reform. The farm wing, led by Alberta's Henry Wise Wood (1860–1941), wanted to scrap the existing party system and its discipline. It sought instead to focus on farmer grievances. The only actions the two wings could agree upon were negative. The Progressives would not become the official opposition, and they would not join in coalition with the Liberals, now led by William Lyon Mackenzie King (1874–1950). As a result, the inexperienced farmer MPs were unable to accomplish anything substantial in Ottawa when economic conditions in western Canada worsened. The King government provided token programs to gain the support of moderate Progressives. Meanwhile, drought and the worldwide collapse of wheat prices beginning in 1921 produced a widespread inability to meet mortgage payments. Much of the land in the dry-belt region reverted to the state for unpaid taxes. Its inhabitants went either to the cities or, in many cases, back to the United States. Surviving farmers became too disheartened to support a Progressive Party that had accomplished little in Ottawa, and the party quickly disappeared.

A similar fate befell the major eastern protest, the Maritime Rights Movement. Maritimers had difficulty in joining western farmers in a common cause. The easterners sought not free trade but increased protectionism, as well as lower railway freight rates. The region was acutely conscious of its increasing impotency in Confederation, as its population base continued to decline proportionally to central Canada and the west. By the end of 1921, regional discontent found expression in the Maritime Rights Movement, which combined an insistence on equitable freight rates with a series of particular provincial demands. The result was a widespread, if brief, public agitation. Eschewing the third-party route of the Progressives, the Maritime Rights leaders decided in 1923 to appeal to the remainder of the country over the head of Ottawa. Although a major national advertising and public relations campaign on behalf of Maritime concerns had some success, it was not enough. When Maritimers started voting Conservative in 1923 by-elections, this merely annoyed the King government. After a royal commission investigated Maritime grievances, the Liberals bought off the region with concessions on freight rates, subsidies, and port development. None of these concessions touched fundamental economic problems. In the end, working through the two-party system achieved no more than creating a third party. The inability of regional protest in the Maritimes and the west to find common ground was palpable—and significant. Neither side could see beyond its regional interests. Clever federal politicians, like Mackenzie King, could play the game of divide and rule with impunity.

While the west and the Maritimes produced their ineffectual protests, Quebec turned increasingly inward. It pursued a nationalism that was at least partly a reaction against its increasing sense of isolation from the remainder of

Canada. The chief outlet for this nationalism was the journal *L'Action Française*, founded on the eve of the Conscription Crisis by the *Ligue des droits de français*. This movement began with a crusade to save the French language, but gradually shifted into broader issues. Inspiration for both movement and journal came from the Abbé Lionel Groulx (1878–1967). Groulx worried about the survival of the traditional religion and culture in the face of an ever more materialistic environment. From the French-Canadian perspective, that environment was increasingly 'in the middle of an immense Anglo-Saxon ocean' (quoted in Cook 1969b:193). In the 1920s Groulx denied that he was a separatist, although his arguments pointed in that direction. He called for a commitment in building the Quebec economy, preparing for a future in which Confederation came to an end. By the late 1920s, Groulx had proved more successful at refashioning the history of French Canada than at gaining widespread public support.

THE DEPRESSION AND ITS RESPONSES

The good times were brief. The stock market failed in October 1929, with Wall Street leading the way for a record collapse of stock prices everywhere in North America. Contrary to popular opinion, this disaster was fairly independent of the Depression that followed it. That Depression was really the cumulative result of the worldwide fall in prices, which had never readjusted from the inflation of wartime and the deflation of the postwar period. An international inability to buy left Canada and other resource producers, such as Argentina and Australia, with decreased orders for their products. Trade deficits quickly mounted. Nations that owed Canada money were unable to pay. The dollar fell, and in 1931 so did a number of major Canadian financial institutions, brokerage agencies, and insurance companies. The country would not recover until after the eruption of another war in 1939. For most Canadians, the 1930s depression was always the Great Depression. Canadians lived in its shadow for decades to come. Those generations who had experienced its effects were always sympathetic to calls for social justice.

What the Depression meant, first and foremost, was unemployment. Official statistics are totally meaningless as a measure of the extent of joblessness, much less its significance. According to the publication *Historical Statistics in Canada* (1983), reflecting contemporary government data, unemployment in Canada rose from 116,000 in 1929 to 741,000 in 1932 to 826,000 in 1933, ultimately declining to 411,000 in 1937 and increasing to 529,000 in 1939. These figures, while substantial enough in a nation of only 10 million, hardly reflected the reality. No farmers or fishermen, or their families, counted among the ranks of the unemployed at this time. The government regarded them as self-employed businessmen. Women out of work did not count either. Thus

A Depression soup line (National Archives 306 NT-165319).

unemployment in the depths of the Depression, around 1933, ran to over 27 per cent in the non-agricultural sector, but probably over 50 per cent overall. At the same time, a farmer whose expenses exceeded his income was probably better off than a jobless city dweller whose expenses similarly exceeded his income. Farmers at least had some land on which food could be grown. Moreover, provincial governments tended to respond to the plight of the farmers, who made up a substantial proportion of the electorate in many provinces. The rural population actually grew in this decade as members of farm families returned from the city to the family farm.

The fall in prices meant that times were good for those with jobs, although almost everyone held their breath each time payday rolled around. As for Canadian business corporations, outside the financial sector there was little permanent damage. Most large corporations ruthlessly retrenched and waited for better times. Canadian business corporations actually suffered losses only in 1932 because they had been too slow to limit operations. In 1933, the lowest point on the economic curve, they ended collectively in the black.

The real victims of the Depression were the urban unemployed, who found that their relief became the great political football of the period. Traditionally Canadian municipalities and private charities had cared for the poor and

Collecting Relief in Winnipeg During the Depression

[In November 1930 James Gray's employer went out of business. Without a job, he was forced to apply for relief. In his book, *The Winter Years: The Depression on the Prairies*, he described the relief system in Winnipeg. *Source*: J. Gray, *The Winter Years: The Depression on the Prairies* (Toronto: Macmillan, 1966):15–17.]

The Winnipeg system, like that of all other prairie cities, was designed only to bridge the winter for those who were seasonally unemployed and could prove they were completely destitute. Those who were aided—a few hundred families each winter—worked off their relief sawing cordwood into stove lengths at the city Woodyard. The city Relief Department was an adjunct of the Woodyard—departmentally and physically. . . . A crowd of several hundred milled around in the yard and I elbowed my way through to the shed. Inside, at the far end of the shed, were three doors leading into the main office. One was marked APPLICATIONS. The second was marked RENT AND FUEL, and a third was marked GROCERIES. There were long lines in front of each door and the APPLICATIONS line extended the full length of the shack and out into the yard. . . . I was feeling a lot better when I reached the end of the line that afternoon and a harried clerk took my application and explained the system to me. I became entangled in the regulations before we even got on relief. . . . In the end the supervisor let me apply for everybody, and I went home to await the arrival of an investigator who would come around to inspect us. Two days later an investigator turned up, made a few perfunctory inquiries, and approved my application. . . . I was to take my approved application back to the Woodyard on Tuesday. Thereafter, save when sickness intervented, I was a regular Tuesday visitor to the Woodyard for the next two years. When I arrived on the first Tuesday, the system had been somewhat reorganized from the week before. There was now a 'NEW CARD' line parallel to the 'APPLICATIONS' line. The end of the line for new cards was again outside the shack and it took the better part of an hour to get in out of the cold. Eventually I reached the clerk who was handing out the cards. He took the slip the investigator had given me and laboriously copied the particulars onto a printed card some-

jobless. The challenge in the 1930s was more than any city could handle, at least without the full cooperation and assistance of senior levels of government. R.B. Bennett (1870–1947), prime minister from 1930 to 1935, personally assisted from his own pocket many people who wrote him begging letters while he was in office, but Bennett had long opposed the dole system and insisted that the provinces were responsible for social welfare. The provinces, in turn, maintained that they lacked the appropriate taxing potential. They passed the problem to the municipalities, which had to support the unemployed on declining revenue from property taxes that provided about 80 per cent of municipal revenue. Municipal assistance was grudging, almost always in the

what larger than a driver's licence. Across the top of the card were a number of headings, viz.: 'Groceries,' 'Bread,' 'Milk,' 'Rent'. Under each the clerk inserted code numbers after I had named the store, bakery, meat market, and creamery with which we dealt. I spent the rest of the day going from line to line picking up vouchers. One qualified me to receive seven quarts and seven pints of milk, a second provided for seven loaves of bread, a third was worth sixty-five cents at the butcher's, and the fourth was for $2.38 in groceries. This was the new world of vouchers in which no cash ever passed from hand to hand. . . . A family of three such as ours was allowed $16 a month for food and $10 to $13 a month for rent. Householders got a winter allowance of $6 to $10 a month in cord-wood for fuel. It was possible to live on these allowances because of the collapse in the price structure. . . . In the late winter of 1931, milk was ten cents a quart, bread six cents a loaf, chuck roasts sold for ten cents a pound, hamburger was nine cents, a rib roast was twelve cents, sausage was three pounds for a quarter, and potatoes forty-five cents a bushel. Even these prices would seem high a year later, when milk sold for six cents a quart in Winnipeg, bread was three loaves for a dime, butter sold for fifteen and twenty cents a pound, and eggs were fifteen cents a dozen. For people accustomed to shopping with money, operating a household with vouchers took a lot of getting used to. Everything had to be bought in small quantities. If we had been given our grocery allowance for the month in a single voucher, instead of once a week, advantage could have been taken of quantity buying. But many months were to pass before the fact was recognized and allowances were distributed on a fortnightly basis. While becoming accustomed to voucher shopping was slow, people settled into the relief system itself with little difficulty. We had lived in a continuing food-and-shelter crisis for a month, and once these problems were solved by going on relief we were freed from the feeling of being incessantly driven. We relaxed and made a start at sorting out our family problems. On an invitation from relatives, my father and brothers emigrated via cattle train to Ontario to look for work in the textile mills. My mother stayed on with us until they could send her transportation. We found a house we could rent for the $13 a month the relief department would allow and settled down to wait for spring and a job. Two months later I came down with tuberculosis.

form of credit vouchers to be redeemed at local stores rather than as cash, which might be spent on 'frivolities' or worse. The relief lines were not called 'the dole' for nothing. For the single unemployed male, the city often advised him to go elsewhere and even paid his rail tickets out of town. The constitutional wrangling between the provinces and the federal government seemed quite irrelevant to Canadians looking for help.

Only in 1935, on the eve of a federal election, did R.B. Bennett become a convert to interventionist strategies. He announced his new policy, a 'New Deal' for Canada, in a live radio address to the nation early in January 1935, saying, 'I am for reform. I nail the flag of progress to the mast. I summon the power of the state to its support.' Bennett spoke of legislation regulating working conditions, insuring against unemployment, and extending credit to the farmer. Unfortunately for Bennett, his radio proclamations ran well ahead of the practical legislative program he and his cabinet had ready for Parliament. The Canadian electorate, moreover, was understandably suspicious of last-minute conversions. Instead, the voters brought back Mackenzie King's Liberals, who offered few promises but had the solid backing of Quebec.

R.B. Bennett's 'conversion' to New Dealism involved more desperation than returning to office. It also represented a growing realization by large parts of the Canadian business and professional communities that stabilizing the nation's economy was necessary to prevent a more serious upheaval. Many leading businessmen and financiers were in favour of state intervention, not so much because they believed in social justice as because they sought to produce economic stability for capitalism. The prevailing political and economic system of Canada was under attack from many directions in the 1930s. Canadian politicians and businessmen did not need to look to Germany or Italy to find examples of radical responses to economic problems. What European experience did point out, however, was that radicalism was not necessarily confined to the traditional left, to be associated with organized labour, socialism, or communism. The great fear was of the demagogue of any political persuasion, offering simple but final solutions to a frustrated electorate. Canada had its share of prospective demagogues. Most of their success came on the provincial rather than on the federal level, however. All were advocates of provincial rights. This blunted their national effectiveness. Agreeing to bash Ottawa together was never a very creative strategy unless agreement could be reached on what to do next. About all these leaders had in common were their own curious mixtures of radical rhetoric and fundamentally conservative attitudes.

Perhaps the most successful radical response came in Alberta, where the Social Credit Party mobilized a population that had suffered heavily from drought and depression. The leader of Social Credit in Alberta was a Calgary radio preacher, William Aberhart (1878–1943), who since 1924 had used his Sunday broadcasts for the Prophetic Bible Institute over CFCN (Canada's most powerful radio station at the time) to build up a substantial personal following attracted to Protestant fundamentalism. In 1932 Aberhart added a secular dimension to his broadcasts, following his personal conversion to the economic ideas of a Scottish engineer named C.H. Douglas. An unconventional monetary theorist, Douglas claimed that capitalism's failure was in its inability to translate its production into purchasing power for the mass of people. Douglas advocated distributing money, in the form of 'social credit', to bridge the gap between production and consumption. Neither Aberhart nor his Alberta audience ever truly understood Douglas's monetary theories, but both understood that the state would issue a social dividend, eventually set by Aberhart at $25 per month, to all citizens as part of their cultural heritage. With the assistance of Ernest Manning (1908–96), Aberhart organized the Social Credit Party early in 1935. The new party swept to success at the polls, taking fifty-six of sixty-three seats and winning 54 per cent of the popular vote. The federal government (and courts) opposed much of its original legislative program, particularly mortgage, debt, and banking legislation, eventually disallowing thirteen Alberta acts. Social Credit moved to more traditional fiscal practices, blaming Ottawa and eastern big business for its inability to enact its program. (Under Aberhart and, following his death in 1943, under Manning, Social Credit won nine successive elections in Alberta and governed the province until 1971.)

The emergent popular leader in Quebec was Maurice Duplessis (1890–1959). Duplessis came from a family of Conservatives. In 1933 he became leader of the highly fragmented Conservative Party of Quebec. He found allies in two burgeoning Quebec movements of the early 1930s: the Catholic social action of the *École social populaire*, and the Liberal radicalism of the *Action libérale nationale* (ALN). From Catholic social action Duplessis took a program of government intervention to redistribute wealth, protect farmers and workers, and regulate large corporations, all within the context of the Christian law of justice and charity. From the ALN he took an emphasis upon economic nationalism that called for liberation from colonial oppression through agrarian reform, new labour legislation, the promotion of small industry and commerce, and the destruction of the great financial establishments of the province. Duplessis negotiated the merger of the ALN with the Conservatives in 1935 to form the *Union Nationale*. The new party campaigned on the ALN's reform platform, winning an easy victory in the 1936 election of seventy-six seats and 58 per cent of the popular vote. Now 'prime minister' of Quebec, Duplessis quickly abandoned the reform program that had brought him to power. Instead, he concentrated power in his own hands. His considerable success in office relied on a nationalistic concern for provincial autonomy in federal-provincial relations, anticommunism, and calculated paternalistic grants and patronage for the disadvantaged. He carefully cultivated the Catholic hierarchy in the province. The *Union Nationale*'s economic program consisted chiefly in giving American entrepreneurs a free hand to develop the province's resources.

Other provinces besides Quebec and Alberta also produced populistic political leaders, although within the context of traditional party labels. In British Columbia, T. Dufferin (Duff) Pattullo (1873–1956) had led his Liberal Party to power in 1933 without sounding very radical. In office, however, Pattullo gradually became a convert to state activism of the New Deal variety.

The Regina Manifesto, 1933

[In July 1933 the first national convention of the Co-operative Commonwealth Federation, held in Regina, Saskatchewan, adopted as its manifesto a document that had been drafted in advance by Frank Underhill and several other members of the League for Social Reconstruction. What follows is the preamble to that manifesto.]

The CCF is a federation of organizations whose purpose is the establishment in Canada of a Co-operative Commonwealth in which the principle regulating production, distribution and exchange will be the supplying of human needs and not the making of profits.

We aim to replace the present capitalist system, with its inherent injustice and inhumanity, by a social order from which the domination and exploitation of one class by another will be eliminated, in which economic planning will supersede unregulated private enterprise and competition, and in which genuine democratic self-government based upon economic equality will be possible. The present order is marked by glaring inequalities of wealth and opportunity, by a chaotic waste and instability; and in an age of plenty it condemns the great mass of the people to poverty and insecurity. Power has become more and more concentrated into the hands of a small irresponsible minority of financiers and industrialists and to their predatory interests the majority are habitually sacrificed. When private profit is the main stimulous to economic effort, our society oscillates between periods of feverish prosperity in which the main benefits go to speculators and profiteers, and of

His government was arguably the most interventionist in Canada, held back only by the province's shortage of revenue. In Ontario, Mitchell Hepburn (1896–1953) led a Liberal government with a series of flamboyant political gestures designed chiefly as self-advertisement. He achieved national prominence in April 1937, in the midst of a strike at the General Motors plant in Oshawa, Ontario. More than 4,000 workers struck for an eight-hour day, better wages and working conditions, and recognition of the new union of United Automobile Workers. This union was an affiliate of the recently formed Congress of Industrial Organization, which was organizing throughout the United States. Hepburn sided with General Motors and clashed publicly with the prime minister over Mackenzie King's refusal to send RCMP reinforcements for the local police. The premier organized a volunteer force called Hepburn's Hussars. Both Pattullo and Hepburn got great political mileage out of their well-publicized clashes with Ottawa.

None of the prominent provincial political leaders of the 1930s had any serious socialist leanings. The most important alternative political response of the Depression years based in the socialist tradition came from the Co-opera-

catastrophic depression, in which the common man's normal state of insecurity and hardship is accentuated. We believe that these evils can be removed only in a planned and socialized economy in which our natural resources and the principle means of production and distribution are owned, controlled and operated by the people.

The new social order at which we aim is not one in which individuality will be crushed out by a system of regimentation. Nor shall we interfere with cultural rights of racial or religious minorities. What we seek is a proper collective organization of our economic resources such as will make possible a much greater degree of leisure and a much richer individual life for every citizen.

This social and economic transformation can be brought about by political action, through the election of a government inspired by the ideal of a Co-operative Commonwealth and supported by the majority of the people. We do not believe in change by violence. We consider that both the old parties in Canada are the instruments of capitalist interests and cannot serve as agents of social reconstruction, and that whatever the superficial differences between them, they are bound to carry on government in accordance with the dictates of the big business interests who finance them. The CCF aims at political power in order to put an end to this capitalist domination of our political life. It is a democratic movement, a federation of farmer, labor and socialist organizations, financed by its own members and seeking to achieve its ends solely by constitutional means. It appeals for support to all who believe that the time has come for a far-reaching reconstruction of our economic and political institutions. . . .

tive Commonwealth Federation (CCF). A convention in Calgary in 1932 founded the CCF as a coalition of farmers' organizations, labour unions, and labour-socialist parties in the four western provinces. The League for Social Reconstruction (LSR) served as the CCF's midwife. The LSR, organized in 1931 by a number of prominent Canadian academics, believed in Fabian socialism. Like the Fabians, it was proudly non-Marxist and non-revolutionary, although vehemently committed to a welfare state and the state's take-over of key industries. At its first annual convention at Regina in 1933, the newly founded CCF adopted a political manifesto that promised a heady brew of political reform. The Regina Manifesto called for the nationalization (with compensation for the owners) of all industry 'essential to social planning'. It advocated a series of universal welfare measures for Canada—hospitalization, health care, unemployment insurance, and pensions—after amendments to the British North America Act to remove these areas from provincial jurisdiction.

The new party was an uneasy alliance of academics and public activists. It chose as leader the former Methodist minister James Shaver Woodsworth. Pacifist, idealist, and moralist, Woodsworth had since 1921 led a small cadre of labour-supported MPs in Ottawa. The new party attracted over 300,000 votes in the 1933 British Columbia provincial elections, more than 30 per cent of the popular vote. In the 1935 federal election it obtained 8.9 per cent of the popular vote, which translated into seven CCF seats. During the 1930s the party would flourish only in BC and Saskatchewan, however. It did not attract broad-based popular support, particularly east of Ontario.

The nation's politicians and businessmen grimly viewed the CCF as a threat from the radical left, completely failing to appreciate that the new party provided a far more restrained left-wing approach than the Communist Party of Canada (CP). At the outset of the Great Depression, only the CP had sought to organize popular discontent, especially among the unemployed. The Communists operated under several disadvantages, however. One was the charge that they were members of an international conspiracy. The other was the Canadian government's willingness to repress the party in any way possible. Ottawa used section 98 of the Criminal Code, introduced in 1919 at the time of the first 'Red Scare', to outlaw the advocacy of revolution. It arrested eight Communist leaders in August of 1931. The courts quickly convicted and sentenced them, although the government gradually released them from prison after continual public demonstrations on their behalf. Nevertheless, the repression arrested the momentum of the party. After 1933 the CCF took away some CP support. By mid-decade the CP found itself caught up in rapidly changing orders from the USSR and by events in Europe. In 1937 many Canadian Communists entered the European struggle by joining the Mackenzie-Papineau Battalion to fight in the Spanish Civil War.

The CP took the credit for organizing, through the Workers' Unity League, a mass march on Ottawa in 1935 known as the On-to-Ottawa Trek. The marchers came out of the unemployment relief camps in BC, where unemployed young men found their only refuge. Conditions in the camps were degrading. Not even the Communists claimed that the discontent was anything but spontaneous. The trek began in Vancouver and ended in Regina. The RCMP allowed a delegation of eight marchers to take their grievances to Ottawa. The talks broke down and the delegation returned to Regina. At this point the Mounties moved in with baseball bat batons. The ensuing riot reduced downtown Regina to shambles and put 120 protesters in jail. Most of the remaining trekkers accepted offers of transportation back home. While the 1930s were punctuated from time to time by outbreaks of public discontent that turned to violence, such as in Regina, two points must be emphasized about these occurrences. The first is that with most of the spontaneous popular demonstrations, most of the damage to persons and property resulted from the authorities' efforts to break up what they regarded as ugly crowds. The second point is that much of the violence of the period resulted from confrontations between organized labour and the authorities. Clashes between police and strikers were common, as they always had been.

CANADIAN SOCIETY BETWEEN THE WARS

For more than half a century before 1919, Canada had been making a gradual transition from frontier nation to modern industrial state. This process basically continued unabated between the wars. Most of the emerging social patterns were not very much different from those that affected all heavily industrialized countries. Urbanization advanced while rural (and especially agricultural) society declined in importance. The traditional family unit seemed under attack. Technology rapidly altered communication and transportation. It also profoundly affected the ways in which Canadians entertained themselves.

Demographic Trends

As in all industrial countries, Canada experienced profound demographic changes. Some of these had been somewhat disguised by the federal government's failure, until 1921, to keep accurate national statistics beyond the census. Enormous infusions of new immigrants before 1914 also helped prevent the new demographic trends from becoming easily apparent, but they existed. By the 1941 census more Canadians lived in urban rather than rural places, a result of a substantial increase in urban residents, especially during the 1920s. Moreover, the 1941 census would be the last in which rural numbers and farm dwellers grew absolutely in number. Even before 1941, the impact of urbanization and industrialization was apparent.

First, mortality rates declined. In the critical area of infant mortality, the death rate had been steadily declining since the nineteenth century. Infant mortality took another major drop in the 1930s, while the overall death rate drifted perceptibly downward. By 1946 the median age at death was 63.1 for males and 65.3 for females. For the first time, Canadian society had begun to produce substantial numbers of people who would live beyond the age of productive labour; a rise in concern for old-age pensions in this period was hardly accidental. The main exception to the national trend was in the Aboriginal population. Their death rates ran four times the national average; infant mortality was at least twice that of Canadian society as a whole. Large numbers of Native mothers died in childbirth. Moreover, Indians suffered up to three times more accidental deaths than Canada's population overall. They had a high suicide rate. Before 1940 most Aboriginal peoples died of communicable rather than chronic disease, with tuberculosis as the big killer. The decreasing death rate for Canadians as a whole resulted from an improved standard of living and better medical treatment. In 1921–6, 270 out of every 1,000

Canadian deaths came from pulmonary and communicable disease. By 1946 such fatalities dropped to just over sixty out of every 1,000 Canadian deaths. Cardiovascular problems, renal disease, and cancer—all afflictions of an aging population—became more important killers.

Then fertility rates declined. The extent to which the fall in the birth rate resulted from conscious decisions on the part of women is not entirely clear, but the two were plainly related. Increased urbanization made large families less desirable. Industrialization took more women out of the home and into the workforce, where they found difficulties in caring for children. More women, especially over thirty, began to limit their number of births, practising some form of contraception. Birth rates had begun to fall in Canada before 1919 and continued their fall in the 1920s and 1930s. They recovered from an extremely low point in the middle of the Depression after 1941, increasing sharply after 1945. There were some significant internal differentials. One was between Quebec and the remainder of Canada. The birth rate in French Canada remained substantially higher than in Anglo-Canada, although it shared in the general decline. There was also a difference between urban and rural, with substantially higher birth rates in the latter. A third differential occurred between Catholic and Protestant, although certain Protestant subgroups, such as Mennonites and Mormons, had higher rates than the overall Catholic one. Finally, Aboriginal birth rates ran at least twice the national average.

As for other demographic factors, several require consideration. One was immigration, which (despite the upheavals in Europe) did not return to its pre-1914 incidence after the Great War. Public opinion, as reflected in government policy, did not favour massive new immigration. Many Canadians felt that since most agricultural land was now settled, newcomers would compete for jobs while altering the ethnic make-up of the population. Immigration ran at around 125,000 per year in the 1920s and then fell to 20,000 per year during the 1930s when the government discouraged most immigration. Canadian immigration policy operated on a preferred-nation basis, discouraging new arrivals from outside northern Europe and demonstrating hostile indifference to immigrants from non-European nations. Canada was not at all officially receptive, moreover, to the plight of refugees, mainly Jewish, from Nazi persecution. The nation took only a relative handful (about 6,000) of these people.

Another important factor was divorce. The year 1918 saw 114 divorces in all of Canada, a rate of 1.4 per 100,000 people. By 1929 the divorce rate had reached 8.2 per 100,000, rising to 18.4 per 100,000 in 1939 and to 65.3 per 100,000 by 1947. Higher rates occurred partly because more Canadians gained access to divorce courts; Ontario courts obtained divorce jurisdiction in 1930. The increase also resulted from a changed attitude, particularly among women, who instituted most divorce actions. Divorce statistics did not begin to measure the extent of marital dissolutions, however. Most dissolutions never reached a court. Especially during the Depression, they were the result of a husband's desertion of his wife. Many contemporaries saw the increase in divorce as evidence of the disintegration of the Canadian family.

Technological Change

Despite the nation's uneven economic record between 1919 and 1945, Canadians in these years experienced an increase in the rate and nature of technological change. The new technologies had enormous impact upon all aspects of Canadian life. On one level they forced governments to adopt a myriad of new policies. On another level they had tremendous psychological impact, particularly by militating against communalism in favour of the individual, family, or household.

One evident area of change was in the mass acceptance of the internal combustion engine in the form of the automobile and the tractor. Before 1920 automobile ownership had been almost entirely an urban phenomenon, but by 1920 it had become more general. In 1904 there were fewer than 5,000 motor vehicles in Canada. By 1920 there were 251,000, most of them built during the war. From 1918 to 1923 Canadian manufacturers, allied to US companies, were

A Toronto traffic jam in 1924. The motorists are out for a Sunday drive on the newly built Lakeshore Boulevard (City of Toronto Archives, James Collection 2530).

the second-largest car producers in the world. Canada was a major exporter, especially to the British empire. By 1930 only the United States had more automobiles per capita than did Canada. In that year Canada had 1,061,000 automobiles registered. Also significant was the increase in the number of tractors employed on the nation's farms after 1918.

The automobile was individually owned and operated as an extension of a household. It represented private rather than public transportation. No other single product operated so insidiously against communalism as the automobile. It also had tremendous spin-off consequences. Automobiles required roads, which were a provincial and municipal responsibility. More than one-quarter of the $650 million increase in provincial and municipal debt between 1913 and 1921 resulted from capital expenditures on highways, streets, and bridges. Road mileage in Canada expanded from 385,000 mi. (619,580 km) in 1922 to 565,000 mi. (909,254 km) in 1942. Motorists wanted not only roads but properly paved ones. Although in 1945 nearly two-thirds of Canadian roads were still of earth construction, the other third had been paved or gravelled at considerable expense. Automobiles ran on petroleum products. Not only did they encourage petroleum production, chiefly in Alberta, but they also created the gasoline station, the garage, the roadside restaurant, and the motel as new service industries to provide for a newly mobile population. Door-to-door rather than station-to-station mobility was one of the principal effects of the automobile revolution. Both the automobile and the truck competed with the railways, which began their decline in the 1920s. Although the automobile provided an important source of tax revenue for both federal and provincial governments, neither Ottawa nor the provinces made any serious effort to control the use or construction of motor vehicles, aside from some fairly minimal rules of the road and the issuance of drivers' licences to almost all comers. Despite its importance, the automobile and its 20,000 parts were produced entirely according to manufacturers' standards and consumers' desires. The car quickly became the symbol of North American independence and individuality. It also served as a combined status and sex symbol.

Unlike the automobile, the federal government treated radio as a public matter deserving of regulation. Broadcasting of programs, rather than the radio receiver itself, became the target. The transmission and reception of sound via radio waves had initially been developed before the Great War as an aid to ships at sea. The 1920s saw the mass marketing of the radio receiver in North America. In order to sell radios, it was necessary to provide something to listen to. By 1929 eighty-five broadcasting stations were operating in Canada under various ownerships. Private radio broadcasting in Canada was not all bad, but it was most uneven. A royal commission on broadcasting—the Aird Commission, appointed in 1928 and reporting in 1929—recommended the

This photograph, though staged, conveys the avid interest in radio in 1935. For those who could afford one, the receiver was a large piece of living-room furniture, like the walnut-veneer cabinet of this Canadian General Electric radio (National Archives of Canada C-80917).

nationalization of radio. Its advice was not immediately taken. The Bennett government eventually introduced the Broadcasting Act of 1932, however, which led to the formation of the Canadian Radio Broadcasting Commission to establish a national network and to supervise private stations. In 1936 this commission became the Canadian Broadcasting Corporation, with extensive English and French networks, and operated with federal financial support as an independent agency. No other Canadian cultural institution of its day was so closely associated with Canadian nationalism and Canadian culture than was the CBC. The CBC was not only pre-eminent but often unique in fostering of Canadian culture. Often the battle seemed to be uphill, since Canadians usually preferred listening to the slick entertainment programming produced in the United States.

Prohibition and Church Union

The impetus for the reform movement died after 1918. To some extent, reform was a victim of its own successes. For many Canadians, the achievement of prohibition and women's suffrage—the two principal reform panaceas of the prewar period—meant that the struggle had been won. To some extent, reform was a victim of the Great War. Reformers had exhausted themselves in a war effort that had produced devastation but no final victory. The war had been a disillusioning experience for many.

The failure of the prohibition experiment symbolized the decline of reform. Despite considerable evidence that the elimination of alcoholic beverages had made a social difference—the jails were emptied in most places, since they were usually filled with prisoners who had committed alcohol-related offences—the supporters of prohibition were unable to stem the tide. The Ontario Alliance for the Total Suppression of the Liquor Trade claimed in 1922 that the number of convictions for offences associated with drink had declined from 17,143 in 1914 to 5,413 in 1921, and drunkenness cases decreased in the province's major cities from 16,590 in 1915 to 6,766 in 1921. Nevertheless, various provinces went 'wet' between 1920 and 1924, and the Liquor Control Act replaced the Ontario Temperance Act in 1927. Opposition to prohibition after the war found a new argument to add to the old one that private conduct was being publicly regulated: attempts to enforce prohibition encouraged flouting the law, even created organized crime and vice. Too many people were prepared to ignore the law, said prohibition's opponents, who found more acceptable slogans of their own in 'Moderation' and 'Government Regulation'. In many provinces, the possibility of obtaining provincial revenue for tax-starved coffers led to the introduction of government control over the sale of alcohol. Taxing bad habits rather than forbidding them became part of the Canadian tradition.

While prohibition was dying, in 1925 the Methodist, Presbyterian, and Congregational churches (the first two were among Canada's largest denominations) merged as the United Church of Canada. As three of the most 'liberal' denominations in Canada, home of much of the Social Gospel commitment to Christian reform of secular society, they hoped to rejuvenate reform fervour through unification. Not all members of the three denominations were equally enthusiastic. Opposition to union was particularly strong among the Presbyterians. In the end, congregations could vote to stay out of the union. Thus 784 Presbyterian and eight Congregational congregations so declared, while 4,797 Methodist, 3,728 Presbyterian, and 166 Congregational congregations joined in the United Church of Canada. The new denomination became the most substantial Protestant communion of Canada, generally committed to liberal thinking and reform.

Racism

Canadian society between the wars continued to be profoundly racist. That point was demonstrable in a variety of different ways, although it must be emphasized that very few Canadians saw their racial and exclusionist attitudes as either socially undesirable or disfunctional.

Imported from the United States, the Ku Klux Klan flourished in Canada during the 1920s. In the United States the revived Klan spread anti-Black and anti-Catholic hate propaganda under the guise of a fraternal organization. In its secret rituals, fundamentalist Protestantism, and social operations, the Klan appeared to some Canadians to be little different from a host of other secret societies. The Klan assumed a Canadian face, posing as the defender of Britishness against the alien hordes and calling itself the 'Ku Klux Klan of the British empire'. Although the Klan had some success everywhere in Canada, it made particular headway in the late 1920s in Saskatchewan, where by 1929 there were over 125 chapters. In that province it found support from a number of Protestant ministers, who objected to the increasingly liberal leanings of the main-line Protestant churches. Much of its appeal was to a beleaguered conservative Protestant population in Saskatchewan. It also gained acceptance as a way of opposing the patronage-style politics of the provincial Liberal government. Few of its members associated it with American-style cross burning or midnight lynch mobs.

Canada's treatment of its Aboriginal population continued to display both belief in the superiority of its culture and its antagonism towards the Native peoples. The Department of Indian Affairs assumed that assimilation was the only possible policy. Deputy Minister Duncan Scott asserted in 1920 that 'Our object is to continue until there is not a single Indian in Canada that has not been absorbed into the body politic, and there is no Indian question, and no Indian Department.' Indian Affairs employed a variety of policies. It forced Aboriginal children into schools, usually residential ones far removed from their families. It forbade and actively suppressed the practice of traditional Native rituals like the potlatch. It carried out the Canadian government's legislative provisions to enfranchise the Indians, thus in theory making them full citizens and no longer wards of the state. Most of the Aboriginal resistance to these measures was passive, although there was the beginning of organization. The first congress of the League of Indians convened at Sault Ste Marie in September 1919. The league's objectives were 'to claim and protect the rights of all Indians in Canada by legitimate and just means', and to assert 'absolute control in retaining possession or disposition of our lands' (quoted in Cuthand 1978:31–2). The league and its successors met regularly thereafter.

In British Columbia, an anti-Oriental movement flourished during the interwar years. Much of the criticism of the 'menace' from Asia came from economic fears, although there was also a general concern for the racial integrity of the province as a White civilization. The general argument was that the newcomers would not assimilate, although there was considerable evidence that the Japanese, at least, were acculturating rapidly. Moving onto small holdings in the Fraser Valley and into salmon fishing along the coasts, the Japanese appeared to pose a potential military threat should their homeland—which was militarily aggressive in the Pacific throughout the century—attempt to expand into Canada. If people from Asia were highly visible in some areas and in some industries, that fact was partly explained by their exclusion—in law and in practice—from so much of the life of the province.

In the later 1930s, the Canadian government showed little interest in accommodating refugees from the Nazi pograms in Europe. Despite the Jewish community's continued efforts in Canada, the government refused to adopt a generous policy. Immigration officials systematically rejected highly skilled professionals and intellectuals (including doctors, scientists, and musicians) as inadmissible applicants. One government mandarin wrote, 'We don't want to take too many Jews, but, in the present circumstances particularly, we don't want to say so.' For a nation as deficient in world-renowned scientific, intellectual, and cultural talent as Canada, the result was a cruel, if totally deserved, shortfall. Other countries, particularly the United States, benefited greatly from immigrants in fields as diverse as physics, medicine, theatre, music, and education. Canada did not. Even in the most crass of non-humanitarian terms, Canadian policy was a disaster, but from a country that was constantly lecturing the world in moral terms, it was inexcusable.

Women

Canadian women emerged from the Great War with the vote in hand. A few feminist critics had argued that the vote was no panacea for women's second-class position in Canadian society. It did not even assure a high level of political involvement. Between the wars women did not very often run for public office or constitute a recognizable voting bloc. The flapper, with her bobbed hair, short skirts, and spirit of independence, was the symbolic 'new woman' of the 1920s, but she was hardly typical. Most Canadian women did not smoke or sip cocktails or dance the Black Bottom. About all they had in common with the flapper was that, like her, they worked outside the home. More women worked in Canada in 1931 than in 1921, mostly in dead-end jobs. The Depression was particularly difficult for women. Public opinion turned against married women holding jobs that could be done by men. Most relief programs were geared to men, partly because it was not thought that women would threaten the social order by rioting and demonstrating. Many husbands deserted their wives, and even where the family remained together, the wife did most of the work to keep it functioning.

CANADIAN CULTURE BETWEEN THE WARS

A resurgence of Canadian nationalism characterized the 1920s. The larger stories of the interwar period, however, were the blossoming of Canada's love affair with American popular culture and the simultaneous emergence of a number of substantial home-grown writers and artists. By the 1930s Canadians no longer had to be apologetic about their cultural achievements, although the number of individuals who could actually make a living from their creative work remained fairly small.

The Great War may have been fought for the British empire, but both its course and outcome made Canadians more conscious of their nation's distinctiveness. In the 1920s Canadian nationalism wore a dual face. On the one hand, it had to reflect Canada's new international status. On the other, it felt it had to protect the country from being overwhelmed by foreign culture. The painter Arthur Lismer (1885–1969) wrote, 'After 1919, most creative people, whether in painting, writing or music, began to have a guilty feeling that Canada was as yet unwritten, unpainted, unsung. . . . In 1920 there was a job to be done' (quoted in Thompson and Seager 1985:158). That job was not simply to write books, paint pictures, and compose music that captured the true Canadian spirit. The task was also to organize national cultural organizations and institutions that would mobilize a new sense of national consciousness. A number of Canadian magazines and journals made their appearance to serve as vehicles for Canadian ideas. The *Canadian Bookman* appeared in 1919, and the *Canadian Forum*, the *Canadian Historical Review,* and *The Dalhousie Review* in 1920. The Canadian Authors' Association, founded in 1921, backed campaigns promoting Canadian writers. In 1937 it succeeded in persuading the governor-general—the famous Scottish novelist John Buchan (1875–1940), Lord Tweedsmuir—to establish the prestigious Governor-General's awards. In art, the Group of Seven consciously sought to create a Canadian mythology. According to their first exhibition catalogue of 1920, their vision was simple: 'An Art must grow and flower in the land before the country will be a real home for its people' (quoted in Thompson and Seager 1985:162).

Between 1920 and 1940 over 750 Canadian novels were published. While most of these works were of escapist fiction, a number of Canadian novelists achieved national and even modest international reputations as being skilful at their craft. Perhaps even more important, a small number of strong, confident, realistic novels appeared that formed the foundation of modern Canadian fiction. An unsentimental stream of writing was necessary to unite two important contemporary perspectives on literature. International critical standards of the time insisted upon such an approach. At the same time, realism was also the most efficient way to reflect the Canadian environment, thus providing the distinctively Canadian content that nationalism demanded. As for the visual arts, particularly during the Depression when most artists had to live at subsistence level, much work we now value highly was produced. Few visual artists in Canada could make a living from their work alone, but art schools were now sufficiently

Emily Carr in the Cariboo, 1904.

common in the larger Canadian cities to provide employment for painters and sculptors. British Columbia's Emily Carr (1871–1945) united art and literature in a highly original way. Combining French Post-Impressionism with Indian form and colour, Carr gradually created a powerful and distinctive visual landscape. She also won a Governor-General's award for *Klee Wyck* (1941), a collection of stories based on her visits to Indian villages. By the time of her death, Carr's paintings were probably the visual icons the average Canadian could most easily associate with an individual artist. She had triumphed not only over the disadvantages of Canadian geography but over the limitations faced by any woman who aspired to more than a genteel 'dabbling' in art.

During the interwar period, radio, motion pictures, and the great expansion of professional sports all represented major American influences on the Canadian consciousness. In popular culture Canada made little effort at national distinctiveness. The loudest critics of insidious Americanization usually had no alternatives to offer other than a somewhat outworn Britishness. At the same time, Canada and Canadians were hardly innocent victims of American cultural imperialism. As a nation Canada had choices it failed or refused to exercise. As a people Canadians were willing—indeed, active—collaborators in the cultural process, both at home and in the United States itself. A closer examination of motion pictures and hockey in this period is instructive.

In the world of film, Hollywood's success was also Canada's, since there was no shortage of Canadian talent involved in the formative years of Tinseltown. Mack Sennett, Sidney Olcott, Louis B. Mayer, Jack Warner, Walter Huston, Mary Pickford, Norma Shearer, and Marie Dressler—some of Hollywood's biggest and most influential names in its formative years—were Canadian-born. Pickford, Warner, and Mayer founded three of the major Hollywood studios between 1919 and 1924. At the same time, Canada itself had only the beginnings of a Canadian film industry, comprising mainly the seven films produced by Ernest Shipman, of which *Back to God's Country* (1919) is a Canadian silent-film classic. Otherwise film making in Canada was confined chiefly to newsreels and documentaries often appended to American features. By 1922 American studios were including Canadian receipts as part of domestic revenue, and in 1923 Famous Players' Canadian Corporation, a subsidiary of Pickford's studio, took over the leading Canadian cinema chain, Allen Theatres. At the height of the silent-film era, Hollywood succeeded in monopolizing the distribution of film in Canada, although the Canadian exhibitors and cinema owners were Canadians who were not much concerned where the product had originated so long as it was profitable.

Other nations around the world took some sort of defensive action against the Hollywood juggernaut, either placing quotas on imported films or providing tax incentives for native productions. Canada did neither, partly because its citizens were so closely connected with the American film industry, partly because Canadians so clearly preferred Hollywood films to the alternatives. During the Great Depression, when the Dream Factory provided blessed release from the cares and woes of everyday life for millions of Canadians, that dream was plainly American. Canadians continued to love American movies despite the inaccuracy with which Hollywood persistently treated Canadian geography, society, and history. Symbolically, the successive and successful film portrayals of that quintessential American, Abraham Lincoln, by two Canadian actors, Walter Huston (1884–1950) and Raymond Massey (1896–1983), only solidified the close identification of Canadians and Americans in the popular mind on both sides of the border.

The situation with hockey was even more interesting. The National Hockey Association (NHA) was organized in 1909 in eastern Canada. On the West Coast, Frank and Lester Patrick, in 1911–12, formed the Pacific Coast Hockey League (PCHL), which defeated an NHA team for the Stanley Cup in 1915. In 1917 the National Hockey League (NHL) formed out of the NHA. The PCHL folded in 1925. That same year, the NHL granted a franchise lease to the Boston Bruins and became the top professional hockey league in North America. The New York Rangers and the Pittsburgh Pirates soon followed, and Chicago and Detroit received NHL franchises in 1927. Most of the American clubs were owned or managed by Canadians, and the players were almost entirely Canadian. Indeed, the Patrick brothers had brought players from their PCHL teams to the American-based NHL teams they acquired in the 1920s. The Toronto Maple Leafs acquired a physical presence when Maple Leaf Gardens was built as their home. At the opening on 12 November 1931, Foster Hewitt (1902–85) broadcast his first 'Hockey Night in Canada', describing the game from a gondola overlooking the rink. For three decades thereafter, his high-pitched voice—and his excited refrain, 'He shoots! He scores!'—was hockey for most Canadians. 'Hockey Night in Canada' was the one and only Canadian-produced radio program on CBC that consistently outdrew American offerings with the Canadian listeners. Although the Depression benefited professional sports by providing a desperate need for escape, not all Canadians could afford to pay for admission. In Toronto, for example, ticket prices of 50¢ and $1.25 resulted in many empty seats. By 1939 the NHL had suffered the loss of all but two of its Canadian teams, the Maple Leafs and the Montreal Canadiens. The centre of professional hockey power shifted to the United States, although Canadians still knew that virtually all the players came from Canada.

THE SECOND WORLD WAR

Canada went back to war on 10 September 1939. This time the government waited a week after the British declaration of war against Germany to join the conflict, thus emphasizing Canada's 'independent' status. The nation's entry into the war helped complete the process of economic recovery. Unprepared militarily, as in the Great War, Canada proved capable of mobilizing resources remarkably swiftly when required. Canada quickly accepted the British Commonwealth Air Training Plan as its major war commitment. The details of the scheme were agreed upon by Britain and Canada on 17 December 1939. Within months the program's first graduates emerged from Camp Borden, Ontario. It eventually graduated 131,533 Commonwealth airmen, 72,835 of whom were Canadian, at a cost of $1.6 billion. A nation of less than 12 million people would eventually put over 1 million of them into uniform. Using the War Measures Act, Canada succeeded in mobilizing economic resources in a way that had seemed impossible during the Depression. Tax arrangements between the Dominion and the provinces were restructured during the emergency, with the federal government collecting most of the revenue and making grants to the provinces to recover their operating expenses.

The economy was totally managed and regulated, a process associated with Ottawa's wartime economic czar, Clarence Decatur Howe (1886–1960). By 1943 unemployment was well under 2 per cent, a figure regarded in most quarters as full employment. Federal spending rose from 3.4 per cent of the gross national product (GNP) in 1939 to 37.6 per cent of GNP by 1944, totalling a full $4.4 billion in that later year. Industrial growth was better distributed across the regions than in 1914–18, inflation was controlled, and consumption was regulated by shortages and rationing. Canada's total GNP rose from $5.6 billion in 1939 to $11.9 billion in 1945. The nation became one of the world's major industrial giants, producing 850,000 motorized vehicles and over 16,000 military aircraft during the war. The government borrowed heavily from its own citizens, partly in the form of war bonds. While the achievement was impressive, it suggested that the riddle of social justice remained unsolved. Canada appeared far more capable of efficient utilization of its productive capacity to fight destructive wars abroad than to battle domestically with poverty and unemployment.

As in the Great War, Canadians fought well whenever called upon. As in the previous conflict, they were often employed as shock troops. In the disastrous landing of the 2nd Canadian Division at Dieppe in August 1942, nearly 2,700 of the 5,000 Canadians who embarked were either killed or captured. The First Canadian Army, formed in 1942 under the command of General A.G.L. McNaughton (1887–1966), was composed of five divisions that were eventually split between Italy and northwest Europe. This army was independently commanded, although the Royal Canadian Air Force and the Royal Canadian Navy were mainly integrated with their British counterparts. Canada ultimately had the third largest navy among the Allied powers, the fourth largest air force, and the fourth largest army. Such a contribution ought to have made it something of a power in the world, although the major powers—Britain, the United States, and the USSR—routinely treated Canada as little different from Allied nations like Chile or Brazil, which had only token forces in the war.

Canada fought chiefly in the European and North Atlantic theatres. Canadian assistance to American and British efforts in the Pacific and Southeast Asia was fairly minimal. In December 1941, however, two Canadian battalions were involved in the surrender of Hong Kong. The 1,421 men who returned home after years in Japanese prison camps had to fight for twenty-three years to win proper veteran's benefits from the Canadian government. As in the Great War, casualties in this conflict were heavy, with 42,642 Canadians giving up their lives. One innovation in this war was the active military service of women. As in 1914–18 large numbers of women were employed in the war industry, but by 1945 over 43,000 women were actually in uniform. A Gallup

Life at Sea in a Canadian Corvette During the Second World War

[One of Canada's major military functions during the war against Hitler was to provide escort service against Nazi submarines for convoys of ships plying the dangerous North Atlantic route. Much of this duty was carried out in small ships called corvettes. Built in Canadian shipyards and originally intended for coastal duty, the corvettes were manned by nearly 100,000 young Canadian sailors. Life aboard them was dangerous and uncomfortable, as the following account from Howard Cousins, leading signalman aboard HMCS *Algoma* in 1941–2, suggests. *Source*: M. Johnston, *Corvettes Canada: Convoy Veterans of WWII Tell Their True Stories* (Toronto: McGraw-Hill Ryerson, 1994):113–15.]

The ship was your home and the weather had a direct effect on the degree of comfort that home provided. When the wind and seas built up, the comforts of your home were virtually non-existent. As the ship rolled and pitched, you were thrown around continuously, not daring to move without holding fast to something. The bridge was wet with spray, sometimes solid water.

The highly developed storm gear we have today was not available then. An oilskin coat worn over a duffel coat, a sou'wester on your head and sea-boots on your feet was the rig of the day. In theory, the oilskin coat overlapped the tops of the sea-boots. In practice, the wind whipping around the bridge caused the skirt of the coat to lift and flap. Before long water had seeped into your boots and soon your feet were wet and cold. Water also found its way down your neck. Some of us wore a towel around our neck, but before long the towel became soaked and water trickled down your chest and back.

A corvette on the crest of the wave could have one-third of the forward portion clear of the water. As the ship rolled and dropped down into the trough, it was almost a free fall. The poor blokes

poll taken in 1944 indicated, however, that most Canadians, including 68 per cent of the women polled, believed that men should be given preference for employment in the postwar reconstruction. As a result, the machinery for women's participation, including day care centres, was dismantled with unseemly haste at the war's end.

As in the Great War, dissent was met with persecution. The Canadian government proved almost totally insensitive to pacifists' beliefs. It interned thousands of Canadians without trial, often for mere criticism of government policy. The most publicized abuse of the state's power was the treatment of the Japanese Canadians. Although the King government did not for a minute believe that Japanese Canadians represented any real military danger, it yielded to pressure from British Columbia and forcibly evacuated most Japanese from the West Coast. Many were sent to internment camps in the interior of BC, and others were scattered across the country, their land seized and their property sold at auction. 'National emergency' was also used to justify the dissemination

in the forecastle felt virtually weightless; anything on the lockers, shelves, and tables, including your meal, frequently floated off. When the ship smashed into the back of the next wave, it felt as if the ship had been dropped on concrete.

Drawing meals from the galley was awkward, to say the least. The galley was located aft of the wheelhouse and the duty messman had to collect the meals for his mess on a tray, then carry that tray along the open deck to the forecastle. With no hand available to hang on with, seas breaking over the side and down from the break of the forecastle, it was a perilous trip. Some meals did not make it.

I remember one occasion when the messman, having successfully made the trip, proudly stood at the head of the table as someone removed the oilskin protecting the food. The messman was starting to boast how good he was when the ship fell rapidly over the crest of a wave. When the ship was brought back up with the usual jolt, the messman and our food were thrown across the deck.

Bad weather also involved the laws of physics in the basic act of getting into your bed, which was a hammock suspended from steel rods on the deckhead. To get into your hammock, you grabbed the rod and swung yourself up and in. Timing was essential. If the ship was lifting to a sea, it was virtually impossible to push yourself off the deck, let along swing up into the hammock. On the other hand, if you waited until the ship was falling off the crest, a slight push of the toes was enough for you to float effortlessly up to the hammock.

Everyone's job became more difficult under bad weather conditions. . . . The cook often gave up and resorted to sandwiches. . . . No, home was not a place of comfort in bad weather, which did have one good thing going for it—there was very little chance that the convoy would be troubled with submarine attacks.

of propaganda, now called 'management of information'. Citizens needed to be educated in order to maintain faith and hope and to eliminate 'potential elements of disunity', a euphemism for criticism of the government. One major institution of information management was the National Film Board of Canada, under Scottish-born John Grierson (1898–1972), who believed in the integration of 'the loyalties and forces of the community in the name of positive and highly constructive ideas'. Grierson saw 'information services—propaganda if you like—' as an inevitable consequence of the government's involvement in the crisis (quoted in Young 1978:217–40).

Internal policies of the war revolved around two major questions: conscription and postwar reconstruction. In a national plebiscite held on the question of conscription in the spring of 1942, the nation voted 2,945,514 to 1,643,006 to release the government from an earlier pledge not to conscript for overseas service. Quebec voted strongly in the negative. The conscription issue emerged again in 1944, when the military insisted (as in 1917) that it was neces-

Japanese Canadians leaving for an eastern destination via the CNR (Vancouver Public Library 1386).

Anticonscription demonstrators in downtown Montreal, March 1942 (*Montreal Gazette*/National Archives of Canada).

sary to ship overseas conscripts who had been drafted with the promise that they would not be required to serve abroad. In the end, although conscripts were sent to Europe, few served as combatants before the war ended in May 1945. For the King government, the increasing threat from the CCF became a problem as nagging as that of Quebec. As early as 1941 many Canadians had apparently come to realize that the failure to make a concerted assault on social injustice had been a result mainly of governments' refusal to act. Canada was now in wartime demonstrating how thoroughly the country could be mobilized if the will to do so was present. Public opinion in Anglo-Canada began turning to the social promises of the CCF. By the time of the September 1943 federal election, the CCF received the support of 29 per cent of the electorate at the polls. In 1944 the Saskatchewan CCF wiped out a long-standing Liberal government in an election fought over social services.

King's Liberals had dragged their heels over social welfare reform. Federal unemployment insurance had been introduced in 1940, but other progressive legislation remained on hold. Now, in 1944, King declared in the House of Commons 'a wholly new conception of industry as being in the nature of social service for the benefit of all, not as something existing only for the benefit of a favoured few'. The introduction of social reform was not only necessary to deal with the threat from the CCF but also to prevent possible public disorder at the conclusion of the war and to assert the authority of the federal government. Once the political decision was made to implement social reform, there were plenty of schemes available, including a package in the 'Report on Social Security for Canada' tabled in the House of Commons Special Committee on Social Security by economist Leonard Marsh (1906–82) in 1943. In the end, a full program of progressive legislation was never actually enacted before the end of the war. The Liberal government did introduce the Family Allowances Act of 1944, Canada's first social insurance program with universal coverage. It provided benefits to mothers of children under age sixteen. In 1944 the Liberals also passed the National Housing Act, described as 'An Act to Promote the Construction of New Houses, the Repair and Modernization of Existing Houses, the Improvement of Housing and Living Conditions and the Expansion of Employment in the Postwar Period.' The King government turned to the postwar period, however, with intentions of attacking the problem of social justice and the constitutional limitations of the British North America Act simultaneously.

Despite war fatalities, injustices, and some deprivation, the Second World War was, on balance, a unifying and positive experience for most Canadians. Full employment helped a good deal. Rationing provided a better balanced diet. Limited leisure time and the absence of big-ticket consumer items, such as

The Marsh Report on Social Security, 1943

[In 1943 Leonard Marsh submitted his 'Report on Social Security for Canada' to the House of Commons Special Committee on Social Security. In preparation for several years along with other documents on the postwar reconstruction, this report called for a vast overhaul and expansion of Canada's social insurance system. In the following excerpt, Marsh explained the reasons for his call. *Source*: Special Committee on Social Security, *Report on Social Security for Canada, Prepared by Dr L.C. Marsh for the Advisory Committee on Reconstruction* (Ottawa: King's Printer, 1943):12–13.]

The purpose of this report is to look forward, not backward. It would not serve this purpose if it were not geared closely to consideration of the vast economic and social changes which are going on now, and which must continue only with the difference of changes in purpose and direction, once the war is over. There have been certain compelling arguments for the community types of social provision ever since the growth of large industrial communities. But there are additional reasons, and some reasons which change the force of the old ones, for planning the overhaul and extension of our social legislation at this time.

The first is that social security has become accepted as one of the things for which the peoples of the world are fighting. It is one of the concrete expressions of 'a better world' which is particularly real to those who knew unemployment, destitution, inadequate medical care and the like in the depression periods before the war. To others the idea of better social security measures may be less of a reaction from previous hard experience; but it is an intelligible recognition that it is one way of realizing nationally a higher standard of living, and of securing more freedom and opportunity through the use of such income as is available once social insurance has taken care of the minimum.

automobiles and household appliances, forced many Canadians to save, often by purchasing war bonds and savings stamps. By war's end, a fifteen-year deferral of expectations had built up a powerful urge among Canadians to enjoy material comforts, free from concern over life's vagaries and hazards. This population was fully conscious of the dangers of assuming that social protection could be left to the private individual. It was equally aware that the state could intervene in the process, if it so desired.

Whatever assessment may be placed on the first and rather broad interest in social security, a second one is completely realistic and timely. The end of the war means demobilization of much of the civilian as well as the uniformed population and, no matter how short may be the period of transition, there are risks and difficulties attached to the process of re-employment against which all appropriate facilities must be mobilized. It should not be forgotten, in this connection, that the re-employment problems of the post-war period include the reassembling of many thousands of families.

A third and equally realistic consideration is that the transition period will show in more marked contrast than any other, differences in respect of social provision for Canadian citizens when they are in the army or in some other branch of the services, and when in ordinary civilian life. The provisions which the state extends to its armed forces and their dependents in time of war, and to ex-service men's families after war, go far along all the avenues of what is usually comprised in 'social security'— provision for children's maintenance, widowhood, medical care, disability, unemployment, retraining, and other contingencies. . . .

The final point in gauging the need and validity of a social security programme in post-war Canada is only indirectly a welfare matter at all, but it is a strategic factor in economic policy generally whose importance cannot be over-emphasized. One of the necessities for economic stability is the maintenance of the flow of purchasing-power at the time when munitions and other factories are closing down and war activity in many other spheres is being liquidated. Sound social insurance, which is a form of investment in physical health, morale, educational opportunities for children, and family stability, is a desirable and a comparatively easy vehicle of expenditure. It is not only an eminently appropriate peacetime alternative for expenditures now being devoted to destruction: it is also a form of using some of the deferred backlog of consumer expenditure to which reference is so often made only in terms of radios, frigidaires and other tangible consumers' goods.

Major Events, 1945–1960

1945   Liberal government is re-elected. Dominion-Provincial Conference on Reconstruction is convened. United Nations is founded in San Francisco.

1947   Imperial Oil brings in Leduc, Alberta, oilfield. Prime Minister Mackenzie King acknowledges Canada's 'moral obligation' to refugees and displaced persons from Europe.

1948   Mackenzie King resigns and is replaced by Louis St Laurent. Newfoundland holds two plebiscites on its future, choosing to join Canada.

1949   Asbestos strike in Quebec. Newfoundland joins Confederation. Royal Commission on National Development in the Arts, Letters, and Sciences (Massey Commission) is appointed. North Atlantic Treaty Organization is formed.

1950   Canada joins the Korean War. Interprovincial oil pipeline is built from Edmonton to Superior, Ontario.

1951   Old Age Security Act of 1951 is passed by Ottawa. Employees strike at Eaton's department stores. Aluminum Company of Canada begins the Kitimat project in British Columbia.

1952   The first CBC television stations are opened.

1953   Quebec's Tremblay Commission on Constitutional Problems makes its report. Mackenzie Highway is completed to Northwest Territories. Transmountain oil pipeline is built from Edmonton to Vancouver.

1954   British Empire Games in Vancouver sees first four-minute mile run by both Roger Bannister and John Landy. St Lawrence Seaway opens. First iron ore leaves Ungava, Quebec.

1955   Canso Causeway is opened in Nova Scotia, linking Cape Breton to the mainland.

1956   Canadian Labour Congress is formed from a merger of the Canadian Congress of Labour and the Trades and Labor Congress of Canada. The Unemployment Assistance Act is passed by Parliament. Trans-Canada Pipeline debate weakens the Liberal government. First transatlantic telephone cable is completed between Newfoundland and Scotland.

1957   Liberal government passes the Hospital Insurance Diagnostic Services Act. Diefenbaker's Tories win a minority government; St Laurent steps down. Lester B. Pearson wins the Nobel Peace Prize. The Canada Council is created.

1958   Inco strike. Lester B. Pearson is chosen Liberal leader. Diefenbaker Tories sweep the nation, including Quebec. Great Slave Railway is begun.

1959   Diefenbaker government decides to scrap the Avro Arrow. Maurice Duplessis dies.

1960   Royal Commission on Government Organization is appointed.

9

Prospering Together, 1945–1959

✦

The post-Second World War era, particularly before 1960, was a period of unparalleled economic growth and prosperity for Canada. Production and consumption moved steadily upward. Employment rose almost continuously. Canada substantially increased its workforce. Inflation was steady but almost never excessive. Interest rates were relatively low. The nation was in the midst of an uncharacteristic natural increase in its population growth rate that would become known as the baby boom. At the same time that many Canadians took advantage of the good times by conceiving children and moving to new homes in the suburbs, both the federal and provincial governments became active in providing new programs of social protection for their citizens. That network was not created without controversy, particularly of the constitutional variety, although the debate was still relatively muted until the 1960s. By that time, Canadian governments at all levels had become interventionist in a variety of ways, however, including the public nurture of culture.

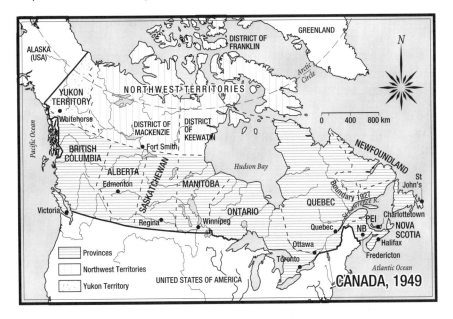

AFFLUENCE

At the base of all developments from 1946 to 1960 (and beyond) was economic prosperity and growth. Almost all aspects of planning in both the public and private sectors were based on assumptions of constant growth, and such thinking seemed to work. Between 1946 and 1960, per capita income in Canada nearly doubled, thus increasing the Canadian standard of living. Canadians could be forgiven for believing that there were no limits to growth. Great Depressions were disasters of the past, standards of living could continue to rise. Both politicians and their expert advisers argued that governments could now manage economies. They could correct for negative movements soon after they began. The operative economic wisdom was Keynesianism, named after the English economist John Maynard Keynes, whose writings provided much of the theoretical underpinning of affluence.

Quebec's Tremblay Commission on Constitutional Problems well described the prevailing wisdom in 1953:

> The objective envisaged was the maintenance of economic stability and full employment.... Both expenditures and investments, by individuals as well as by companies, should, therefore, be encouraged. Moreover, the government should take a part in this, and co-operate in stabilizing the economy and in ensuring full employment by its own expenditures and investments. This would demand from it an appropriate fiscal and monetary policy, as well as a programme of carefully planned public works.... The new policy necessarily entailed a considerable number of social security measures regarded as indispensable for the correction of variations in the economic cycle (Kwavnick 1973:183–4).

In truth, the overall pattern of affluence was neither solely attributable to government management nor distinctive to Canada. It was general across the Western industrial world. It started, in part, with the rebuilding of the war-torn economies of Europe and Asia. It continued with heavy expenditures on military defence during the cold war. Then prosperity continued on its own momentum for a time.

Foreign trade was an important component of Canadian affluence. The volume of both imports and exports increased substantially. Canada became integrated into the American trading market as Great Britain decreased in importance as a trading partner. The government set the value of the Canadian dollar in terms of the American dollar, and attempted to control Canadian foreign exchange and Canadian domestic banking through the Bank of Canada. After 1954 banks were allowed to move into consumer credit and mortgage loans, although before 1967 they were limited in the interest they could charge. Canada's monetary policy was to increase the supply of money in circulation, producing an inflation that would eventually run out of control.

The relative importance of various sectors of the domestic economy shifted. Agriculture declined from 25 per cent of the total workforce in 1946 to 11 per cent in 1961. The real growth area was in the public sector, particularly in public administration and services necessary to manage the new state. In 1946 just over 15 per cent of Canadians were employed in the public sector, while by 1961 that figure had increased to just over 25 per cent. Many of the public-service employees were highly educated white-collar workers, and by 1960 over half of Canadians held white-collar jobs. In manufacturing, regional disparities continued and even grew. Central Canada, especially Ontario, experienced most of the gains in manufacturing. Ontario produced over 50 per cent of total manufacturing value added in the nation. Ontario dominated the manufacture of durable goods and big-ticket consumer items in many industries. In 1957, for example, Ontario turned out 98.8 per cent of Canada's motor vehicles, 90.7 per cent of its heavy industrial goods, 90 per cent of its agricultural implements, and 80.7 per cent of its major household appliances. Canadian manufacturing served two principal markets. One was the domestic consumer market, which exploded after fifteen years of doing without. The other was a huge market for military hardware to equip Canada's armed forces, which greatly increased in number after 1950. Canada had a natural ambition to produce home-grown equipment, but had to settle for subcontracting parts of Canadian orders through American branch plants. The Diefenbaker government's decision to scrap the Avro Arrow in 1959 marked the last serious Canadian venture in the independent development of military hardware.

The resource economy did reasonably well. Beginning in 1947, when Imperial Oil brought in the major oilfield at Leduc, in southern Alberta, there was significant expansion in western Canadian oil and gas. Most of the risk taking was done by Americans, and the Alberta oil industry was quickly taken over by multinational firms. Oil and gas began to be transported by pipeline from the west into the major centres of population and industry. Potash provided a major new resource for Saskatchewan, and uranium was a short-lived bonanza for northern Ontario. The burning of fossil fuels and the development of nuclear power were the growth areas in the energy industry. Hydroelectric generation, which accounted for almost 95 per cent of Canada's electrical capacity in 1946, had dropped to just over 75 per cent by 1960 and would be down to only half that by the 1970s, despite massive hydroelectric projects in many provinces, especially Quebec and British Columbia.

In this period of affluent growth, nobody paid much attention to environmental issues and pollution. Nuclear experts insisted that nuclear accidents were extremely unlikely, and did not worry about the disposal of long-life nuclear wastes. Petrochemical plants dumped waste into surrounding waters, and paper-processing plants dumped poisonous mercury into rivers and lakes. Solid industrial waste was usually buried, often used as landfill to create new housing estates near large urban centres. Many inland rivers and lakes deteriorated into veritable cesspools of industrial waste and human sewage. Acid rain spread unrecognized as an international problem. Farmers dumped chemical fertilizers and weed-killers into the soil, where they eventually ended up in underground aquifers. Economic growth and development were the measures of all things.

The boom of the postwar years encouraged the growth of American direct investment in Canada and the rise of the multinational corporation, which usually had headquarters in the United States and a branch-plant operation in Canada. By 1950 more than three-quarters of total foreign investment in the country was American, chiefly in mining, manufacturing, and petroleum. In 1959 foreign-owned companies controlled nearly 60 per cent of assets in Canadian mining, over 60 per cent of the oil and gas industry, and over 50 per cent of Canadian manufacturing. The extent of foreign ownership of all major Canadian industries in 1959 was 34 per cent, of which 26 per cent was owned by United States residents. American ownership was especially prevalent in the highly profitable consumer area, where production flourished on the backs on American technology and American promotion of goods and brand names. American advertising and cultural values created consumer demand on a continental basis, and Canadian subsidiaries fulfilled it for the Canadian market. Not until 1957, however, did American investment and the growth of multinationals become an important public issue. As late as 1956, one of the leading textbooks in Canadian economic history referred to foreign investment as 'one of the mainsprings of progress' without mentioning its less desirable aspects (Easterbrook and Aitken 1956:402). The foreign investment issue was first brought to the public's attention by the Royal Commission on Canada's Economic Prospects, chaired by Walter Gordon. The report of the commission, released after the Liberal government that had appointed it was defeated in 1957, observed that 'No other nation as highly industrialized as Canada has such a large proportion of industry controlled by non-resident concerns' (*Royal Commission on Canada's Economic Prospects* 1958:384). The commission's concern was not immediately shared by the public, however.

Part of the critique of American multinationalism was related to Canada's scientific research and development policy. Critics noted that Canada spent a far smaller proportion of its science dollar on the development side of research and development. They added that industry in Canada contributed a far smaller share of scientific activity than in any other highly industrialized

Table 9.1
_____

Ontario's Portion of Certain Manufacturing Industries in Canada, 1957

Manufacturing Industries	Per cent of National Total
Large Industries	
Motor vehicles	98.8
Motor vehicle parts	94.5
Heavy electrical goods	90.7
Primary iron and steel	77.4
Telecommunications equipment	77.0
Iron castings	69.9
Fruit and veg. preparations	67.6
Sheet metal products	59.1
Industrial machinery	58.9
Misc. chemical products	58.1
Printing and bookbinding	57.8
Brass and copper products	57.5
Acids, alkalies, and salts	55.3
Medium-size Industries	
Agricultural implements	90.9
Soaps and washing compounds	88.4
Major household appliances	80.7
Household and office machines	79.7
Hardware, tools, and cutlery	74.0
Heating and cooking apparatus	68.3
Confectionery	57.7
Small Industries	
Machine tools	100.0
Tobacco processing	94.7
Bicycles	90.0
Prepared breakfast foods	90.6
Leather tanneries	85.0
Batteries	70.7

Source: Statistics Canada, *Manufacturing Industries of Canada 1957*, section D (31–206) (Ottawa: Queen's Printer, 1957):5–6.

nation. The reasons for these lags, many insisted, were to be found in Canada's ability as a branch-plant economy to import technology developed elsewhere. In 1959, for example, industry was responsible for only 39 per cent of scientific research in Canada, as opposed to 58 per cent in Britain and 78 per cent in the United States. By this time the federal government's outlays in scientific activity were in excess of $200 million per year, while in 1959 Canadian industry spent only $96.7 million on research and development at home. Between 1957 and 1961, moreover, 95 per cent of all Canadian patents involved foreign applicants, nearly 70 per cent of them American. Clearly Canada spent large sums of public money on scientific research, but was not getting much industrial advantage from the expenditures. Canadian scientists had cooperated with American counterparts to produce the IBM 101 electronic statistical machine in time for it to analyse the 1951 Canadian census data. But the new technology became American, and Canadians were never in the front lines of the microchip revolution of later years. In 1962 expenditure on research and development as a proportion of sales averaged 0.7 per cent by all Canadian manufacturers, as opposed to 2 per cent by American ones and even larger proportions in Germany and Japan.

An increased role for organized labour accompanied other economic trends of the affluent society. Union membership increased and unions were organized in a number of new industries. The Second World War had marked a major turning-point for Canadian labour. It had fought any number of bitter strikes during the Depression in search for recognition of an unfettered right to bargain collectively with employers. It received precious little support from government in this effort, however. The percentage of union members in the total civilian labour force had actually declined slightly between 1929 and 1939. During the war, however, the federal government had decided to co-opt labour into the war effort. Both it and the provinces began the slow process of altering labour legislation to recognize and protect the rights to organization and collective bargaining. The key breakthrough came in 1944 when the federal government, by wartime Order in Council, introduced PCO 1003. This order combined older Canadian labour principles of investigating disputes with recently adopted American principles of compulsory recognition and bargaining. By 1946, 17.1 per cent of all workers and 27.9 per cent of non-agricultural workers belonged to unions.

With bargaining rights achieved, labour unions went on to hammer out working relationships with most of Canada's traditional industries. Improved working conditions and higher wages were the result. The process of coming to terms with employers was hardly a painless one. Throughout the 1950s there were never fewer than 159 strikes per year across Canada, involving between 49,000 and 112,000 workers annually. Important strikes that achieved national prominence included the great asbestos strike of 1949 in Quebec, the Eaton's strike of 1951, and the Inco strike of 1958 in Sudbury. A major breakthrough for public-sector unionism came at the very end of the 1950s when the postal employees organized and began demanding the right of collective bargaining. In 1956 the two largest Canadian umbrella organizations for labour—the Trades and Labor Congress of Canada and the Canadian Congress of Labour—merged as one consolidated body called the Canadian Labour Congress (CLC). This merger reduced jurisdictional disputes at the top of Canada's table of labour organization, although it did not deal with the question of the domination of so-called 'international' unions by their American members.

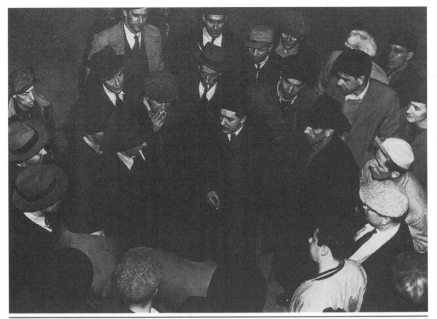

The 1949 Asbestos Strike in Quebec (Metropolitan Toronto Reference Library).

THE BABY BOOM AND THE SUBURBAN SOCIETY

Canadians emerged from the Second World War with twenty years of disruption behind them. Normal expectations for family life had been interrupted in various ways. During the Depression, marriage and birth rates had decreased and the average age of marriage had risen. Between 1939 and 1952 the marriage rate jumped substantially, especially among the young. More family units were formed each year, while both the birth rate and the annual immigration intake rose. Birth rates rose because of early marriages combined with earlier and more children born by mothers who remained at home. The result was a substantial increase in the total numbers of children in Canada between 1941 and 1961. This was the baby boom. These children went through each stage of life in waves, which in sheer numbers put heavy pressure on facilities to deal with them. The phenomenon would first hit education in the primary grades in the 1940s and would then roll progressively through Canadian society as the baby boomers got older. Secondary schools were affected in the 1950s, universities in the 1960s, employment needs in the later 1960s, and so on.

We do not entirely understand why this demographic blip occurred. Pent-up deferral of expectations before the early 1940s is part of the answer. The fulfilment of deferred expectations, however, does not explain why an entire nation should suddenly decide to marry earlier and raise larger families. A better explanation is probably to be found in the fantasy package of a better life for postwar Canadians, fuelled by postwar affluence. The urge affected Quebecers as well as anglophone Canadians. Pierre Vallières described his father's postwar dream: 'We'll be at peace. The children will have all the room they need to play. We'll be masters in our own house. There will be no more stairs to go up and down. . . . Pierre won't hang around the alleys and sheds any more. . . . The owner was prepared to stretch the payments out over many years. . . . Life would become easier. . . . He would enlarge the house. A few years from now, Madeline and the "little ones" would have peace and comfort' (Vallières 1971:98). In 1945 the Vallières family moved to Longueuil-Annexe, one of the 'mushroom cities' that grew up around Montreal.

What Canadians thought they wanted—and what the media told them was desirable—was a detached bungalow, preferably in a nice suburban neighbourhood, surrounded by green grass and inhabited by a traditional nuclear family. This fantasy included a wife who stayed at home and a houseful of perfect children. Suburbia was always less a geographical reality than a mental and emotional space. It is a convenient term that can be used to describe the fantasy world of the postwar period. After the war there was a popular domesticization of values that cut well into the ranks of the lower-middle and traditional working classes. Postwar suburbia was not only highly traditional in its gender roles but it tended to be retrogressive in its emphasis on the role of the female as child bearer and nurturer. In its consumer orientation, as well as in its child centredness, it was a powerful force.

Houses became homes, easily the most expensive physical object possessed by their family-owners. So much time and emotional energy could be devoted to the edifice that it often seemed to possess its owners. The house focused the life of the nuclear family, while at the same time permitting individual members to have their own private space. Ideally each child got a bedroom, for example, and a large recreation room in the basement provided a place for the children to play and gather. The kitchen was often too small for gathering, and the living-room was, increasingly after 1950, the home of the television set. Advertising and articles in the media both exalted the roles of housewife and mother as the epicentre of this world. Radio, television, and the record-player all made it possible for popular culture to be consumed without ever leaving the house.

Central to any postwar middle-class household were its children, around whose upbringing the parents' lives increasingly revolved. The baby-boom generation of children grew up in a child-centred atmosphere in both home and school. Older standards of discipline and toughness in the parent-child relationship were replaced by permissiveness. New child-rearing attitudes found their popular expression in *The Pocket Book of Baby and Child Care* by Benjamin Spock, MD, which outsold the bible in Canada after the war. An

American paediatrician, Spock replaced more austere Canadian manuals. Many Canadian mothers referred to him as 'God'. The book was one of the earliest mass-market paperbacks, sold over the counter at drugstores and supermarkets for less than 50¢. In its pages the reader could find continual reassurance. Use your common sense, said Spock, for almost anything reasonable is okay. 'Trust Yourself' was his first injunction. The good doctor came down hard against the use of coercion of any sort. In toilet training, for example, he insisted that 'Practically all those children who regularly go on soiling after 2 are those whose mothers have made a big issue of it and those who have become frightened by painful movements.' Spock explained that children passed through stages. Once parents recognized what stage of development their child had reached, they could appreciate that seemingly incomprehensible behaviour, and that exceptional problems were really quite common.

The permissively raised Spock generation combined with the new affluence to produce large numbers of adolescents, segmented from and sandwiched between childhood and adult society. More and more young people were encouraged to remain in school longer. The schools and progressive education treated them as a distinct social phenomenon. The authors of Crestwood Heights, a study of a wealthy Toronto suburb (1956), found a central theme in the 'difficulties experienced by the child in living up to the expectations of both parents and the school for "responsibility" and "independence".' They labelled the ages sixteen to nineteen as 'Dependent Independence'. The loss of community through urbanization and suburbanization provided a real challenge for social control. Kept out of the workforce, teenagers did not become full adults. Law and custom combined to prevent them from enjoying full adult privileges. These kids had considerable spending power. Encouraged to live at home, the youngsters were not often required to contribute their earnings (if any) to family maintenance. Instead, their parents gave them pocket money or allowances. Canadian teenagers rapidly became avid consumers, providing a market for fast food, clothing fads, acne medicine, cosmetics, and popular music. Melinda McCracken has explained that 'to be a real teenager you had to drink Cokes, eat hamburgers [known as nips in Winnipeg because the local Salisbury House chain sold them as such], French fries [known in Winnipeg as chips, in the English fashion], go to the Dairy Queen, listen to the Top Forty and neck' (McCracken 1975:72).

Between 1946 and 1960 Canadian education, responding partly to the baby boom, partly to changing social expectations, transformed itself entirely. Canadians had long accepted the concept of universal education in the primary grades. In the 1940s and 1950s education for all was extended to secondary levels by raising the school-leaving age to sixteen. In 1945 there were 1,741,000 children in provincially controlled schools. By 1960–1 that figure had risen to 3,993,125. The expenditure per pupil in public schools nearly tripled between

1945 and 1958. Thousands of new schools had to be built to accommodate the increased student population. Teachers who had before 1946 enjoyed a year or two of teaching-training college now required a university degree. In 1956 the authors of *Crestwood Heights* observed that the flagship suburban community they had studied was 'literally, built around its schools'. In Crestwood Heights, education was 'aimed primarily at preparing pupils for a middle-class vocation in a highly-industrialized culture' (Seeley, Sim, and Loosley 1972:224). Such was the goal of baby-boomer education all across Canada by the early 1960s.

Not all the nation's population growth came from natural increase. Immigration also played its part. After the Second World War, European wives of Canadian soldiers (the war brides) were admitted virtually without question. Beginning in 1946, Canadian residents were allowed to sponsor relatives for immigration purposes, which was the earliest introduction of the sponsorship feature of Canadian immigration policy. In 1947 Prime Minister King announced a characteristic one step forward, one step backward immigration strategy. On the one hand, immigration into Canada would be governed by the nation's absorptive capacity, which many Canadians took to mean economic and racial considerations. On the other hand, King for the first time recognized Canada's moral obligation to refugees and displaced persons from wartorn Europe. Over the ensuing decade, a substantial number of refugees of European origin were allowed to come to Canada, over 1,200,000 in total. Of that number, 34.1 per cent originated in the British Isles, 30.2 per cent in northwestern Europe, 15.1 per cent in central and eastern Europe, and 15.3 per cent in south-eastern and southern Europe. Another 3.5 per cent were of Jewish origin, leaving only 1.7 per cent of 'other origin'. Old patterns died hard, however. Despite the formation of the Department of Citizenship and Immigration in 1950, immigrants received very little assistance from the Canadian government beyond employment placement once they entered Canada, especially in terms of sensitizing Canadian society to their presence and their needs. The goal of the government and the many volunteer organizations that assisted immigrants, proclaimed the official Canadian yearbook in 1959, was to see the immigrant 'develop a sense of belonging to the Canadian community' (*Canada Year Book* 1959:177). The onus was on the immigrant to make the adjustment.

Immigration was a privilege, and the government felt no obligation to explain its choices. By the late 1950s immigration department statistics indicated that most sponsored immigrants (the vast majority of newcomers) would not have otherwise qualified for admission. Between 1946 and 1952, Canada took nearly 165,000 displaced persons, while the United States took 329,000 and Australia 172,000. In 1956 a Canadian mission selected thirty-nine families for admission to the country from among some 900,000 refugees from the Arab-Israeli conflict, using discretionary powers allowed the minister of immigration under a new immigration act passed in 1952. That same year, nearly 20,000 refugees from the Hungarian Revolution were admitted into Canada, the largest single intake of exiles since the Loyalists. The disparity between Middle Eastern and Hungarian admissions was obvious.

THE GROWTH OF THE STATE

Government at all levels—federal, provincial, and municipal—grew extremely rapidly after the war. For the Dominion government, the extension of its power and authority represented a continuation of wartime momentum. For provincial governments, extensions of power were necessary to counter federal incursions in areas traditionally reserved for the provinces. All levels of government found the Canadian public responsive to the piecemeal introduction of new social services. The emergence of a much more powerful and costly public sector was fuelled partly by increased social programs, partly by the growth of a Canadian public-enterprise system after the war.

While the Canadian public-enterprise system went back to the nineteenth century, the development of Crown corporations greatly accelerated during and especially after the Second World War. Both federal and provincial governments created Crown corporations, publicly owned and operated. They modelled management structures on private enterprise and usually administered the corporation on a hands-off basis. Many Crown corporations came into existence to provide important services that could not be profitably offered by private enterprise. There was a tendency for public enterprise, almost by definition, to risk unprofitability. The CCF Saskatchewan government employed the Crown corporation frequently from the time of its election in 1944. One of the largest public enterprises of the 1950s, the St Lawrence Seaway, was a Crown corporation. For many rural Canadians the extension of electricity into all but the most remote corners of the country was a great development of the postwar period. Many provinces consolidated electric utilities in Crown corporations after the war to extend services. The federal government had hoped to expand Canada's social services after the Second World War, at least partly to justify continued control of the major tax fields it had acquired under wartime emergency conditions. At the Dominion-Provincial Conference on Reconstruction, which began on 6 August 1945 (the day the first atomic bomb was dropped on Japan), Ottawa discovered that not all the provinces were willing to withdraw permanently from the fields of personal and corporate income tax. Quebec and Ontario, particularly, were equally unenthusiastic about surrendering their constitutional rights to social services. The provincial rebuff to Ottawa in 1945 did not mean that the Dominion gave up on social security measures. Both funding and constitutional haggling, however, would be a continuing problem.

While we often talk about the Canadian welfare state, there is little evidence that many people in Canada, much less in the federal government, had any notion of a truly comprehensive and integrated national social security system that would include full employment, housing, and education as part of the social rights of all Canadians. Social protection in Canada would instead grow on a piecemeal basis through the activities of all levels of government. Sometimes new programs responded to overt public demand, sometimes they met obvious public need. Frequently job creation was the immediate rationale for a social program. Oftimes a particular program of social protection was intended to provide a platform on which a government or political party could campaign. Political proponents of such programs hoped that the opposition would demur, thus providing a convenient election issue. Oppositions frequently failed to take the bait, thus skirting the issue by accepting the program. A patchwork of social programs thus emerged in fits and starts.

Canada ended the war with a limited federal pension program, a universal family allowance scheme, and a housing act designed chiefly to provide employment. In 1945 Ottawa had also proposed to the provinces a national universal pension scheme for Canadians over seventy (with a means test program provincially administered for those sixty-five to sixty-nine), a national public assistance scheme for the unemployed, and a health insurance scheme to be shared by the provinces and the federal government. The almost inevitable demise of the Dominion-Provincial Conference on Reconstruction meant that federal progress on social protection moved ahead extremely slowly. Apart from the creation of the Central Mortgage and Housing Corporation to assist in providing low-cost mortgage loans to Canadian families and a limited home-building program (10,000 houses per year), little happened on the housing front in the fifteen years after 1945. On the health care front, the government in 1948 established a fund for health research and hospital construction, but did little else on health until 1957 when it passed the Hospital Insurance and Diagnostic Services Act. This legislation allowed the federal government to provide 50 per cent of the cost of provincial hospital insurance plans. A new Old Age Security Act of 1951 provided a $40 per month pension to all Canadians over the age of seventy, but still insisted on a means test for those between sixty-five and sixty-nine. In 1956 a limited federal Unemployment Assistance Act with a needs test passed Parliament. Education remained almost entirely a provincial matter before 1960.

In 1945, the last year of the war, federal expenditure was just over $5 billion, with another $451 million spent by the provinces and $250 million by municipalities. In 1960 the Dominion still spent $5 billion, although far less on the military, but provincial governments now spent $2.5 billion and municipalities another $1.7 billion. Much of the increase was on social services. The result was a vast expansion in the number of government employees. In 1945, the last year of the war, the Dominion had 30,240 permanent civil servants and 85,668 temporary ones. At the beginning of 1961, it employed 337,416 Canadians, most of them 'regular' and many of them female. Both provincial and municipal employment grew even faster. The provinces employed 50,000 in 1946 and 257,000 twenty years later, while the municipalities increased from 56,000 in 1946 to 224,000 in 1966. By 1960 there was a sense (on at least the federal level) that matters could get out of hand. The Diefenbaker government in that year created the Royal Commission on Government Organization to improve efficiency and economy. It was chaired by J. Grant Glassco (1905–68).

THE SHAPE OF POLITICS

At the federal level there were only two major parties, the Liberals and the Progressive Conservatives. In this period there were a variety of other federal parties as well, chiefly the CCF and Social Credit. The nature of the Canadian electoral system—particularly the 'first past the post' method of determining victorious candidates in single-member constituencies—combined with the continued presence of a multiplicity of parties to reduce to inconsequence the relationship between the popular vote and the number of seats in the House of Commons. True political mandates were difficult to find in such electoral results. The Liberals never won more than 50 per cent of the popular vote in any election in the period 1945–60, although they came close to it in 1949 and 1954. Only the Diefenbaker government of 1958 was elected by more than half of actual votes cast. The correlation between popular vote and number of seats could be quite low for both major and minor parties. The system tended to translate any edge in the popular vote for a major party into considerably larger numbers of seats, and to dissipate votes for other parties. Third parties were much better off if their support was concentrated in a few ridings (as was true for Social Credit) and not spread widely across the country (as was the case for the CCF). In 1953, for example, the Liberals had 48.8 per cent of the popular vote to 31 per cent for the PCs, 11.3 per cent for the CCF, and 5.4 per cent for the Social Credit Party. These percentages translated into 171 Liberal seats, fifty-one PC, twenty-three CCF, and fifteen Social Credit.

The Liberals had a number of advantages in the pursuit of continued federal power, of which two were absolutely critical. Above all they had the ongoing support of Quebec, which elected one of the largest blocks of seats in the House of Commons. Support from francophone Quebec had come to the Liberals in the 1890s, was solidified during the Conscription Crisis of the Great War, and was further confirmed by Mackenzie King's management of that same issue during the Second World War. The Liberals did not lose a federal election in Quebec between 1896 and 1958, usually winning more than three-quarters of the available seats. To triumph nationally without Quebec's support, an opposition party needed to win the vast majority of seats in the remainder of the country, including Ontario (in which the two major parties were always fairly evenly matched). The Tories did win anglophone Canada in 1957. Such a victory could produce only a minority government, however. The Diefenbaker sweep of 1958 was the exception that proved the rule. In other elections the Liberals were able to persuade Quebec's francophone voters that the competing parties were unsympathetic to French Canada.

The apparent Liberal stranglehold on Quebec had its impact on the other parties, particularly in terms of choice of leaders and electoral strategies. During this period, neither the Progressive Conservatives nor the CCF ever seriously considered a leader from Quebec, much less one who spoke French fluently or was a French Canadian. Nor did the other parties make much of an effort to campaign in French Canada, except in 1958. The Liberal Party, therefore, continued its historic collaboration with francophone Quebec. It alternated its leaders between anglophone and francophone Canada, following Mackenzie King (1919–48) with Louis St Laurent (1948–57) and Lester B. Pearson (1958–68). This association tended to polarize Canadian federal politics. The Liberals also did well with other francophone voters, particularly the Acadians of New Brunswick.

But the Liberal political advantage was not confined to support from francophones. While national political parties needed to appeal to a broad spectrum of voters across the nation in order to gain power, only the Liberals consistently succeeded in this appeal, chiefly by staking out their political ground outside French Canada slightly to the left of centre. Mackenzie King had specialized in adopting the most popular goals of the welfare state, often lifting them shamelessly from the platform of the CCF, a practice his successors continued. The Liberals preferred to find urbane, well-educated leaders from the professional middle classes, oriented to federal service and politics. Each man had his own expertise. Mackenzie King was a professional labour consultant and negotiator who had studied economics at Chicago and Harvard and had written a well-known book entitled *Industry and Humanity* (1918). St Laurent was a former law professor at Laval, who became a highly successful corporation lawyer and president of the Canadian Bar Association. Pearson had begun as a history professor at the University of Toronto before joining the Department of External Affairs as a mandarin and professional diplomat. None of these men had earned a doctorate, but all held appointments that in our own time would probably require one.

The Progressive Conservative Party also had three leaders in this period: John Bracken (1942–8), George Drew (1948–56), and John Diefenbaker (1956–67). Bracken and Drew had been successful provincial premiers with little federal experience, while Diefenbaker had been an opposition spokesman in the House of Commons from 1940. Bracken had been a university professor (of field husbandry) and administrator before entering politics. The other two had been small-town lawyers. All three were regarded as being to the left of their parties, and the PC party platforms of these years looked decidedly progressive. Diefenbaker was *sui generis*, a brilliant if old-fashioned public orator and genuine western populist. All the PC leaders had strong sympathies for the ordinary underprivileged Canadian, although only Diefenbaker managed to convince the public of his concerns. None of these men spoke French comfortably, and left what campaigning was done in Quebec to others.

The Co-operative Commonwealth Federation had emerged from the war with high hopes, gaining 15.6 per cent of the popular vote and twenty-eight Members of Parliament in the 1945 federal election. Its popularity decreased regularly thereafter, however. By 1958 it was reduced to eight MPs and 9.5 per cent of the popular vote. This erosion of support came about partly because the CCF was mistakenly thought by some to be associated with international communism, and partly because much of the Canadian electorate regarded it

T.C. (Tommy) Douglas at the founding convention of the New Democratic Party in July 1961 when he became its first leader (National Archives of Canada C-36219).

as both too radical and too doctrinaire. The CCF showed no strength east of Ontario and was not a credible national alternative to the two major parties. After its 1958 defeat, the CCF remobilized through an alliance with organized labour (the Canadian Labour Congress), which in 1961 would produce the New Democratic Party under the leadership of former Saskatchewan premier T.C. (Tommy) Douglas. The Social Credit Party won some scattered seats in Alberta and Saskatchewan after the war, but would achieve prominence only after Robert Thompson (b. 1914) became president of the Social Credit Association of Canada in 1960 and party leader in 1961.

Liberal dominance before 1957 was moderated less by the opposition parties than by other factors. One was the increased size and scope of the apparatus of bureaucracy, including a 'mandarinite' at the top of the civil service. Powerful senior civil servants stayed in their posts despite changes of minister or government. They provided most of the policy initiatives for the government. Another important limitation was the force of public opinion, which often restrained policy initiatives and provided a public sense of fair play. The Liberals under St Laurent lost the 1957 election for many reasons, but one of the most critical was a public sense that they had become too arrogant. Government closure of debate over the Trans-Canada Pipeline in 1956 served as a symbol for Liberal contempt of the democratic process. As the new leader in 1958, Lester

Prime Minister Louis St Laurent in December 1953 (National Archives of Canada PA-144069).

Pearson blundered in challenging the minority government of John Diefenbaker to resign in his favour without offering any compelling reasons for so doing.

At the provincial level, few provinces enjoyed genuine two-party politics. Governing parties were common, and even in Atlantic Canada, where there was a long tradition of trying to keep provincial and federal governments of the same party, the party in power was not necessarily Liberal. The Tories, under Robert Stanfield, took over Nova Scotia in 1956; Tories ran New Brunswick from 1951 to 1961. Quebec was controlled by Maurice Duplessis's *Union Nationale*. The 'Big Blue Machine' ran Ontario, while Alberta (1935–72) and British Columbia (beginning in 1952) were governed by Social Credit. In British Columbia, W.A.C. Bennett (1900–79) took advantage of an electoral change (the preferential ballot), designed by a warring coalition to keep the socialists out of power, to win enough seats to form a minority government in 1952. Continuing to exploit brilliantly the social polarities of a province divided into free enterprisers and socialists, Bennett never looked back. The CCF governed Saskatchewan. There was no provincial Liberal government west of Quebec between 1945 and 1960, although the coalition government of Manitoba was usually headed by a Liberal.

Liberal success in Newfoundland was a product chiefly of unusual local circumstances. Joseph R. Smallwood (1900–91) parlayed strong Liberal support for Confederation with Canada into an unbroken tenure as first premier from 1949 to 1971. After a somewhat complicated journey, Newfoundland joined Canada in 1949. Effectively bankrupt, the province had surrendered its elective government to Great Britain in 1933. It was governed until 1949 by an appointed commission, which balanced the budget but was not very popular. After 1945 the British government sought to get rid of its colonial obligations, and ordered a national convention elected in 1946 to decide Newfoundland's future. In a preliminary referendum in 1948 69,400 voters (44.5 per cent) voted for a return to the pre-1933 situation, 64,066 (41.1 per cent) voted for Confederation with Canada, and 22,311 (14.3 per cent) voted for the continuation of commission government. A second ballot held on 22 July 1948, which had an 84.9 per cent turnout, saw 78,323 Newfoundlanders (52.3 per cent) vote for Canada, and 71,344 (47.66 per cent) for the resumption of Crown colony status. Confederation did best outside the Avalon Peninsula and St John's. The Canadian cabinet accepted the decision on 27 July 1948, allowing Smallwood, now leader of the Liberal party, to head an interim government that easily won the province's first election in many years.

FRENCH CANADA AFTER THE SECOND WORLD WAR

The scope of social and economic change in French Canada, especially after 1939, went largely unheralded in the remainder of the nation until the 1960s. In English-speaking Canada, the popular press (before 1960) was fascinated with

Lament for a Nation

[In 1965 the Canadian philosopher George Grant published his *Lament for a Nation: The Defeat of Canadian Nationalism*, which catapulted Grant to prominence as a popular hero of the counterculture. Grant's success with the young was a curious one. He was middle aged, a philosopher, and a political Tory who saw the failure of Canada encapsulated in the downfall of John Diefen-baker. But like the young he was critical of the military industrial complex. In the following excerpt he comments on Diefenbaker's policy towards French Canada. *Source*: G. Grant, *Lament for a Nation: The Defeat of Canadian Nationalism* (Toronto: Macmillan, 1965):21–2.]

There was one aspect of Diefenbaker's nationalism that was repugnant to thoughtful French Canadians, however attractive to English-speaking Liberals and New Canadians. He appealed to one united Canada, in which individuals would have equal rights irrespective of race and religion; there would be no first- and second-class citizens. As far as the civil rights of individuals are concerned, this is obviously an acceptable doctrine. Nevertheless, the rights of the individual do not encompass the rights of nations, liberal doctrine to the contrary. The French Canadians had entered Confederation not to protect the rights of the individual but the rights of a nation. They did not want to be swallowed up by that sea which Henri Bourassa had called 'l'américanisme saxonisant.' Diefenbaker's prairie experience had taught him to understand the rights of ethnic and religious communities, such as the Ukrainians and the Jews. He was no petty Anglo-Saxon homogenizer who wanted everybody to be the same. He had defended the rights of communities to protect their ancient cultural patterns. But in what way was this different from the United States, where Polish and Greek Americans keep their remembrances while accepting the general ends of the Republic? The French-Canadian nation, with its unique homeland and civilization, is quite a different case. The appeal of a nation within a nation is more substantial than that of the Ukrainians or the Jews.

Maurice Duplessis and his *Union Nationale*. Duplessis mixed heavy-handed attacks on civil liberties and trade unions with *laissez-faire* economic policy, while ignoring the underlying social changes and debates occurring within Quebec. For many English-speaking Canadians, Quebec remained stereotyped as a priest-ridden rural society inhabited by a simple people. That Quebec had been lagging in the socio-economic aspects of modern industrialism made its rapid catch-up more internally unsettling and externally bewildering. Certainly by the 1950s Quebec was no longer behind the remainder of Canada in most social and economic indicators.

Many Canadian commentators outside Quebec who were aware of the province's transformation assumed that the continued electoral success of Duplessis and the *Union Nationale* represented confusion on the part of many

For Diefenbaker, the unity of all Canadians is a final fact. His interpretation of federalism is basically American. It could not encompass those who were concerned with being a nation, only those who wanted to preserve charming residual customs.

This failure to recognize the rights of French Canadians, *qua* community, was inconsistent with the roots of Canadian nationalism. One distinction between Canada and the United States has been the belief that Canada was predicated on the rights of nations as well as on the rights of individuals. American nationalism was, after all, founded on the civil rights of individuals in just as firm a way as the British appeal to liberty was founded on these rights. As the price of that liberty, American society has always demanded that all autonomous communities be swallowed up into the common culture. This was demanded during the Civil War; it was demanded of each immigrant; it is still the basis of the American school system. Diefenbaker appealed to a principle that was more American than Canadian. On this principle, the French Canadians might as well be asked to be homogenized straight into the American Republic. In so far as he did not distinguish between the rights of individuals and the rights of nations, Diefenbaker showed himself to be a liberal rather than a conservative.

Diefenbaker's nationalism included contempt for the intellectual community, particularly the one found in the universities. . . . Did not Diefenbaker know that the existence of Canada depended on a clear definition of conservatism? Did he not know that there had been diverse formulations of the meaning of Canadian history? For most of his appointments to Royal Commissions and other bodies, Diefenbaker chose the established wealthy or party wheelhorses. When he did choose from the university community, he turned to administrators and technicians, to those with the minimum of intellectual conviction. In the election of 1963, Diefenbaker had no support from the intellectual community, although he was standing on the attractive platform of Canadian sovereignty. This is a measure of how far he had carried yahooism in his years of office. He acted as if friendship with public-relations men and party journalists was a sufficient means to intellectual nationalism.

French Canadians. Since social and economic modernization ought in the long run to produce French-Canadian assimilation into the majority society of North America, said external observers, in the short run it must be causing internal chaos. Neither of the standard postwar assumptions about Quebec's modernization—that it meant short-term confusion and long-term loss of distinctiveness—was particularly valid. The socio-economic transformation was accompanied by a series of profound ideological shifts within Quebec society that shook its foundations to the very core. The patterns of that development ought to have been comprehensible to anyone familiar with what was happening elsewhere in developing societies. Traditional forms of defensive nationalism, including the power and authority of the Roman Catholic Church, were being swept away by a new secular nationalism that had become fully articulated under Duplessis. The main opposition to the new nationalism came less from the old nationalism than from a renewed current of nineteenth-century liberalism adapted to twentieth-century Quebec conditions. In the 1960s these two competing ideologies would find popular labels as 'separatism' and 'federalism'.

The new nationalism was profoundly different from the old in its intellectual assumptions, however similar the two versions could sound in rhetorical manifestos. In the first place, while often espousing Catholic values, the new nationalism was profoundly anticlerical. It opposed the entrenched role of the Church in Quebec society. In the second place, the new nationalism had no desire to return to a golden age of agricultural ruralism, but instead celebrated the new industrial and urban realities of modern Quebec. It insisted that Quebec nationalism had to be based on the aspirations of the newly emerging French-Canadian working class, which meant that nationalists had to lead in the battle for socio-economic change. While scorning international socialism because it would not pay sufficient attention to the particular cultural dimensions of French Canada, the new nationalists pre-empted much of the vocabulary and economic analysis of Marxism, including the essential concept of proletarian class solidarity. In their insistence on nationalism, they were hardly traditional Marxists. The postwar world, however, saw many examples of sim-ilar movements that combined Marxist analysis with national aspirations. The new nationalists—particularly the younger, more militant ones—were able to find intellectual allies and models everywhere. The external neo-Marxism most commonly cited came from the French ex-colonial world or from Latin America. The new nationalists had long insisted that the key to their program was an active and modern state. The homogeneous secular state represented the highest articulation of the nation, and was the best means of liberating humanity. Traditionalist forces in Quebec had historically collaborated with forces in Canada to keep French Canadians in their place. The active state envisioned by the nationalists was Quebec, not Canada.

Opposition to the new nationalism came from a tiny but influential group of small-l liberal intellectuals centred on the journal *Cité libre*. This publication was founded by Pierre Elliott Trudeau (b. 1919) and Gérard Pelletier (b. 1919), among others, at the height of the Duplessis regime, to which it was a reaction. These liberals were as revisionist in spirit as the new nationalists, but simultaneously suspicious of what they regarded as simplistic doctrinaire thinking. They were committed to the new rationalism of the new social sciences. As Trudeau wrote in an oft-quoted manifesto: 'We must systematically question all political categories bequeathed to us by the intervening generation. . . . The time has arrived for us to borrow from architecture the discipline called "functional," to cast aside the thousands of past prejudices which encumber the present, and to build for the new man. Overthrow all totems, transgress all taboos. Better still, consider them as dead ends. Without passion, let us be intelligent' (quoted in Behiels 1985:69). Trudeau's small group was even more fiercely anticlerical than the new nationalists, perhaps because its members still believed in the need for a revitalized Catholic humanism and criticized the Church from within. It was equally critical of traditional French-Canadian nationalism, which it regarded as outdated, inadequate, and oppressive. *Cité libre* preferred to locate French Canada within an open multicultural and multinational state and society. Not only traditional nationalism but all nationalism was unprogressive and undemocratic.

At the end of the 1950s most Quebec intellectuals had arrived at some similar conclusions, however different the routes. The traditional nationalism in Quebec—of Catholicism, of the *Union Nationale*—led nowhere. The dead hand of the Church had to be removed. A modern state, secular and interventionist, was needed to complete Quebec's modernization. There was some disagreement over the nature of this modern state. The new nationalists were inclined to see it as a liberating embodiment of French-Canadian collectivities, while the *Cité libre* people saw it more as a regulating mechanism. It only remained to persuade the general populace of the province of the need for change.

FEDERAL-PROVINCIAL RELATIONS

The 1945–6 Dominion-Provincial Conference on Reconstruction had served as the arena for the renewal after the war of constitutional conflict between the Dominion and its provinces. In August 1945 the federal government tabled a comprehensive program for an extended welfare state based on the tax collection and economic policy of a strong central government. It sought the cooperation of the provinces to implement its plans. Ottawa wanted agreement that it could keep the emergency powers it had acquired to fight the war, especially the power to collect all major taxes. The conference adjourned for study, finally meeting again in April 1946. At this point Quebec and Ontario in tandem simultaneously denounced centralization while insisting on a return to provincial autonomy. Ontario had some social programs of its own in the planning stages. Quebec, led by Duplessis, wanted to keep control of social powers in order not to have them used. In the wake of this meeting, the federal government offered a 'tax rental' scheme to the provinces, whereby it would collect certain taxes (on incomes, corporations, and successions to estates) and distribute payment to the provinces. Ontario and Quebec went their own way, but the remaining provinces (and Newfoundland after 1949) accepted tax rental, which (along with suitable constitutional amendment) had been recommended by the Rowell-Sirois royal commission in 1940.

Constitutional revision was no easy matter to contemplate. As we have seen, conflict had been literally built into Confederation by the British North America Act. The Dominion of Canada was a federal state, with a central government in Ottawa and local governments in the provinces. While the intention of the Fathers of Confederation had been to produce a strong central government, they had been forced by the insistence of the provinces (especially what would become Quebec) to guarantee them separate identities. These identities were protected through an explicit division of powers between federal and provincial governments in sections 91 and 92 of the British North America Act of 1867. The division thus created reflected the state of political thinking of the 1860s. It gave the federal arm the authority to create a viable national economy. It gave the provinces the power to protect what at the time were regarded as local and cultural matters. Some of the provincial powers, such as those over education, were acquired because the provinces demanded them. Others, such as the powers over the health and welfare of provincial inhabitants, were not regarded by the Fathers as critical for a national government. Lighthouses and post offices were more important than public medical care in the 1860s.

Over time the division of powers had found the provinces with responsibility, in whole or in part, for many of the expensive aspects of government, including health, education, and welfare. Provincial ability to raise a commensurate revenue was limited, however. Many important aspects came to be shared among governments. The BNA Act's division of powers was clearly dated, ambiguous, and contentious. Despite the miracle of Canada's survival, the Constitution was constantly strained. Then, as now, critics of the existing system stressed its tensions, while its defenders lauded its capacity for survival.

One of the key problems was the settling of disputes over interpretation of the BNA Act itself. The act provided for a judicature modelled on British arrangements, with a Supreme Court at the top. This court, established in 1875, was not always the court of final recourse on constitutional matters. Until 1949 constitutional questions could be finally appealed to a British imperial court, the Judicial Committee of the Privy Council of the United Kingdom. In the years after Confederation, this committee had interpreted the Constitution in ways highly favourable to the provinces. Even with the successful elimination after the war of this example of continued colonialism, amendment of the Constitution was extremely difficult. Amending procedures were not spelled out in the act itself. The convention had grown up that amendment required the consent of all provinces, which was not easy to obtain. Moreover, such amendment could ultimately be achieved only by an act of the British Parliament.

By the mid-twentieth century, Canadian political leaders had worked out a variety of informal means for dealing with matters of constitutional disagreement. One of the most important was the federal-provincial conference, which was not only employed regularly after 1945 to deal with financial business but gradually came to address constitutional matters as well. So long as the *Union Nationale* government of Maurice Duplessis represented Quebec at these gatherings, Quebec stood by a traditional view of the 1867 arrangement. The province protected its existing powers fiercely, but did not particularly seek to expand them. Another dimension was added to the postwar constitutional situation through John Diefenbaker's insistence on the introduction of a Canadian Bill of Rights, however. The Americans had produced their Bill of Rights (the first ten amendments to their 1787 Constitution) as part of the process of ratifying the Constitution. In Canada, the British constitutional tradition insisted that Parliament was supreme, while the courts automatically protected against the abuse of power. The BNA Act had protected some minority rights, but had displayed little interest in the rights of the individual so crucial to the American approach. This notion of spelling out rights—for individuals or collective groups—was a potentially profound change in the Canadian Constitution. Diefenbaker's Bill for the Recognition and Protection of Human Rights and Fundamental Freedoms, fulfilling campaign promises of 1957 and 1958, passed the federal Parliament in 1960. As it was limited to the federal level, with the rights it protected capable of being overridden by national emergencies, it had little immediate impact. A full ten years would go by before the Canadian Supreme Court would hear a case based upon the Bill of Rights, but its implications for constitutional reform—particularly when combined with the growth of new conscious minorities in the 1960s—were substantial.

At the end of the 1950s the Canadian Constitution stood on the cusp of great change. Canadians ought to have recognized that neither constitutional nor federal-provincial problems were solely the product of the presence of Quebec in Confederation. Nevertheless, the issue of Quebec became inextricably bound up with increasing federal-provincial tensions. Constitutional reform would become the panacea for what divided the nation.

THE RISE OF CANADIAN CULTURE

Culture in Canada and Canadian Culture (the two were never quite synonymous) after the Second World War became major public issues. This emergence was a major development of the postwar period. Culture had not been entirely ignored before 1945, but it had always taken a back seat to political and economic matters. Canada's cultural performance (or lack of it) was explained chiefly in terms of priorities. Culture was a luxury that would come only with political and economic maturity. Such maturity was now at hand. A number of parallel developments affecting culture occurred after 1945. One of the most obvious saw both federal and provincial governments attempt to articulate and implement public cultural policy. The policy initiatives were driven chiefly by concerns to protect indigenous culture from being overwhelmed by external influences. They helped create a variety of new cultural institutions in the post-war period. On the creative level, many contemporary artists began deliberately cultivating a naive or native style, with considerable public success, thus help-ing to breach the older boundaries of art and culture. Other artists enthusiast-ically joined international movements.

Canada was hardly alone in discovering that culture in its various forms was an important matter in the postwar world. Few nations, however, had a greater need for conscious cultural policy than Canada. It was a nation without a single unifying language and with at least two of what many after 1945 began to call founding cultures. At the same time, francophones and anglophones often meant something quite different when they talked about culture. While nobody doubted that French Canada's culture was distinctive, defining that of the remainder of the nation was more problematic. More than most nations, Canada was exposed to external cultural influences, particularly from its behe-moth neighbour to the south, the United States. The Americans purveyed to Canada and then to the world a profoundly American cultural style, anchored in popular culture.

In 1945 (or at any point earlier), Canada had considerably more cultural activity than most Canadians would have recognized at the time. One of the problems was that cultural commentators relied on highly restrictive critical canons and categories. Much of Canada's cultural life occurred outside the boundaries of what critics and experts usually regarded as Culture with a capi-tal C. Canadians became involved in culture on a non-professional basis for their own pleasure. The resultant culture came from folk traditions more than from high art. Moreover, it was not necessarily distinctly Canadian. By 1945, Canadian government—particularly at the federal level with the Public Archives, the National Gallery, the National Film Board, and the Canadian Broadcasting Corporation—already had a substantial if largely unheralded role in culture. Prime Minister St Laurent was told during the 1949 elections that the Liberals might lose votes to the CCF from 'those Canadians who have a distinct national consciousness and feel that more should be done to encour-age national culture and strengthen national feeling'. St Laurent appointed the Royal Commission on National Development in the Arts, Letters, and Sciences, usually known after its chairman, Vincent Massey, as the Massey Commission.

The Massey Commission existed because its time had come. It did not invent a cultural policy but merely publicized it. While its recommendations were crucial in increasing government involvement in the arts, they were precisely the ones envisioned in the commission's terms of reference, which were in turn a product of considerable lobbying by well-established arts groups. The commission held extensive public meetings, receiving 462 briefs and listening to 1,200 witnesses. The witnesses, reported its chairperson, represented '13 Federal Government institutions, 7 Provincial Governments, 87 national organizations, 262 local bodies and 35 private commercial radio stations' (*Report of the Royal Commission on National Development in the Arts, Letters and Sciences* 1951:8). In most respects the Massey Commission looked backward instead of forward. It attempted to promote a Victorian vision of culture. It may have established most of the agenda of federal cultural policy for at least a generation to follow, but that agenda was narrowly conceived.

Despite its mandate to articulate a national cultural policy, especially in radio and television broadcasting, the commission was chiefly interested in élite culture and élitist ways of dealing with it. What needed to be preserved was a culture of excellence that was 'resolutely Canadian'. In 1952 it recommended the creation of a national television service as quickly as possible. It also wanted both radio and television broadcasting to be 'vested in the Canadian Broadcasting Corporation'. This monopoly would help 'to avoid excessive commercialism and to encourage Canadian content and the use of Canadian talent' (*Report of the Royal Commission on National Development in the Arts, Letters and Sciences* 1951:305). It supported the expansion of the National Film Board, the National Gallery, the National Museum, the Public Archives, the Library of Parliament, and the Historic Sites and Monuments Board of the National Parks Service. It also recommended the extension of the concept of the National Research Council (for scientific research) into the humanities and social sciences through the creation of a Council for the Arts, Letters, Humanities, and Social Sciences. Much of its agenda would be implemented in piecemeal fashion by federal governments over the next decade. The Canada Council, for example, was established in 1957.

Another royal commission on television appeared in 1955, chaired by Robert Fowler (1901–80) of Montreal. It made its final report in 1957. The Fowler Commission had to deal with the shift from radio to television and the prevalence of American production on both media. It insisted that the century-old Canadian answer to Americanization was for the government to provide 'conscious stimulation' through financial assistance. In addition to subsidies and protective measures, the Fowler Commission recommended another cultural strategy: regulated competition with a 'mixed system of public and private ownership'. The Diefenbaker government translated Fowler's recommendations into its Broadcasting Act of 1958, creating the Board of Broadcast Governors to monitor broadcasting to ensure that the service would be 'basically Canadian in content and character' (*Report of the Royal Commission on Broadcasting* 1957:8–11).

After the war a handful of Canadian intellectuals became fascinated by the media's role in modern society. Given Canada's long history of wrestling with communications, this was perhaps not surprising. The Canadian scholar Marshall McLuhan (1911–80) became the chief international guru of media culture. His first book, *The Mechanical Bride: Folklore of Industrial Man* (1951), examined comic strips, advertisements, and other promotional imagery of the American press to convey insights into 'that very common condition of industrial man in which he lives amid a great flowering of technical and mechanical imagery of whose rich human symbolism he is mainly unconscious' (McLuhan 1951:4). Like his mentor, Harold Adams Innis (1894–1947), McLuhan took the media seriously. Unlike Innis, however, McLuhan was not prepared to condemn the mechanization process and its introduction of a 'mass' dimension.

Categorizing culture has never been simple. One of the principal artistic developments of the postwar period—the commercialization of Inuit art— well demonstrates the problems. The Inuit of the Arctic had for centuries carved a complex image world in ivory and other materials, mainly for their own pleasure. In the late 1940s several Canadian artists working in the north, led by James Archibald Houston (b. 1921), encouraged the Inuit to offer their carvings for sale in the south through cooperative marketing. Later in the 1950s Houston would teach the Inuit how to translate their striking images into prints. The federal government encouraged commercialization, with the assistance of the Canadian Handicrafts Guild and the Hudson's Bay Company. Inuit art quickly produced some of Canada's most distinctive images, known around the world. Its combination of folk tradition and deliberate commercialization, while not unique in this or any other period, resisted facile generalizations.

Against a backdrop of economic prosperity and substantial population growth, Canada after the war finally appeared to be fulfilling its promise. Substantial strides were made on fronts as different as social welfare and cultural policy. 'Progress' was everywhere. Quebec and the Constitution had not yet emerged as a serious problem for the federal government, which by 1959 appeared to have emerged as a typical twentieth-century centralized state.

Major Events, 1960–1972

1960 Introduction of Enovid. Royal Commission on Government Organization is created. Jean Lesage and the Liberals win in Quebec. Bill of Rights passes federal Parliament.

1961 National Indian Council is founded. Canadian content regulations are introduced for television. CTV is formed. New Democratic Party is organized.

1962 Federal election returns a Diefenbaker minority government. Hydro-Québec is formed. Lesage government wins again with slogan 'Maîtres chez nous.'

1963 Lester Pearson becomes prime minister at the head of a Liberal minority government. Parent Commission reports on education in Quebec. Royal Commission on Bilingualism and Biculturalism is formed.

1964 Family allowances are expanded. Brock University is founded. New Canadian flag is adopted.

1965 Student Union for Peace Action is founded. National Pension Plan is introduced, with a separate plan for Quebec. War on Poverty begins. Simon Fraser University and York University are opened.

1966 Federal Medical Care Act of 1966 is passed. Union Nationale defeats the Liberals in Quebec.

1967 Canadian Centennial Year celebrations. New national anthem is adopted. Royal Commission on the Status of Women is appointed. National Hockey League expands, with no new Canadian teams. René Lévesque resigns from the Liberal Party in Quebec.

1968 Michel Tremblay's play Les Belles-Soeurs is produced. Federal divorce reform is introduced. Canadian Métis Society and the National Indian Brotherhood are formed. Special Senate Committee on Poverty is established.

1969 Criminal Code amendments dealing with abortion and homosexuality are introduced. Sir George Williams Computer Centre is occupied. Montreal Expos begin to play. White Paper on Indian Affairs is published. Pierre Trudeau's Liberals are elected with large majority. Official Languages Act is passed.

1970 Ledain Commission on non-medical use of drugs reports. Robert Bourassa's Liberals win over the Union Nationale in Quebec. October Crisis of 1970.

1971 New federal Unemployment Insurance Plan of 1971.

1972 'Waffle' purged from Ontario NDP. First Canada-Russia hockey series.

10

Edging Towards the Abyss, 1958–1972

❁

Periods in history are seldom neat and tidy. Decades and centuries have a nasty tendency to spill over their technical dates. The era from 1958 to 1972 in Canada will always be labelled 'the sixties'. Life in those years was a bit like riding in a roller-coaster. Revolution was in the air, although it never quite arrived. Everything seemed to be happening at roller-coaster speed. Although the ride was frequently quite exhilarating, the view from the front seemed to open into a bottomless abyss. Almost every positive development had its downside. The Canadian economy continued to grow, but the unpleasant side-effects became more evident. Government sought to reform the legal system regarding divorce while the rates of marital breakdown reached epidemic proportions. The Roman Catholic Church internationally introduced a series of unprecedented reforms, but Canadians stopped attending all churches in record numbers. An increasing number of students at Canadian universities became concerned about American influence in Canada, only to become wrapped up in the fallout from the American student reaction to the war in Vietnam. A variety of collective minorities began insisting on their rights, the acceptance of which would require the complete remaking of social justice— and indeed society—in Canada. The nation celebrated its Centennial in 1967, the most memorable event of which was an off-the-cuff public exclamation by a foreign visitor.

The usual picture of Canada after the Second World War limns a naive and complacent society that, with the aid of imported American ideas, suddenly questioned virtually all its values. There are a number of important qualifications to such a view. There was more ferment under the surface in postwar Canada than was recognized at the time. In many respects, ideas and behaviour that had previously been underground suddenly shifted into the public arena. Discontent was mounted on the back of the rising expectations caused by economic affluence. As is so often the case, much confrontation occurred because institutions did not change rapidly enough. While American models were influential, Canadians had their own home-grown concerns. One of the chief reasons that Canadians were able to take over so much of the American critical vocabulary was because of their profound suspicions of the American system. Social critics in the United States struck a respondent chord in

Canadians who had similar feelings about the contradictions of American society and culture.

THE 'RADICAL SIXTIES'

The era 1958–72 involved complex currents and countercurrents. Discussion of even the most major movements can only scratch the surface. Nonetheless, any account of the sixties must begin by considering three of the period's most striking developments: a broad societal shift towards liberalization; the appearance of a youth-centred counterculture; and the emergence of newly energized collective minorities in Canadian society. Sixties rhetoric was able to find a venue on radio and television. The reformers were the first radicals ever to have access to colour television. Only a few contemporaries ever managed to get beneath the rhetoric to understand the substance of the critique.

The Emancipation of Manners

The sixties have been credited with (or blamed for) a revolution in morality in which the traditional values of our Victorian ancestors were overturned virtually overnight. Firmly held moral beliefs do not collapse quite so rapidly or easily, of course. Rather, a belief system that was already in a state of decay and profoundly out of step with how people actually behaved in their daily lives was finally questioned and found wanting. A previous Canadian reluctance to examine morality was ended. The brief contemporary upsurge of formal Christianity that characterized the postwar era suddenly terminated. Canadians ceased attending church in droves. The phenomenon was especially evident in Catholic Quebec. The shifts involved were international ones that went much further elsewhere in the industrialized world than in Canada. By comparison with Sweden or California, for example, Canadian manners appear in retrospect to have remained quite old fashioned.

The liberation of manners occurred simultaneously on several visible levels. The old media taboos against sexual explicitness, obscenity, and graphic depiction of violence virtually disappeared. Television attempted to maintain the traditional standards, but TV news itself constantly undermined that self-restraint with its coverage of what was happening in the world. The sixties was probably not a more violent period than any other in human history. However, constant television coverage of its more brutal features, increasingly in living colour, brought such events into everyone's living-room. The memories of any Canadian who lived through the period include a veritable kaleidescope of violent images: the assassinations of John F. Kennedy, his brother Robert, and Martin Luther King; the Paris and Chicago student riots of 1968; scenes in Vietnam (including the My Lai murders of innocent civilians and the defoliation of an entire vegetation). Closer to home, there was the October Crisis of 1970. Canadians liked to believe that violence happened outside Canada, especially in the United States. Canadians somehow were nicer. On the eve of the October Crisis, the Guess Who, a Canadian rock group, had a monster hit, the lyrics of which pursued some of the most common metaphors of the time. 'American Woman' identified the United States with violence and Canada's relationship with its southern neighbour in sexual terms, a common conceit of the time.

As for sexuality, it became more explicit. Canadians began to talk and write openly about sexual intercourse, contraception, abortion, premarital sex, and homosexual behaviour. In place of the winks and nudges that had always accompanied certain 'unmentionable' topics, a refreshing frankness appeared. Many of the issues of sexuality revolved around women's ambition (hardly new) to gain control of their own bodies and reproductive functions. The rapid spread of the use of Enovid, the oral contraceptive widely known as 'the pill' after its introduction in 1960, was part of the new development. The pill seemed to offer an easier and more secure method of controlling conception. Its use became quite general before some of its unpleasant side-effects came to light. One of the pill's advantages was that the woman herself was responsible for its proper administration. The birth rate had already begun declining in 1959, and probably would have continued to decline without the pill. Enovid symbolized a new sexual freedom—some said promiscuity—for women that gradually made its way into the media. By the mid-1960s, popular magazines that had previously preached marriage, fidelity, and domesticity were now featuring lead articles on the possibility of premarital sex, marital affairs, and cohabitation before marriage.

Language, at least as the media used it, was equally rapidly liberated. Canadian writers—whether in fiction, poetry, drama, film, or history—had usually employed a sanitized and almost unrecognizable version of spoken French or English. Earl Birney's comic war novel *Turvey* (1949) suggested the use of profanities by Canada's soldiers by means of dashes in the text. But *Turvey* only hinted at the larger reality. In everyday life many ordinary Canadians relied heavily not only on profanities but on a rich vocabulary of vulgar slang that could be found in few dictionaries of the day. In French Canada, daily language was called *joual*. While earlier writers like Gabrielle Roy and Roger Lemelin had suggested its use, later writers such as Michel Tremblay (b. 1942) actually began to employ it. Tremblay's play *Les Belles-Soeurs*, written in 1965 but not produced until 1968 because of concerns about its language, cast its dialogue in *joual*. His later plays added sexually explicit themes, including transvestism and homosexuality. By 1970 both language and themes previously considered unsuitable became public across the country.

Gabrielle Roy in the 1950s (National Archives of Canada C-18347).

Earle Birney, winner of the 1950 Leacock Medal (National Archives of Canada C-31956).

The state played its own part in the reformation of manners. Pierre Elliott Trudeau (b. 1919) achieved a reputation that helped make him prime minister by presiding over a reformist Department of Justice from 1967 to 1968. He became associated with the federal reform of divorce in 1968, as well as with amendments (of 1969) to Canada's Criminal Code dealing with abortion and homosexuality. Trudeau's remark that the state had no place in the bedrooms of the nation struck a responsive chord. He was prime minister in 1969 when a commission was appointed to investigate the non-medical use of drugs. While its report, published in 1970, did not openly advocate the legalization of soft drugs, such as marijuana, its general arguments about the relationship of law and morality were symptomatic of the age. The commission maintained that the state had the right to limit the availability of potentially harmful substances through the Criminal Code. At the same time it added that it was not necessarily 'appropriate to use the criminal law to enforce morality, regardless of the potential for harm to the individual or society' (Addiction Research Foundation 1970:503–26).

The concept that it was not the state's function to enforce morality flew in the face of the Canadian tradition, which had always embodied morality in the Criminal Code. The new liberalism informed many of the legal reforms of the later 1960s. A number of Roman Catholic bishops, in a brief to a special joint committee of the legislature on divorce in 1967, stated that the legislator's goal should not be 'primarily the good of any religious group but the good of all society' (*Proceedings of the Special Joint Committee of the Senate and House of Commons on Divorce* 1967:1515–16). Such liberated thinking not only paved the way for a thorough reform of federal divorce legislation, making divorce easier and quicker to obtain, but also amended the Criminal Code in 1969 regarding abortion. Termination of pregnancy became legal if carried out by physicians in proper facilities, and following a certification by a special panel of doctors that 'the continuation of the pregnancy of such female person would or would be likely to endanger her life or health'. The Criminal Code was also amended in 1969 to exempt from prosecution 'indecent actions' by consenting couples over the age of twenty-one who performed such acts in private.

The reformation of manners, if not morals, based on the twin concepts that the state had no place in enforcing morality and that individuals were entitled to decide on the ways they harmed themselves, was largely in place by 1969. There were clear limits to liberalization, however. Since 1969 Canada has witnessed a resurgence of demands for state intervention in areas where liberalization was held to produce adverse consequences. Thus many women's groups have come to advocate stricter legislation on obscenity and

Justice Minister Pierre Elliot Trudeau with Prime Minister Pearson at the federal-provincial conference of February 1968 (National Archives of Canada C-25001).

indecency, particularly in the media, in order to protect women and children from sexual abuse.

The Counterculture

One of the most obvious manifestations of the ferment of the sixties was the rebellious reaction of young baby boomers against the values of their elders, a movement that has come to be known as the counterculture. Many Canadian rebels of the decade took much of the style and content of their protest from the Americans, although they had their own home-grown concerns, especially in Quebec. As in the United States, youthful rebellion in Canada had two wings, never mutually exclusive: a highly politicized movement of active revolution, often centred in the universities and occasionally tending to violence; and a less overtly political one of personal self-reformation and self-realization, centred in the 'hippie'. Student activists and hippies were often the same people. Even when different personnel were involved, the culture was usually much the same, anchored by sex, dope, and rock music. The participants in the two Canadian branches of youthful protest also had in common distinctly middle-class backgrounds, for these were movements of affluence, not marginality.

The United States was the spiritual home of the sixties' counterculture in English Canada. Americans had gone further than anyone else both in suburbanization and in universalizing education. The rapidly expanding university campus provided an ideal spawning ground for youthful rebellion. The campus had helped generate, in the civil rights movement, a protest crusade that served as a model for subsequent agitation. Civil rights as a public concern focused attention on the rhetorical contradictions of mainstream American society, which preached equality for all while denying it to Blacks. It also mobilized youthful idealism and demonstrated the techniques of the protest march and civil disobedience, as well as the symbolic values of popular song. French-Canadian youths could identify with Pierre Vallière's *White Niggers of America*. When some American Blacks left the movement, convinced that only violence could truly alter the status quo, they provided models for urban guerrilla activity, including the growing terrorist campaign in Quebec that was associated with separatism.

In English Canada, what really ignited the revolt of youth was the war in Vietnam. In retrospect, the extent to which Vietnam dominated the period becomes even clearer than it was to contemporaries. The war became the perfect symbol for the sixties generation of everything that was wrong with mainstream American society. It was equally exportable as an emblem of American Evil, representing everything that the rest of the world hated about the United States, including its arrogant assumption that it was always morally superior. Vietnam was central to the Canadian counterculture in a variety of ways. Hostility to American policy in Vietnam fuelled Canadian anti-Americanism, as a paperback book about the United States entitled *The New Romans: Candid Canadian Opinions of the U.S.* demonstrated in 1967. This hostility also connected young Canadians with the burgeoning American protest movements. Many Canadian university faculty members recruited during the decade were Americans, most of them recent graduate students critical of American policy. They were joined in their sympathies by an uncounted number of American war resisters (some said as many as 100,000 at the height of the war), the majority of whom sought refuge in communities of university students or hippies in large Canadian cities.

The youthful reaction advocated an eclectic kind of socialism—Marxist-influenced, democratically oriented, and idealistically verging on romanticism—which is usually referred to as the New Left. The movement was much better at explaining what was wrong with the present system than at proposing workable alternatives. It had no example of a large-scale society that operated on its principles. Nevertheless, student activists rose to positions of power in their universities, establishing several national organizations, such as the Student Union for Peace Action in 1965. Student radicalism flourished at a few universities, such as Simon Fraser, York University, and the Université de Montréal. Many of the less extreme student activitists joined the Waffle wing of the NDP, which attempted to radicalize that party in the direction of economic nationalism and social reform. Perhaps the most publicized student protest in Canada occurred in February 1969 when the computer centre at Sir George Williams University (now Concordia University) in Montreal was occupied for two weeks to protest racial intolerance and the 'military, imperialistic ambitions of Canada in the West Indies' (quoted in Forsythe 1971:9). The student protesters ended their occupation on 11 February by smashing the computers and damaging the university's equipment and records estimated in the millions of dollars. Ninety occupiers were arrested, including forty-one Blacks, many of whom came from the Caribbean region.

Despite the incident at Sir George Williams, youthful protest was not quite the same in Quebec as in Anglo-Canada. While Quebec's young were no less alienated than their anglophone compatriots, their anger found an outlet in opposition to Canadian federalism's colonial oppression of their province. Young people of university age (although seldom at university) formed most of the active cells of the FLQ, including the one that provoked the October Crisis of 1970. FLQ rhetoric and tactics during the crisis were clearly modelled on extreme movements of protest in the United States and Europe. English-speaking Canadian students talked of the 'student as nigger', but French Canadians saw their entire society as comparable with that of the Blacks or an oppressed

Third World nation (quoted in Kostash 1980:250). Radical young Quebecers were able to become part of a larger movement of protest and reform that cut across the age structure of Quebec society. Unlike their counterparts in English Canada, young protesters in Quebec were not cut off from the mainstream of adult society.

'The bureaucratic forms of organization shared by communism and capitalism', wrote one American activist, 'were embodiments of insult to the ideals of individualism, spontaneity, mutual trust and generosity that are the dominant themes of the new sensibility' (quoted in Kostash 1980:250). Such ideals motivated the hippies, who accordingly dropped out of mainstream society. Earlier generations of middle-class Canadians had dutifully struggled up the ladder of success. Many of the sixties generation lacked such ambition or direction. They were their parents' children, searching for personal self-fulfilment through any possible means. For some, the quest led to vulgarized versions of Eastern mystical religions. For others, it led to communes close to nature, often on remote islands. For the vast majority, it certainly meant experimenting with hallucinogenic drugs, particularly cannabis, and a sexual freedom bordering on promiscuity in an age when sexually transmitted diseases seemed easily treatable with antibiotics. Such experiments, together with a revolution in popular music, were the core of the sixties for participants and onlookers alike. Rock music was almost impossible to define, incorporating as it did so many musical styles ranging from Black rhythm and blues to traditional folk music to Indian *ragas* to medieval Gregorian chant. Nevertheless, rock served as the symbol that both united the young and separated them from their parents.

It is impossible to define a precise moment at which the bubble of the sixties' youth energy burst. Many of the characteristics and tendencies of the period continued in fragmented fashion into the succeeding decades. But at the end of the sixties the naive beliefs of the young received a series of shocks when American student activitists were ruthlessly suppressed at Chicago (1968) and Kent State (1970). At the same time, the central rallying point—American involvement in Vietnam—was gradually removed. In Canada, the founding of the *Parti Québécois* in 1968 provided a place *within* the system for many Quebec student activists. Two years later the October Crisis demonstrated how far some activists were prepared to go in the use of violence, and how far the Canadian state was prepared to go in suppressing it. The purging of the NDP's Waffle movement in 1972 perhaps completed the process of neutralizing activism, at least in Anglo-Canada. Some observers explained the collapse of the sixties youth movements in terms of demography. They got older and acquired jobs. Perhaps. In any event, by 1973 only memories of the 'good old days', often in the form of the lyrics of rock songs, were left for most of the sixties generation.

The Radical Sixties: The Rise of Militant Collectivities

While much youthful protest disappeared at the end of the decade, the baby boomers had joined in some movements that outlasted the era. The sixties saw a number of previously disadvantaged groups in Canadian society emerge with articulated positions and demands. These included, among others, Native peoples, Blacks, women, and homosexuals. To some extent, all these groups shared a common sense of liberation and heightened consciousness during the heady days of the sixties, as well as some common models and rhetoric. The several Black movements in the United States, especially civil rights and Black power, were generally influential. It was no accident that almost every group, including French Canadians, compared itself with American Blacks. While on one level other emerging collectivities could hardly avoid sympathizing with French Canada, on another level the arguments and aspirations of Quebec often seriously conflicted with those of other groups. Many collectivities sought to mobilize federal power to achieve their goals, often seeing the provinces and provincial rights as part of their problem.

As with so many other long-standing Canadian problems, that of the Aboriginal peoples moved into a new activist phase in the 1960s. Native activism built partly on its own traditions of constructing organizations to speak for Indian and Inuit concerns. In 1961 the National Indian Council was founded 'to promote unity among Indian people, the betterment of people of Indian ancestry in Canada, and to create a better understanding of Indian and non-Indian relationships' (quoted in Patterson 1972:177). This organization was formed chiefly by urbanizing Indians who hoped to combine the concerns of status and non-status Indians, as well as Métis. In 1968 political incompatibility led to the dissolution of the National Indian Council and the formation of two new groups: the Canadian Métis Society (which in 1970 renamed itself the Native Council of Canada) representing Métis and non-status Indians, and the National Indian Brotherhood (which would become the Assembly of First Nations) representing status Indians. Activists were also able to take advantage of American models and Canadian federal policy, particularly the 1960 Bill of Rights. The search for new sources of raw materials for exploitation in the Canadian north threatened Aboriginal ways of life, forcing them into the political mainstream. By the end of the decade, an emerging Native militancy confronted a federal government attempt to rethink the Aboriginal problem.

In 1969 the Department of Indian Affairs, under Jean Chrétien (b. 1934), published a White Paper on federal policy. All encompassing in its reassessment, the document had three controversial recommendations: the abolition of the Indian Act (and the Department of Indian Affairs), which would eliminate status Indians; the transfer of Indian lands from Crown trust into the hands of the Indian people; and the devolution of responsibility for Indians to the provinces. The White Paper touched off bitter criticism in all quarters, not least because it had been generated with little prior consultation with Native groups. It produced the first popular manifesto for Canadian Aboriginals in Harold Cardinal's *The Unjust Society: The Tragedy of Canada's Indians* (1969), which argued for the re-establishment of special rights with the strengthened contexts of treaties and the Indian Act.

The White Paper was consistent with federal policy towards all minorities, including French-Canadians, at the end of the 1960s. It called for the advancement of the individual rather than the collective rights of Native peoples: 'The Government believes that its policies must lead to the full, free, and non-discriminatory participation of the Indian people in Canadian society. Such a goal requires a break with the past. It requires that the Indian people's role of dependence be replaced by a role of equal status, opportunity, and responsibility, a role they can share with all other Canadians' (*A Statement of the Government of Canada on Indian Policy* 1969:5). An assimilationist document, the White Paper insisted that treaties between the Crown and Aboriginals had involved only 'limited and minimal promises' that had been greatly exceeded in terms of the 'economic, educational, health, and welfare needs of the Indian people' by subsequent government performance (*A Statement of the Government of Canada on Indian Policy* 1969:5). Allowing Indians full access to Canadian social services (many of which were administered provincially) would mark an advance over existing paternalism. Ottawa seemed surprised that Indians responded so negatively to the White Paper, conveniently ignoring its implications for the concepts of treaty and Aboriginal rights. Prime Minister Trudeau defended the policy as an enlightened one, noting that 'the time is now to decide whether the Indians will be a race apart in Canada or whether they will be Canadians of full status'. He added, 'It's inconceivable, I think, that in a given society one section of the society have a treaty with the other section of the society. We must all be equal under the law' (Indian-Eskimo Association of Canada 1970:Appendix 8).

Like other collectivities that discovered a new voice in the 1960s, Canadian women had been quietly preparing for their emergence (or re-emergence) for many years. Whether or not one took a patient view of the lengthy period of quiescence from the enfranchisement of women to the blossoming of women's lib—and most modern feminists understandably did not—some things had changed, and some political experience had been acquired. The Committee on Equality for Women, which organized in 1966 to lobby for a royal commission on the status of women, consisted of experienced leaders from thirty-two existing women's organizations united by their feminism. Their first delegation to Ottawa was ignored. Laura Sabia (1916–96), president of the Canadian

Federation of University Women and leader of the call for a national evaluation of women's status, responded with a classic sixties' threat: she would lead a women's protest march on the capital. The Pearson government behaved characteristically. Although not convinced that women had many legitimate grievances, it dodged trouble by agreeing to an investigation 'to inquire and report upon the status of women in Canada, and to recommend what steps might be taken by the federal government to ensure for women equal opportunities with men in all aspects of Canadian society' (*Report of the Royal Commission on the Status of Women in Canada* 1970:vii). The Royal Commission on the Status of Women, established in 1967, examined areas under provincial as well as federal jurisdiction and made its recommendations based on four operating assumptions: the right of women to choose to be employed outside the home; the obligation of parents and society to care for children; the special responsibilities of society to women because of maternity; and, perhaps most controversially, the need for positive action to overcome entrenched patterns of discrimination. The commission's report provided a program that would occupy mainstream feminism for decades to come.

Virtually simultaneous with the royal commission was the emergence of the movement usually known as women's liberation. This articulate and militant branch of feminism had begun in the United States as an offshoot of the student movement, partly a product of the failure of male student leaders to take women seriously. Women's liberation shared much of its rhetoric with other leftist movements of decolonization. '[Woman] realizes in her subconscious what [Herbert] Marcuse says', went one manifesto: 'Free election of masters does not abolish the masters or the slaves' (quoted in Kostash 1980:169). Not surprisingly, the liberationists found their organizing principles in issues of sexuality, particularly in the concept that 'woman's body is used as a commodity or medium of exchange' (quoted in Kostash 1980:196). True liberation could come only when women could control their own bodies, especially in sexual terms. Thus birth control and abortion became two central political questions, along with more mundane matters, such as day care and equal pay for equal work. Such concerns brought feminists into conflict with what became known as male chauvinism at all levels of society. At the beginning of the 1970s, the women's movement stood poised at the edge of what appeared to be yet another New Day.

The minority that was perhaps most closely linked to the women's liberationists was composed of homosexuals and lesbians. Like the libbers, the gays (a term they much preferred to other more pejorative ones) focused their political attention on sexuality, particularly the offences enshrined in the Canadian Criminal Code. By the late 1950s more advanced legal and medical thinking had come to recognize the value of decriminalizing homosexual activity, at least between consenting adults. The sixties would see the expansion of this view, partly because of public lobbying by a number of gay organizations, such as the Association for Social Knowledge (1964), that emerged in the period. An increasing number of gay newspapers and journals also made their appearance. Like other minority groups, homosexuals and lesbians began to concentrate on constructing a positive rather than a destructive self-identity. The 1969 revisions to the Criminal Code did not legalize homosexuality and lesbianism, but they did have a considerable effect on the gay community. It was now possible, if still courageous, to acknowledge one's homosexuality (the usual term was 'coming out of the closet'). The ranks of openly practising gays greatly expanded. It was also possible to become more aggressive in support of more homosexual rights, and the first gay liberation organizations were formed in Vancouver, Montreal, Toronto, and Ottawa in 1970 and 1971. These groups led the way in advocating the protection of sexual orientation in any human rights legislation adopted by the government.

By the early 1970s a number of collectivities were making new demands for constitutional reform and political change. The political and constitutional agenda of Canada was no longer confined to such matters as extending the welfare state, satisfying Quebec, or redefining the federal-provincial relationship. It now had to take into account a variety of organized and articulate subgroups of Canadian society—of which Aboriginal peoples, Blacks, women, and gays were only the most vocal—demanding that their needs also deserved attention.

A STILL BUOYANT ECONOMY

Behind all the reform sentiment of the sixties lurked a persistently prosperous economy. Inflation (which ran at an annual average rate of 2.1 per cent between 1959–68) and interest rates continued to be manageable. The nation continued to provide jobs for most of its expanding population, with unemployment rates under 6 per cent for most of the period. Critics might note that these rates were substantially higher than in other highly industrialized nations, where unemployment was under 2 per cent. But for the vast majority of Canadians, the performance of the economy seemed more than satisfactory, particularly after 1963, when a veritable explosion of construction projects began and foreign trade blossomed. Everywhere there were the visible signs of prosperity in the form of cranes and hard hats. Montreal and Toronto built subway systems. Large and small shopping malls sprouted up everywhere. Cultural facilities proliferated. Each province put up new university buildings. Less visible but equally important were a number of projects in the north, usually associated with hydroelectric expansion. The bellwether of the Canadian economy continued to be Ontario, still the only province with a mixed economy

Table 10.1

Unemployment Rates by Region, 1961–1970

Year	Atlantic	Quebec	Ontario	Prairies	BC	Canada
1961	11.3	9.3	5.5	4.6	8.5	7.2
1962	10.8	7.5	4.3	3.9	6.6	5.9
1963	9.6	7.4	3.8	3.7	6.4	5.5
1964	8.2	6.3	3.3	3.1	5.3	4.7
1965	7.4	5.4	2.5	2.6	4.2	3.9
1966	6.4	4.7	2.5	2.1	4.6	3.6
1967	6.6	5.3	3.1	2.3	5.2	4.1
1968	7.3	6.5	3.6	2.9	6.0	4.8
1969	7.5	6.9	3.1	2.9	5.0	4.7
1970	7.6	6.9	4.3	4.4	7.7	5.9

Source: Department of Regional Economic Expansion, *Major Economic Indicators, Provinces and Regions* (Ottawa: Queen's Printer, 1971):Table 2.4

Table 10.2

Percentage of Employment in Manufacturing by Region, 1961 and 1969, and Average Wage in Manufacturing, 1969

Region	Employment 000	1961 Share %	1969 Share %	Average Wage $
Atlantic	76.8	4.6	4.5	4,995
Quebec	527.0	33.6	31.2	5,542
Ontario	836.9	47.8	49.5	6,228
Prairies	119.8	6.9	7.1	5,888
BC	130.7	7.7	7.7	6,591

Source: Department of Regional Economic Expansion, *Major Economic Indicators, Provinces and Regions* (Ottawa: Queen's Printer, 1971):tables 3.3, 3.1.

Table 10.3

Average Income of Salaried Males in Fourteen Ethnic Groups, Quebec, 1961

Ethnic Group	In Dollars	Index
General Average	3,469	100.0
British	4,940	142.4
Scandinavian	4,939	142.4
Dutch	4,891	140.9
Jewish	4,851	139.8
Russians	4,828	139.1
Germans	4,245	122.6
Poles	3,984	114.8
Asians	3,734	107.6
Ukrainians	3,733	107.6
Other Europeans	3,547	102.4
Hungarians	3,537	101.9
French Canadians	3,185	91.8
Italians	2,938	84.6
Native Indians	2,112	60.8

Source: *Canadian Dimension* 5, no. 8 (February 1969):17.

balanced between manufacturing and primary production. Ontario contained such a large proportion of the nation's people that its successes consistently raised national averages.

The averages disguised marked discrepancies and disparities. Some of them were regional. Overall, the most seriously disadvantaged area was the Atlantic region—the Maritime provinces plus Newfoundland. Per capita average income in this region was persistently more than 30 per cent below the figures for the other provinces, and a much larger proportion of the population than elsewhere worked in marginal primary resource extraction, which was often seasonal in nature. Even after taxes, Ontario's per capita income in 1970 was 70 per cent higher than Newfoundland's. Many commentators insisted, however, that the real regional disparity was between the industrial heartland of central Canada and the resource hinterland that constituted most of the remainder of the country. Canadians were naturally drawn to the more prosperous regions, while both the Atlantic region and Saskatchewan-Manitoba lost population in the 1960s through out-migration. A perception of disparity underlay much of the nation's political discontent. Some disparities were not regional at all, although they often had geographical overtones. Low wages, high unemployment, low labour force participation, and a limited tax base (constraining the financing of public services) together created higher incidences of inequality in some provinces. Young people under twenty-five were twice as likely to be unemployed as Canadians over that age, for example, and youth unemployment sky-rocketed in marginal areas. Substantial evidence was advanced in this period that indicated that an individual's ethnic group, racial origin, and gender also affected economic success. And then there were the poor. What constituted real poverty in Canada remained a matter of continual debate. What was indisputable, however, was the inequality of national personal income in Canada. The highest 20 per cent of Canadians earned over 40 per cent of the income, and the lowest 20 per cent earned less than 6 per cent. Most of those in the lowest 20 per cent, it should be added, were employed.

Some of Canada's endemic economic problems did become better publicized (if not better resolved) in the 1960s. There were a number of obvious weak points. One was in the food-producing sectors. Canadian farmers continued to find that increased mechanization and use of fertilizers meant that fewer hands were needed to produce larger crops. Canadian farms became ever more capital intensive, marginal lands less attractive, yet returns to the farmer remained sluggish. Most increases in food costs to the consumer were caused by non-agricultural factors, such as transportation and processing, rather than by an increased return to the farmer. The farm population in Canada had been declining absolutely for decades, and this era was no exception. Between the

1961 and 1971 censuses, the number of farm residents fell from 2,072,785 to 1,419,795. Drops were especially marked in Prince Edward Island and Manitoba. As for the fishery, the admission of Newfoundland to Confederation in 1949 only increased the numbers of fishermen in serious difficulty. Experts' warnings about overfishing were ignored by governments eager to create programs to aid fishermen.

By the end of the period, a handful of environmentalists had begun pointing out the damage being done by those reaping resources without concern for conservation practices. Moreover, the issue of foreign ownership, first introduced by the Gordon Commission in 1958, took on a new life in the later 1960s when it became associated with American multinational corporations. Radical younger scholars—such as Mel Watkins (b. 1932), who headed the Task Force on the Structure of Canadian Industry, which in February 1968 released its report entitled *Foreign Ownership and Structure of Canadian Industry* (the Watkins Report)—called for the repatriation of the Canadian economy. Critiques of American multinationalism merged with a widespread Canadian hostility to the policies of the United States, especially in Vietnam, as well as with the concerns of those worried about the maintenance of a distinctive Canadian identity. Public opinion shifted considerably between 1964 and 1972 over the question of further investment of US capital in Canada. According to a 1964 Gallup poll, only 46 per cent of Canadians thought there was already enough American investment, and 33 per cent wanted more. By 1972, 67 per cent said that was enough, and only 22 per cent wanted further amounts.

Canadian nationalism emerged in the labour movement as well in the 1960s. This issue combined with others, particularly discontent among younger workers with the traditional nature of union leadership and organization. The older union leaders were not much interested in broad reform issues. They tried to dampen the reactions against local branches of international (i.e., American-dominated) unions that were seen as collaborators with American multinationals in both the 'sell-out' of Canada and the maintenance of the 'military industrial complex'. By the later 1960s many rank-and-file union members expressed discontent with American domination. The Americans took more money out of the country in dues than they returned in assistance; they failed to organize outside traditional industrial sectors; they often supported American military adventurism abroad; and, finally, they did not understand Canada and treated Canadian members with contempt, at least so went the complaints. Withdrawal from international unionism began seriously around 1970, and would increase in volume over the next few years as wholly Canadian unions grew in numbers and membership. One of the major factors in the home-grown union movement was the success of public sector unionism in the 1960s. In 1963 the Canadian Union of Public Employees organized, and in 1967 thousands of civil servants repudiated staff associations and formed the Public Service Alliance of Canada. Outside the civil service, but within the public sector, unionization was particularly marked in the teaching and health-care professions. Strikes by postal workers, teachers, and even policemen irritated large sectors of the Canadian public. Anger at the interruption of what many Canadians saw as essential services would eventually help make the unions easy targets in the 1970s as scapegoats for Canada's newly emergent economic problems.

POLITICAL LEADERSHIP

For much of the period, the Liberal hegemony of the King/St Laurent years appeared to be broken or at least bending. Not until the arrival of Pierre Trudeau did the Liberals get back on track, and that was at least partly because Trudeau represented a new style of political leadership, consonant with the age of television. John Diefenbaker, who became prime minister in 1957 and swept to a great victory in 1958, had a very old-fashioned political style. His bombastic speeches sounded as if they had been rhetorically crafted in the nineteenth century, and he revelled in being a House of Commons man, good in the specialized cut and thrust of debate in that legislative body. Diefenbaker inspired tremendous loyalty from some members of his party, but he seldom created confidence in his capacity to master public affairs. As a prime minister, he was a good leader of the opposition. Diefenbaker held a variety of contradictory positions; his latest biographer calls him a 'Rogue Tory'. He was a populist reformer at the head of a party that contained many genuine conservatives. He was simultaneously a Cold Warrior and a Canadian nationalist, holding both positions equally fervently. Despite his electoral successes in Quebec in 1957 and especially 1958, Diefenbaker was always associated (and associated himself) with English Canada.

During much of Diefenbaker's tour of leadership of the Progressive Conservative Party from 1956–67, his chief political opponent was Lester B. (Mike) Pearson. The contrast between the two men was instantly apparent, and the 'Dief and Mike' show (in the Commons and outside) was the joy of political cartoonists and satirists for the entire decade between 1957 and 1967. Pearson was a soft-spoken former diplomat who had won a Nobel Peace Prize for conciliation in the Suez Crisis of 1956. Quietly ambitious, he had little House of Commons or domestic political experience. Apart from the 1958 election, the nation never gave either Pearson or Diefenbaker a mandate to govern, thus perhaps reflecting its suspicion of their qualifications. The voters preferred Diefenbaker in 1957, 1958, and 1962 (the first and the third elections producing minority governments), and Pearson in 1963 and 1965 (both times in a minority situation). Pearson was better able to govern with a minority, since his party could arrive at unofficial understandings with the CCF/NDP, something not possible for the Diefenbaker Tories. Pearson was no more able than Diefenbaker to rein in ambitious colleagues or provinces, however. The decade 1957–67 was one of constant federal political turmoil and federal-provincial hassles.

The victory of Pierre Trudeau in 1968 marked a new era, which by the early 1970s saw a return to Liberal hegemony. The Tories had chosen Robert Stanfield (b. 1914) to succeed Diefenbaker. The soft-spoken Stanfield seemed a good match for Lester Pearson, but could not compete with the trendy and articulate Trudeau. Like the pop stars he seemed to emulate, Trudeau was capable of repackaging his image (and his policies) to suit changing conditions 'blowin' in the wind'. Not only was Trudeau a thoroughly bilingual French Canadian who was likely to appeal to Quebec, but he was continually able to

John Diefenbaker and Lester B. Pearson, 30 January 1958 (Photo by Duncan Cameron/National Archives of Canada PA-117093).

convince the electorate that he was far more of a reformer than either his electoral pronouncements or subsequent policies would indicate. After years of
apparently irresolute national leadership, Trudeau also seemed to be a strong
figure. In some respects he was, as his behaviour in the October Crisis of 1970
demonstrated. The prime minister did not hesitate for a moment to invoke the
War Measures Act and employ the military against the FLQ. Most of the nation
appreciated his decisiveness.

The era was also characterized by a number of long-serving and highly
visible provincial premiers, who provided considerable stability for the provincial cause in the regularly held Dominion-provincial conferences. While federal
leadership had been ineffective before Trudeau, almost all the provinces had
seemingly strong leaders. There continued to be little genuine two-party politics anywhere in Canada. Instead, dominant parties were usually in control. In
Newfoundland Joey Smallwood still governed virtually unopposed. In New
Brunswick Louis Robichaud was in control from 1960–70. Ontario had John
Robarts, Manitoba had Duff Roblin, Saskatchewan got Ross Thatcher, while
Alberta still had Ernest Manning and British Columbia was led by W.A.C.
Bennett. Few of these governments were Liberal. Ross Thatcher (1917–71)
headed the only provincial Liberal government west of Quebec between 1945
and 1972, and he was a vociferous critic of federal Liberalism. By the early
1970s the only provincial governments controlled by the Liberals were in
Prince Edward Island and Quebec. Pierre Trudeau's conception of liberalism
and federalism certainly did not accord with that of Quebec's Liberal premier,
Robert Bourassa (1933–96).

No matter who was in charge and at what level, the size and scope of the
apparatus of bureaucracy continually expanded. The scope of bureaucracy had
political as well as economic implications. The larger it got, the harder it was to
manage. A host of popular commentators and the press attacked governments
at all levels for mismanagement and waste, but as one commentator astutely
pointed out, 'It is true that the initial motive for reforms may be the outsider's
simple-minded belief that gigantic savings can be effected. But once set an
investigation afoot and the economy motive gets quickly overlaid with the
more subtle and difficult problems of improved service and efficiency'
(Hodgetts 1968:7–18). The Royal Commission on Government Organization,
appointed by Diefenbaker in 1960, found itself unable to effect major changes
in the bureaucracy, particularly in downscaling the scope of operations. All
governments, including federal Liberal ones, increasingly found themselves
entrapped by the actions of their predecessors and by the difficulties of
dismantling systems once created. Government was becoming more difficult
and the nation increasingly impossible to lead.

THE EXPANSION OF THE WELFARE STATE

Part of the reason for the continual expansion of government bureaucracy, of course, was continual (if uncoordinated) expansion of the Canadian welfare state. Politicians viewed expanded social services as popular vote-getters and no political party strenuously opposed the principles of welfare democracy. Although the Diefenbaker government was not associated with any major program, it had initiated a number of reviews and royal commissions, the recommendations of which would pass into legislation under the Liberals. The minority Pearson government was pushed towards improved social insurance by the NDP, its own reforming wing, and competitive pressures from an ambitious Quebec and other provinces. Were Ottawa not to introduce new national programs, the federal government could well lose control of them to the wealthier and more aggressive provinces. The expansion in 1964 of family allowances to include children up to the age of eighteen who were still in school merely imitated something introduced by the Lesage government in 1961. In 1965 the federal government attempted to introduce a national contributory pension scheme, settling for one that allowed Quebec its own plan.

The changing demography of Canada guaranteed that there would be continual pressures on the government to improve the pension system. Those who wanted improved benefits were able to make common ground with those who sought to control costs. Both could agree on the superiority of a contributory scheme. The Medical Care Act of 1966 built on provincial initiatives with a cost-sharing arrangement. By 1968 all provinces and territories had agreed on cost-sharing arrangements with Ottawa that produced a social minimum in health care. For most Canadians, access to medical service (doctors and hospitalization) would thereafter be without charge. Occasionally cynicism triumphed. Early in 1965 the prime minister wrote his cabinet ministers asking for suggestions of policy initiatives that would shift attention from political harassment by the opposition over mistakes and difficulties. The result was a Canadian variation of Lyndon Johnson's War on Poverty, which proposed 'a program for the full utilization of our human resources and *the elimination of poverty among our people*'. Actual reforms were not very significant.

The first Trudeau government, responding to the reform euphoria of the era, actually contemplated shifting the grounds of social protectionism in 'the Just Society'. To the late 1960s the emphasis of mainstream reform had been to carry out the agenda of the 1940s for the establishment of a 'social minimum' providing basic economic security for all Canadians. Now, at least briefly, the bureaucrats and politicians debated the possibility of expanding the welfare state to include some measure of income distribution. Poverty became seen as

Table 10.4

Expenditures on Personal Health Care as a
Percentage of Gross Provincial Product and
Personal Income, Ontario, 1960–1975

Year	GPP	Personal Income
1960	3.76	4.62
1961	3.95	4.98
1962	4.04	5.04
1963	4.14	5.17
1964	4.15	5.40
1965	4.18	5.47
1966	4.08	5.35
1967	4.43	5.67
1968	4.69	5.99
1969	4.76	6.04
1970	5.06	6.32
1971	5.32	6.57
1972	5.17	6.18
1973	6.56	6.05
1974	6.38	8.23
1975	6.94	8.57

Source: K.J. Rea, *The Prosperous Years: The Economic History of Ontario 1939–75* (Toronto: University of Toronto Press, 1985):119.

a serious problem worthy of public focus. The Economic Council of Canada in 1968 described the persistence of poverty in Canada as 'a disgrace'. Later that same year a Special Senate Committee on Poverty was established under Senator David Croll's chairmanship. In 1971 this committee produced a report, *Poverty in Canada*, which insisted that nearly 2 million people in Canada lived below the poverty line. More radical critics, in *The Real Poverty Report* that same year, put the figure much higher.

Poverty not only characterized the lives of millions of Canadians, but it was structural, regional, and related to racial and sexual discrimination. A number of schemes were suggested, including guaranteed income for low-income families as part of the family allowance package. The year 1970 had already seen the publication of a federal White Paper called 'Income Security for Canadians', which pointed out the escalating costs of social insurance and criticized the principle of universality that had previously governed Canadian policy. The ultimate result was the new Unemployment Insurance Plan of 1971, which extended and increased coverage without actually confronting the concept of a guaranteed minimum income for all Canadians. At about the same time, Ottawa eliminated a separate fund for Canada pension contributions and began considering them as part of the general revenue of the government.

Reformers had long insisted that access to education was one of the social rights to which all Canadians were entitled. Increasing access meant new facilities. The presence of the baby-boom generation gave urgency to that implication. Parents were much attracted to the practical benefits of education in providing future employment and a better life for their children. The results in the 1960s were enormous pressures on education budgets and increasing demand for the production of more and better teachers. School authorities attempted to ease some of their problems by consolidating rural education through use of the ubiquitous yellow school bus, a process that continued into the early 1970s. Teachers acquired more formal credentials, became better paid, and organized themselves into a powerful professional lobby, sometimes even unionized. By the late 1950s virtually everyone could agree on universal high school education, and by 1970 over 90 per cent of Canadian children of high school age were in school. Increasing numbers of high school graduates were entitled to a university education, and the decade of the 1960s was the golden age of university expansion in Canada. Not only were new facilities constructed but 20,000 new faculty members were recruited, most of them from the United States. By 1970 public spending on education had risen to 9 per cent of the gross national product, and represented nearly 20 per cent of all taxes levied by all three levels of government.

Before 1970 the disagreement between the universalists and the means testers had been relatively muted. Both sides could agree that there had been an absence of overall integrated planning in the growth of the welfare state. Little attention had been paid to the long-range implications of any policy. Bureaucracies and programs had been allowed to expand with no thought for tomorrow. The later 1960s had introduced a new ingredient into the mix, however. Governments began routinely spending more money than they were receiving.

QUEBEC

The 1960s was the decade in which the average Anglo-Canadian discovered that Quebec was unhappy with Confederation. That discovery was part of the completion of Quebec's transformation into a secularized, urbanized, and industrialized region that differed little in many respects from its central Canadian neighbour, Ontario. The transformation was often associated with the Quiet Revolution in the first half of the decade, a term used by the media to describe the modernization of Quebec. The structural changes to French-Canadian society had already taken place before 1960, however. At the close of the 1950s traditional French-Canadian nationalism in church and state, symbolized by the *Union Nationale*, still seemed to prevail. But the critique of tradition had already been elaborated and the program of reform for Quebec was well articulated. All that remained was to fit the government of Quebec and popular aspirations together. That task was begun by the provincial Liberal Party, led by Jean Lesage, which defeated the *Union Nationale* and came to power in 1960. The leading Liberal strategists did not realize at the time just how ready Quebec was for change, or how easily the traditional institutions and ways would crumble once they were confronted by an activist government composed from Quebec's new middle and professional classes.

The first major step had to do with hydroelectricity. The tradition that had to be overcome was the long-standing Quebec fear, nurtured for decades by the *Union Nationale*, of anything resembling economic statism (or socialism or communism). *Anti-étatisme* in Quebec was not the same thing as a do-nothing government. Under Duplessis, the provincial government had spent a lot of

Lesage Endorses Hydro-Québec

[In 1962 René Lévesque, as Quebec's minister of natural resources, had publicly committed himself to the nationalization of private hydroelectric companies in the province without gaining the support of his premier and party leader, Jean Lesage. In his memoirs, Lévesque recounted the resolution of the problem. *Source*: R. Lévesque, *Memoirs*, translated by P. Stratford (Toronto: McClelland and Stewart, 1986):174–6.]

After having wished me in hell at one time because of my ideas on hydro, Lesage had curiously enough avoided opening the subject again. Since the others were thus prevented from expressing their opinions, I was left free to sell my wares. But certain ministers were growing more and more nervous, and others didn't hesitate to say I was taking up too much room and should be shut up or such talk would eventually put the government in danger. When the fall session came, then, suspense had built up even more. It was becoming urgent to put our cards on the table.

Thus, on September 3, cabinet was summoned to a special meeting in the chalet at Lac-à-l'épaule. Driving up there I reviewed all the elements to the dossier, including some last-minute figures that seemed to me to clinch the feasibility of our plan. But could one ever know? In politics so often there are reasons logic has nothing to do with.

The first night reinforced these doubts. The atmosphere was heavy. Most of my colleagues were in an ugly mood. Some really had it in for me, this nobody, this black sheep who was the cause of all their woes. Discussion seemed to start up, only to fizzle out again in back-room bickering. Some had taken a glass too many, and since Lesage was one of these, it soon became apparent that the evening was a write-off. It was so depressing I wondered if I hadn't better let the whole thing drop. But I had promised the team not to come back without a clear decision one way or another. So I stayed on and passed a very bad night.

Next morning things didn't look much better. Mornings after the nights before are always gloomy. At last, about eleven, Lesage decided to call the meeting to order and, to get the ball rolling, gave me the floor. After distributing copies of our last memo, which certain members shoved disdainfully aside, I made a special effort to be as concise as possible, just hitting the highlights.

In rebuttal George Marler did his best to demolish me. . . . An old Liberal leader returning to Montreal after a tour

money on public services, including many hydroelectric projects to assist rural electrification. What the minister of natural resources, René Lévesque, proposed on 12 February 1962, without consulting his colleagues, was the enforced government consolidation of all existing private hydroelectric companies into a massive Hydro-Québec. Hydroelectricity was an ideal place to fight the battle of nationalization, partly because electrical generation and supply was a public enterprise right across North America, partly because it

of duty in Ottawa, he had been named to that little provincial senate called the Legislative Council, and it was from here Lesage had invited him to join the cabinet as his right-hand man in financial matters. He was reputed to have a very tight grasp on the purse strings. . . . That day Marler was not the eminent and phlegmatic notary who never raised his voice. . . . Insisting on the cost of the operation, on the danger of isolation Quebec might be exposed to, and on the opposition that was being manifested, particularly by the Chambers of Commerce, Marler had the bad idea to conclude by suggesting he might possibly resign. Lesage sat bolt upright and indignantly adjourned the meeting for lunch. . . .

Then suddenly everything was back on track again when early in the afternoon Lesage reopened the session and, after briefly summarizing the proposition, turned to Georges-Émile Lapalme, whom we hadn't heard from yet. 'Well, George, haven't you got anything to say? What do you think of this business?'

Lapalme took his time. As usual, behind those heavy glasses with their black frames that made him look like an evil owl, he stared long and without indulgence at the man who had taken his place. He had been leader of the opposition during the last Duplessis years until he was replaced by Lesage in 1958, just on the eve of that string of events that at

long last brought the Liberals back to power. Although he had consented to remain in the government, he was serving under a successor who would always be a usurper for him. This visibly gnawed at his vitals, and even though he adored the Ministry of Cultural Affairs that had been expressly created for him, he was too sensitive and deeply embittered to carry on much longer. In a few months he would be gone. But for the time being he was saving a surprise for us.

'Well, yeah . . .' he said, stretching his pauses, '. . . is the project a good one? As for me, I'd say yes. . . . Is it feasible? . . . Yes, again. . . . But how should we go about it? That's the question. . .'

'Do you think,' Lesage continued, 'that we could make it an election issue?'

'Well, . . . it's a big deal. . . . Before we get involved in it, it wouldn't be a bad idea to go for a new mandate.'

'Good. Well, let's see now,' said Lesage, leafing through an agenda he had just pulled out of his pocket. 'How does November 14 strike you?'

directly touched the pocketbook of the rural Quebecer, who was most likely to oppose state action. Despite a famous '*Jamais!*' from Premier Lesage, nationalization was quickly accepted by the Liberal cabinet as a winning campaign issue, and the Liberals took it to the province in 1962 with the slogan '*Maîtres chez nous*'. Led by Lesage and a compelling Lévesque, the Liberals managed to turn Hydro-Québec into a symbol of the economic liberation of Quebec from its colonial status, thus co-opting the new nationalism with a vengeance.

Liberal expenditure on welfare state reform and public enterprise tripled the provincial budget in the early 1960s, which saw a provincial government involvement in almost every economic, industrial, and social activity in the province.

The other great symbolic reform of Lesage's Quiet Revolution was the secularization and modernization of Quebec's educational system. Since before Confederation, education had been in the hands of the Catholic Church, which staffed it chiefly with priests and nuns teaching a curriculum slow to change from the nineteenth-century classical one. By 1960 the Church itself was in trouble, not just in Quebec but around the world. Criticism of Quebec education was led by a Catholic clergyman, Brother Jean-Paul Desbiens (b. 1927), who published the best-selling *Les Insolences de Frère Untel,* based on a series of letters he had written to *Le Devoir* in 1959. The spate of responses to Frère Untel, many of them in the form of letters to editors of newspapers, demonstrated that he had struck a chord in the province. Lesage responded with a provincial commission of enquiry into education, chaired by the vice-rector of Laval University, Monseigneur Alphonse-Marie Parent. The commission's hearings produced a battery of complaints and indictments against the Quebec system, most of which the commission endorsed in its 1963 report. The Parent Commission called not only for modernization along North American lines but for administration by a unitary secular authority. Armed with this endorsement, in 1964 the Lesage government passed Bill 60, which for the first time placed education in Quebec under provincial administration. Quebec education was thereafter rapidly brought up to national standards.

The Lesage government also sensed the importance of Frère Untel's call for the preservation and extension of French-Canadian culture and the French language. It had already created the Ministry of Cultural Affairs in 1961, which presided happily with grants and other forms of support over a veritable explosion of French-Canadian art and writing in the 1960s. The Ministry of Cultural Affairs in many ways typified the Quiet Revolution. The Lesage government was not so much the agent of change in Quebec as its *animateur.* As such it was the beneficiary of years of preparation by others. What the Liberals did was to identify some of the key problems, thus liberating the new-found aspirations of Quebec. Nevertheless, Lesage's government was defeated in 1966 by a rejuvenated *Union Nationale* under Daniel Johnson (1915–68), chiefly because it had failed to follow to its nationalist conclusion the logic of the revolution over which it had presided. The *Union Nationale* continued the Lesage program with louder nationalist rhetoric. In 1970 the party in turn was defeated by the Liberals under the new party leader, Robert Bourassa, partly because too many of its leaders had suffered fatal heart attacks, partly because it was squeezed between the Liberals and the PQ.

Quebec's attitude towards Confederation changed perceptibly during the 1960s. Under Duplessis, Quebec supported provincial rights to prevent Ottawa from exercising them. Under Lesage and his successors, provincial powers were something to be exercised positively as Quebec built its own welfare state and accompanying bureaucracy. Quebec's newly empowered middle class became increasingly conscious of the powers beyond their reach. A substantial separatist movement developed in the province, its most visible example the *Front de libération du Québec* (FLQ). This organization, founded in March 1963, soon began a terrorist campaign to publicize its views. More traditionally, in November 1967 René Lévesque resigned from the Quebec Liberal Party and began organizing a new party, the *Parti Québécois*, which was devoted to some form of independence. Along with increased constitutional militancy came increased fears for the future of the French language, with many French-Canadians turning a suspicious eye to the immigrant groups in Quebec who were still educating their children in English. By 1970 no Quebec politician wanted to be publicly associated with anything less than provincial autonomy. The first round of separatist agitation came to a climax in October 1970 when two cells of the FLQ kidnapped a British diplomat (Trade Commissioner James Cross) and a Quebec cabinet minister (Pierre Laporte), murdering the latter.

Prime Minister Trudeau arrives at the Church of Notre-Dame, Montreal, on 20 October 1970 for the funeral of Pierre Laporte. A cell of the FLQ had seized Laporte on 10 October, and his body was found on the 17th at St Hubert airport in the trunk of a car. His murder justified to the federal government the imposition of the War Measures Act (National Archives of Canada PA-113490).

The Ideology of the FLQ

[On 5 October 1970 two armed men kidnapped British Trade Commissioner James Cross from his home in Montreal. A few hours later a communiqué from the abductors, a cell of the *Front de libération du Québec*, was received. It was later broadcast as demanded by the abductors. Sandwiched in the middle of the document between specific demands, the FLQ summarized its ideology. *Source*: Quoted in J. Saywell, *Quebec 70: A Documentary Narrative* (Toronto: University of Toronto Press, 1971):37–8.]

. . . Through this move, the Front de libération du Québec wants to draw the attention of the world to the fate of French-speaking Québécois, a majority of which is jeered at and crushed on its own territory by a faulty political system (Canadian federalism) and by an economy dominated by the interests of American high finance, the racist and imperialist 'big bosses.'

When you examine the origins of Confederation you are in a better position to understand what were the true interests ($$$) which inspired those who were called the Fathers of Confederation. Besides, in 1867, the Quebec people (Lower Canada) were not consulted as to the possibility of creating a Confederation of existing provinces. It was a question of big money and these questions are only sorted out by interested parties, the capitalists, those who possess and amass capital and the means of production and who, according to their sole needs and requirements decide on our whole lives as well as those of a race of people.

Thousands of Québécois have understood, as did our ancestors of 1837–38, that the only way to ensure our national as well as economic survival is total independence.

The Front de libération du Québec supports unconditionally the American blacks and those of Africa, the liberation movements of Latin America, of Palestine, and of Asia, the revolutionary Catholics of Northern Ireland and all those who fight for their freedom, their independence, and their dignity.

The Front de libération du Québec wants to salute the Cuban and Algerian people who are heroically fighting against imperialism and colonialism in all its forms, for a just society where man's exploitation by man is banished.

However, we believe that the only true support we can give these people moving towards their liberations is to liberate ourselves first. During and after our struggle we shall offer much more than the usual sympathy of shocked intellectuals confronted with pictures showing aggression in a peaceful and blissful setting. . . .

WE SHALL OVERCOME. . . .

THE NATION AND QUEBEC

Although John Diefenbaker had come to power with the assistance of the Quebec voter, neither 'the Chief' nor his English-Canadian supporters ever really attempted to understand Quebec's aspirations. It was left to the Liberal minority ministries of Lester Pearson to respond to what was obviously a more feisty Quebec. To some extent, most Canadians were prepared to be sympathetic with Quebec, since few could conceive of a nation without its franco-phone province. Pearson adopted three strategies. One was cooperative federalism, a concept exemplified in a series of agreements (1963–5) between Ottawa and the provinces, which accepted the need for great consultation and flexibility, chiefly by having Ottawa give up many of the constitutional pretensions it had been insisting upon since the 1940s. This strategy ran aground because, as one political scientist put it, 'Quebec's demands for autonomy appeared to be insatiable' (Smiley 1970:48–66). Later critics would regard Ottawa's concessions as the beginning of the end for a strong federal state.

A second strategy dealt with the symbols of sovereignty, with the government looking towards reform before 1967 and the Centennial Year of Confederation. A new Canadian flag was adopted by Parliament in 1964 after closure, a new national anthem was approved in 1967. Centennial Year gave everyone a chance to display the new flag and sing the new anthem. Substantial amounts of money were spent on the celebration, with its centrepiece the Canadian Universal and International Exhibition at Montreal, familiarly known as Expo 67. The show was attended by millions of Canadians.

The final policy initiative of the Pearson Liberals was the concept of equal partnership, including the notions of cultural dualism and 'two founding races'. The Royal Commission on Bilingualism and Biculturalism was set up in 1963 to implement equal partnership. The commission discovered, to its surprise, that not all Canadians believed in cultural dualism. It ended up recommending some acceptance of multiculturalism as well as an official bilingualism implemented by the Official Languages Act of 1969. By the time bilingualism was formally adopted, Quebec had passed well beyond the stage of accepting its implications. Many political leaders were calling for a policy of unilingualism within the province. After the earlier entrance of Quebec's 'Three Wise Men' (Jean Marchand, Gérard Pelletier, and Pierre Trudeau) into Parliament and the cabinet in 1965, Pearson's resistance to Quebec had stiffened, however.

Quebec was not the home of all French Canadians, for there were hundreds of thousands of francophones living outside that province. The need to provide continuing protection for this outlying population was a principal argument of the federalists within Quebec. Francophones outside Quebec were understandably ardent federalists, and they were the chief beneficiaries of blingualism and biculturalism. Only in New Brunswick were the francophones (the Acadians)

The Canadian Pavilion at Expo 67, dominated by a huge inverted pyramid. The dome alongside it was clad with rows of enlarged photographs of Canada.

sufficiently concentrated geographically and sufficiently numerous to regard themselves as a distinct people. The 1960s saw a renaissance of Acadian culture and a new sense of political awareness that Acadian interests had to be served. Thus both major New Brunswick parties supported bilingualism, French-language education (including a university at Moncton), and the entrenchment of Acadian culture in the province. Bilingualism and biculturalism helped rejuvenate francophones elsewhere in Canada, most of whom were fluently bilingual. Not only did they gain advantages in obtaining federal employment in their regions, but their educational and cultural facilities came to receive a good deal of financial assistance from the federal government as well.

CANADIAN CULTURE

In some senses, Canadian culture came of age in the 1960s. The cumulation of years of the development of cultural infrastructure within the private sector, combined with a new government recognition of the need for conscious cultural policy and an enormous expansion of the Canadian university, brought at least élite culture to a flowering in the decade. A national cultural policy, first articulated by the Massey Commission, was actually implemented under Diefenbaker and Pearson. Intended to foster a distinctive Canadian identity in the face of the ubiquitous Americans, it employed all possible cultural strategies, ranging from subsidies (the Canada Council) to protectionism (periodical policy and Canadian content regulations for television introduced in 1961) to regulated competition (the Board of Broadcast Governors, established in 1958, licensed new television stations, which became CTV, a new television network, in 1961). Within the realm of 'serious' culture Canadian governments at all levels were prepared to spend large amounts of money to produce international standards. To a considerable extent they succeeded. Whether the culture that resulted was Canadian Culture was, of course, another matter entirely.

Perhaps the greatest success story was in Canadian literature. Before the 1960s the market for, and interest in, works of literature by Canadian writers was not strong. There was no tradition of indigenous literary criticism, few literary periodicals, and almost no sense of a literary community anywhere outside Quebec. In 1976 critic Northrop Frye noted 'the colossal verbal explosion that has taken place in Canada since 1960' (Frye 1976:849). That explosion saw a number of Canadian writers—Mordecai Richler, Margaret Laurence, Robertson Davies, Mavis Gallant, Marie-Claire Blais, and Margaret Atwood— achieve international critical recognition. It also saw the creation of a number of small presses across the nation, and the emergence of 'Can Lit' as an accept-

Marie-Claire Blais (*c.* 1959) (Wheler-Scott Ltd).   Northrup Frye (*c.* 1967) (Brigdens Limited).

able field of study at the university. By 1970 virtually every Canadian university offered an undergraduate course in Canadian literature, and a critical canon had more or less been established, which naturally emphasized the distinctly Canadian qualities of Canadian writing. Without a new breed of scholarly critics who were prepared to take Canadian writing seriously—as well as the subsidies that helped sustain author, critic, teacher, and journals—that writing would have developed more slowly. For many critics, the challenge was to reveal quintessential Canadian-ness in the imaginative elements of the literature. Québécois fiction shared in the cultural flowering, with the anger and violence of language and subject matter, radical changes in syntax and formal structure, not only mirroring but fostering the spirit of liberation and the new goals of Quebec society.

A new maturity and international acceptance of culture produced in Canada was to be found everywhere. We can see one major shift in the performing arts, where an amateur tradition of the 1950s was transformed quite swiftly into a full-fledged professional system operating from coast to coast. For example, Winnipeg—a middle-size geographically isolated urban centre with no particular tradition of cultural patronage—by 1970 was supporting a fully professional symphony orchestra; the Royal Winnipeg Ballet and other dance companies; an opera association mounting several works each year; the Manitoba Theatre Centre, an acclaimed model for regional theatre, whose impressive mainstage opened in 1970; an active art gallery; and a major concert hall. Thanks to various centennials, similar facilities and institutions existed in every major urban centre across Canada. By 1970 no important Canadian city or region was without its own professional theatre company, art gallery, and symphony orchestra.

Created with substantial public monies in the form of block grants from all levels of government, new institutions initially relied heavily on recent immigrants to Canada for professional expertise and, as had been hoped, many of these professionals became teachers and sponsors of spin-off activities. It was not long before highly qualified younger Canadians were ready to step into these companies and organizations, and a substantial local audience had been developed. One of the secrets of public success in music and theatre was the introduction of annual subscription campaigns. Unlike audiences in New York, London, Paris, or Berlin, where tickets were sold for individual events, patrons in Canada's performing arts were asked to buy blocks of tickets in advance to guarantee an audience. If by 1970 the personnel in the performing and exhibitory arts were Canadian, the repertoire on display tended to be largely an international one, both in origin and in style. Canadian artists, playwrights, composers, and choreographers had some trouble in gaining any place and audience within the repertoire regardless of their style. How they could be distinctly Canadian was another matter entirely. Nevertheless, this question ate away at the hearts of many Canadian creative people throughout the period.

The 1960s was also a critical decade for popular culture, particularly that valiant effort to keep the Canadian identity from being totally submerged by American influences. The record was mixed, as developments in Canadian sports well demonstrate. Nothing could be more quintessentially Canadian, for example, than hockey. But that sport entered the postwar period in the hands of the American entertainment industry, and the situation never really altered. By the 1960s only at the National Hockey League (NHL) level did Canadian teams have any real representation (two of six teams, in Toronto and Montreal). At the minor-league level only Vancouver had a professional team. The NHL finally expanded in 1967, adding six new American franchises in hockey hotbeds like St Louis and Philadelphia. Not even Vancouver, to its chagrin, could get a look-in. The chief argument against new Canadian teams was related to television. American TV viewers would not watch professional sports played by 'foreign' teams, said the experts, and the secret of expansion's success was a US national television contract. In 1969, on the other hand, the National Baseball League granted a franchise to a Montreal team to be called the Expos, demonstrating that if the local markets were big enough, the moguls could be won over. As for the Canadian Football League, it entered its most successful decade to date. Teams became totally professional and drew considerable crowds. The fans appeared quite satisfied with the Canadian game and its differences from the American one—the size of the field, the number of downs, the 'rouge'—and with the large number of Canadians who, thanks to a quota system on imports, played it.

In 1961 the federal government finally took some initiative on the problem of sports in Canada. Bill C-131, intended to 'encourage, promote and develop fitness and amateur sport in Canada', passed both Houses of Parliament unanimously in September of that year. Much of its bipartisan political support was a result of public outcry over Canada's poor performance in international competitions, including hockey, and was part of the cold war. Speaking about amateur sports at that time, Opposition leader Lester Pearson (who had played lacrosse and hockey while at Oxford) said: 'all the publicity attached to international sport and the fact that certain societies use international sport, as they use everything else, for the advancement of prestige and political purposes, it is a matter of some consequence that we in Canada should do what we can to develop and regain the prestige we once had, to a greater extent than we now have in international competition' (quoted in Morrow 1989:328). Although the act was deliberately vague, it allowed the government to subsidize amateur coaches and teams, particularly in national and international competitions. In 1968 the National Advisory Council, set up under the act to recommend policy and its implementation, was shunted to one side in favour of professional bureaucrats within the Ministry of National Health and Welfare. Amateur sports in Canada had been taken under the wing of the welfare state. In that same year Pierre Trudeau promised in the election campaign a new study of sports in Canada. The 'Report of the Task Force on Sports for Canadians' was published in 1969. Despite the increased government involvement in and subsidization of amateur sports, in 1976 Canada acquired the dubious distinction of becoming the first (and so far only) nation to host the Olympic Games without winning a gold medal at the ones it hosted.

Sports developed in ways remarkably similar to those of other cultural sectors, and indeed of the nation in general. By the early 1970s sports had been thoroughly drawn into the net of federal and provincial government policy, turned over to the bureaucrats and bean counters. It had not yet resolved the question of whether excellence and Canadian-ness were truly compatible, however, although the sense was that a sufficient expenditure of money would in the end resolve all problems. Unbeknownst to its participants, however, sports in Canada was about to share with other aspects of the Canadian experience a new sense of existing on the edge of some kind of precipice, about to free fall into new and unknown territory. What directions the fall would take were anybody's guess, although there were increasingly loud mutterings about the limits of growth. After 1972 Canadians would have to explore together the implications of a world in which not all things were possible. They would discover, as money and resources became more limited, that the infighting could be extremely fierce.

Major Events, 1972–1992

1972 Canada-Russia hockey series. Trudeau Liberals win in close election. NDP defeats W.A.C. Bennett in British Columbia.

1973 OPEC raises the price of oil. Robert Bourassa's Liberals are elected in Quebec, but the *Parti Québécois* finishes strong.

1974 Trudeau Liberals win in a close election. Trudeau imposes wage and price controls.

1976 Canadian Airline Pilots Association Strike. Montreal Olympics are held. *Parti Québécois* wins power in Quebec. Joe Clark is chosen as leader of the Tories.

1977 Quebec government passes Bill 101.

1978 Task Force on National Unity tours Canada.

1979 Joe Clark's Tories win minority government.

1980 Quebec referendum results in 60 per cent *Non* and 40 per cent *Oui* on sovereignty association. The Clark government falls, and Trudeau Liberals are swept back to power. Trudeau proposes constitutional reform.

1981 Supreme Court rules on federal constitutional initiative. The PQ is re-elected in Quebec. 'Gang of Nine' cuts a deal on the Constitution. Revised constitutional package passes Parliament.

1982 A revised Constitution is approved by British Parliament.

1983 Brian Mulroney replaces Joe Clark as Tory leader.

1984 Trudeau retires and is succeeded by John Turner. Brian Mulroney leads Progressive Conservatives to a federal sweep.

1985 PQ is defeated by Bourassa's Liberals.

1986 Mulroney government negotiates Free Trade Agreement with the US.

1987 Meech Lake agreement is arranged.

1988 Mulroney's Tories win again. Mulroney signs redress agreement with National Association of Japanese Canadians. Ben Johnson wins a gold medal at the Seoul Olympics, which is later revoked because of a positive steroid test.

1989 Fourteen female engineering students are gunned down in Montreal.

1990 Meech Lake Accord fails. Lucien Bouchard forms the *Bloc Québécois*. Mohawks confront Quebec government at Oka. Audrey McLaughlin is chosen as first female party leader in Canada.

1991 GST is officially introduced. Jean Chrétien becomes Liberal leader.

1992 Charlottetown Accord is reached. Toronto Blue Jays win the World Series. National referendum rejects the Charlottetown Accord.

Coming Apart, 1972–1992

✤

After a quarter-century of optimism, the years after 1972 presented Canadians with a different picture. Everything, from the economy to the very nation itself, suddenly seemed to be in a state of disintegration bordering on confusion.

THE PROBLEMS OF FEDERAL LIBERAL NATIONALISM

Until the early 1970s the postwar era had been for most Canadians one of affluence and optimism. It was characterized by a nationalism anchored by strong central federal government. This relatively positive climate had been achieved by policies dominated by twentieth-century small-l 'liberalism', a delicate balancing act that accepted an economic system based on private enterprise and corporate capitalism while also attempting to provide a social welfare safety net for the nation's citizens. Not all the resulting policies were influenced by Keynesian economics, but many of them were. Such policies were the operative ones for governments throughout the Western industrialized world. They were non-partisan. All major Canadian political parties, for example, at all levels of government—ranging provincially from the Socreds of the west to the separatists of Quebec—were essentially exponents of variants of liberalism with a small 'l'.

If the political consensus sought by all democratic governments in this period was formally dominated by liberal economics, the constitutional framework in which the liberalism was to operate increasingly produced conflict. For much of the period before 1970, the Liberal Party had combined liberal economics with a constitutionally centralized federalism nationalism. Although the Progressive Conservatives, in their six years of power between 1957 and 1963, had demonstrated different emphases, even they had not seriously contemplated overturning the broad framework. As we have seen, the Liberal consensus had come under attack in the 1960s, mainly from the left. It began seriously unravelling in the 1970s, and was in tatters by the beginning of the 1990s.

The Canadian political arena seemed incapable of dealing with both economic problems and constitutional problems simultaneously, at least at the same level of intensity. The period after 1972 saw an alternation of focus between the Constitution and the economy. The two questions were not entirely divorced, of course. One of the major arguments of the federalists was that only strong national policies could deal with the problems of the economy, and with the demands of minorities not geographically embodied into provinces and regions. Moreover, while constitutional matters were largely under the control of Canadians, economic ones were chiefly world oriented. After the election of a Tory government under Brian Mulroney in 1984, both nationalism and federalism were jettisoned for free trade and Meech Lake, while the principles of liberal economics were replaced by privatization, clawbacks, and deregulation.

No single factor or event can possibly be isolated as responsible for the collapse of the federal liberal-national consensus in Canada. Instead, a cumulation of what Marxist analysts would call 'contradictions'—matters that simply could not be resolved within the consensus—would eventually defy attempts at management, compromise, or hopeful neglect. The contradictions would come together at centre-stage to produce a series of what the media liked to call 'crises'. Many of the pressures were not really of Canada's own making but were part of international trends over which no Canadian government had very much control. Increasingly both politicians and the public came to feel that all political responses were defensive reactions to unmanageable situations, and that all policies were merely band-aids placed over festering wounds. Public trust in the nation's political leaders declined as the consensus disintegrated and was not replaced by a new paradigm. Cynicism became entrenched at the core of the Canadian national psyche. To some imponderable extent, the increase in cynicism and the gradual emergence of ever more unalloyed self-interest as the mainspring of human action contributed to the further deterioration of the old consensus. The Second World War had been fought on the basic principles of the deferral of expectations and the need for national sacrifice for the greatest good of the greatest number—a classic liberal utilitarianism. Canadians, whether as private individuals or as voting citizens, became increasingly less willing to buy such arguments. They became ever more prepared to accept the calls of leaders who, by implication or open assertion, opposed either waiting or sharing.

In 1973 a cease-fire agreement allowed the United States to withdraw from Vietnam, and the American process of national disillusionment continued with the Watergate affair, in which an apparently successful president was eventually forced to resign on 9 August 1974 rather than risk removal from office by impeachment for years of lying to the public. In Canada, Vietnam seemed less important than the October Crisis, bringing to the fore the *Parti Québécois*, which succeeded in electing seven candidates in the 1970 Quebec election. Then on 6 October 1973 the Arabs and Israelis went to war, as they had done periodically for many years. On this occasion, however, events in the Middle

East had an immediate impact on the world and on Canada. The Arab oil exporters (who dominated the world market) embargoed shipments of oil to nations supporting Israel. Shortly thereafter, the Organization of Petroleum-Exporting Countries (OPEC), which for thirteen years had been a toothless cartel, managed to agree on another even more substantial price increase than the modest one announced before the Yom Kippur War. The price of oil per barrel more than tripled in 1973, and all Western industrialized nations suddenly realized how much their economies had depended on a constant supply of cheap oil.

Perhaps more than any other single commodity of the postwar era, oil symbolized the economics of the age of affluence as well as its North American contradictions. Cheap oil made possible the development of large, powerful, and comfortable automobiles—the 'Yank Tanks' as they were called in Canada before they briefly became the 'Detroit Dinosaurs'—that sat in every suburban driveway and clogged every freeway. Those freeways, of course, had been paved with materials conjured out of petroleum derivatives. The manufacture and sale of instantly obsolescent gas-guzzling automobiles, as well as the construction of roads that connected thousands of new suburban developments and shopping malls, were major components of postwar economic prosperity in both the United States and Canada. Some saw the car as a symbol of postwar progress, while others saw it as a sex symbol. Either way, a 20-horsepower electric engine could hardly provide the same effect. The typical Detroit automobile not only consumed gas and oil as if there were no tomorrow, but it also discharged harmful hydrocarbons, which were principal contributors to the air pollution that increasingly affected everyone's health. Detroit engineering had never been renowned for its flexibility. It proved very slow to respond to a new need for fuel efficiency brought about by significantly higher oil prices. By the time it had moved to smaller vehicles, the Japanese had taken command of the North American automobile market, a fact that strongly suggested a new world trading order.

If petroleum—literally as well as symbolically—fuelled the contradictions of the North American economy, it also exposed Canadians to a number of distinctly home-grown problems. Many of these matters had already been newsworthy before OPEC pulled the plug, but they seemed more urgent and apparent as the nation searched for a viable energy policy to respond to the 'crisis'. The Canadian petroleum industry, located chiefly in Alberta, was almost entirely owned and operated by multinational corporations, most (though not all) of them American based. Oil, indeed, was one of those resources that most obviously epitomized the problems of foreign ownership that were addressed by a series of governments and task forces in the early 1970s. Moreover, although the petroleum still in the ground was a Crown resource, the Crown involved was the province and not the federal state. When the problems of jurisdictions over offshore oil were added to provincial control of oil as an internal natural resource, the result was a key item of potential dispute in federal-provincial relations. Most of the consumption of oil in Canada occurred in the industrialized east, while most of the raw material was in the resource-rich west, a discrepancy that exacerbated regional tensions. Finally, increased petroleum prices had a ripple effect throughout both the Canadian and world economies. Prices rose overnight, and an already steady inflation soared to new highs at a time when Canadian labour unions had only recently succeeded in establishing themselves in many key industries, especially in the public sector. Having achieved full recognition of collective bargaining, union organizers next moved for improved working conditions and higher wages to match the cost of living. OPEC's price increases, with promises of more to come, thus affected Canada in several vulnerable areas: foreign ownership, federal-provincial relations, regional conflicts, and labour relations.

Virtually the only long-standing problem that oil did not seem to affect directly was Quebec. On 29 October 1973, only three weeks after the start of the Yom Kippur War, Quebecers went to the polls to elect a new provincial government. From the outset of the contest between the Liberals of Robert Bourassa and the *Parti Québécois* headed by René Lévesque, the chief issue had been the desirability of a separate Quebec. Both parties had worked to polarize the electorate on this simple issue. The result, on the surface, was a resounding victory for the Liberals: 1,600,000 votes (54.8 per cent of the total votes cast) to 897,000 for the PQ, and 102 seats in the legislature to six for the PQ and two for the *Créditistes*. Nonetheless, the *Péquistes* had improved their performance over the 1970 election in almost every riding, and did exceptionally well among younger voters in Montreal. Postelection studies suggested that the majority of Liberal supporters had favoured federalism and a majority of PQ supporters independence for Quebec. The anglophone voters were much more staunchly federalist than the francophones. In any event, separatism had suddenly become respectable. While no other province was prepared to join the PQ in the front lines of the quest for a new constitutional arrangement for Canada, resource-rich provinces like Alberta certainly favoured new guarantees of constitutional autonomy for the provinces.

The relationship between Quebec separatism and Canada's economic problems after 1973 did not lie so much in positive as in negative polarities. In 1976 the PQ won a somewhat surprising victory, not necessarily to be interpreted as a mandate for separatism or sovereignty association, although one of its pre-election platform planks was the promise of a referendum on sovereignty association. When the referendum was held in May 1980, the *Nons*—those opposed to sovereignty association—won 60 per cent to 40 per cent. The PQ, however, were re-elected the next year. Especially after the referendum, the federal government under Pierre Trudeau turned its attention from the economy to the Constitution. Trudeau himself was not only a federalist Quebecer but a constitutional lawyer far more comfortable with the intricacies of the British North America Act than with oil-price equalization or economic planning. Oil and the Constitution were scarcely the only issues after 1973, but they were certainly front and centre for many years. The various attempts to resolve the problems they helped to create (as well as the ones they obscured) precip-itated the deterioration of the postwar consensus.

Pressure for continual expansion of the welfare state came from many directions before 1980, one scholar has noted, because income security became essential to the federal government's power, representing as it did the main link between Ottawa and the people. After 1980, however, contrary tendencies became evident and eventually dominant. Canada's involved economic and social problems would continue to produce demands for expansion of social insurance, but with the erosion of revenue and intense international competition, the federal government increasingly focused on restraint and privatization. Before 1992, no major element of the existing welfare net had actually been eliminated, however. Pension benefits for the elderly even improved. But the government cumulatively reduced the universality of the system of family benefits through the income tax system. In unemployment compensation, revised regulations increased the waiting period, making it more difficult to use unemployment funds as income supplements. The notorious goods and services tax (GST) was a thoroughly regressive tax that hit hardest at the poor. The greatest irony of government policy towards social welfare remained unchanged from the earlier part of the century, however. The government of Brian Mulroney was continually concerned about spending and the deficit, but had no trouble finding funds to support its military cooperation in the Gulf War of 1990. The unsolved riddle of social justice was still a challenge.

THE SHAPE OF FEDERAL POLITICS

The Ottawa scene from 1972 to 1992 divides in two periods, broken in 1984. During most of the first period the Liberals under Trudeau clung tenaciously to power in a series of very close elections (1972, 1974, 1979, and 1980), although they were replaced in office briefly, in 1979, by a minority Tory administration headed by Joe Clark. This period was one of a gradual Liberal Party deterioration paralleling the unravelling of the small-l liberal consensus of the postwar era. In 1984 the Tories under Brian Mulroney swept to power in the most decisive election since 1945, exceeding even the Diefenbaker sweep of 1958 in percentage of popular votes and number of seats. As with most decisive electoral shifts in Canada, the one in 1984 involved a massive reorientation of votes in Quebec and Ontario. The change in Quebec was particularly critical, although it was not clear whether Quebec's party shift was a long-term one, or precisely what it meant. At the end of their tenures of office, both Trudeau and Mulroney engendered enormous currents of fierce voter hostility in a general atmosphere of public mistrust of politicians.

Whether Mulroney's Tories actually represented a different political vision that could serve as the basis for a new consensus was always an open question. Certainly they sought to move to the consensual centre, which public opinion polls and voting behaviour suggested had become dubious about many of the old assumptions, but there was no clear evidence that a new political paradigm was emerging from the shards of the old liberal one. Instead, the events of his second administration suggested that Mulroney, like Diefenbaker a generation earlier, was simply perplexed and confounded by the chaos of the disintegration of federalism. The problem of Quebec, which came to dominate public attention across Canada in the late 1980s and early 1990s, contributed to further confusion.

The Liberals

The fortunes of the federal Liberal Party between 1968 and 1984 became increasingly associated with Pierre Elliott Trudeau, its leader for most of that period. The identification was partly due to television's relentless search for visual images and Trudeau's brilliant mastery of the medium. But it was also a

Prime Minister Pierre Elliot Trudeau and Robert Bourassa, the newly elected premier of Quebec, at the federal-provincial conference in Ottawa, September 1970 (Photo by Duncan Cameron/National Archives of Canada PA-117468).

result of Trudeau's operation as a loner, not encouraging strong colleagues to emerge around him. Trudeau's 'arrogance', the term most often used to describe his behaviour, was personal, not political. As a French Canadian who had always firmly opposed Quebec separatism, he had little scope for manoeuvre as public opinion polarized in that province. As an equally strong federalist, he had as little time for western expressions of provincial or regional autonomy as for Quebec's. A central-Canadian urbanized intellectual, he could not empathize with the problems of either the Atlantic region or western Canada. The east never deserted him, but by 1980 'western alienation' had reduced the number of Liberal MPs west of Ontario to two (both from Manitoba).

Never a fervent party man, Trudeau did not cultivate the grassroots. The powerful Liberal political organizations that had flourished before 1970 were allowed to wither away in most provinces, surfacing when federal patronage was to be dispensed but not at federal election time. Trudeau distressed many Canadians with forthrightness ('Just watch me'), vulgarity bordering on obscenity (one four-letter word in the House of Commons was transcribed as 'fuddle duddle', a raised-finger gesture to a western crowd appeared in newspapers across the nation), and personal unconventionality. Perhaps most damaging of all was an increasing tendency to treat almost everyone (members of his own caucus, the opposition, reporters, the voters) as ill-informed and irrational. Trudeau's public persona oscillated between that of a genial swinger (who could date Barbra Streisand) and that of a university professor facing a particularly stupid class.

Trudeau had announced his intention of retiring in 1979 following the Liberals' unexpected electoral defeat. But the Clark minority government fell before his replacement could be chosen. The Liberal caucus persuaded him to lead the party into the unanticipated election of 1980, and he remained in power for four more years. In 1984 Trudeau made his retirement stick. He was succeeded by John Turner (b. 1929), who had waited in the wings for years. Chosen on 16 June 1984 as Liberal leader and becoming prime minister two weeks later, Turner dissolved Parliament on 9 July for the fateful 1984 election. Turner was born in England, but was thoroughly bilingual. His decision regarding the election was a difficult one. He chose to run as a fresh face, on the momentum of his selection as leader, rather than remaining in office to attempt to improve the government's image. He had no new policies. Instead he was encumbered by the twin albatrosses of Trudeau's mounting unpopularity and the growing collapse of the liberal consensus. To everyone's surprise, he also proved utterly inept on television. The weak Liberal showing of 1984 (forty seats in Ottawa) was hardly unexpected. Something better was expected in 1988, however. In that election the Liberals did even worse in Quebec than in 1984, and Turner was a lame duck on election night. He was finally replaced in the summer of 1990 by Jean Chrétien (b. 1934), another veteran of earlier Liberal governments. Chrétien was a loyal party man and a proven campaigner. His leadership opponents had labelled him 'Yesterday's Man' with some justification, but lacked sufficient credibility or charisma to beat him.

The Progressive Conservatives

Robert Stanfield led the Tories to three successive defeats at the hands of the Trudeau Liberals. He was too low-key and uncompelling. Stanfield spoke French badly and his party did poorly in Quebec during his leadership (four seats in 1968, two in 1972, and three in 1974). He was followed as Tory leader by Alberta MP Joe (Charles Joseph) Clark (b. 1939), who emerged from nowhere as the compromise 'progressive' candidate at the 1976 leadership convention. 'Joe Who?' never did establish a distinct personality with the voters, except as a man who was accident-prone. In 1979 his Tories received 136 seats to 114 for the Liberals. Clark formed a minority government despite having won only two seats in Quebec (to sixty-seven for the Liberals). He tried to govern as if he had a majority, mistakenly assuming either that other parties would support him in Parliament rather than face another election or that the nation would rally to his banner in a new election. Neither assumption worked. The NDP refused to support Clark, especially over the privatization of Petro-Canada. His government fell on a motion of non-confidence about the budget, involving gasoline pricing. Clark remained party leader after the disastrous election of 1980, but in June 1983 was replaced by 'the Boy from Baie Comeau', Brian Mulroney (b. 1939).

Brian Mulroney entered Canadian politics at the highest level without ever having held public or elected office, although he had been active in the political back rooms for years. Unlike Clark, whose public utterances were unpolished and delivered in a boyish tenor (he reportedly took elocution lessons to lower his voice), Mulroney was a fluent speaker, perfectly bilingual, and possessed of one of the richest and most mellifluous voices ever heard in Canadian politics. He was an experienced labour lawyer and corporation executive, at his best at behind-the-scenes conciliation. Mulroney understood the need for Tory success in Quebec, and he brought a number of new faces into the campaign, some of whom were refugees from the old *Union Nationale*. In 1984 he successfully captured the centre of the new Canadian political spectrum. Although Mulroney's Tories promised they would not dismantle the existing welfare state, they put an ominous emphasis on 'fiscal responsibility'. They were equally committed to better relations between Canada and the United States, which meant less economic nationalism, as well as improved relations between Ottawa and the provinces (especially Quebec), which meant surrendering federalist pretensions.

Brian Mulroney in 1983, the year he became leader of the Progressive Conservative Party, MP for Central Nova, and leader of the Opposition. He became prime minister the following year (Photo by Ed McGibbon/National Archives of Canada PA-146485).

The ten provincial premiers and Prime Minister Brian Mulroney at Meech Lake, 30 April 1987 (Canapress Photo Service/Charles Mitchell).

Once in office with an enormous majority, including fifty-eight seats from Quebec, Mulroney succeeded in 1986 in negotiating a free trade agreement with the United States and the Meech Lake constitutional accord with the provinces. On the coat-tails of these successes the Tories won again in 1988, with sixty-three of its 169 seats from Quebec. Mulroney's second term was an unmitigated disaster. Given the amount of public support he had enjoyed in 1984 and 1988, the rapid growth of hostility to Mulroney in the early 1990s was quite remarkable. A variety of things went wrong. Government spending got quite out of hand. What was supposed to be a progressive tax reform, the GST, proved to be the most unpopular tax ever introduced in Canadian history, even less popular for the way the Tories adopted it over Senate opposition. The GST replaced previously hidden levies with an all-too visible tax computed at the cash register. Unlike provincial sales taxes, it was applied to everything without exemption. With the provincial taxes, the GST meant a surcharge of nearly 20 per cent in several provinces on most consumer spending. Meech Lake failed, and in a national referendum in October 1992 the nation rejected its successor, the Charlottetown Accord. Much of Canada came to believe that the Tory constitutional deals, especially with Quebec, not only made too many concessions but had actually stirred up unnecessary trouble.

Other National Parties

Throughout this period the New Democratic Party remained the constant third party. Its continuity was exemplified by the steadiness of its popular vote in federal elections, which ran between 15 and 20 per cent, and by the steadiness of its policies, which were indisputably federalist, nationalist, and liberal. Some complained that the party was not sufficiently socialist. It had certainly purged its socialist wing, the Waffle, in the early 1970s. But it was still unable to make inroads east of Ontario, consistently the big loser when the popular vote was translated into parliamentary seats. From 1971 to 1975 the NDP was led by David Lewis (1909–81), the son of Russian immigrants to Canada and a Rhodes scholar who had spent a lifetime associated with the CCF/NDP. His selection as leader followed a bitter fight with the ultra caucus within the party. From 1972 to 1974 the Lewis-led NDP propped up the minority Liberal government, arguably turning it to the left, but paying for the collaboration at the polls in 1974.

In 1975 Ed Broadbent (b. 1936), a former political science professor at York University, succeeded Lewis. Broadbent's national position in Canada in the 1980s was a peculiar one. He consistently headed the polls as the most popular and trustworthy national leader, but his party was never able to increase its public support. In 1990 Broadbent was replaced by Audrey McLaughlin (b. 1936), a former social worker from the Yukon Territories who spoke halting French and had no appeal in Quebec. Her selection as the first female party leader in Canada, however, marked the NDP as yet again in advance of the other parties, for feminist issues were part of the unresolved agenda of Canadian politics in the 1990s.

THE PROVINCES, THE CONSTITUTION, AND THE CHARTER OF RIGHTS

The Shape of Provincial Politics

The provinces continued to have difficulty generating truly viable two-party or multiparty systems. Instead, most provinces operated through a single dominant party (often outside the two major federal ones) that remained in office in election after election, producing what C.B. Macpherson described for Alberta as a 'quasi-party' system. A single dominant party, Macpherson argued, satisfied voters and mediated local conflict by insisting that the important battle was against external forces symbolized by the Canadian federal government. Conflict with Ottawa had been an endemic feature of provincial politics and government since Confederation. Offers to outbash the opposition regarding Ottawa were standard fare in provincial elections, particularly highly contested ones. Party identification with government in Ottawa was always extremely dangerous when provincial rights issues were on the table.

In some ways the 1970s were hard on dominant parties in the provinces. Four long dominant provincial parties went down to defeat: the Liberals in Newfoundland and Quebec, and the Socreds in Alberta and British Columbia. It was never clear whether the coincidence of these defeats was part of a much larger political shift, the product of changing economic circumstances, or mere accident. In any event, political veterans like Joey Smallwood, Ernest Manning, and W.A.C. Bennett were replaced by younger leaders such as Peter Lougheed (b. 1928) in Alberta, Brian Peckford (b. 1942) in Newfoundland, and Bill Bennett (b. 1932) in British Columbia. For the younger men, Dominion-provincial relations were not conditioned by depression, war, or postwar prosperity so much as by provincial self-interest ruthlessly pursued.

Federal-Provincial Relations

The 1970s

Throughout the 1970s federal-provincial relations were dominated by oil, Quebec, and abortive constitutional reform. In June 1971, at the premiers' conference held in Victoria, the Trudeau administration made another effort to agree on a formula for constitutional repatriation that would satisfy Quebec's aspirations. Three points are worth noting about the 1971 discussions: first, entrenching rights in a charter was regarded as one way to reassure those who feared losing British protection of an act of Parliament; second, Quebec did not achieve a sufficiently distinctive place in Confederation to suit its demands; and finally, only Quebec and Ontario were given perpetual vetoes (other provinces could together mount a veto only using complicated cooperative formulas). The question of constitutional reform was not picked up again until 1980, by which time much had changed for both Canada and its provinces. Oil and the whole question of resource management had become subjects of continual tension between some of the provinces (led by Alberta) and the federal government after 1973. Before OPEC pulled the plug, Alberta had often singlehandedly opposed Ottawa over resource management. With non-renewable resources now hot commodities, more provinces recognized the advantages of provincial autonomy. Only PEI, Manitoba, and New Brunswick were left to visualize their provincial self-interest as best served by a strong federal government. By 1980 the rich provinces, usually led by hard-headed businessmen who insisted that they put balance sheets ahead of sentiment, were ready to help dismantle Ottawa's centralized arrangements.

The Parti Québécois and the Constitution

The occasion for a new round of constitutional discussions was provided by the *Parti Québécois*, not through its electoral victory of 1976 but through its referendum on sovereignty association of 1980. The PQ victory came as a shock to English-speaking Canada, although it was really quite predictable. The Bourassa government in Quebec had been badly shaken by charges of scandal and corruption on top of its seeming inability to deal expeditiously with either the separatists or Pierre Trudeau. It had lost considerable face when the Canadian Airline Pilots Association produced a national strike in June 1976, ostensibly over safety but really over bilingualism, which only the federal government could resolve. Rumours of cost overruns and construction disasters in the preparations of the 1976 summer Olympics in Montreal had been rife for years. Bourassa's government was not directly involved in the problems, which were the primary responsibility of Jean Drapeau's Montreal government, but Drapeau was a Liberal ally and Bourassa had waffled over intervening. The province took over the Olympics construction only at the last minute. There were similar concerns over the control of James Bay hydroelectric development, but in the summer of 1976 these were not so immediately visible in Montreal as the Olympics fiasco. A resurgent *Union Nationale* won many of the non-PQ votes, as the electorate simultaneously rejected Bourassa's Liberals and embraced Lévesque's PQ.

Issues are never tidy in any election. No evidence suggested that the PQ, despite its resounding victory, had received any mandate for its well-publicized sovereignty association. The *Péquistes* had insisted that they would not act unilaterally on separation without a provincial referendum. Voters could thus support the reformist social-democratic zeal of the PQ without signing on to its extremist constitutional position. English-speaking Canada, however, responded to the Quebec election by assuming that separatism had triumphed in Quebec. The nation had to be saved at any cost. Had Lévesque sought to renegotiate the constitutional issues in the immediate wake of the victory, he might have been offered some sort of two-nations formula, but the PQ was committed both to internal Quebec reform and to a democratic approach to separation.

In office Lévesque's PQ successfully pursued policies of economic and linguistic nationalism. Its most controversial legislation was Bill 101, which went well beyond an earlier piece of Bourassa legislation (known as Bill 22) in turning Quebec into a unilingual francophone province. Bill 101 made it necessary for most Quebecers, regardless of their background or preference, to be educated in French-language schools. Only those temporarily resident in Quebec or whose parents had been educated in English-speaking schools in the province were exempted. The bill also insisted that French was the only legal medium in business and government, requiring the elimination of virtually all English-language signs in the province. In 1979 the Quebec government produced a White Paper detailing what it meant by sovereignty association. It wanted 'a free, proud and adult national existence' within the context of a series of joint Quebec-Canada institutions, including a court of justice and a monetary authority (Québec conseil exécutif 1979). A totally independent Quebec, it insisted, would still have access to Canada and its economy. Outside the ranks

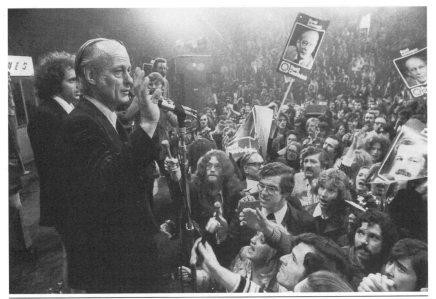

René Lévesque on provincial election night, 29 October 1973 (Photo by Duncan Cameron/National Archives of Canada PA-115039).

of the converted, the scheme seemed far too lopsided in Quebec's favour. The proposal was a unilateral Quebec initiative.

As had been promised, there was a referendum, eventually scheduled for 20 May 1980. Referendums are notoriously tricky political instruments. They often encourage No votes. Certainly the non-francophone population of Quebec (less than 20 per cent of the whole), although vehemently opposed to a *Oui* vote, were not by themselves numerous enough to reject sovereignty association, but in the end almost 60 per cent of the province's voters and even a bare majority (52 per cent) of its francophones voted *Non*. This fairly decisive result left 40.5 per cent of the Quebec population, and just under half of its francophones, in favour of sovereignty association. Nevertheless, Quebec had publicly rejected separation from Canada. The nation responded by breathing a collective sigh of relief and calling for a new federalism. Forgotten for the moment was the simple truth that pressure for change of the fundamental sort represented by separatism does not go away because of one set-back at the ballot-box.

The First Round of Constitutional Revisions

Canadians had discussed and debated both national unity and constitutional change since the PQ victory in 1976. More than enough proposals for reform floated about the country. Many surfaced in the travelling road show (known as the Task Force on National Unity) sent across Canada in 1978. Out of the flurry of activity and the myriad suggestions, several points were clear. One was that many Canadians—including a fair proportion of academics and lawyers, if not its historians—were prepared to make relatively major alterations in the British North America Act that served as the nation's Constitution. A second was that the vast majority of anglophone Canadians were prepared to make substantial concessions to keep Quebec within Confederation. A third point, perhaps less well understood by the public, was that the anglophone provinces of Canada— led by the western provinces of Alberta, British Columbia, and Saskatchewan, and strongly supported by Nova Scotia and Newfoundland—had developed their own agenda for constitutional reform. These provinces saw Ottawa's federalism as operating almost exclusively in the interests of central Canada. They were quite prepared to take advantage of Quebec's moves towards greater autonomy, particularly if these pressures reduced Quebec's influence within Confederation and allowed for constitutional change in the best interests of other provinces. What the other provinces wanted chiefly was unrestricted control over their own natural resources and a reform of some of Ottawa's governing institutions, notably the Senate and the Supreme Court, to reflect regional interests. The Trudeau government had seemed on the verge of conceding much of the provincial program when it was defeated in 1979. The Clark government had not dealt with the issue when it too failed at the polls.

The opportunity presented to Prime Minister Trudeau by the Quebec referendum, as he called a first ministers' conference for early June 1980, was real, if dangerous. Once the box of constitutional revision was opened, it might never be closed. From the federalist perspective, it was necessary to deal with Quebec's aspirations without conceding too much to the other provinces, none of which was controlled by a Liberal government and all of which had their own versions of change. Ottawa's most consistent ally was Ontario, confirming regional charges that it had been the chief beneficiary of the old federalism. Quebec did not participate in the new discussions, but it could not be churlish about them. Its best strategy was to allow the anglophone provinces to initiate the dismantling of Confederation. Indeed, one of the principal characteristics of this round of constitutional discussion was that Quebec's concerns were not front and centre. General consensus was developed on economic issues, balancing provincial resource control against federal economic planning. But other questions remained difficult to resolve. Ottawa wanted to entrench a Charter of Rights in any new constitutional document, chiefly to guarantee francophone linguistic rights across the nation, but the majority of the provinces (including Quebec) objected to such a Charter as threatening their own rights. The provinces, for their part, wanted an amending formula that allowed all provinces the right of veto and the right to opt out of any amendments that they regarded as threatening their powers. This round of discussions broke down in September 1980. As Prime Minister Trudeau had been threatening for months, Ottawa prepared to take unilateral action.

Politically the federal constitutional package developed in Ottawa was carefully calculated. As an ardent federalist, a trained constitutional lawyer, and an exponent of *realpolitik*, Pierre Trudeau was clearly in his element. The new proposal called for the elimination of recourse to the British Parliament for amendment of the British North America Act ('repatriation'). It contained a Charter of Rights, plus a number of qualifications on their applicability. The inclusion of the rights of other collective minorities sought to prevent the French Canadians from being treated as an exceptional case. The package also provided for a new method of amendment in the event of provincial obstructionism through national referendum initiated in Ottawa. The Trudeau government was prepared to pass the package through the federal Parliament and send it to Britain for approval without recourse to either the Supreme Court of Canada or the provinces, although it clearly infringed on the informal 'right' of the provinces to consent to constitutional change. Not surprisingly, the federal NDP supported this position, leaving the Progressive Conservative minority in Parliament to oppose it and voice the objections of nearly all the

Chronology of Quebec Separatism

March 1963	*Front de libération du Québec* is founded.
November 1967	René Lévesque resigns from the Quebec Liberal Party and begins organizing the *Parti Québécois*.
25 June 1968	Pierre Trudeau is elected with a large Liberal majority.
7 July 1969	Canada becomes officially bilingual through the Official Languages Act.
October 1970	Kidnapping of James Cross and Pierre Laporte. War Measures Act is invoked.
29 Oct. 1973	*Parti Québécois* wins six seats in the Quebec election and becomes the official opposition.
15 Nov. 1976	PQ wins majority in Quebec election and takes over government.
26 Aug. 1977	Bill 101 makes French the official language of Quebec.
15 April 1980	Quebec sovereignty referendum opens campaign.
14 May 1980	Trudeau promises constitutional reform.
20 May 1980	Sovereignty association is defeated by 60–40 per cent.
2 Oct. 1980	Trudeau announces the Constitution will be repatriated.
13 April 1981	PQ wins a majority in the Quebec election.
2–5 November	Ottawa and nine anglophone provinces reach a deal on the Constitution. Lévesque claims he has been stabbed in the back.
1 July 1982	Queen gives royal consent to a new Constitution.
21 July 1985	René Lévesque retires.
3 October 1985	Pierre-Marc Johnson, new leader of the PQ, becomes Quebec premier.
2 Dec. 1985	Liberals under Bourassa defeat Johnson's PQ and form a new government.
3 June 1987	Meech Lake Accord is negotiated.
1 Nov. 1987	Death of René Lévesque.
17 March 1988	Jacques Parizeau is elected new leader of the PQ.
2 June 1990	Meech Lake Accord fails when Manitoba and Newfoundland fail to ratify within deadline. Quebec says it will not take part in further constitutional deals.
25 June 1990	Seven independent Quebec MPs, led by Lucien Bouchard, form the *Bloc Québécois*.
28 Jan. 1991	Quebec Liberal Party calls for a decentralized Canada.
27 March 1991	Bélanger-Campeau Commission recommends a referendum on sovereignty by November 1992 if there is no deal with Canada.

24 Sept. 1991	Ottawa proposes a recognition of Quebec as a distinct society, Senate reform, Aboriginal self-government, economic union, and adjustments to federal-provincial powers to give provinces more control.
12 March 1992	First formal federal-provincial meeting since the failure of Meech Lake.
7 July 1992	Federal government, nine provincial premiers (less Quebec's), and Aboriginal leaders agree on a new formula for reform.
4 August 1992	Bourassa meets with other premiers and PM Mulroney.
19-23 Aug. 1992	Charlottetown Accord is negotiated, including Senate reform, Aboriginal self-government, expanded House of Commons, some new power arrangements, and a provincial veto over future change to federal institutions.
18 Sept. 1992	National referendum campaign on Charlottetown begins.
26 Oct. 1992	Canadian voters reject Charlottetown 54–45 per cent.
25 Oct. 1993	Federal Liberals under Chrétien demolish the Tories and NDP; Bouchard's *Bloc Québécois* forms the official opposition in Commons with fifty-five seats.
11 Jan. 1994	Bourassa resigns and is succeeded by Daniel Johnson.
12 Sept. 1994	PQ elected in Quebec and promises referendum on sovereignty.
12 June 1995	Parizeau, Bouchard, and Mario Dumont (of *Parti l'Action Démocratique du Quebec*) form a coalition to fight for *Oui* on referendum.
30 Oct. 1995	Sovereignty rejected by Quebec referendum 50.7–49.3 per cent; voter turnout is incredible 93.5 per cent of eligible voters.
31 Oct. 1995	Parizeau resigns as PQ leader.
11 Jan. 1996	Lucien Bouchard is chosen PQ leader and Quebec premier.
18 Jan. 1996	Bouchard resigns as BQ leader.
17 Feb. 1996	Michel Gauthier is chosen as head of BQ.
Sept. 1996	Quebec nationalist Guy Bertrand wins right in Quebec Superior Court to seek a court injunction against a new sovereignty referendum.

minority in Parliament to oppose it and voice the objections of nearly all the provinces except (again not surprisingly) Ontario.

Parliamentary amendments eliminated some of the least saleable features of the original proposal and introduced some new wrinkles, including the specific affirmation of 'aboriginal and treaty rights of the aboriginal peoples of Canada' (McWhinney 1982:176). The Liberal government had neatly set against each other two sets of rights, one the human rights protected in the entrenched Charter and the other the provincial rights ignored in both the amending process and the Charter itself. Eight of the provinces (excluding Ontario and New Brunswick), often unsympathetically referred to in the media as 'the Gang of Eight', organized as the leading opponents of unilateral repatriation, although Quebec and the English-speaking premiers had quite different views on positive reform.

The first major hurdle for the federal initiative was the Supreme Court of Canada, to which constitutional opinions from several provincial courts had gone on appeal. If the federal government won support from the Supreme Court, it would render untenable the provincial claim that the package was unconstitutional. While the Supreme Court deliberated, René Lévesque and the PQ won a resounding electoral victory in Quebec. The win did not, of course, resolve the deep contradiction that the PQ represented a separatist party committed to non-separatist action, but it did reactivate Quebec on constitutional matters. Although the British government had refused to deal officially with the provincial premiers (much as it had in 1867 when Nova Scotia sent Joe Howe to London), Canada's Native peoples set up their own lobbying office in London. They had some claim to direct treaty connections with the British Crown, and a decent legal case. The Supreme Court of Canada handed down its ruling on 28 September 1981. Many Canadians had trouble comprehending both the process and the decision, since neither the constitutional nor the political role of the Canadian court was as well understood as that of its American equivalent.

As one constitutional expert commented, the decision was in legal terms 'complex and baffling and technically unsatisfactory' (McWhinney 1982:80). In political terms, such complexity was doubtless exactly what the Supreme Court intended. Essentially, by a decision of seven to two, it declared the federal patriation process legal, since custom could not be enforced in courts. It then opined, by a decision of six to three, that federal patriation was unconventional. Since most of the legal arguments against the process revolved around violations of constitutional 'convention' (or custom), these two opinions were mutually contradictory, although in law Ottawa had won. What the politicians could make of a result that said, in effect, that the federal package of repatriation was strictly speaking legal but at the same time improper was another matter.

In the end the nine English-speaking premiers, including seven of the original Gang of Eight, worked out a deal with Prime Minister Trudeau on 5 November 1981. Trudeau made considerable concessions, for example, abandoning the provision for a referendum. Ontario joined Quebec in agreeing to drop its right of veto in favour of a complex formula that ensured that either one or the other (but not both) would have to agree to any amendment. This represented less a loss for Ottawa than for the central provinces, especially Quebec. At the same time, provinces that had refused to concur with constitutional change had the right to remain outside its provisions until choosing to opt in, a considerable move from Trudeau's earlier positions. Trudeau's greatest concessions were in the Charter of Rights, particularly the so-called 'notwithstanding' clause, which allowed any province to opt out of clauses in the Charter covering fundamental freedoms and legal and equality rights, although not other categories of rights, including language rights. There was disagreement over the intention of the negotiations regarding Native peoples, resulting in a temporary omission of the clause guaranteeing Indian treaty rights, which subsequently had to be restored by Parliament. As for definition of those rights themselves, there was to be a constitutional conference to identify them.

The final compromise satisfied the nine anglophone premiers. It certainly strengthened in theory the rights of the provinces to opt out of the Charter on critical issues, including both Native rights and women's rights, through use of the 'notwithstanding' clause. Perhaps understandably, both Native groups and women's groups vowed to fight on in opposition to the package as revised. As for Quebec, it had lost little except much of its self-perceived distinctive status in Confederation. That loss would prove fairly crucial, however, for Quebec would consistently refuse to accept the constitutional reforms on the grounds that Canada's two 'national wills' had not been consulted. That position would lead to another attempt at provincial unanimity at Meech Lake in 1987.

The revised constitutional package passed the Canadian Parliament in December 1981 and the British Parliament early in 1982. The latter had resolutely refused to become involved in the various protests against the new agreement, thus surrendering its role as court of last resort against unconstitutional actions within Canada. Canadians did not at the time fully appreciate what had happened constitutionally, or what the changes would mean. The principle of patriation had been purchased at considerable expense by the Trudeau government. The Charter of Rights did reflect the principle that collective and individual rights transcending the existent British North America Act (and its conception of relevant players) had to be carefully guarded. But in place of the earlier British constitutional position that the legislature (federal and provincial) was the source of protection, the Charter established the American constitutional notion that the court system would enforce fundamental rights over the legislature and the government responsible to it. In place of the earlier concept that Parliament was supreme, it introduced a whole new series of formal checks and balances limiting parliamentary supremacy. The principles of the Charter did contribute to the signature of Brian Mulroney on 22 September 1988 on a Redress Agreement between the National Association of Japanese Canadians and the Canadian government regarding the handling of Japanese Canadians during and after the Second World War. In letters to 20,000 Japanese Canadians in 1990, the prime minister acknowledged that the wartime treatment 'was unjust and violated principles of human rights as they are understood today'.

The new Constitution not only gave new powers to the provinces, it also recognized new and rather amorphous political collectivities in the Charter of Rights, which was somewhat less concerned than the American Bill of Rights in defining the individual rights of Canadians and somewhat more concerned in delineating their collective rights. Thus, in addition to providing equality before the law for individuals facing discrimination 'based on race, national or ethnic origin, colour, religion, sex, age or mental or physical disability' (section 15.1), the Charter also specifically permitted in section 15.2 'any law, program, or activity that has as its object the amelioration of conditions of disadvantaged individuals or groups', including (but not limiting itself to) those disadvantaged by discrimination as in section 15.1. Moreover, Aboriginal and treaty rights of the Aboriginal peoples, although deliberately not defined, were entrenched, as were sexual equality and multiculturalism. Although at first glance these Charter provisions seemed to represent the ultimate triumph of liberalism, in several respects they were not. In the first place, the liberal Charter provisions were balanced by the increased power given to the provinces to control their own resources and to call their own shots about the applicability of the Charter and any constitutional amendments. In the second place, the constitutional introduction of a whole series of new collectivities provided further complications for an already overloaded political process. In the end this would help stifle the liberal impulse itself. Finally, the well-publicized antics of the politicians over the Constitution contributed to a further reduction in the esteem with which those politicians were held by an increasingly cynical Canadian public.

Constitutional Revision: Rounds Two and Three

The 1982 Charter, with its explicit and implicit recognition of both collective and individual rights, was hardly the last word on the subject. An ongoing body of case-law would have to be developed by the courts, especially the Supreme Court of Canada, which became the ultimate arbiter for interpreting the vague terminology of the document. Governments did not produce further detail. The Charter simply became a wild card exercised by the Supreme Court of Canada on behalf of Canadians, arguably more amenable to change than the parliamentary system.

In 1987 the Mulroney government fastened on one of the loose ends of the 1982 constitutional process, Quebec's refusal to accept the 1982 Constitution. By this time René Lévesque had retired (in June 1985) and the PQ had been defeated in December 1985 by a Liberal Party under a rehabilitated Robert Bourassa. Once again in power, Bourassa offered to compromise. Mulroney summoned a new 'Gang of Ten' to a closed-door session on 30 April 1987 at Meech Lake, where a revised constitutional arrangement acceptable to Quebec was worked out. While Quebec was to be constitutionally recognized as a 'distinct society' and given further concessions, including a veto over most amendments to the Constitution, there were also inducements to the other provinces, which would share with Quebec some of the new features of autonomy. The federal government would compensate all provinces for programs they refused to join. Each province was given a veto over further amendments. There was to be regular discussion of Senate reform, although no particular formula was agreed upon. Nevertheless, there was a consensus among participants that the federal Parliament, and the legislatures of all ten provinces, would have to approve the agreement by early June 1990, the lengthy timeframe allowed for public hearings and feedback, or the arrangement was dead.

The three years permitted between the Meech Lake meeting and its ultimate acceptance created many difficulties. While the Mulroney government understandably insisted that no changes could be made in the agreement until it had been formally approved, not every provincial government felt bound by the particular terms of controversial understanding accepted by whoever happened to be its premier in April 1987. The subsequent public debate made clear that not all Canadians agreed with what was perceived as a further dismantling of central authority in favour not merely of Quebec but of all the provinces. The poorer have-not provinces—led by Manitoba, New Brunswick, and eventually Newfoundland—were concerned that few new federal programs would be mounted if the richer provinces had the option of receiving federal funds for their own versions. Other collectivities, such as Aboriginal peoples and women, worried that their rights were being bartered away to the provinces. Across the country suggested revisions sprung up almost like grass, many of them offering structural panaceas, such as a reformed and more effective Senate.

As the deadline for acceptance loomed, only Manitoba and Newfoundland held out, the latter having rescinded an earlier legislative endorsement after Brian Peckford's Tories were defeated by the Liberals under Clyde Wells (b.

1937). Prime Minister Mulroney tried the time-honoured tactics of the labour scene on the premiers, calling them into closed-door sessions designed to shame them into support on the eve of the deadline. This tactic appeared to work, but in the subsequent sessions of the Manitoba legislature, Indian leader Elijah Harper (b. 1949) refused to give the unanimous consent necessary to beat the deadline. Since Manitoba was not going to approve, Newfoundland's Wells backed off a previous commitment to supply his province's legislative endorsement. In the end, the two provinces refused endorsement and Meech Lake failed. Ominously, in the last days of Meech Lake, several Conservative MPs from Quebec, led by Minister of the Environment Lucien Bouchard (b. 1938), left the government to form a pro-separatist *Bloc Québécois*.

In the post-mortems on Meech Lake, a number of points stood out. One was that after 1987 the popular support for Brian Mulroney (and the federal PCs) and Meech Lake had declined together. Quebec understandably interpreted the mounting hostility to Meech Lake in English-speaking Canada as directed specifically against the 'distinct society', but the fact was that most Canadians appeared to be prepared to allow Quebec its autonomy. What people objected to was the extension of that autonomy to the other provinces, a process that would balkanize the nation. Moreover, Elijah Harper's action called attention to Meech Lake's incompatibility with the collective rights recognized by the Canadian Charter. During the summer of 1990 the failure of Meech Lake was followed by an extremely nasty confrontation between Aboriginal peoples in Quebec, led by the Mohawks of Oka, and the Bourassa government. Bourassa called in the federal armed forces, as he had done in the October Crisis of 1970.

The crushing defeat in early September 1990 of one of the main supporters of Meech Lake, Premier David Peterson of Ontario, by the NDP led by Bob Rae (b. 1948) was perhaps another straw in the wind. Certainly the NDP's achievement of power (for the first time) in Ontario suggested that there might be a resurgence of the left. The NDP's victory proved illusory, based chiefly on hostility to Peterson's government. Subsequent 1991 NDP victories in British Columbia and Saskatchewan only demonstrated the electorate's discontent and the NDP's inability to provide a new political paradigm.

The federal government spent most of 1991 attempting to figure out how to allow for 'democratic input' into the process of constitutional revision. The Mulroney administration was far too unpopular simply to force through legislation. Public hearings were followed by weekend conferences, none of which provided much direction. Canada had no tradition of consultative reform. In the end, another series of closed-door meetings between Ottawa and the anglophone provinces, subsequently joined by Quebec in August 1992 at Charlottetown, produced a revised package. This one offered Quebec a distinct society, the provinces a veto, the Aboriginal peoples self-government,

Table 11.1

Results by Province of the 26 October 1992 Referendum on the Charlottetown Accord

Province	Percentage Yes	Percentage No
Newfoundland	62.9	36.5
Nova Scotia	48.5	51.1
Prince Edward Island	73.6	25.9
New Brunswick	61.3	38.0
Quebec	42.4	55.4
Ontario	49.8	49.6
Manitoba	37.9	61.7
Saskatchewan	45.5	55.1
Alberta	39.6	60.2
British Columbia	31.9	67.8
Northwest Territories	60.2	39.0
Yukon	43.4	56.1
National	44.8	54.2

and the country both Supreme Court and Senate reform. The nation voted on the package at a referendum on 26 October 1992, the day after the Toronto Blue Jays won the World Series. (The World Series was named after the New York newspaper the *World* and had no international implications.) To the simultaneous amusement and consternation of Canadians, in the opening ceremonies, the United States Marine Corps had inadvertently carried the Canadian flag upside down. The eventual victory produced an outpouring of Canadian nationalism across the country. Some commentators openly feared for a country that could find togetherness only by celebrating the success of a collection of highly paid foreign athletes. How the win factored into the referendum is not known.

Six provinces (including Quebec) voted No. The national totals were 44.8 per cent in favour and 54.2 against. Polls indicated that Charlottetown failed because the majority of Canadians regarded the agreement as a bad one. Poorer provinces favoured Charlottetown, while poorer, younger, and less well-educated Canadians opposed it. According to one poll, household income of $60,000 per year was the economic cut-off between Yes and No, while a university degree was the educational one. Most of those who voted No believed that their vote would have no negative consequences for the nation. Perhaps.

THE ECONOMY

One of the many reasons for the failure of the paradigm justified by Keynesian economics was that after 1972 the system no longer worked very well. Government management, even wage and price controls, could not prevent runaway inflation, high interest rates, high levels of unemployment, and substantial poverty. With the manufacturing economies of the industrialized world fully recovered and new competition from the industrializing world emerging daily, Canadian manufacturing was in serious structural trouble. So too were the farmer and the fisherman. Symptomatically, the government's complex oil policy after 1973, attempting to create a new national energy policy based on a federally owned petroleum company to be called Petro-Canada, created only controversy.

As usual, Canadians had trouble understanding the intersection of international and domestic economic problems. They sought a reassuring way of comprehending their difficulties, for the notion that the country was internationally uncompetitive could not be seriously entertained. There were several potential scapegoats at hand. The bankers could have been blamed for the interest rates, or the businessmen for the unemployment. Instead, the country chose to fasten on the most visible and immediate of the trinity of troublesome indicators—inflation—and on a single factor to explain it. Polls taken in 1975 indicated that Canadians were willing to believe that the chief culprits on the inflation front were overpowerful labour unions demanding unreasonable wage settlements. Labour unions were understandably attempting to protect their members from the new economic situation. They wanted wage increases to keep pace with inflation, and opposed management efforts to rationalize or modernize their workforces through lay-offs or redundancies. Strikes in many industries, including a much-publicized postal strike in the summer of 1975, made the demands of labour appear unreasonable. When policemen, firemen, nurses, and teachers began taking similar steps, Canadians became alarmed. Not only were key public services threatened with interruption, but wage settlements in the public sector would have to be financed either with higher taxes or with deficit spending.

Although the extent of government deficits became a major public issue later, by the early 1970s all levels of Canadian government were well into deficit financing. High interest rates made the government debt much more expensive to service. The economic problems of the period set into motion a series of automatic mechanisms, built into the social services safety net, that greatly increased public expenditures. Even without those economic problems, spending on social services constantly escalated according to some mysterious laws of increased demand and expectation. The propensity to expand the civil service had its own logic. A variety of conservative economists now appeared to criticize the government's spending principles. Like the public, Pierre Trudeau's federal Liberals talked about the need for structural reform of the economy, but they were unable to confront the problems before the dangers posed by the PQ victory led to a renewed concern with the Constitution. Like all other governments around the world, Ottawa continued to spend more than it collected in taxes and revenue. In 1970 the per-capita debt figure of the Canadian government was $795. By 1990 it was $14,317 per Canadian. Between

Table 11.2

Federal Government Debt (Million Dollars)

Dates	Net Federal Debt	Gross Federal Debt	Components of the Gross Debt					
			Marketable Bonds	Treasury Bills	Savings Bonds	Other Securities	Pension Plans	Other Liabilities
1866–7	76	93	69	—	—	—	—	24
1917–18	1,192	1,863	1,428	75	—	—	5	355
1949–50	11,645	16,723	12,882	450	891	850	175	1,475
1974–5	23,958	55,289	14,490	5,360	12,915	51	12,378	9,825
1983–4	162,250	210,841	58,994	41,700	38,204	3,228	37,988	30,727
1990–1	385,047	443,278	147,104	139,150	34,444	4,514	74,807	43,259

Source: Canada Year Book 1994 (Ottawa: Statistics Canada, 1994):304.

1981 and 1990, the total debt of the federal government soared from $100 billion to $380 billion. The last budget surplus had been in fiscal 1972–3.

Like the government, the Canadian consumer lived increasingly in Tomorrowland. Canadian consumer debt more than doubled in the 1980s, increasing in small but steady stages from 18.7 per cent of personal income to over 20 per cent. Much of that debt was incurred through the medium of plastic credit cards. In the last year of the decade alone, the number of bank credit-card transactions increased from just over 100 billion to 150 billion. Residential mortage debt nearly tripled. Over ten years Canadian personal consumer debt (including mortgages) increased from 54.1 per cent of disposable personal income to 71.7 per cent, despite heavier taxes and truly debilitating interest rates. One of the most popular automobile bumper stickers proudly proclaimed, 'We're spending our children's inheritance.'

Despite its talk of privatization, such as the selling of the assets of the Canada Development Investment Corporation, the Mulroney government backed away from an open confrontation with the welfare system. Instead, it took back benefits (such as the mothers' allowance) from those with higher incomes and concentrated on increasing revenue through improving economic prosperity. The main vehicle for prosperity was to be a new economic relationship with Canada's largest trading partner, the United States. The eventual Free Trade Agreement, characteristically negotiated in secret during 1986 and 1987, ran to 3,000 pages of legal technicalities. Tariffs would gradually be removed, leaving Canadians astonished to discover that tariffs were not much responsible for the disparity between what goods cost in American and Canadian stores. Canadians were equally surprised to find that 'free trade' did not apply to ordinary people shopping in the United States and returning to Canada with their purchases. The national debate over the deal generated little useful information. Not even the economic experts could safely predict the ultimate effects of the treaty, although most favoured it in principle. Some critics complained that the Canadian negotiators had traded a less than useful access to the American market in return for continental economic integration. This was a futile argument, since most of that integration had already occurred. Only a fraction of total Canadian-American trade was actually affected by the treaty.

The most telling criticism was that the Free Trade Agreement did *not* revolutionize Canadian-American economic relations. Instead, the FTA was merely a cosmetic overhaul of the existing continental arrangement. Including the Mexicans in the North American Free Trade Agreement in the early 1990s was perhaps potentially more significant, but many observers could see few advantages to Canada in an economic partnership with a nation possessing a lower standard of living and cheaper workers.

After 1975 the Canadian economy more or less settled down to rates of unemployment, inflation, interest charges, housing costs, and taxation that would have previously been regarded as disastrous. Only food costs remained unaffected, which was not good news for the farmer. There were economic slow-downs in the early 1980s and early 1990s. From the standpoint of its conservative intentions, the welfare state worked. In both slow-downs the social protection net clicked in, and while more families fell below the poverty line, there were few demonstrations in the streets. Canadians became conscious that jobs were harder to get and harder to keep. The young responded to the lack of jobs by seeking further education in courses that promised some immediate economic pay-off, but they did not become radicalized. Perhaps they were too busy working to keep up the payments on their credit cards.

CANADIAN SOCIETY

A number of social trends characterized Canadian society in the 1970s and 1980s. One was a constant increase in the traditional indicators of 'instability'—marital breakdown, divorce, suicide, rape, crime, and sexually transmitted diseases. Canada seemed to be coming apart socially as well as constitutionally and economically. Another was an oscillation between abuse (often violent) of others and extreme self-indulgence, both products of alienation. These trends were also linked to the power of the media, which on the one hand publicized what had long been occurring beneath the surface, and on the other hand produced new consumer fads, fashions, and even needs. A third trend involved the working through the system of the baby-boom generation, which was coming up to early retirement by the 1990s. The baby boomers would at retirement meet a fourth trend, the enormously increased number of elderly Canadians. A final development of the era was the increased visibility of racial minorities, resulting in new social problems.

In 1974 a study had found that suicide had become Canada's fifth-ranked cause of 'early death' (i.e., death between the ages of one and seventy). Suicide rates continued to rise, and were especially serious among young males in general and young Aboriginal males in particular, reaching epidemic proportions in some communities. A 1984 National Task Force on Suicide in Canada indicated that the causes were 'complex and multifactorial', adding that 'interprovincial studies appear to show that there has been a change in the contemporary fabric of society with lessened self-restraints and lowered morals (anomie). This coincides with a period of expanding economy, greater affluence as a whole, high-technology industrialization, and increased unemployment' (National Task Force on Suicide in Canada 1984:9). A similar explanation could have been advanced for many of Canada's 'morbidities'. Another set of rising statistics related to crimes of violence against the person. From 1982 to 1987 crimes against property increased 0.1 per cent, while crimes of violence increased 30.1 per cent. From 1987 to 1991 violent offences increased another 29.8 per cent, while total criminal offences increased by only

Table 11.3

Offences by Type, 1987–1991

Type	1987	1988	1989	1990	1991	Percentage change, rate/100,000, 1987–91
Violent offences	219,381	232,606	248,579	269,381	196,680	+29.8%
Property offences	1,468,591	1,457,361	1,443,048	1,551,278	1,726,226	+12.8%
Other offences	1,276,036	1,265,861	1,300,005	1,343,397	1,470,454	+10%
Total	**2,960,908**	**2,955,828**	**2,992,632**	**3,164,056**	**3,440,671**	**+11.5%**

Source: *Canada Year Book 1994* (Ottawa: Statistics Canada, 1994):222.

11.5 per cent. On 6 December 1989 a lone gunman, apparently a misogynist, killed fourteen female engineering students at the *École Polytechnique* in Montreal. This horrifying event occurred near the close of a year in which, according to one estimate, over 32,000 Canadian women had been raped. The number of divorces had been 32,389 in 1972, rising to 90,985 in 1987 before beginning to decline slightly in numbers. By the late 1980s it was estimated that well over half of all Canadian children born after 1980 would at some point experience life in a broken home. If divorce increased, marriage declined. Moreover, the number of common-law relationships more than doubled between 1981 and 1991.

Whether abuse actually increased in incidence became a hotly debated topic. The general professional consensus was that it had less altered in extent than become a matter of general attention, more likely to be reported to someone. Racial and sexual excesses that might have gone unrecorded in previous generations were now openly publicized. Wife-beating—for decades the most common domestic crime on the police blotter—became a matter of public concern. Not surprisingly, much of the abuse was directed against the less powerful—children, women, Aboriginal peoples, and visible minorities—by traditional authority

The Failure of the Criminal Justice System in Nova Scotia

[In 1989 a royal commission in Nova Scotia reported on the case of Donald Marshall, a young Micmac Indian wrongfully convicted of murder in 1971. It condemned the criminal justice system in the province in no uncertain terms, as the following extract indicates. *Source: Royal Commission on the Donald Marshall, Jr, Prosecution, vol. 1: Findings and Recommendations* (Halifax: The Commission, 1989):15–17.]

On May 28, 1971, four people came together in a brief, unplanned nighttime encounter in Wentworth Park in Sydney, Nova Scotia. One of them, a 17-year-old black youth named Sandford (Sandy) William Seale, was killed. Another, a 17-year-old Micmac Indian named Donald Marshall, Jr, was wrongfully convicted of his murder, and was sentenced to life imprisonment in November 1971. Eleven years later, after Marshall's lawyer, Stephen Aronson, brought forward information suggesting Marshall did not commit the murder, the RCMP reinvestigated the case for a second time. After that investigation confirmed that Marshall did not kill Seale, he was released on parole and subsequently acquitted by the Supreme Court of Nova Scotia (Appeal Division) in May 1983. A third man, Roy Newman Ebsary, who was one of the four people who had come together in Wentworth Park that night, was charged with killing Seale and was convicted of manslaughter following three trials. He was sentenced to three years in prison. In 1986, the Court of Appeal reduced his sentence to one year. He died in 1988.

The events that took place in Wentworth Park in those few moments on that spring night in 1971 have spawned numerous official inquiries and proceedings, including three formal police investigations, two preliminary inquiries, four trials, three appeals to the Supreme Court of Nova Scotia (Appeal Division), a Reference to the Court of Appeal and two Royal Commissions, including this one. The cost in dollars has been tremendous. The toll in human anguish has been incalculable.

The principal task of this Royal Commission has been to determine why Donald Marshall, Jr was wrongfully convicted and to make recommendations to ensure that such a miscarriage of justice does not happen again.

figures ranging from fathers to pastors to teachers to policemen to judges. On one level it was possible to take solace in the fact that such maligned behaviour was now being addressed. On another it was possible to argue that what had changed was not authority behaviour but society's willingness to tolerate its excesses. Yet on a third level both the extent of the abuse and the undermining of authority to which it contributed were distressing. Canadians could no longer believe, as before, that they were all good guys living in the Peaceable Kingdom, nor could they continue to believe in the inherent beneficence of authority figures or the fairness of the Canadian judicial system. The revelations of the post-1972 period, particularly in the 1980s, could only contribute to a growing national mood of

First, what did go wrong? Although we will examine in detail each of the relevant events of the Marshall case from its beginning on May 28, 1971, to our appointment on October 28, 1986, we can begin with the following general conclusions that flow from our consideration of all of the evidence.

The criminal justice system failed Donald Marshall, Jr at virtually every turn, from his arrest and wrongful conviction in 1971 up to—and even beyond—his acquittal by the Court of Appeal in 1983. The tragedy of this failure is compounded by the evidence that this miscarriage of justice could have—and should have—been prevented, or at least corrected quickly, if those involved in the system had carried out their duties in a professional and/or competent manner. . . .

This Commission has concluded that Donald Marshall, Jr was not to blame for his own conviction and that the miscarriage of justice against him was real.

That is the inescapable, and inescapably distressing, conclusion we have reached after listening to 113 witnesses during 93 days of public hearings in Halifax and Sydney in 1987 and 1988 and after sitting through 176 exhibits submitted in evidence during those hearings.

But concluding that Donald Marshall, Jr was the victim of a miscarriage of justice does not answer the complex question of why Marshall came to be wrongfully convicted and imprisoned in the first place. Was it because he was a Native? Was it because he was poor?

To answer those admittedly difficult questions, this Commission has looked not only at how the criminal justice system in Nova Scotia operated in the Marshall case, but it has also compared the handling of the Marshall case with the way in which the system dealt with cases involving powerful and prominent public officials. At the same time, we commissioned independent research studies to find out how Natives and Blacks are treated in the criminal justice system.

From all of that, the evidence is once again persuasive and the conclusion inescapable that Donald Marshall, Jr was convicted and sent to prison, in part at least, because he was a Native person.

sullen cynicism with regard to authority, which was hardly appeased by the unimaginative and self-seeking behaviour of the politicians.

Much of the abuse of Canadians was self-inflicted, often related to short-term gratification without regard for long-term consequences. The availability of drugs continued to increase steadily. Alcohol abuse continued unabated, along with substance abuse of many descriptions, including gasoline sniffing, and the use of steroids by athletes became common. Canada's most notorious substance abuser was the Olympic sprinter Ben Johnson (b. 1961), whose gold medal at Seoul in 1988 was ignominiously stripped from him for the use of steroids he initially denied but eventually acknowledged at another well-publicized public enquiry. The most dangerous drug of all was tobacco. Canadian adults, reflecting the health consciousness of the baby boomers, led the way internationally in quitting smoking during the late 1980s. The young, however, remained undeterred by cigarette prices, which were often in excess of $6 per pack. One calculation revealed that tobacco would ultimately kill eight times as many fifteen year-olds as automobile accidents, suicide, murder, AIDS, and drug abuse combined. Self-inflicted abuse was part of the new world of self-indulgence. Those who made their way to the top could reward themselves with luxuries and expensive toys. Sniffing cocaine became an indulgence of choice among the affluent. As for the poor, they had access to little pleasure that was not addictive and physically harmful.

In many ways the post-1970 era was dominated by the baby-boom generation. Before 1970 the boomers had their chief impact on the educational system. Now they put pressure on the employment system not only by their sheer numbers but by their educational qualifications. Not all were able to get the jobs for which they had prepared. The tightness of the job market, combined with the increased consumer requirements of the boom generation, produced more childless working couples and further lowered fertility rates. By the 1980s the baby boomers' demand for detached housing drove up housing prices in most of the nation's larger cities. Even after the inevitable bust, prices could never return to previous levels. In cities of premium-priced housing (such as Toronto and Vancouver), it was estimated that less than a quarter of those seeking to purchase their first house could qualify for a mortgage. Many boomers had money to spend on nice things: 'My Tastes Are Simple', read one popular bumper sticker, 'I Like the Best.' Marketing strategies to reach these consumers included slick magazines distributed free to homes in targeted neighbourhoods with the appropriate demographics. Articles on various aspects of affluent lifestyles—home (re)decorating, gourmet foods eaten at home or in restaurants, and luxury travel—were some of the subjects featured. The boomers continued their fascination with the 1950s and 1960s pop and rock music of their youth. The music nostalgia industry thrived. Radio stations that for decades had tried to appeal to the kids suddenly shifted their programming to the 'Golden Oldies' in a blatant attempt to capture the largest single audience segment: middle-aged baby boomers.

The progressive aging of the Canadian population was neither a new development of the post-1970 period nor a distinctly Canadian one. By 1991 life expectancy for Canadian men had reached seventy-four years, and over eighty years for women. The leading causes of death in Canada were all diseases of the old. The emerging conception of a 'crisis' was primarily connected with what seemed to be the increased costs associated with the elderly—pensions and health care—in the welfare states of the advanced world. Part of the problem

Table 11.4

Leading Causes of Death, 1990

	Male		Female	
	No.	Rate	No.	Rate
Diseases of the circulatory system	38,823	296.3	36,266	269.0
Cancer	28,865	220.3	23,560	174.8
Respiratory diseases	9,351	71.4	6,921	51.3
Accidents and adverse effects	9,064	69.2	3,993	29.6
Diseases of the digestive system	3,961	28.2	3,303	24.5
Endocrine diseases, etc.	2,533	19.3	2,939	21.8
Diseases of the nervous system	2,275	17.4	2,580	19.1
All other causes	9,358	71.2	8,434	62.7
Total, causes	**104,230**	**793.3**	**87,996**	**652.8**

was that the proportion of the population who were productive members of the workforce able to finance the care of the aging was constantly declining. In 1983 in Canada there were eighteen people over sixty-five for every 100 between eighteen and sixty-four. One prediction suggested that there would be fifty-two people over sixty-five for every 100 between eighteen and sixty-four by 2031.

Pensions had always been based on the notion that the working generation supported the retired one. One study in the mid-1980s argued that by the year 2021 the funds required for public pensions would be three and one-half times greater than in 1976, given the continuation of the 1976 level of payments. Without a high level of pension support, the elderly would become an even greater proportion of Canadians below the poverty line. In 1986 46.1 per cent of unattached females over the age of sixty-five were below that level. Longer life obviously meant more demands on the health care system, culminating in the potential need for expensive nursing home facilities. In 1986, only 9 per cent of Canada's elderly could be accommodated in nursing homes. Studies demonstrated that the cost of medical care for the last year of life was substantially greater than for the entire earlier lifespan. The problem was deciding when the last year had come, or what medical strategy to adopt.

The increased visibility of racial minorities was especially evident in the nation's larger cities, where they tended to congregate. This concentration only encouraged racism. Despite higher levels of media attention, government expenditure, and Aboriginal self-consciousness, the demographic realities of Native life, while improving, continued to recall conditions in nations generally regarded as the most backward on the planet. Infant mortality and overall death rates ran high. Conditions on many remote reserves continued to be absolutely deplorable. It was not surprising that many Aboriginals migrated to cities like Winnipeg, where they met considerable social disapproval. After 1973 new immigrants to Canada came chiefly from the non-European Third World. In that year, Hong Kong, the Philippines, Jamaica, Trinidad, and India appeared on the list of top-ten countries of origin for Canadian immigrants. Reform of

Table 11.5

Immigrants Arriving by Place of Birth, 1981–1990

Place	Number	Percentage
Europe	351,511	26.4
Great Britain	81,460	6.1
Portugal	38,630	2.9
France	15,256	1.1
Greece	6,884	0.5
Italy	11,196	0.8
Poland	81,361	6.1
Other	116,724	8.8
Africa	72,941	5.5
Asia	619,089	46.5
Philippines	67,682	5.1
India	90,050	6.8
Hong Kong	96,982	7.3
China	74,235	5.6
Middle East	90,965	6.8
Other	199,175	15.0
North & Central America	114,073	8.6
US	63,106	4.7
Other	50,967	3.8
Caribbean & Bermuda	89,908	6.7
Australasia	5,877	0.4
South America	67,936	5.1
Oceania	10,040	0.8
Other	375	
Total	**2,416,423**	

Source: *Canada Year Book 1994* (Ottawa: Statistics Canada, 1994):116.

immigration legislation in 1976, 1978, and 1987 further encouraged immigration from non-traditional sources. Beginning in 1986, individuals with substantial amounts of capital could invest this money in approved projects and thereby gain access to Canada. People of Third World origin, who represented less than 1 per cent of the Canadian population in 1967, represented 4.6 per cent by 1986. In that year, Canadian residents from the Third World totalled 30 per cent of all foreign-born.

CANADIAN CULTURE

After 1972 Canadians discovered that culture not only had moral, intellectual, and aesthetic dimensions but powerful economic implications as well. Canadian bureaucrats began to talk about 'cultural industries' instead of just culture, measuring jobs and spin-offs as well as enlightenment. At about the same time, governments began to discover how much money they had been putting into various aspects of culture since the halcyon days of the 1950s and

1960s. An additional debate over cultural policy focused on both how to limit and supplement the vast public expenditures on activities ranging from university research to art events. To the extent that it was regarded as a non-essential, culture was extremely vulnerable to budget cutting. Not only limitation but pay-off became a live issue. Canadian cultural policy was hotly debated, particularly since the politicians sought to use cultural policy to other ends, notably in the area of multiculturalism. The always artificial distinction between commercial and non-commercial culture had now been partially overcome by the inclusion of cultural enterprise in the economy. Thus popular culture (including sports) became more frequently recognized as a legitimate part of culture.

Certainly one of the defining events of a lifetime for many Canadians was the Canada-Russia hockey series of 1972. The largest television audience ever assembled in Canada was glued to the TV, mesmerized by an unofficial sporting event, played for no historical trophy or recognized world title. Paul Henderson of the Toronto Maple Leafs scored the game- (and series-) winning goal with thirty-four seconds remaining in regulation time. Despite this moment of national togetherness, the schism between francophone and anglophone cultures was constantly widening, and all levels of government cont-inued to jostle for advantage. The result was a strong sense of diffusion and decentralization—some would say regionalization (although not merely geography was involved)—of what had once been perceived as a monolithic cultural establishment. Such developments parallelled and reinforced the retreat of centralism in the political and constitutional area, as well as contributing to the sense that Canadian society was unravelling.

By 1990 the *Canada Year Book* could call the cultural sector 'the fourth largest employer in Canada' (*Canada Year Book* 1990). A few years earlier, a 1985 Statistics Canada compendium entitled *Arts and Culture: A Statistical Profile* had estimated that in 1982 culture's share of the gross domestic product was $8 billion, calculated that there were 280,000 Canadian arts-related jobs in the 1981 census, and insisted that arts jobs were growing at a faster rate than the total labour force in all provinces. The 1986 Task Force on Funding in the Arts revised the economic dimensions of the cultural sector upwards to $12 billion and the job numbers to 415,000. Despite the billions of dollars of public support, however, government spending on arts-related culture represented only about 2 per cent of the total of government expenditure at all levels. Moreover, little of the vast sums spent on culture trickled down to the primary producer—the writer, painter, actor, and composer. Government surveys of artists from 1978 to 1984 indicated that very few Canadians could make a living from the sale of their work or talents. Most held other employment, often in teaching. At the same time, the fact that even a few thousand Canadians could

Table 11.6

Percentage of Television Viewing Time Devoted to Canadian and Foreign Programming in Prime Time (7 p.m.–11 p.m.)

| | ENGLISH | | | |
| | 1984–5 | | 1992–3 | |
	Canadian	Foreign	Canadian	Foreign
CBC	62.0	38.0	81.7	18.3
CTV	20.8	79.2	17.3	82.7
Global	7.9	92.1	17.4	82.6
Independent	16.4	83.6	17.9	82.1
	FRENCH			
SRC (Radio Canada)	72.1	27.9	90.9	9.1
TVA	46.2	53.8	66.3	33.7
TOS	54.8	45.2	47.6	52.4

Source: *Globe and Mail* (1 February 1996):A21.

conceive of making a living as professional producers of culture certainly distinguished the post-1970 period from earlier times.

Little enough changed in terms of the distinctive Canadian content of culture in Canada, still conceived to be a major problem by many observers. The statistics were revealing enough. In book publishing, for example, titles published in Canada in 1984 (most written by Canadian authors) accounted for only 25 per cent of books sold. Nearly half the books sold to Canadians came directly from foreign sources. Twelve foreign-controlled firms in 1984 had 89 per cent of the sound-recording market in Canada, most for recordings made outside Canada. In one week in 1986 the top seven TV shows in English-speaking Canada were all American. The situation was quite different in French Canada, where all top seven shows were locally produced. In the 1980s there was great hope for satellite and cable technology, but while these improved access for many Canadian viewers, they did little for actual Canadian content.

Government support for High Culture further aided a respectable Canadian showing in areas of traditional activity, such as painting and litera-ture. But as Canadian High Culture achieved international recognition, it further continued a process of diffusion, which produced tensions between what came to be labelled 'national' and 'regional' culture, both in Canada as a whole and in the linguistic dualities of French and English. Before the late 1960s, a major problem for Canadian creators was receiving public exposure outside Toronto and Montreal. The small presses and galleries that cropped up in the country, especially after 1970, became possible for several reasons. One was the allocation of new provincial funding for the arts, often from the revenues of publicly authorized gambling activities. In Quebec, cultural subsi-dies were a matter of high politics. Another was the emergence of local cultural entrepreneurs in what was now a large enough market for culture in second-tier cities such as Quebec, Halifax, and Winnipeg. Almost inevitably the new publishers and galleries tended to stress local themes and settings. Cultural regionalism grew to match political regionalism. It began to appear that the very concept of a Canadian National Culture was an artificial one, impossible for most Canadian artists to realize in a fragmented nation. Precious few books published in Quebec were ever translated into English, for example.

In early 1991, when the Quebec government of Robert Bourassa finally responded to the collapse of Meech Lake, it listed immigration, health and manpower, and cultural matters as the key areas in which it would demand increased constitutional powers. 'As far as culture is concerned, yes we should be in charge', announced Liberal Minister of Cultural Affairs Liza Frulla-Herbert in January 1991. 'We have to work toward being the one and only one giving the pulse of Quebec culture. Listen, culture belongs to Quebec' (*Winnipeg Free Press* 25 January 1991). No Canadian could doubt that in Quebec, culture was lively and distinctive, certainly better able to withstand American influence than elsewhere in Canada. Whether Quebec Culture was a National Culture became, in the end, a question more susceptible to political than intellectual answers.

Major Events, Canada's External Relations

1871   Sir John A. Macdonald signs Treaty of Washington.

1884   Canadian voyageur volunteers go to Sudan.

1899   Canada sends volunteers to South Africa.

1903   Alaska Boundary Dispute between Canada and the United States is handed over to a joint commission of six 'impartial jurists of repute'.

1909   Department of External Affairs is created.

1914   Canada joins the Allies in the Great War.

1917   Canada joins the Imperial War Council.

1919   Canada attends Paris Peace Conference as part of the British empire delegation.

1920   Canada becomes a member of the League of Nations.

1921   Chanak Crisis.

1925   O.D. Skelton is appointed to External Affairs.

1926   Canadian minister to Washington is first appointed.

1930   Westminster Conference of 1930.

1931   Statute of Westminster makes Canada legislatively independent of Great Britain.

1932   International Trade Conference at Ottawa.

1935   Most-favoured-nation treaty signed with the US.

1939   Canada declares war on Germany.

1940   Ogdensburg meeting between Canada and the US. Lend-lease exchanges destroyers for Newfoundland bases.

1941   Hyde Park Declaration.

1945   Canada helps found the United Nations.

1946   Gouzenko affair. Cold war begins.

1948   Canada becomes part of the Marshall Plan.

1949   North Atlantic Treaty Organization is created.

1950   Canada joins the UN force in Korea.

1954   Canada joins a joint commission on Vietnam.

1955   Distant Early Warning line is established.

1957   Lester B. Pearson wins the Nobel Peace Prize. Canada joins NORAD.

1959   Avro Arrow is cancelled.

1962   Cuban Missile Crisis.

1964   Canada sends a peacekeeping force to Cypress.

1972   Trudeau proposes 'Third Option'.

1989   Berlin Wall is opened.

1990   Canada participates in the Gulf War.

1992   Canada sends first peacekeepers to Bosnia.

1993   Canada agrees to peacekeeping in Somalia. Canada closes the last two military bases on German soil. Canada withdraws peacekeepers from Cyprus.

1994   NAFTA takes effect. Last troops withdrawn from Lahr, Germany.

1995   Fisheries crisis with Spain.

12

Facing the World

❀

As a result of both its geographical position and its colonial situation, Canada before 1914 was able to enjoy relative isolation from the turmoil of international politics, concentrating on its own domestic development. Like Americans, most Canadians were relatively inward looking, even isolationist, in their attitudes towards the wider world. Most French Canadians saw themselves as an autonomous people without close European or international connections, while Canadians of British origin felt varying degrees of loyalty to Great Britain, which looked after most international affairs in the name of the British empire. Canada's corps of diplomats was tiny, confined to Washington, London, and Paris. After 1909 a small Department of External Affairs supervised and coordinated the nation's sporadic formal relations with the world. While most Canadians felt no need to be citizens of the world before 1914, they were not necessarily ignorant of it. The larger daily newspapers covered foreign affairs far more assiduously than their modern equivalents, for example.

After the Great War, Canada's international position changed rapidly. In the interwar period, Canada broke its imperial ties and began to construct its own foreign policy and diplomatic apparatus. Before 1939–40, direct American influence over Canadian foreign and defence policy was minimal; as late as the 1920s the Canadian military still thought of the United States as a potential enemy rather than as an ally. The Second World War completed the process of withdrawal from the British umbrella and initiated the process of Canada's integration into an informal American empire. Canada's scope for genuinely autonomous action in the world was never very great, although most Canadians were reasonably content with the nation's situation as they understood it. Until the late 1980s, Canada stood as a junior partner of the United States in the international struggle with communism known as the cold war. Then suddenly the USSR collapsed. The cold war ended. What would replace it was another matter.

THE 1920S AND 1930S

Even before the First World War, many Canadians appreciated that Canada had no voice in the affairs of the British empire. The war brought the point home in increasingly graphic fashion, however. Prime Minister Borden took the lead in pressing for change. He argued privately in 1916 that 'it can hardly be expected that we shall put 400,000 or 500,000 men in the field and willingly accept the position of having no more voice and receiving no more consideration than if we were toy automata' (quoted in Stacey 1981:192). The British eventually invited Dominion ministers to sit in imperial council as a token gesture. The Dominions insisted on full representation as participants in the Paris Peace Conference of 1919, in the end settling for being part of the British empire delegation. Nevertheless, Borden himself led a strong Canadian delegation to Paris, pressing successfully for full membership in the League of Nations and various collateral League bodies.

Once Canada was admitted to the League of Nations as a full member, it became a regular (if uninfluential) participant, occasionally surfacing to lecture the world on its failures. During the 1920s the major energy of external relations was spent redefining the nation's role in the British empire. The ultimate result was the Westminister Conference of 1930, attended by Mackenzie King's successor, R.B. Bennett. The resulting Statute of Westminster (1931) made six Dominions—Canada, Australia, New Zealand, the Irish Free State, South Africa, and Newfoundland—legislatively independent. As Bennett himself said at the time, with the adoption of the Statute of Westminster 'the old political Empire disappears'. But, he went on to add, he hoped that it would be replaced by 'the foundations of a new economic Empire' (quoted in Stacey 1981:135). The 1920s also saw the expansion of the Department of External Affairs, initially under undersecretary O.D. Skelton (1878–1941). Skelton recruited a number of young men of talent, albeit from a fairly narrow male, upper middle-class spectrum of Canadian society, who served the nation abroad until the 1950s. Under Skelton's tutelage, external affairs expanded abroad. A Canadian minister to Washington was appointed in 1926. Similar legations opened in Paris and Tokyo in 1928. A few foreign embassies opened in Ottawa.

The decade of the 1930s, in terms of foreign affairs, divides at 1935. Between 1930 and 1935 foreign relations were dominated almost exclusively by economic considerations. Even at the Westminster Conference, Canada was really more interested in economic than constitutional matters. The result was a conference in Ottawa in 1932 intended to re-examine imperial economic policy. The meeting was not a success, beyond a bit of tariff reform. Canada set the tone by bargaining almost exclusively in terms of its own immediate advantage. As for Canadian-American relations, the two neighbours had exchanged high protective tariffs in 1930. Gradually they resumed more normal cooperative relations. Mackenzie King made American negotiations one of the first points on the government's agenda after his electoral success in 1935. The result was a most-favoured-nation treaty with the United States signed on 15

November 1935. By this time, the Italian invasion of Ethiopia had made all the nations of the world realize the dangers of the military rearmament undertaken by Germany, Italy, and Japan. Canada clearly needed friends, for the Canadian military was in no position to defend it in an age of renewed aggression. The nation spent only pennies per capita on its military. A regular force of 3,000 and the militia were maintained to provide domestic security, but the country had no modern antiaircraft guns, not a single operational aircraft, and enough artillery ammunition for ninety minutes of firing 'at normal rates'.

After 1935 international events moved inexorably towards another conflagration. Canadians displayed an increased interest in external affairs and in foreign policy. In 1937 the first serious debate over external affairs in years occurred in Parliament. The pacifist J.S. Woodsworth moved a resolution of strict Canadian neutrality 'regardless of who the belligerents might be' (quoted in Stacey 1970:195–6). The government's response was that its hands should not be tied. At the 1937 Imperial Conference connected with the coronation of George VI, Mackenzie King refused publicly to make commitments, but privately admitted to British leaders that Canada would again support Britain in a war against European aggressors. In a meeting with Adolph Hitler early in the summer of 1937, King was mesmerized by the Nazi leader's personality and persuaded by his assertions that Germany did not want a war. Fully understanding the threat of war, Canada quietly supported the British policy of appeasement. Such a policy was arguably necessary since Canada was even more ill-prepared than other Western democracies to resume a shooting conflict. Less defensible was Canadian policy towards the victims of the Nazi pogroms in Europe, especially the Jews, as discussed in Chapter 8.

CANADIAN EXTERNAL RELATIONS IN WARTIME, 1939–1945

The greatest value of appeasement, apart from buying a bit of time for reinvigorating long-neglected military establishments, was that it delayed war until only the most ardent pacifist or isolationist could deny its necessity. By the summer of 1939 no informed observer could doubt that the next German aggression would be met firmly by the allied governments. On 10 September Canada responded to the German invasion of Poland by joining Britain and France in a separate declaration of war against Germany. The Canadian government had no intention of rushing troops overseas. Instead, it emphasized a Canadian air training program, economic assistance, and an intermediary's role with the United States, which did not join the Allies until December 1941. Despite official American neutrality, Canada found the Roosevelt administration receptive to mutual defence undertakings. When France fell to the Germans in 1940 and Britain stood virtually alone in Europe against the Nazi war machine, Canada simultaneously supported the British while creeping quietly under the American military umbrella.

From the outset of war, it was obvious that Canada's connections with Britain would be reduced as a consequence of it. After Dunkirk, the Americans sought desperately to prop up the tottering British. Washington's friendship with its northern neighbour made it possible to use Canada to facilitate assistance to the British while still remaining officially neutral. In August 1940

Mackenzie King at the San Francisco Conference, April-June 1945 (National Archives of Canada PA-23272).

Franklin Roosevelt on his own initiative invited Mackenzie King to Ogdensburg, New York, where the two leaders, according to their joint press statement, 'agreed that a Permanent Joint Board on Defence shall be set up at once by the two countries'. Canada could serve not only as a conduit to Britain, but with its economy legally able to gear up for wartime production, could assist in American rearmament. Shortly after Ogdensburg, the Americans sent the British fifty destroyers in return for long leases on military bases within the British empire, including Newfoundland. Since that island had surrendered its Dominion status in 1933 as an alternative to bankruptcy and was now technically a British colony, its government was not consulted about the deal. In April 1941 Canadian-American cooperation was advanced by the Hyde Park Declaration, which consisted of a statement that 'each country should provide the other with defence articles which it is best able to produce, and above all, produce quickly, and that production programmes should be coordinated to this end' (Cuff and Granatstein 1977:Appendix A). The Americans ordered military equipment made in Canada under a program using American technology and money. Until the Americans were legally at war and even beyond that date, the Canadian production would prove quite useful.

Prime Minister King and his advisers seemed reasonably satisfied—most of the time—with Canada's role as a secondary power under the tutelage of Winston Churchill's Britain and Franklin Roosevelt's United States. Canada had difficulty gaining information about many high-level decisions, but never pushed for access to the inner corridors of power. It did try for representation on middle-level coordinating bodies, such as the Munitions Assignment Board, the Combined Production and Resources Board, and the Combined Food Board. It also insisted that it deserved to be fully represented on any formal international organizations, such as the United Nations Relief and Rehabilitation Administration, which was formed in 1943. A Canadian rationale for these efforts was developed at the Department of External Affairs in the spring of that year. Called 'functionalism', it expressed a Canadian posture to international organizations that continued well into the 1960s. Canada insisted that authority in world affairs be neither concentrated solely in the hands of a few superpowers nor distributed equally among states regardless of size. Instead, 'representation on international bodies should be determined on a functional basis so as to permit the participation of those countries which have the greatest stake in the particular subject under examination.' Along with functionalism went multilateralism, another governing principle of Canadian diplomacy for generations. Multilateralism insisted on Canadian involvement in multination arrangements rather than bilateral partnerships with nations that would inevitably seek to dominate it. Both functionalism and multilateralism led to Canada's interest in the United Nations. The Canadian delegation at the 1945 San Francisco Conference, which drafted the UN charter, consisted of a veritable Who's Who of Canadian mandarins and diplomats. The Canadians made some major contributions to the Charter's ultimate acceptance as an international document. Most important, they fully supported the notion that security issues were no more critical than economic and social ones in establishing any new basis for world peace.

THE COLD WAR

By 1945, Canada was probably already too deeply enmeshed in its linkages with the United States ever to cast them aside. Great Britain, financially strapped, was not likely to provide much of a counterweight. Canadian involvement in the cold war was almost inescapable. There were numerous signs in the latter years of the war that the Russians and the Americans were the emergent world superpowers, eager to carve up the world into respective spheres of influence. Countries like Canada found themselves virtually excluded from the process of peacemaking with the defeated enemies, as well as from most of the significant diplomatic manoeuvring of the postwar period. Canada quickly withdrew from Europe after 1945, chiefly because it was not being treated in a manner commensurate with its contribution. As a result of the war, Canada substantially increased its overseas diplomatic contacts, with twenty-five posts abroad in 1944 and thirty-six by 1947, but it hardly improved its international position. Towards the close of the war Canada tried to create some diplomatic distance from the Americans in their continual arm-wrestling with the Russians, but the notorious Gouzenko affair made it difficult for Ottawa to remain sympathetic with the Russians.

Igor Gouzenko (1919–82) was an obscure cipher clerk in the Russian Embassy in Ottawa. In September 1945 he brought to the RCMP material that demonstrated how the Russians had organized a spy ring in Canada during the war. Nowadays spying is taken for granted, but at the time, Gouzenko's information and the subsequent arrests of Canadian citizens (including one Member of Parliament) were absolutely shocking. Canada did not exchange ambassadors again with the Russians until after 1953. In public opinion polls in 1946 Canadians proved far more willing than people in other nations to believe that Russia sought to dominate the world. The Gouzenko business would also send shock waves across the Western world, for loose ends from the files made it apparent that the Russians had not merely suborned Canadians. Moreover, the tight security connected with research on atomic energy carried on in Montreal had been breached. The Russians had received secret information that may have aided them in developing their own atomic bomb in 1949. With the two superpowers both possessing nuclear capability, the stand-off that characterized the cold war began in earnest. Unlike the British and French, the Canadian government declared its refusal to use nuclear power for military purposes.

Economic considerations impelled Canada in the same inevitable direction as the nuclear stand-off. Prime Minister King was leery of a complete economic integration proposed by the Americans late in the war—and supported by many of his own civil servants—but Canada and the United States became closer trading partners than ever before. Moreover, when the American Congress approved the Marshall Plan early in 1948—by which the United States proposed to rebuild war-torn Europe with unrestricted gifts of money and goods—Canada was forced to do something. If European reconstruction was limited solely to American goods, Canadian trade would shrink to nothing. Canada needed market access into the American program, permission for Europe to use American money to buy Canadian goods. The US readily agreed. King used North Atlantic security as a way out of continental free trade. A security treaty would not only deflect reciprocity but, as a multilateral arrangement, might provide a much-needed international counterbalance against American military domination. The Americans were not enthusiastic about a multilateral arrangement for North Atlantic security, but the Canadians pressed hard. Some Canadian diplomats even wanted non-Atlantic Commonwealth countries admitted, and Escott Reid (b. 1905), the deputy undersecretary of state for external affairs, sought a treaty that encompassed social and economic issues as well. The Americans ultimately accepted the North Atlantic Treaty's military and security provisions, particularly the centralization of command under what would inevitably be an American general. They quietly scuttled other aspects of the alliance.

THE SEARCH FOR MIDDLE-POWER STATUS

By the time NATO was established in 1949, the cold war had extended beyond Europe into Asia, where a communist government headed by Chou En-lai had taken over China. Communism made gains in other places like Indochina and Korea, which had been partitioned after the war. The United States always saw these communist governments as mere extensions of international communism rather than as movements of legitimate national liberation. In 1950 North Korea invaded American-supported South Korea. The Americans took advantage of a temporary Soviet boycott of the Security Council of the United Nations to invoke universal collective security. The Canadian government was in a quandary. It had neither a peacetime military nor enthusiasm about collective security under the American aegis. Eventually a Canadian Army Special Force of 20,000 volunteers served in Korea, suffering 1,557 casualties and 312 fatalities. Most of the Canadians were involved after the Chinese had intervened on behalf of North Korea. Canada was more eager than the United States for an armistice, but usually supported the Americans in public.

Korea's chief effect was to pressure further for a military build-up. By 1953 the defence budget stood at nearly $2 billion, up tenfold since 1947. Public opinion in the 1950s consistently supported rearmament. The policy makers at the Department of External Affairs did their best to give Canada an autonomous international presence, developing a Canadian reputation for sending small numbers of soldiers to trouble spots to supervise international agencies and to monitor local conditions. This peacekeeping occurred in Indochina and the Middle East, especially Cyprus. The nation's standing reached its high point in 1957 when Lester B. Pearson won the Nobel Peace Prize for his efforts to end the 1956 hostilities in Suez. Pearson, with American support, found a way for Britain and France to back out of an impossible situation created by their ill-conceived invasion of Egypt to protect the Suez Canal. Canada had earned its place among the 'middle powers', a characterization that became popular with Canada's international-relations specialists at the same time that it flattered the nation's pretensions. But the world changed rapidly after Suez, and middle-power status altered with events.

THE RETREAT FROM INTERNATIONALISM

Part of the gradual change in Canada's place in the world was a result of technology. When, in 1953, the USSR added a hydrogen bomb to its nuclear ar-senal, Canadians became even more conscious than before that their nation sat uneasily between the two nuclear giants. Everyone's attention turned to air defence. Canada expanded the RCAF and began development of the famed CF-105 (the Avro Arrow). The United States pushed for increased electronic surveillance in the Arctic. In 1955 Canada agreed to allow the Americans to construct at their own expense a series of northern radar posts called the Distant Early Warning (or DEW) line. The Americans also pressed for an integrated bilateral air-defence system, the North American Air Defense Command (NORAD), which was agreed to by the Diefenbaker government soon after it took office in 1957. Diefenbaker's administration simultaneously gave way on the big principles to the Americans, while balking over the unpleasant consequences and details. Diefenbaker, moreover, was thoroughly detested by American President John F. Kennedy, who referred to 'the Chief' as one of the few men he had ever totally despised. Three related issues—the decision to scrap the Avro Arrow, the acceptance of American Bomarc-B missiles on Canadian soil, and the government's reaction to the Cuban Missile Crisis of 1962—suggest the government's problems.

When Diefenbaker terminated the Avro Arrow project early in 1959, he did so for sound fiscal reasons. The plane had no prospective international market and would be inordinately expensive to make only for Canadian needs. The prime minister justified his decision in terms of changing military technology and strategy. An aircraft to intercept bombers would soon be obsolete, said Dief, and what Canada needed were missiles obtainable from the Friendly Giant. It turned out that Canada still needed fighters, however, buying some very old F101 Voodoos from the Americans. By cancelling Canada's principal technological breakthrough into the world of big military hardware in return for an agreement whereby parts of equipment purchased by Canada from the American defence industry would be assembled in Canada, Diefenbaker probably accepted reality. But the Bomarc-B missile was armed with a nuclear warhead, and Canada had a non-nuclear policy. Diefenbaker thus refused to allow the Bomarcs to be properly armed, erroneously insisting that they could be effective with non-nuclear warheads. The question took on new urgency in 1962 after President Kennedy confronted the USSR over the installation of Russian missile bases in Cuba. As Soviet ships carrying the missiles cruised westward towards Cuba and Kennedy threatened war if they did not turn back, NORAD automatically ordered DEFCON 3, the state of readiness just short of war. Neither Diefenbaker nor his ministers were consulted—much less informed—about this decision. The prime minister was furious that a megalomaniac American president could, in effect, push the button that would destroy Canada.

An artist's drawing of a CF 105 Avro Arrow (National Archives of Canada PA-111546).

In the end Nikita Khrushchev backed down in the fearsome game of nuclear chicken, but Cuba changed Canadian public opinion, which had tended to be against nuclear armament. The crisis provoked considerable media discussion of the government's prevarications and inconsistencies over nuclear and defence policy. NATO made it quite clear that Canada was part of the nuclear system. Liberal leader Lester Pearson announced that the Liberals would stand by the nation's nuclear commitments even if the government that had made them would not. There was no point in housing nuclear weapons on Canadian soil if they could not be instantly deployed in the event of a crisis. Such defence blunders did Diefenbaker no good in the 1962 election. By January 1963 defence issues had reduced his cabinet to conflicting factions. The minority government fell shortly afterwards. Traditional Canadian nationalism as practised by John Diefenbaker was simply not compatible with the missile age.

The returning Liberals, who regained power in 1963 under Pearson, spent most of the 1960s attempting to implement the integration of Canada's armed forces, chiefly on the grounds that duplication of resources and command structures was an expensive luxury the nation could not afford. A unified Canadian military would be both leaner and meaner, capable of remaining within budget figures that the nation could afford. The country and its politicians, however, continued their schizophrenic attitudes towards the Canadian military, its foreign obligations, and Canada's overseas role. Canada wanted to control its own destiny, which probably required a neutral stance internationally. Neutrality in international affairs would cost even more than the American and NATO alliances, however, so everyone pretended that Canada could hold the line on military spending and still honour its commitments through administrative reform.

Despite Prime Minister Pearson's high profile as a successful world diplomat, his governments were not distinguished for their triumphs in the international arena. In fairness to Pearson, the world was changing in other ways not sympathetic to Canada's self-proclaimed role as a middle power. After 1960 the United Nations General Assembly opened its doors to dozens of Third World countries, most of them recently emerged from colonial status and quite hostile to the Western democracies. The new complexities of politics and expectations at the assembly, and in the various collateral UN organizations, worked against a highly developed and industrialized nation such as Canada—populated chiefly by the descendants of White Europeans—which also happened to be a junior partner of the United States. In UN bodies Canadian diplomats found themselves in the embarrassing position of defending the country's internal policy, particularly towards Aboriginal peoples, in the face of criticisms of racism and insensitivity to human rights. Canada was not in the same league as South Africa, perhaps, but its record on human rights was a hard one to explain internationally. At the same time, the success of the European Economic Community (first established in 1958) made western European nations more important international players, while Japan had succeeded in restoring its industrial position. As a result, Canada became less important in the league table of industrial nations at the same time that it became unable to lead the Third World.

It was not only the configuration of world politics that had altered by the 1960s. So had the policy of the United States. President Kennedy and his successor, Lyndon B. Johnson, were actually more hard-bitten and confrontational Cold Warriors than their predecessors, Truman and Eisenhower. The latter had been extremely embarrassed in 1960 when the Russians shot down an American U-2 spy plane and captured its pilot, Francis Gary Powers. Kennedy authorized dirty tricks by the CIA in foreign countries with no compunction or apology when they were exposed. His only regret about the abortive 1961 Bay of Pigs invasion of Cuba by US-backed Cuban exiles, for example, was that it had failed. Most important, however, both Kennedy and Johnson permitted their governments to become ever more deeply involved in the quagmire of Southeast Asia. Like Korea, Indochina had been partitioned into communist and non-communist states after the Second World War. When the French government proved incapable of retaining its colonial control against armed 'insurgents' from the Democratic Republic of Vietnam (North Vietnam, governed by Ho Chi Minh), Canada in 1954 had become involved in attempts at international control. It served as one of three members, with Poland and India, of a joint commission. Canada was actually eager to participate, as part of its middle-power pretensions in the world. The 1954 commission set the pattern for the next twenty years: one Iron Curtain nation, one Western ally of the United States, one neutral power, with votes often going against Canada as the American supporter. From the outset Canada had deceived itself into believing that it had a free hand to carry out its work without either upsetting the Americans or appearing to act merely as a lackey of the United States.

When the American administration gradually escalated both US involvement and the shooting war in Vietnam after 1963, Canada's position became increasingly anomalous, both on the commission and outside it. Lester Pearson was still hoping to mediate in April 1965 when he used the occasion of a speech in Philadelphia to suggest that the American government might pause in its bombing of North Vietnam to see if a negotiated settlement was possible. He was soon shown the error of his ways in no uncertain terms. In a private meeting with Lyndon Johnson shortly thereafter, the American president shook Pearson by his lapels and criticized Canadian presumptuousness with Texas profanity. Vietnam certainly contributed to a new Canadian mood in the later 1960s, both in Ottawa and on the main streets of the nation. Canadians now sought to distance themselves from the policies of the 'Ugly Americans', although never by open withdrawal from the American defence umbrella.

After Pierre Trudeau succeeded Pearson in April 1968, an undeclared and never coordinated policy of retreat from middle-power pretensions was accelerated. Trudeau had long been critical of Canada's foreign and defence policies. Soon after his accession to office, he initiated formal reviews, which the departments of national defence and external affairs found most threatening. The prime minister was particularly eager to raise 'fundamental questions', such as whether there was really a Russian threat to world order, or 'Will the US sacrifice Europe and NATO before blowing up the world?' (quoted in Granatstein and Bothwell 1990:17). The bureaucrats were not comfortable with such questions, nor were several of Trudeau's cabinet colleagues. Trudeau had a reputation as an internationalist, but he disliked the military, and ultimately proved much more comfortable with domestic matters than external ones. For Trudeau, protecting the sovereignty of Canadian territory was far more important than international peacekeeping. Defence budgets were cut and active Canadian involvement in NATO was pared to the lowest limits of allied acceptability. The best-known armed action by the Canadian military was in occupying Quebec during the October Crisis of 1970. In 1973 Canada sent a large military mission to Vietnam to serve on a revised International Commission for Control and Supervision. Its purpose was to allow the Americans to withdraw from that troubled corner of the world, but the commission was not able to act effectively. The Trudeau government called it home in mid-1973. Canada was no longer a self-defined middle power. It had no clear conception of its place or role in world affairs.

INTERNATIONAL DRIFTING

Canada's problem in the world was basically simple. Its economic indicators entitled it to major-league status, but its population was small and its close relationship with the United States made it a minor-league subsidiary player. The Canadian image abroad was as perplexing as its policies. On the one hand, it continued its habit of preaching from on high to nations that did not regard themselves as morally inferior. Catching Canada in hypocritical moral contradictions became a favourite international game. On the other hand, Canada continued to be one of the most favoured destinations for immigrants from around the world. Ordinary people accepted that life was better in Canada. Indeed, surveys regularly listed Canada at the top of the international standard-of-living table.

Whatever the Department of External Affairs was or was not doing, Canadians themselves became citizens of the world in a way that would have been incomprehensible to earlier generations. By the early 1970s, relatively cheap airplane tickets to go anywhere in the world had become an accepted part of life. In the 1960s kids had travelled the world, carrying backpacks festooned with the Canadian flag and sleeping in youth hostels. Now their parents followed them, staying in hotels that were just like those at home. Almost every Canadian family had at least one member with photographs of a major overseas expedition. Cheap air fares also brought relatives from abroad to Canada. All this travel combined with new immigration to make Canada an increasingly cosmopolitan place to live. Canadians drank less beer and more wine, much of it imported. They ate in restaurants with exotic cuisines, learned to cook similar food at home, and insisted on their availability at their local supermarkets.

Pierre Trudeau's attempt to reorient Canadian foreign policy met with limited success. He managed to reduce Canada's military commitment to NATO and to reduce the size of Canada's armed forces. In 1972 the government produced a policy document that recommended a 'Third Option': less dependence upon the Americans, but if Canada moved away from the Americans, where would it go? The obvious answer was to Europe. Canada had waited too long and had become too closely identified with (not to mention integrated in) the American economy. The fizzle of the European initiative was followed by a similar effort in Asia, with perhaps slightly better success. After 1975, however, Canada returned to closer ties with the United States. Aside from perennial concern over trade figures and the occasional international conference attended by the prime minister, Canada's relations outside North America assumed a very low profile during the 1980s. Canadians expected precious little from foreign policy initiatives. The Free Trade Agreement with the Americans merely confirmed what everyone knew.

The key international developments of the 1980s were totally beyond Canada's control. The first was *glasnost*, the process of liberation from the repression of communism in the Soviet Union. The Soviet regime had been opening up for decades, but no one was prepared for the rapid changes of the later 1980s when the Russians made it clear that they were no longer prepared to prop up unpopular governments in eastern Europe and wanted to shift their own internal priorities in what appeared to be capitalistic and democratic directions. The most obvious symbol of collapse was the razing of the Berlin Wall, which was demolished, along with the government of East Germany, in November 1989, clearing the way for German reunification in late 1990. This event ultimately permitted Canada to close its last two bases on German soil in 1993. The demise of communism did not occur without difficulty. In many of the Iron Curtain nations, it turned out that the communist regime had been the only force supporting unity and stability, whatever the price. Movements of national liberation tore apart the USSR itself, as well as other ethnically complex constructions, such as Yugoslavia. Civil war among Serbs, Croats, and Muslims in Bosnia became an international concern. The transition to a capitalistic economy was so painful that many citizens of the old Soviet bloc began voting in free elections for their former communist masters. By the mid-1990s it was clear that the cold war was indeed dead. What would replace it as a principal of international dynamics was another matter entirely.

The elimination of communist repression did not necessarily save the world for democracy. As if to demonstrate the fragility of international peace, in the summer of 1990 the Iraqi army invaded Kuwait, one of the small independent oil-rich principalities on the Persian Gulf. The world witnessed the unusual spectacle of American-Russian cooperation at the United Nations, and elsewhere, in opposition to Saddam Hussein's move. With Russian approval, President George Bush sent American forces to the Persian Gulf. Canada contributed three ancient destroyers to the international force. In some ways the collapse of the cold war temporarily opened up new ways for Canadians to offer their services to the world. Canadian peacekeepers were in constant demand around the world, ultimately serving in trouble spots like Somalia and Bosnia with a singular lack of effectiveness. Whether the 800 Canadian troops serving under UN auspices in Haiti would do any better was another matter. Canada also flirted with the dangers of diplomatic isolation in 1995, as its attempts to enforce limitations on offshore fishing led to an open confrontation with the Spaniards. Fortunately, there was enough support for the Canadian position behind the scenes to discourage Spanish militancy. The crisis was resolved peacefully.

Lack of success, lack of funding, and some nasty scandals reduced the credibility of Canada's military to the point that by 1996 the nation could fully anticipate that Canada's armed forces would no longer be serving anywhere in the world but at home. A total withdrawal from Europe had been delayed by peacekeeping in Yugoslavia, but in early 1996 Canada announced it was acting unilaterally. Somalia and Bosnia were both public-relations disasters. In the former, supposedly highly disciplined Canadian soldiers brutalized the locals. In the latter, Canadian peacekeepers seemed unable to accomplish anything positive, while often being held as impotent hostages by the warring factions. Only Haiti was left, but whether 'propping up a legitimately elected government' was actually peacekeeping was another matter. The Liberal government of Jean Chrétien cancelled several large orders for new hardware the military commanders deemed necessary to keep the forces competitive. Public exposure of Canadian soldiers' racism and brutality towards one another did little for either image or morale. One battalion of paratroopers, the Canadian Airborne, was ultimately totally disbanded.

The disarray of the military seemed symptomatic of Canada's international posture. The idealism of earlier days was now replaced by failure and incompetence.

Freefalling Towards the Twenty-first Century

❧

If one listened to the journalists and the media pundits, Canada and Canadians lived in a constant state of crisis and turmoil in the 1990s, lurching from one emergency to the next without any road-map to the future. While such may well be the case, in this view there is little perspective. The 'news' almost by definition has no sense of history. Certainly Canada was not unique in its problems, which almost without exception were occurring regularly around the world. Even the potential disintegration of the Canadian Confederation was hardly unique. Movements of national liberation were everywhere, and as Bosnia, the USSR, and Sri Lanka, to name but a few troubled nations, suggested, at least in Canada the conflicting sides were not yet armed camps. Moreover, despite the nation's well-publicized problems, most of the population of the remainder of the world would have probably traded their situation for that of the average Canadian. Canada continued to rank at or near the top of everyone's world standard-of-living table. As far as the absence of direction was concerned, while this condition prevailed in the 1990s, it had equally applied *at the time* in every past era. With hindsight, historians can offer some notion of what the direction was and what the ultimate outcome would be. We can see an inexorable line from the Great Depression through the Second World War to the social service state, for example. Those who live in the midst of the maelstrom, however, can have little sense of the eventual resolution of the unresolved issues and paradoxes of the moment. Nor can the participants in the chaos of the moment tell whether the resolution will be progressive or retrogressive, apocalyptic or gradual. About all we can say with assurance is that the future—as it always has been—is uncertain. That fact is not by itself a crisis.

POLITICS

At the federal level, the major political development of the mid-1990s was the triumph of the Liberal Party in the 1993 election, combined with the absolute collapse of the Progressive Conservative Party and its replacement by two openly antagonistic regional parties. National political parties had failed abysmally at the polls before (the Liberals in 1918, the Tories in 1940). Regional parties (such as the Progressive Party) had temporarily risen to prominence.

Jean Chrétien talks to reporters in Ottawa, 21 December 1993 (Canapress Photo Service/Chuck Mitchell).

What was new about the election of 1993, of course, was the emergence in the House of Commons of two regional parties of equal strength, the Reform Party and the *Bloc Québécois*, each committed to irreconcilable policies and their combined seats unequal to the large Liberal majority. These two regional parties both tended to draw their strength from voters who had previously supported the Tories. At the same time, the Liberals did win a major victory, but without any evidence of new policies.

By the close of 1992 it was clear that Prime Minister Brian Mulroney's popularity ratings, consistently lower than any other Canadian prime minister had ever previously experienced, were not likely to improve with time. At the inevitable leadership convention that ensued in June 1993, Kim Campbell (b. 1947) was chosen to lead the party on the second ballot. Campbell, a British Columbian who had originally been associated with the Social Credit party in that province, thus became Canada's first female prime minister. Although a relative newcomer to federal politics, she had more experience than Brian Mulroney at the time of selection. She had held two major cabinet portfolios beginning in 1989. The Tories apparently hoped that her gender and her

Preston Manning, leader of the Reform Party, 2 December 1987 (Canapress Photo Service).

refreshing 'candour' would lead the country to see Campbell as a fresh face, although her credentials in French Canada were hardly up to those of the man she had beaten out (Jean Charest of Quebec). Some observers, particularly among feminists, argued that Campbell had been chosen as a 'sacrificial lamb' to bear the brunt of the inevitable election defeat about to occur. In any case, like John Turner a decade earlier, Campbell inherited the enormous unpopularity of her predecessor. She had little time to establish a new government image before having to call an election. Jean Chrétien's Liberals were in some ways well prepared for the contest, certainly financially, although the party platform was somewhat schizophrenic, committed to carrying on the welfare state while balancing the budget and reducing the deficit. Chrétien was hardly a brilliant campaigner, but he proved adequate to the task, much aided by a series of blunders by Campbell and her advisers. The worst occurred shortly before the end of the campaign, when Campbell was unable to distance herself quickly enough from a negative political ad campaign suggesting that Chrétien was handicapped. Negative campaigning in the media had become common in the United States, but this one backfired by generating popular sympathy for the Liberal leader. Submerged under the national media attention given to Campbell and Chrétien were a series of fascinating local races featuring a variety of conservative third parties, of which the Reform Party and the *Bloc Québécois* proved on the day to be the most attractive to the voters. The Liberals

Lucien Bouchard, 20 December 1995 (Canapress Photo Service/Paul Chiasson).

did not so much receive a mandate as triumph over an otherwise badly divided field headed by the singularly inept Tories.

The Reform Party had been organized in October of 1987 by (Ernest) Preston Manning, son of the great Alberta Social Credit leader, Ernest Manning. Its backbone was in traditional Alberta and British Columbia Socred constituencies, but it had some appeal as far east as Ontario among retired Canadians and first-time young voters. Manning was a professional management consultant. He was a colourless speaker, but his lack of charisma was somewhat redeemed by a sense of humour and irony seldom seen among major political leaders, as well as by a wry sense of self-deprecation. The Reform Party stood four-square for the traditional, often populist, values of the Anglo-Canadian west. It wanted to cut federal spending, to reform Parliament to make it more responsive to the popular will, and to provide for the equal treatment of provinces and citizens alike. The party had no time for the sovereigntist pretensions of Quebec or for French-Canadian culture. Reform liked multiculturalism little better than biculturalism. Manning indicated his willingness to contemplate new limitations on immigration to Canada, although he was not pressed hard on the issue.

As for the *Bloc Québécois*, it was associated both within and without Quebec with its major campaign issue, the separation of that province from the Canadian Confederation, and with its leader, Lucien Bouchard. Born in St-Coeur de Marie in 1938, Bouchard had been a lawyer in Chicoutimi before his appointment as Canadian ambassador to France in 1985 by the Mulroney government. In the election of 1988, he had run as a successful PC candidate, but had left the party before the 1992 referendum on the Charlottetown Accord to sit as an independent committed to a sovereign Quebec. In terms of their responses to him, Bouchard was an interesting example of some curious cultural differences between French Canadians and Anglo-Canadians. While many *Québécois* found Bouchard compelling and charismatic in the traditional pattern of *le chef* (the best example of which had been Maurice Duplessis), anglophones within and without the province were not attracted to him in the slightest.

Not only were the PCs—soon led by Jean Charest (b. 1958)— reduced to a mere two seats on 25 October 1993, but both they and the NDP (with nine seats) lost official standing in the House of Commons. This loss of standing was particularly serious for the NDP, which had relied heavily on Commons financial support for its Ottawa infrastructure. With fifty-four seats to Reform's fifty-three, the *Bloc Québécois* became the official opposition, offering the somewhat anomalous spectacle of 'Her Majesty's Loyal Opposition' committed to the destruction of the institution in which it was participating. The Liberals had a pretty easy time in most respects, since the opposition was unable to agree on very much and lacked numerical strength anyway. In power, the Chrétien government continued to exhibit the schizophrenia of its campaign platform, simultaneously trying to reduce federal expenditure and the deficit without doing serious damage to any of the major social programs—or its image. A major review of the entire welfare and unemployment system, headed by Lloyd Axworthy (b. 1939), ended up making essentially cosmetic changes to the system designed to make it more difficult to remain for long periods on social assistance or to use welfare to subsidize seasonal employment. The government predictably sought to save money by cutting deeply into cultural programs and the military, and by reducing the amount of transfer payments to the provinces for health and higher education. As the time for another election approached, the Liberals had precious little in positive accomplishment to take to the nation, however.

Developments at the provincial level confirmed the split personality of the electorate. The public was concerned about the size of the deficits and was unalterably opposed to higher taxes, but at the same time was not enthusiastic about deep cuts into social programs. Whether these sentiments were held by the same people or by different groups of voters was not clear. In Alberta, the Tory government of Ralph Klein (b. 1942) won a big election victory in 1993 on a platform of realistic government budgeting. Klein carried through with major budget cuts, although because of Alberta's relative wealth, these probably hurt less than they would have in a province like Newfoundland. In Ontario, the NDP government of Bob Rae (b. 1939), which had not succeeded in controlling finances and had run afoul of the province's trade union movement in its attempts to cut the costs of its civil service, was demolished in 1995 by the Tories led by Mike Harris (b. 1945). The chief campaign issue was government spending. When Harris actually began to cut spending, however, the cries of outrage were substantial. In Ontario, as elsewhere, there was some evidence from the polls that Canadians were actually prepared to pay higher taxes to preserve some of their social benefits, particularly in the health care sector. The reasons for the 1994 electoral victory of the *Parti Québécois*—or the mood of the electorate in that province—were, as usual, clouded if not obfuscated by the sovereignty issue. The Bourassa government had not controlled spending, but the PQ did not present itself in the campaign as the party of fiscal restraint. What was evident everywhere in Canada was that no politician or political party had any fresh ideas for resolving the fiscal dilemma.

THE CONSTITUTION

Any hope that the referendum defeat of the Charlottetown Accord had put a lid on constitutional matters was ended by the 1994 PQ victory in Quebec. Led by Jacques Parizeau (b. 1930), the PQ moved inexorably towards another Quebec referendum on sovereignty. Parizeau had initially opposed sovereignty association, but gradually came to see it as a way to satisfy some soft nationalists. Realizing that one of the major problems with the 1980 referendum had been the uncertainty regarding both the question and consequent action, Parizeau sought to tie down the new question. He had legislation passed defining the terms. In June 1995 he and two other separatist leaders, *Parti Action Démocratique* leader Mario Dumont (an ex-Liberal who advocated sovereignty association) and *Bloc Québécois* leader Lucien Bouchard, agreed on a plan. Quebecers would be asked to authorize the Quebec government to open negotiations with Ottawa on sovereignty association. If the province gave a mandate and if an agreement with Canada was not reached within a year, Quebec would unilaterally declare sovereignty. The cooperation of all three leaders was intended to prevent fears that the Quebec government would, in Parizeau's words, 'jump the gun' on a declaration of sovereignty. The vote was soon set for 30 October 1995. The official question was 'Do you agree that Quebec should become sovereign, after having made a formal offer to Canada for a new

Economic and Political Partnership, within the scope of the Bill respecting the future of Quebec and of the agreement signed on June 12, 1995?'

In the beginning the federalist (or *Non*) forces seemed to be well in control of the situation. Experts expected the usual ballot bonus for the federalists, who would turn out a higher proportion of their supporters. They also anticipated the usual conservative response to uncertainty. For the most part, Ottawa kept its distance from the campaign, allowing Liberal leader Daniel Johnson to carry the *Non* message to the electorate. The federal strategy was to do as little as possible to fuel the sovereigntist position. Then, with polls showing a marked advantage for the *Non* side, Lucien Bouchard actively entered the fray. Bouchard had only recently recovered from a rare bacterial infection that cost him a leg and nearly his life. He had not been originally expected to be an important campaigner, but the province was clearly not excited by Parizeau and Dumont. Bouchard introduced a new level of emotion into the campaign, simplifying the issues considerably. For many Quebecers, the need to move forward on the constitutional front became the key question in the referendum. When the need for constitutional change rather than the need for sovereignty became the real referendum question, the situation rapidly deteriorated for the federalist forces. What had earlier been a ho-hum campaign suddenly turned into a real barn-burner. At the last minute, Prime Minister Chrétien suggested the panic in Ottawa by offering Quebec concessions, including yet another 'distinct society' constitutional proposal.

Jacques Parizeau speaks to business people while campaigning for the *Oui* side, 3 October 1995 (Canapress Photo Service/Jacques Boissinot).

The vote turned into a real cliff-hanger as virtually every eligible resident of Quebec cast his or her ballot. The final turnout—over 94 per cent of the total electorate—was seldom matched except in police states with compulsory elections. Millions of Canadians remained tuned to their television sets until late in the evening, waiting for the decisive result. Finally, it became clear that the *Non* forces had won a narrow victory. In the end, 2,362,355 Quebecers (or 50.6 per cent) of the total voted *Non*, while 2,308,054 (or 49.4 per cent) voted *Oui*. The young, the francophone, and the Quebecer outside Montreal led the way in voting *Oui*. There were many informal complaints about voting irregularities, but the vote was allowed to stand. Premier (or Prime Minister) Parizeau had prepared a gracious speech of conciliation to accompany a sovereigntist victory. In his bitter acknowledgement of failure on national radio and television, he blamed anglophones and ethnics for thwarting the aspirations of francophone Quebec. As Parizeau spoke, the cameras panned around the crowd of people gathered at *Oui* headquarters. Many were in tears. Parizeau's impulsive attack turned much public opinion against him, even within his own party. Within hours he announced his resignation. In February 1996 he would be officially replaced by Lucien Bouchard.

In the wake of the referendum, the Chrétien government passed a unilateral declaration in the Canadian Parliament that recognized Quebec as a distinct society, but as virtually everyone had come to appreciate, this gesture was too little too late. French Canadians in Quebec had made clear their desire for a new constitutional relationship with Canada. Virtually the only question remaining was whether or not a sovereign Quebec would remain within some sort of Canadian Confederation. Postreferendum polls continued to emphasize that Quebecers wanted to remain within Canada, but not under its present Constitution. Canadians turned to debate the next step in the ongoing constitutional process. One of the most difficult parts of this debate was trying to figure out a process for generating a new constitutional arrangement, since most of the previous ones employed appeared discredited.

Any new constitutional arrangement would have to deal with more than merely the aspirations of Quebec. One of the most important additional items on the agenda for constitutional reform was the First Nations, who wanted the constitutional entrenchment of their conception of Indian self-government. In many ways this demand parallels that of Quebec, which refuses to accept sovereigntism within its jurisdiction. This refusal helps explain the insistence of the Quebec government in early 1996 that 'Quebec is indivisible.' The Constitution Act of 1982, while entrenching the existing Aboriginal and treaty rights of the Indians, had not really come to terms with Indian self-government, chiefly because the First Nations and Ottawa were so far apart on the subject. The Indians have insisted that their government should be based on inherent jurisdiction as a historic right. For many Native peoples, this involves sovereign jurisdiction and the independent right to make laws and institutions for their people and their territory, since these rights were not surrendered with treaties. The militants object to the concept of Indian self-government as an equivalent of municipal government, delegated to the First Nations by those jurisdictions (Ottawa and the provinces) that claim the sovereignty under the Crown and Constitution of Canada. As sovereign governments, Indian governments would deal only as equals with Ottawa, which the Native peoples insist still owes them a heavy debt of financial responsibility. As municipal governments, they would become the agents of the senior governments with only those powers allowed them by those governments. To recognize the First Nations (with their more than 500 bands) as sovereign would certainly be more possible in a Constitution that so accepted Quebec. For many Canadians, however, this recognition would not only further balkanize the country but would create independent jurisdictions within Canada that only benefited from their Canadian affiliation but held no concurrent responsibilities under it.

THE ECONOMY

The Canadian economy had now been running for so long without correcting itself that the new standards of performance had become the norm. In the 1990s some of the traditional indicators were positive for economic growth. Inflation was low, interest rates were low and constantly falling, and the Canadian dollar was lower against other world currencies. The resulting economic growth rate was slow, but constantly upward. Foreign trade continued to be buoyant, although mainly in the resource sector and associated industries. On the other hand, construction starts were stagnant and the sale of new automotive vehicles were lower than had been the case since the early 1980s. The Americans chipped ominously away at the Free Trade Agreement whenever it worked to their disadvantage. The buoyant real estate market of the 1980s was no more, even in the still overheated British Columbia economy. Household debt was up to 89 per cent of disposable income. Most important, official unemployment rates were over 10 per cent nationally, while some of the regional figures were alarming, with rates above the national average east of Ontario and below it from Ontario westward. Official unemployment in Newfoundland in 1994 was 20.4 per cent, and in Quebec 12.2 per cent. These figures, of course, only counted the people still looking for work. Many of those previously employed in dead industries like the Atlantic fishery had simply given up, as had quite a few of the young.

Finding a job was not easy. Keeping one was equally difficult. Downsizing continued to be the order of the day. Governments at all levels were attempting to reduce their work forces, and almost every private enterprise was trying (with some success) to make do with less. Even those who still had their jobs lived in constant fear of the next round of rationalization. As for the rationalizers, there was growing evidence that downsizing was no more self-correcting than other economic strategies. According to hopeful economic theory, when business profits were up substantially, excess profits would be reinvested in expansion. This was at least partly the thinking behind keeping business taxes low in what came to be known as 'Reaganomics', after the American president who had campaigned on this view. What often seemed to be happening in the 1990s, however, was that the increasing profits were simply distributed to the shareholders. Nonetheless, governments hesitated to increase the tax rates.

Perhaps as disturbing as the nagging fear of the chop for those who still had jobs was the absence of recognizable new career growth areas for those seeking to prepare themselves for employment. The education counsellors had virtually run out of suggestions for viable careers. There were still plenty of jobs in the part-time, semiskilled (and low-paid) end of the workforce. 'Working at McDonald's' became the catch-phrase encompassing all such employment, which had no attractive future whatsoever and provided no fringe benefits. The younger generation faced with such employment prospects came to label itself Generation X, the post-baby boomers who, through no fault of their own, had arrived at adulthood after all the decent jobs were taken. These Canadians had little to look forward to. Generation X was both hedonistic and bitter, a volatile combination. The creation of new jobs was high on the wish list for most Canadians, but particularly for the young.

One economic growth area continued in household appliances and equipment. What had once been luxury items now became necessities, and new gadgets were being introduced every day. As had been the case for over a century with household equipment, constant reductions in price through technological innovation made mass marketing possible. In 1980 few homes had microwave ovens. By the mid-1990s over 80 per cent of households owned one. By 1994 more than half of Canadian households possessed a gas barbeque, and over 25 per cent of Canadian homes had some kind of air conditioning. Compact-disc players and home computers had exploded from a standing start in the late 1980s to being in over 50 per cent of households in 1995. Much of the electronic household gadgetry was assembled abroad, providing jobs only on the retail sales and highly technical service ends. At the same time, there was obviously room for employment in computers. Canadians established some reputation for software development. Connected to the enormous expansion of the home computer was the growth of e-mail and the use of computer networks for communication, business and personal. By 1996 the Internet—another communications medium in which Canadians had taken the lead—had become so popular and overloaded that it no longer worked very well. Never designed for mass participation, the Internet had grown without any regulation whatsoever, which was part of its attraction and would increasingly become part of its problem. While there was a future in the computer and the microchip, this was a highly technical business that required special skills and special aptitudes. Business publications were full of stories of successful Canadian entrepreneurialism in the glitzy new technologies, but they never explained how this would translate into large-scale employment for the average Canadian.

The private enterprise philosophy associated with the growth of schools of management at the universities had by the 1990s been operative for nearly twenty years. There was precious little evidence, however, that in the end the economic thinking of this philosophy had produced a more satisfactory economy for most Canadians than had Keynesianism. Unemployment still remained high nationally and even higher in certain regions and among certain age groups. Like earlier economic pundits, the private enterprisers insisted that their theories had not yet been given a fair chance, but few Canadians wanted to take the gamble.

CANADIAN SOCIETY

While all the symptoms of social morbidity continued their alarming progress, perhaps the most disturbing trends occurred at the opposite ends of the life cycle, particularly among the aging. The first of the baby boomers were coming up to (early) retirement, soon to be followed by the deluge. That the system was really not ready for this event became increasingly clear. In 1995 the Canadian Institute of Actuaries (CIA) reported that in 1992 retired Canadians (numbering 19 per cent of the working-age population) had paid $9 billion in taxes and received $54.4 billion in public funds in a variety of forms, including medical treatment. By 2030 the percentage of retired Canadians would be up to 39 per cent of those eligible to work. The payout at 1992 rates would be well beyond the capacity of the system to absorb. The present system worked only because the demand upon it had not yet grown sufficiently. The CIA concluded that the present system of social insurance was not 'sustainable in their current form. Contributions will rise. Benefits will be cut; retirement ages deferred; universality curtailed.' Surveys suggested that many Canadians had begun to appreciate the difficulties, although most were still confused and few had any solutions. According to one survey, most Canadians feared that the Canada Pension Plan would be unable to look after their retirement, but fewer than 15 per cent had more than $10,000 put away somewhere apart from their CPP pensions. The age at which most Canadians still expected to retire was fifty-nine, although the experts and the politicians were now suggesting that such an age was simply a pipedream for most people.

Retirement pensions were only part of the problem. The other major concern was health care, the cost of which continued to spiral despite desperate efforts by provincial governments to bring it under control through cost cutting and privatization. Per capita health care expenditure (in constant 1986 dollars) had progressively and annually increased from $1,257.25 in 1975 to $1,896.27 in 1993. The proportion of gross domestic product devoted to health care had gone up from 7.1 per cent in 1975 to 10.1 per cent in 1993. Although these Canadian figures were not as alarming as corresponding American ones—the American proportion of GDP given to health care had increased from 8.4 per cent in 1975 to 14.4 per cent in 1993—they suggested an ultimate financial crisis if not capped somehow. Much of the increasing cost involved health care for the elderly, and life expectancy continued to advance. The baby boom and increased life expectancy together produced the demographic prospect of ever larger numbers of elderly people, obviously making increasing demands on the health care system.

While provincial governments constantly closed hospitals and the number of beds available within them, Canadians began to debate hard questions, such as the extent to which the terminally ill should be offered the expensive treatment that medical science now had at its disposal. Even if the elderly were not given expensive treatment, their increasing numbers provided a housing problem. Only one out of every four Canadians expected to have to look after his or her parents in old age, which was far too low. But even if all Canadians took in their still functioning elderly, the numbers of those requiring extensive care beyond the home were bound to increase enormously. Dealing with seniors was clearly the most important problem facing the social insurance system, particularly given the national sense that deficit financing was already too high. One could only sympathize with a younger generation, unable to establish itself in a career, but still being asked to finance the postretirement years of their elders. According to one study by the Research for Public Policy, younger Canadians would have to pay increasingly more in taxes than they would ever receive in social benefits to maintain the present structure, which was not only 'unsustainable' but 'immoral'.

CANADIAN CULTURE

Economic restraint hit hard at Canada's cultural industries, almost all of which had relied heavily on public subsidies. Cut-backs were inevitably accompanied by exhortations for financial responsibility and the search for assistance in the private rather than the public sector. To the mid-1990s, much of the slack was taken up by cost-cutting and private fund-raising. Ways of raising money became increasingly imaginative and required far more attention from cultural administrators. Too much of the increased revenue, said some critics, came from state-run gambling and privately run lotteries. Public involvement in fund-raising was not necessarily a bad thing, for those in the community who helped raise money were, in the process, bonded to the enterprise. Few of the main-line establishment enterprises in dance, classical music, and the theatre were actually forced out of existence, although everyone complained that there was no room for experimentation and risk taking in the new financial climate. A few more specialized operations bit the dust. Nevertheless, despite the constant cries of crisis, the private sector did seem able to fill most of the gaps in the establishment world of *haute* culture.

Curiously enough, popular culture seemed more genuinely affected by fiscal restraint than did *haute* culture. The long-standing decline of the Canadian Broadcasting Corporation continued unabated, and Parliament carried on with annual cuts to the corporation's operating budget. Across the corporation as a whole, regional production was the first to suffer. The CBC's problems were many. Not all services ought to have been equally in trouble, however. The radio services were generally acknowledged to be the best in the world. Radio Canada's television operation in French consistently outdrew the opposition, producing almost all of the most-watched television programs in Quebec. The sink-hole was English-language television, which had never been able to carve out a satisfactory niche for itself in an increasingly complex viewing world. The introduction of a variety of new Canadian-based cable networks in 1994 further eroded the CBC's position as a Canadian venue. Few seemed willing to scrap the television service, however. Another government commission, this one chaired by Pierre Juneau, recommended an increase in Canadian content, the end of commercial advertising, and additional revenue from taxes on the competing services. CBC TV would no longer have to compete in the world of commercial television, but would instead become a Canadian version of America's Public Broadcasting Corporation, appealing to the higher viewing instincts of the public. There was no certainty with the acceptance of these recommendations. What was definite was that the corporation would have to do with less. Huge staff cuts were announced, with more to follow. Like employees of almost every other enterprise in Canada, those at the CBC could only look forward to further downsizing.

Whether the problems of professional sports in Canada were caused by budgetary restraint in the public sector was another matter, although it was clear that sports teams in Canada could no longer be sustained by massive infusions of indirect aid from the public purse, often in the form of arena facilities. This changing attitude combined with other factors to provide disaster. One was an international market in player salaries with which Canadian teams could not successfully compete. The Canadian Football League, faced with escalating costs and declining attendance in the later 1980s and early 1990s, had

Winnipeg Jets captain Keith Tkachuck (*left*) and team mate Eddie Olczyk say goodbye to Jets fans in Winnipeg, 28 April 1996 (Canapress Photo Service/Joe Bryksa).

responded aggressively to its problems by expanding directly into the United States. This strategy proved absolutely disastrous. The new American franchises all folded after a season or two, leaving behind them nothing but confusion and a trail of debt. As for hockey, American integration finally caught up with it. The Quebec Nordiques left Canada for Colorado in 1995, and the Winnipeg Jets announced their departure for Phoenix, Arizona, early in 1996. Many experts calculated that the Edmonton Eskimos, Calgary Flames, and Ottawa Senators could not be far behind. The National Hockey League, now run by high-powered American business executives, had decided that Canadian franchises in smaller cities were not sufficiently profitable. The League refused to share television revenue equally and made impossible demands in terms of the facilities and financing of arenas, thus literally forcing the franchises to move to greener pastures.

While in the larger scheme of things one pattern of historical development was cyclical, there were few analysts who thought that Canada could ever return to the optimistic prosperity of the 1950s. Instead, the road ahead seemed at best to consist of a series of hard choices. How Canadians and their political leaders would come to terms with such decisions is another matter entirely.

Although Canadians were having some trouble living with the new uncertainties, we should not conclude on a negative note. Today most Canadians live longer, earn more, are better educated, travel more, and possess more consumer goods. Few would wish to return to the period in which there were no life-saving drugs, little family planning, and a minimal welfare and health care system. Not many would prefer the past's adult male suffrage, open ballot, or unabashed sexism and racism. On every international indicator of quality of life—such as health standards, cultural achievement, environmental protection, infrastructure, gross national product per capita, political rights and civil liberties, and per capita purchasing power—Canada continued to rank at or near the top. The statistics only confirmed what Canadians themselves instinctively knew: Canada was a great country and a good place to live.

Suggestions for Further Reading

❄

CHAPTER 1:

Brebner, J.B. 1966. *The Explorers of North America, 1492–1806*. Cleveland: World Publishing Co.

Dickason, O.P. 1984. *The Myth of the Savage and the Beginnings of French Colonialism in the Americas*. Edmonton: University of Alberta Press.

Gordon, B. 1996. *People of Sunlight, People of Starlight*. Ottawa: Canadian Museum of Civilization.

Jaenen, C.J. 1976. *Friend and Foe: Aspects of French-Amerindian Cultural Contact in the Sixteenth and Seventeenth Centuries*. New York: Columbia University Press.

McGhee, R. 1989. *Ancient Canada*. Ottawa: Canadian Museum of Civilization.

Oleson, T.J. 1963. *Early Voyages and Northern Approaches, 1000–1632*. Toronto: McClelland and Stewart.

Ray, A.J. 1996. *I Have Lived Here Since the World Began: An Illustrated History of Canada's Native People*. Toronto: Lester Publishing.

CHAPTER 2:

Dechene, L. 1987. *Habitants and Merchants in Montreal in the Seventeenth Century*. Montreal: University of Montreal Press.

Eccles, W.J. 1990. *France in America*. East Lansing: Michigan State University Press.

Harris, R.C. 1984. *The Seigneurial Regime in Early Canada: A Geographical Study*. Montreal and Kingston: McGill-Queen's University Press.

Reid, J. 1981. *Acadia, Maine, and New Scotland: Marginal Colonies in the Seventeenth Century*. Toronto: University of Toronto Press.

Trudel, M. 1973. *The Beginnings of New France, 1526–1663*. Toronto: McClelland and Stewart.

CHAPTER 3:

Bumsted, J.M. 1982. *The People's Clearance: Highland Emigration to British North America, 1770–1815*. Edinburgh: University of Edinburgh Press.

Clarke, E.A. 1996. *The Siege of Fort Cumberland, 1776: An Episode in the American Revolution*. Montreal and Kingston: McGill-Queen's University Press.

Hitsman, J.M. 1965. *The Incredible War of 1812: A Military History*. Toronto: University of Toronto Press.

Moore, C. 1984. *The Loyalists: Revolution, Exile, and Settlement*. Toronto: Macmillan.

Neatby, H. 1966. *Quebec: The Revolutionary Age, 1760–1791*. Toronto: McClelland and Stewart.

Potter-Mackinnon, J. 1993. *While the Women Only Wept: Loyalist Refugee Women*. Montreal and Kingston: McGill-Queen's University Press.

Stanley, G. 1977. *Canada Invaded, 1775–1776*. Toronto: Stevens.

CHAPTER 4:

Greer, A. 1993. *The Patriots and the People: The Rebellion of 1837 in Rural Lower Canada*. Toronto: University of Toronto Press.

Johnson, J.K. 1989. *Becoming Prominent: Regional Leadership in Upper Canada, 1791–1841*. Montreal and Kingston: McGill-Queen's University Press.

McCallum, J. 1980. *Unequal Beginnings: Agriculture and Economic Development in Quebec and Ontario Until 1870*. Toronto: University of Toronto Press.

Ouellet, F. 1980. *Economic and Social History of Quebec, 1760–1850*. Toronto: Gage.

Ray, A.J. 1974. *Indians in the Fur Trade: Their Role as Trappers, Hunters, and Middlemen in the Lands Southwest of Hudson Bay, 1660–1870*. Toronto: University of Toronto Press.

Sager, E., and L.R. Fischer. 1986. *Shipping and Shipbuilding in Atlantic Canada*. Ottawa: Canadian Historical Association.

Stewart, G. 1986. *The Origins of Canadian Politics: A Comparative Approach*. Vancouver: University of BC Press.

Ward, P. 1990. *Courtship, Love and Marriage in Nineteenth-Century English Canada*. Montreal and Kingston: McGill-Queen's University Press.

Wynn, G. 1981. *Timber Colony: A Historical Geography of Early Nineteenth-Century New Brunswick*. Toronto: University of Toronto Press.

CHAPTER 5:

Careless, J.M.S. 1967. *The Union of the Canadas: The Growth of Canadian Institutions, 1841–1857*. Toronto: McClelland and Stewart.

Forster, B. 1986. *A Conjunction of Interests: Business, Politics, and Tariffs, 1825–1879*. Toronto: University of Toronto Press.

Monet, J. 1969. *The Last Cannon Shot: A Study of French-Canadian Nationalism, 1837–1850*. Toronto: University of Toronto Press.

Morton, W.L. 1964. *The Critical Years: The Union of British North America, 1857–1873*. Toronto: McClelland and Stewart.

Silver, A.I. 1982. *The French-Canadian Idea of Confederation, 1864–1900*. Toronto: University of Toronto Press.

Tucker, G. 1936. *The Canadian Commercial Revolution, 1845–1851*. New Haven: Yale University Press.

Tulchinsky, G. 1977. *The River Barons: Montreal Businessmen and the Growth of Industry and Transportation, 1837–1853*. Toronto: University of Toronto Press.

Waite, P.B. 1962. *The Life and Times of Confederation, 1864–1867: Politics, Newspapers, and the Union of British North America*. Toronto: University of Toronto Press.

CHAPTER 6:

Bolger, F.W. 1964. *Prince Edward Island and Confederation, 1863–1873*. Charlottetown: St Dunstan's University Press.

Bumsted, J.M. 1996. *The Red River Rebellion*. Winnipeg: Watson & Dwyer.

Houston, C., and W. Smyth. 1980. *The Sash Canada Wore: A Historical Geography of the Orange Order in Canada*. Toronto: University of Toronto Press.

Ormsby, M. 1971. *British Columbia: A History*. Toronto: Macmillan.

Reid, D. 1979. *'Our Own Country Canada': Being an Account of the National Aspirations of the Principal Landscape Artists in Montreal and Toronto 1860–1890*. Ottawa: National Gallery of Canada.

Roy, P. 1989. *A White Man's Province: British Columbia Politicians and Chinese and Japanese Immigrants, 1858–1914*. Vancouver: University of BC Press.

Zeller, S. 1987. *Inventing Canada: Early Victorian Science and the Idea of a Transcontinental Nation*. Toronto: University of Toronto Press.

CHAPTER 7:

Berger, C. 1970. *The Sense of Power: Studies in the Ideas of Canadian Imperialism, 1867–1914*. Toronto: University of Toronto Press.

Brown, R.C. 1974. *Canada, 1896–1921: A Nation Transformed*. Toronto: McClelland and Stewart.

Cook, R. 1985. *The Regenerators: Social Criticism in Late Victorian English Canada*. Toronto: University of Toronto Press.

English, J. 1977. *The Decline of Politics: The Conservatives and the Party System, 1901–1920*. Toronto: University of Toronto Press.

Kealey, L., ed. 1979. *A Not Unreasonable Claim: Women and Reform in Canada, 1880s–1920s.* Toronto: The Women's Press.

Nelles, H.V. 1974. *The Politics of Development: Forests, Mines and Hydro-Electric Power in Ontario, 1849–1941.* Toronto: University of Toronto Press.

Owen, W., ed. 1985. *The Wheat King: The Selected Letters and Papers of A.J. Cotton, 1888–1913.* Winnipeg: Manitoba Record Society.

Rutherford, P., ed. 1974. *Saving the Canadian City, the First Phase 1880–1920: An Anthology of Early Articles on Urban Reform.* Toronto: University of Toronto Press.

Voisey, P.L. 1988. *Vulcan: The Making of a Prairie Community.* Toronto: University of Toronto Press.

CHAPTER 8:

Abella, I., and H. Troper. 1982. *None Is Too Many: Canada and the Jews of Europe, 1933–1948.* Toronto: Lester & Orpen Dennys.

Baum, G. 1980. *Catholics and Canadian Socialism: Political Thought in the Thirties and Forties.* Toronto: J. Lorimer.

Berton, P. 1977. *Hollywood's Canada.* Toronto: McClelland and Stewart.

Forbes, E. 1979. *The Maritime Rights Movement, 1919–1927.* Montreal and Kingston: McGill-Queen's University Press.

Granatstein, J.L. 1975. *Canada's War: The Politics of the Mackenzie King Government, 1939–1945.* Toronto: Oxford University Press.

Macpherson, C.B. 1953. *Democracy in Alberta: The Theory and Practice of a Quasi-Party System.* Toronto: University of Toronto Press.

Owran, D. 1986. *The Government Generation: Canadian Intellectuals and the State, 1900–1945.* Toronto: University of Toronto Press.

Safarian, A. 1959. *The Canadian Economy in the Great Depression.* Toronto: University of Toronto Press.

Strong-Boag, V. 1988. *The New Day Recalled: Lives of Girls and Women in English Canada, 1919–1939.* Toronto: University of Toronto Press.

Thompson, J.H., with A. Seager. 1985. *Canada 1922–1939: Decades of Discord.* Toronto: McClelland and Stewart.

CHAPTER 9:

Beheils, M. 1985. *Prelude to Quebec's Quiet Revolution: Liberalism versus Neo-Nationalism, 1945–1960.* Montreal and Kingston: McGill-Queen's University Press.

Creighton, D. 1976. *The Forked Road: Canada, 1939–1957.* Toronto: McClelland and Stewart.

Guindon, H., ed. 1988. *Quebec Society: Tradition, Modernity, and Nationhood.* Toronto: University of Toronto Press.

Kinsman, G. 1977. *The Regulation of Desire: Sexuality in Canada.* Montreal: Black Rose.

Neary, P. 1988. *Newfoundland in the North Atlantic World, 1929–1949.* Kingston and Montreal: McGill-Queen's University Press.

Porter, J. 1965. *The Vertical Mosaic: An Analysis of Social Class and Power in Canada.* Toronto: University of Toronto Press.

Rea, K.J. 1985. *The Prosperous Years: The Economic History of Ontario, 1939–1975.* Toronto: University of Toronto Press.

Report of the Royal Commission on National Development in the Arts, Letters and Sciences. 1951. Ottawa: Queen's Printer.

Rutherford, P. 1990. *When Television Was Young: Primetime Canada 1952–1967.* Toronto: University of Toronto Press.

CHAPTER 10:

Atwood, M. 1972. *Survival: A Thematic Guide to Canadian Literature.* Toronto: Anansi.

English, J. 1992. *Lester Pearson: The Worldly Years, 1949–1972.* Toronto: Alfred A. Knopf Canada.

Joy, R. 1972. *Languages in Conflict: The Canadian Experience.* Toronto: McClelland and Stewart.

Kostash, M. 1980. *Long Way from Home: The Story of the Sixties Generation in Canada.* Toronto: J. Lorimer.

Levitt, K. 1978. *The Silent Surrender: The Multinational Corporation in Canada.* Toronto: Macmillan.

McWhinney, E. 1979. *Quebec and the Constitution, 1960–1978.* Toronto: University of Toronto Press.

Morgan, N. 1986. *Implosion: An Analysis of the Growth of the Federal Public Service in Canada, 1945–1985.* Montreal: Institute for Research on Public Policy.

Newman, P.C. 1963. *Renegade in Power: The Diefenbaker Years.* Toronto: McClelland and Stewart.

Saywell, J. 1971. *Quebec 70: A Documentary Narrative.* Toronto: University of Toronto Press.

Simeon, R. 1972. *Federal-Provincial Diplomacy: The Making of Recent Policy in Canada.* Toronto: University of Toronto Press.

Struthers, J. 1994. *The Limits of Affluence: Welfare in Ontario, 1920–1970.* Toronto: University of Toronto Press.

CHAPTER 11:

Audley, P. 1983. *Canada's Cultural Industries: Broadcasting, Publishing, Records and Film*. Toronto: J. Lorimer.

Banting, K. 1987. *The Welfare State and Canadian Federalism*, 2nd ed. Montreal and Kingston: McGill-Queen's University Press.

Cohen, A. 1990. *A Deal Undone: The Making and Breaking of the Meech Lake Accord*. Vancouver: Douglas & McIntyre.

Hoy, C. 1987. *Friends in High Places: Politics and Patronage in the Mulroney Government*. Toronto: Key Porter Books.

McCall-Newman, C. 1982. *Grits: An Intimate Portrait of the Liberal Party*. Toronto: Macmillan.

Milne, D. 1986. *Tug of War: Ottawa and the Provinces under Trudeau and Mulroney*. Toronto: J. Lorimer.

York, G. 1988. *The Dispossessed: Life and Death in Native Canada*. Toronto: Little, Brown.

CHAPTER 12:

Eayrs, J. 1965–. *In Defence of Canada*, 5 vols. Toronto: University of Toronto Press.

Granatstein, J.L., and R. Bothwell. 1990. *Pirouette: Pierre Trudeau and Canadian Foreign Policy*. Toronto: University of Toronto Press.

Holmes, J. 1979–82. *The Shaping of Peace: Canada and the Search for World Order, 1943–1957*, 2 vols. Toronto: University of Toronto Press.

Levant, V. 1986. *Quiet Complicity: Canadian Involvement in the Vietnam War*. Toronto: Between the Lines.

Stacey, C.P. 1977–81. *Canada and the Age of Conflict: A History of Canadian External Policies*, 2 vols. Toronto: Macmillan of Canada, University of Toronto Press.

Stairs, D. 1974. *The Diplomacy of Constraint: Canada, the Korean War, and the United States*. Toronto: University of Toronto Press.

CHAPTER 13:

Emberley, P.C. 1996. *Zero Tolerance: Hot Button Politics in Canada's Universities*. Toronto: Penguin.

Henighan, T. 1996. *The Presumption of Culture: Structure, Strategy, and Survival in the Canadian Cultural Landscape*. Vancouver: Raincoast Books.

Jenish, D. 1996. *Money to Burn: Trudeau, Mulroney and the Bankruptcy of Canada*. Toronto: Stoddart.

McQuaig, L. 1995. *Shooting the Hippo: Death by Deficit and Other Canadian Myths*. Toronto: Viking.

References

✾

Addiction Research Foundation. 1970. *Summary with Comments on the Interim Report of the Commission of Inquiry into the Non-Medical Use of Drugs.* Toronto: Addiction Research Foundation.

Akins, T.B., ed. 1869. *Selections from the Public Documents of the Province of Nova Scotia.* Halifax: n.p.

Arthur, E. 1986. *Toronto: No Mean City.* Toronto: University of Toronto Press.

Avery, D. 1986. 'The Radical Alien and the Winnipeg General Strike of 1919'. In *Interpreting Canada's Past,* vol. 2, edited by J.M. Bumsted, 222–39. Toronto: Oxford University Press.

Ballantyne, R. 1879. *Hudson's Bay: or, Everyday Life in the Wilds of North America.* London: T. Nelson and Sons.

Behiels, M.D. 1985. *Prelude to Quebec's Quiet Revolution: Liberalism Versus Neo-Nationalism, 1945–1960.* Montreal and Kingston: McGill-Queen's University Press.

Bell, W.P. 1990. *The 'Foreign Protestants' and the Settlement of Nova Scotia: The History of a Piece of Arrested British Colonial Policy in the 18th Century.* Fredericton: Acadiensis Press.

Benson, A.B., ed. 1937. *The America of 1750: Peter Kalm's Travels in North America,* 2 vols. New York: Dover Publications.

Berger, C. 1986. 'The True North Strong and Free'. In *Interpreting Canada's Past,* vol. 2, edited by J.M. Bumsted, 154–60. Toronto: Oxford University Press.

Binnie-Clark, G. 1914. *Wheat and Woman.* Toronto: Bell & Cockburn.

Bliss, M. 1972. 'Canadianizing American Business: The Roots of the Branch Plant'. In *Close the 49th Parallel: The Americanization of Canada,* edited by I. Lumsden, 38. Toronto: University of Toronto Press.

Bourassa, H. 1912. *Canadian Club Addresses 1912.* Toronto: Warwick Bros & Rutter Ltd.

Bowker, A., ed. 1973. *The Social Criticism of Stephen Leacock: The Unsolved Riddle of Social Justice and Other Essays.* Toronto: University of Toronto Press.

Brebner, J.B. 1927. *New England's Outpost: Acadia before the Conquest of Canada.* New York: Columbia University Press.

Brode, P. 1984. *Sir John Beverley Robinson.* Toronto: University of Toronto Press.

Bruce, V., trans. 1977. *Jean Rivard* by A. Gerin-Lajoie. Toronto: McClelland and Stewart.

Bumsted, J.M., ed. 1969. *Documentary Problems in Canadian History.* Georgetown: Irwin-Dorsey.

_____. 1971. *Henry Alline, 1748–1784.* Toronto: University of Toronto Press.

_____, ed. 1986. *Understanding the Loyalists.* Sackville: Mount Allison University Press.

Canada Year Book. 1959. Ottawa: Queen's Printer.

_____. 1990. Ottawa: Queen's Printer.

_____. 1994. Ottawa: Statistics Canada.

Carter, S. 1990. *Lost Harvests: Prairie Indian Reserve Farmers and Government Policy.* Montreal and Kingston: McGill-Queen's University Press.

Clark, C.S. 1898. *Of Toronto the Good: A Social Study.* Montreal: Toronto Publishing Co.

Clark, E.A. 1988. 'Cumberland Planters and the Aftermath of the Attack on Fort Cumberland'. In *They Planted Well: New England Planters in Maritime Canada,* edited by M. Conrad, 49. Fredericton: Acadiensis Press.

Commission on Inquiry into the Non-Medical Use of Drugs. 1970. *Interim Report.* Ottawa: Queen's Printer.

Cook, R. 1969a. *Provincial Autonomy: Minority Rights and the Compact Theory, 1867–1921.* Ottawa: Queen's Printer.

_____, ed. 1969b. *French-Canadian Nationalism: An Anthology.* Toronto: Macmillan.

Craig, G.M., ed. 1963. *Lord Durham's Report.* Toronto: McClelland and Stewart.

Cuff, R.D., and J.L. Granatstein. 1977. *The Ties That Bind: Canadian-American Relations in Wartime from the Great War to the Cold War.* Toronto: Samuel Stevens Hakkert & Co.

Cuthand, S. 1978. 'The Native Peoples of the Prairie Provinces in the 1920s and 1930s'. In *One Century Later: Western Canadian Reserve Indians Since Treaty 7,* edited by I.A.L. Getty and D.B. Smith, 31–2. Vancouver: University of BC Press.

Department of Regional Economic Expansion. 1971. *Major Economic Indicators, Provinces and Regions.* Ottawa: Queen's Printer.

Dollier de Casson, F. 1928. *A History of Montreal 1640–1672,* edited and translated by R. Flenley. London: J.M. Dent & Sons.

Duncan, S.J. 1990. *The Imperialist.* Toronto: McClelland and Stewart.

Durand, E. 1981. *Vignettes of Early Winnipeg.* Winnipeg: Frances McColl.

Dyer, G., and T. Viljoen. 1990. *The Defense of Canada: In the Arms of the Empire 1760–1939.* Toronto: McClelland and Stewart.

Easterbrook, W.T., and M.H. Watkins. 1962. *Approaches to Canadian Economic History.* Toronto: McClelland and Stewart.

_____, and G.J. Aitken. 1956. *Canadian Economic History*. Toronto: Macmillan.

Eccles, W.J. 1983. *The Canadian Frontier 1534–1760*, rev. ed. Albuquerque: University of New Mexico Press.

Ewart, J.S. 1908. *The Kingdom of Canada: Imperial Federation, the Colonial Conferences, the Alaska Boundary and Other Essays*. Toronto: Morang.

Fairley, M., ed. 1960. *The Selected Writings of William Lyon Mackenzie*. Toronto: Oxford University Press.

Fingard, J. 1988. 'The Relief of the Unemployed Poor in Saint John, Halifax, and St John's, 1815–1860'. In *The Acadiensis Reader*, vol. 1, edited by P.A. Buckner and D. Frank. Fredericton: Acadiensis Press.

Fisher, R. 1977. *Contact and Conflict: Indian-European Relations in British Columbia 1774–1890*. Vancouver: University of BC Press.

Forsythe, D., ed. 1971. *Let the Niggers Burn: The Sir George Williams University Affair and Its Caribbean Aftermath*. Montreal: Black Rose.

Frye, N. 1976. 'Conclusion'. In *Literary History of Canada*, rev. ed., edited by C.F. Klinck, 849. Toronto: University of Toronto Press.

Granatstein, J.L., and R. Bothwell. 1990. *Pirouette: Pierre Trudeau and Canadian Foreign Policy*. Toronto: University of Toronto Press.

Grant, G. 1965. *Lament for a Nation: The Defeat of Canadian Nationalism*. Toronto: Macmillan.

Grant, G.M., ed. 1876. *Picturesque Canada*. Toronto: Hunter, Rose & Co. Printers.

Gray, J. 1966. *The Winter Years: The Depression on the Prairies*. Toronto: Macmillan.

Gunn, G.E. 1966. *The Political History of Newfoundland, 1832–1864*. Toronto: University of Toronto Press.

Haliburton, T.C. 1838. *The Clockmaker: or The Sayings and Doings of Samuel Slick, of Slickville*. London: Richard Bentley.

Halpenny, F.G., ed. 1976. *The Dictionary of Canadian Biography*, vol. IX. Toronto: University of Toronto Press.

Harper, S.E. 1992. *A Full House and Fine Singing: Diaries and Letters of Sadie Harper Allen*, edited by M.B. Peck. Fredericton: Goose Lane.

Hatch, R. 1970. *Thrust for Canada*. Boston: Houghton-Mifflin.

Hind, H.Y. 1869. *The Dominion of Canada: Containing a Historical Sketch of the Preliminaries and Oranization of Confederation*. Toronto: L. Stebbins.

Hodgetts, J.E. 1968. 'The Changing Nature of the Public Service'. In *The Changing Public Service*, edited by L.D. Musoff, 7–18. Berkeley: University of California Press.

Indian-Eskimo Association of Canada. 1970. *Native Rights in Canada*. Toronto: Indian-Eskimo Association of Canada.

Innes, H. 1948. *The Diary of Simeon Perkins, 1766–1780*, vol. 1. Toronto: Champlain Society.

Johnston, M. 1994. *Corvettes Canada: Convoy Veterans of WWII Tell Their True Stories*. Toronto: McGraw-Hill Ryerson.

Kealey, G., ed. 1973. *Canada Investigates Industrialism [The Royal Commission on the Relations of Labour and Capital, 1889*, abridged]. Toronto: University of Toronto Press.

Keefer, T.C. 1853. *Philosophy of Railroads, Published by Order of the Directors of the St Lawrence and Ottawa Grand Junction Railway Company*, 4th ed. Montreal: J. Lovell.

Kenyon, W.A., ed. 1980. *The Journal of Jens Munk, 1619–1620*. Toronto: Royal Ontario Museum.

Kostash, M. 1980. *Long Way from Home: The Story of the Sixties Generation in Canada*. Toronto: J. Lorimer.

Kwavnick, D., ed. 1973. *The Tremblay Report*. Toronto: McClelland and Stewart.

Lévesque, R. 1986. *Memoirs*, translated by P. Stratford. Toronto: McClelland and Stewart.

Lucas, C.P., ed. 1912. *Lord Durham's Report*, 3 vols. Oxford: Clarendon Press.

MacBeath, G. 1966. 'Charles de Saint-Étienne de La Tour'. In *Dictionary of Canadian Biography*, edited by G. Brown, 592–6. Toronto: University of Toronto Press.

McCracken, M. 1975. *Memories Are Made of This: What It Was Like to Grow Up in the Fifties*. Toronto: J. Lorimer.

MacDonell, Sister M. 1982. *The Emigrant Experience: Songs of Highland Emigrants in North America*. Toronto: University of Toronto Press.

McLuhan, M. 1951. *The Mechanical Bride: Folklore of Industrial Man*. New York: Vanguard Press.

McWhinney, E. 1982. *Canada and the Constitution 1979–1982*. Toronto: University of Toronto Press.

Masters, D.C. 1936. *The Reciprocity Treaty of 1854*. London: Longmans Green & Company.

Marshall, J., ed. 1967. *Word from New France: The Selected Letters of Marie de l'Incarnation*. Toronto: Oxford University Press.

Monière, D. 1981. *Ideologies on Quebec: The Historical Development*. Toronto: University of Toronto Press.

Moodie, S. 1852. *Roughing It in the Bush, or, Life in Canada*, vol. 1. London: Richard Bentley, 1852.

Morrow, D. 1989. *A Concise History of Sport in Canada*. Toronto: Oxford University Press.

Morton, W.L., ed. 1970. *Monck Letters and Journals 1863–1868: Canada from Government House at Confederation*. Toronto: McClelland and Stewart.

National Archives of Canada. 1745. 'Representation of the State of His Majesty's Province of Nova Scotia' (8 November 1745).

National Task Force on Suicide in Canada. 1984. *Suicide in Canada.* Ottawa: Queen's Printer.

Naylor, R.T. 1975. *The History of Canadian Business, 1867–1914,* vol. 1. Toronto: J. Lorimer.

Neatby, H. 1972. *The Quebec Act: Protest and Policy.* Toronto: Prentice-Hall of Canada.

Nelles, H.V. 1974. *The Politics of Development: Forests, Mines & Hydro-Electric Power in Ontario, 1849–1941.* Toronto: Macmillan.

Patterson, E.P. 1972. *The Canadian Indian: A History Since 1500.* Toronto: Collier-Macmillan.

Pope, Sir J. 1930. *Memoirs of the Rt Hon. Sir John A. Macdonald,* vol. 1. Toronto: Oxford University Press.

Preston, R.A., ed. 1974. *For Friends at Home: A Scottish Emigrant's Letters from Canada, California and the Cariboo 1844–1864.* Montreal and London: McGill-Queen's University Press.

Proceedings of the Special Joint Committee of the Senate and House of Commons on Divorce. 1967. Ottawa: Queen's Printer.

Pryke, K.G. 1979. *Nova Scotia and Confederation, 1864–1874.* Toronto: University of Toronto Press.

Quaife, M.M., ed. 1962. *The Western Country in the 17th Century: The Memoirs of Antoine Lamothe Cadillac and Pierre Liette.* New York: The Citadel Press.

Québec conseil exécutif. 1979. *Québec-Canada, a New Deal: The Québec Government Proposal for a New Partnership between Equals, Sovereignty-Association.* Québec: Québec conseil exécutif.

Raspovich, A.W. 1969. 'National Awakening: Canada at Mid-Century'. In *Documentary Problems in Canadian History,* vol. 1, edited by J.M. Bumsted, 225. Georgetown: Irwin-Dorsey.

Rea, K.J. 1985. *The Prosperous Years: The Economic History of Ontario 1939–75.* Toronto: University of Toronto Press.

Recollections of the War of 1812. 1964. Toronto: Baxter Publishing Company.

Report of the Royal Commission on Broadcasting. 1957. Ottawa: King's Printer.

Report of the Royal Commission on National Development in the Arts, Letters and Sciences. 1951. Toronto: King's Printer.

Report of the Royal Commission on the Status of Women in Canada. 1970. Ottawa: Queen's Printer.

Robertson, J.R. 1911. *The Diary of Mrs John Graves Simcoe, Wife of the First Lieutenant-Governor of the Province of Upper Canada, 1792–1796.* Toronto: W. Briggs.

Royal Commission on Canada's Economic Prospects. 1958. Ottawa: Queen's Printer.

Royal Commission on the Donald Marshall, Jr, Prosecution, vol. 1: Findings and Recommendations. 1989. Halifax: The Commission.

The Royal Society of Canada. 1932. *Fifty Years' Retrospective 1882–1932*. Toronto: University of Toronto Press.

Rubio, M., and E. Waterston, eds. 1987. *The Selected Journals of L.M. Montgomery, vol. 2: 1910–1921*. Toronto: Oxford University Press.

Saywell, J. 1971. *Quebec 70: A Documentary Narrative*. Toronto: University of Toronto Press.

Seeley, J.R., R.A. Sim, and E. Loosley. 1972. *Crestwood Heights: A North American Suburb*. Toronto: University of Toronto Press.

Siegfried, A. 1907. *The Race Question in Canada*. London: E. Nash.

Smiley, D. 1970. 'Canadian Federalism and the Resolution of Federal-Provincial Conflicts'. In *Contemporary Issues in Canadian Politics*, edited by F. Vaughan et al., 48–66. Toronto: Prentice-Hall.

Special Committee on Social Security. 1943. *Report on Social Security for Canada, Prepared by Dr L.C. Marsh for the Advisory Committee on Reconstruction*. Ottawa: King's Printer.

Stacey, C.P. 1970. *Arms, Man and Governments: The War Policies of Canada 1939–1945*. Ottawa: Queen's Printer.

_____. 1981. *Canada and the Age of Conflict: A History of Canadian External Policies, vol. 2: 1921–1948*. Toronto: Macmillan.

Stanley, G.F.G. 1977. *Canada Invaded, 1775–1776*. Toronto: Canadian War Museum.

A Statement of the Government of Canada on Indian Policy. 1969. Ottawa: Queen's Printer.

Statistics Canada. 1957. *Manufacturing Industries of Canada 1957*. Ottawa: Queen's Printer.

Steele, S. 1915. *Forty Years in Canada: Reminiscences of the Great North-West . . . .* Toronto: McClelland, Goodchild & Stewart.

Stephens, H.F. 1890. *Jacques Cartier and His Four Voyages to Canada: An Essay with Historical, Explanatory and Philological Notes*. Montreal: W. Drysdale & Co.

Sykes, E.C. 1912. *A Home-Help in Canada*. London: G. Bell & Sons Ltd.

Thompson, J.H., and A. Seager. 1985. *Canada, 1922–1939: Decades of Discord*. Toronto: McClelland and Stewart.

Traill, C.P. 1846. *The Backwoods of Canada*. London: M.A. Nattali.

Trudel, M. 1973. *The Beginnings of New France 1524–1663*. Toronto: McClelland and Stewart.

Vallières, P. 1971. *White Niggers of America*. Toronto: McClelland and Stewart.

Voisey, P. 1988. *Vulcan: The Making of a Prairie Community*. Toronto: University of Toronto Press.

Waite, P.B. 1962. *The Life and Times of Confederation, 1864–1867: Politics, Newspapers, Union of British North America*. Toronto: University of Toronto Press.

_____, ed. 1963. *Confederation Debates in the Province of Canada*. Toronto: McClelland and Stewart.

Williamson, J.A., ed. 1962. *The Cabot Voyages and British Discoveries under Henry VII*. Cambridge: Hakluyt Society of the University Press.

Williamson, M. 1970. *Robert Harris, 1849–1919: An Unconventional Biography*. Toronto: McClelland and Stewart.

Wright, E.C. 1955. *The Loyalists of New Brunswick*. Fredericton: University of New Brunswick Press.

Wynn, G. 1980. *Timber Colony: A Historical Geography of Early 19th Century New Brunswick*. Toronto: University of Toronto Press.

Young, W. 1978. 'Academics and Social Scientists *versus* the Press: The Policies of the Bureau of Public Information and the Wartime Information Board, 1939 to 1945'. In CHA *Historical Papers, a Selection from the Papers Presented at the Annual Meeting of the Canadian Historical Association* (1978).

Index

❀

Victoria (BC), 144, 158, 238

Vietnam War, 332–3, 336–7, 366, 400, 411–12

Vikings, *x*, 7–8

Vinland, 7–8

Violence, 390–1

Voluntaryism, 163

Voyages (Champlain), 28, 29, 36

Voyageurs, 49

Wacousta (Richardson), 104, 130

Waffle movement (NDP), 330, 338, 374

Waite, R.A., 222

Walker, Sir Edmund, 222

Walker Theatre (Winnipeg), 239

Walsh, Edward, 96

Wandering Spirit (Kapapamahchakwew), 211, 213

War Bonds, 295, 300

Ward system, 239

Warfare and the military: action against civilians: October Crisis (1970), 348, 412; Oka insurrection, 386; strikes and labour unrest, 270–1, 282

Warfare and the military: civil liberties during wartime, 262, 263; pacificism, 296, 403; peacekeeping, 400, 408, 414; traditional Aboriginal practices, 23–4; wartime economies, 260, 263. *See also* Second World War. *See also* specific conflicts (for example, Boer War, First and Second World Wars)

Warfare and the military: conscription: exemption from service, 95; First World War, 216, 220, 221, 261; Military Service Act (1917), 216, 261; Second World War, 297–9, 315

Warfare and the military: military units: air training program, 294, 403; Canadian Airborne, 415; Canadian Army Special Force, 407; integration of armed forces, 410; land grants for, 116; Mackenzie-Papineau Battalion, 282; in New France, 48–9, 80; racism, 414–15; Royal Canadian Air Force, 295; Royal Canadian Navy, 295; volunteer enlistment, 252, 254, 260, 407

Warfare and the military: policy and alliances: defence of British North America, 177; defence of Great Britain, 252, 254–5; defence spending, 408, 412, 414, 420; naval policy, 255; NORAD (North American Air Defence Command), 400, 408, 409; Permanent Joint Board on Defence (1940), 405

Warfare and the military: weapons, 305; Avro Arrow, 302, 305, 400, 408–9; Bomarc-B missile, 408, 409; DEW (Distant Early Warning) Line, 400, 408; nuclear weapons, 406, 408–10

War Measures Act (1970), 294

Warner, Jack, 293

War of 1812, 70, 100–2

War of Austrian Succession (1744–8), 34, 57

War of League of Augsburg (1689–97), 34, 55

War of Spanish Succession (1702–13), 34, 57

Wartime Elections Act (1917), 216, 262

Washington, George, 80, 83

Washington, State of, 148, 155

Washington Treaty (1871), 186, 196, 400

Watkins, Mel, 345

WCTU (Woman's Christian Temperance Union), 186, 204, 257

Wealth of Nations (Smith), 134

Webber, John, 87

Webster-Ashburton Treaty (1842), 144, 148

Welland Canal, 104, 114

Wells, Clyde, 385

West, the: agricultural potential, 258; anglophone population, 215; drought, 272, 273; in 19th century, 155–60, 208–15; Progressive Party, 272–3; role in constitutional revision, 378; settlement, 155, 234; urban growth, 237. *See also* individual provinces

Westminster Conference (1930), 400, 402

Wheat, 186, 216; wheat economy, 232–4, 263, 272–3

Wheat and Women, 233

White, John, 19

White Niggers of America, 336

Willamette Valley, 109

Williams Creek (BC), 160